Introduction

This hard copy of the NIST document is made available to you by www.50page.com. I decided to do this for two reasons. First of all, the NIST documents are great documents. Secondly, as a Security Consultant who works in highly secured environments, I find myself not able to take any printed materials home, and need to reprint them over and over again, which is bad for the environment, and time consuming. With a personal hard copy I can do whatever I want with it.

I was not able to find these documents online to buy. Therefore, I decided to prepare some titles and make them available for print through Amazon at cost price.

Thanks to the US Government, these NIST documents are not subject to copyright, which means I am able to provide you a copy in this form.

To find other NIST documents available in hard copy please check out www.50page.com or www.amazon.com.

Thanks

Emmanuel Aroms

Compiler
www.50page.com

Disclaimer
I not affiliated to the US Government or the National Institute of Standards and Technology (NIST) or the US Department of Commerce. The publication of this document should not in any way imply any relationship or affiliation to the above named organizations and Government.

This document is published without the explicit permission from the NIST. It was done legally based on the fact that these documents are not covered by copyright.

NIST Special Publication 800-53A
Revision 1

Guide for Assessing the Security Controls in Federal Information Systems and Organizations

Building Effective Security Assessment Plans

National Institute of Standards and Technology

U.S. Department of Commerce

**JOINT TASK FORCE
TRANSFORMATION INITIATIVE**

INFORMATION SECURITY

Consistent with NIST SP 800-53, Revision 3

Computer Security Division
Information Technology Laboratory
National Institute of Standards and Technology
Gaithersburg, MD 20899-8930

June 2010

U.S. Department of Commerce
Gary Locke, Secretary

National Institute of Standards and Technology
Patrick D. Gallagher, Director

Reports on Computer Systems Technology

The Information Technology Laboratory (ITL) at the National Institute of Standards and Technology (NIST) promotes the U.S. economy and public welfare by providing technical leadership for the nation's measurement and standards infrastructure. ITL develops tests, test methods, reference data, proof of concept implementations, and technical analyses to advance the development and productive use of information technology. ITL's responsibilities include the development of management, administrative, technical, and physical standards and guidelines for the cost-effective security and privacy of other than national security-related information in federal information systems. The Special Publication 800-series reports on ITL's research, guidelines, and outreach efforts in information system security, and its collaborative activities with industry, government, and academic organizations.

Authority

This publication has been developed by NIST to further its statutory responsibilities under the Federal Information Security Management Act (FISMA), Public Law (P.L.) 107-347. NIST is responsible for developing information security standards and guidelines, including minimum requirements for federal information systems, but such standards and guidelines shall not apply to national security systems without the express approval of appropriate federal officials exercising policy authority over such systems. This guideline is consistent with the requirements of the Office of Management and Budget (OMB) Circular A-130, Section 8b(3), *Securing Agency Information Systems*, as analyzed in Circular A-130, Appendix IV: Analysis of Key Sections. Supplemental information is provided in Circular A-130, Appendix III, *Security of Federal Automated Information Resources*.

Nothing in this publication should be taken to contradict the standards and guidelines made mandatory and binding on federal agencies by the Secretary of Commerce under statutory authority. Nor should these guidelines be interpreted as altering or superseding the existing authorities of the Secretary of Commerce, Director of the OMB, or any other federal official. This publication may be used by nongovernmental organizations on a voluntary basis and is not subject to copyright in the United States. Attribution would, however, be appreciated by NIST.

NIST Special Publication 800-53A, Revision 1, 399 pages

(June 2010)

Comments on this publication may be submitted to:

National Institute of Standards and Technology
Attn: Computer Security Division, Information Technology Laboratory
100 Bureau Drive (Mail Stop 8930) Gaithersburg, MD 20899-8930
Electronic mail: sec-cert@nist.gov

Compliance with NIST Standards and Guidelines

In accordance with the provisions of FISMA,[1] the Secretary of Commerce shall, on the basis of standards and guidelines developed by NIST, prescribe standards and guidelines pertaining to federal information systems. The Secretary shall make standards compulsory and binding to the extent determined necessary by the Secretary to improve the efficiency of operation or security of federal information systems. Standards prescribed shall include information security standards that provide minimum information security requirements and are otherwise necessary to improve the security of federal information and information systems.

- Federal Information Processing Standards (FIPS) are approved by the Secretary of Commerce and issued by NIST in accordance with FISMA. FIPS are compulsory and binding for federal agencies.[2] FISMA requires that federal agencies comply with these standards, and therefore, agencies may not waive their use.

- Special Publications (SPs) are developed and issued by NIST as recommendations and guidance documents. For other than national security programs and systems, federal agencies must follow those NIST Special Publications mandated in a Federal Information Processing Standard. FIPS 200 mandates the use of Special Publication 800-53, as amended. In addition, OMB policies (including OMB Reporting Instructions for FISMA and Agency Privacy Management) state that for other than national security programs and systems, federal agencies must follow certain specific NIST Special Publications.[3]

- Other security-related publications, including interagency reports (NISTIRs) and ITL Bulletins, provide technical and other information about NIST's activities. These publications are mandatory only when specified by OMB.

- Compliance schedules for NIST security standards and guidelines are established by OMB in policies, directives, or memoranda (e.g., annual FISMA Reporting Guidance).[4]

---

[1] The E-Government Act (P.L. 107-347) recognizes the importance of information security to the economic and national security interests of the United States. Title III of the E-Government Act, entitled the Federal Information Security Management Act (FISMA), emphasizes the need for organizations to develop, document, and implement an organization-wide program to provide security for the information systems that support its operations and assets.

[2] The term *agency* is used in this publication in lieu of the more general term *organization* only in those circumstances where its usage is directly related to other source documents such as federal legislation or policy.

[3] While federal agencies are required to follow certain specific NIST Special Publications in accordance with OMB policy, there is flexibility in how agencies apply the guidance. Federal agencies apply the security concepts and principles articulated in the NIST Special Publications in accordance with and in the context of the agency's missions, business functions, and environment of operation. Consequently, the application of NIST guidance by federal agencies can result in different security solutions that are equally acceptable, compliant with the guidance, and meet the OMB definition of *adequate security* for federal information systems. Given the high priority of information sharing and transparency within the federal government, agencies also consider reciprocity in developing their information security solutions. When assessing federal agency compliance with NIST Special Publications, Inspectors General, evaluators, auditors, and assessors consider the intent of the security concepts and principles articulated within the specific guidance document and how the agency applied the guidance in the context of its mission/business responsibilities, operational environment, and unique organizational conditions.

[4] Unless otherwise stated, all references to NIST publications in this document (i.e., Federal Information Processing Standards and Special Publications) are to the most recent version of the publication.

Acknowledgements

This publication was developed by the *Joint Task Force Transformation Initiative* Interagency Working Group with representatives from the Civil, Defense, and Intelligence Communities in an ongoing effort to produce a unified information security framework for the federal government. The National Institute of Standards and Technology wishes to acknowledge and thank the senior leaders from the Departments of Commerce and Defense, the Office of the Director of National Intelligence, the Committee on National Security Systems, and the members of the interagency technical working group whose dedicated efforts contributed significantly to the publication. The senior leaders, interagency working group members, and their organizational affiliations include:

U.S. Department of Defense

Cheryl J. Roby
Acting Assistant Secretary of Defense for Networks and Information Integration/Chief Information Officer

Gus Guissanie
Acting Deputy Assistant Secretary of Defense for Cyber, Identity, and Information Assurance

Dominic Cussatt
Senior Policy Advisor

Office of the Director of National Intelligence

Honorable Priscilla Guthrie
Intelligence Community Chief Information Officer

Sherrill Nicely
Deputy Intelligence Community Chief Information Officer

Mark J. Morrison
Deputy Associate Director of National Intelligence for IC Information Assurance

Roger Caslow
Lead, C&A Transformation

National Institute of Standards and Technology

Cita M. Furlani
Director, Information Technology Laboratory

William C. Barker
Cyber Security Advisor, Information Technology Laboratory

Donna Dodson
Chief, Computer Security Division

Ron Ross
FISMA Implementation Project Leader

Committee on National Security Systems

Dave Wennergren
Acting Chair, CNSS

Eustace D. King
CNSS Subcommittee Co-Chair (DoD)

Peter Gouldmann
CNSS Subcommittee Co-Chair (DoS)

Joint Task Force Transformation Initiative Interagency Working Group

Ron Ross *NIST, JTF Leader*	Gary Stoneburner *Johns Hopkins APL*	Terry Sherald *Department of Defense*	Kelley Dempsey *NIST*
Patricia Toth *NIST*	Esten Porter *The MITRE Corporation*	Peter Gouldmann *Department of State*	Arnold Johnson *NIST*
Bennett Hodge *Booz Allen Hamilton*	Karen Quigg *The MITRE Corporation*	Jonathan Chiu *Booz Allen Hamilton*	Christian Enloe *NIST*

In addition to the above acknowledgments, a special note of thanks goes to Peggy Himes and Elizabeth Lennon of NIST for their superb technical editing and administrative support. The authors also wish to recognize Jennifer Fabius Greene, James Govekar, Terrance Hazelwood, Austin Hershey, Laurie Hestor, Jason Mackanick, Timothy Potter, Jennifer Puma, Matthew Scholl, Julie Trei, Gail Tryon, Ricki Vanetesse, Cynthia Whitmer, and Peter Williams for their exceptional contributions in helping to improve the content of the publication. And finally, the authors gratefully acknowledge and appreciate the significant contributions from individuals and organizations in the public and private sectors, nationally and internationally, whose thoughtful and constructive comments improved the overall quality and usefulness of this publication.

DEVELOPING COMMON INFORMATION SECURITY FOUNDATIONS

COLLABORATION AMONG PUBLIC AND PRIVATE SECTOR ENTITIES

In developing standards and guidelines required by FISMA, NIST consults with other federal agencies and offices as well as the private sector to improve information security, avoid unnecessary and costly duplication of effort, and ensure that NIST publications are complementary with the standards and guidelines employed for the protection of national security systems. In addition to its comprehensive public review and vetting process, NIST is collaborating with the Office of the Director of National Intelligence (ODNI), the Department of Defense (DOD), and the Committee on National Security Systems (CNSS) to establish a common foundation for information security across the federal government. A common foundation for information security will provide the Intelligence, Defense, and Civil sectors of the federal government and their contractors, more uniform and consistent ways to manage the risk to organizational operations and assets, individuals, other organizations, and the Nation that results from the operation and use of information systems. A common foundation for information security will also provide a strong basis for reciprocal acceptance of security authorization decisions and facilitate information sharing. NIST is also working with public and private sector entities to establish specific mappings and relationships between the security standards and guidelines developed by NIST and the International Organization for Standardization and International Electrotechnical Commission (ISO/IEC) 27001, Information Security Management System (ISMS).

Table of Contents

Prologue

"…Through the process of risk management, leaders must consider risk to U.S. interests from adversaries using cyberspace to their advantage and from our own efforts to employ the global nature of cyberspace to achieve objectives in military, intelligence, and business operations… "

"...For operational plans development, the combination of threats, vulnerabilities, and impacts must be evaluated in order to identify important trends and decide where effort should be applied to eliminate or reduce threat capabilities; eliminate or reduce vulnerabilities; and assess, coordinate, and deconflict all cyberspace operations..."

"...Leaders at all levels are accountable for ensuring readiness and security to the same degree as in any other domain..."

-- THE NATIONAL STRATEGY FOR CYBERSPACE OPERATIONS
   OFFICE OF THE CHAIRMAN, JOINT CHIEFS OF STAFF, U.S. DEPARTMENT OF DEFENSE

Preface

Security control assessments are not about checklists, simple pass-fail results, or generating paperwork to pass inspections or audits—rather, security controls assessments are the principal vehicle used to verify that the implementers and operators of information systems are meeting their stated security goals and objectives. Special Publication 800-53A, *Guide for Assessing the Security Controls in Federal Information Systems and Organizations*, is written to facilitate security control assessments conducted within an effective risk management framework. The assessment results provide organizational officials with:

- Evidence about the effectiveness of security controls in organizational information systems;

- An indication of the quality of the risk management processes employed within the organization; and

- Information about the strengths and weaknesses of information systems which are supporting organizational missions and business functions in a global environment of sophisticated and changing threats.

The findings produced by assessors are used to determine the overall effectiveness of the security controls associated with an information system (including system-specific, common, and hybrid controls) and to provide credible and meaningful inputs to the organization's risk management process. A well-executed assessment helps to: (i) determine the validity of the security controls contained in the security plan and subsequently employed in the information system and its environment of operation; and (ii) facilitate a cost-effective approach to correcting weaknesses or deficiencies in the system in an orderly and disciplined manner consistent with organizational mission/business needs.

Special Publication 800-53A is a companion guideline to Special Publication 800-53, *Recommended Security Controls for Federal Information Systems and Organizations*. Each publication provides guidance for implementing specific steps in the Risk Management Framework (RMF).[5] Special Publication 800-53 covers Step 2 in the RMF, security control selection (i.e., determining what security controls are needed to manage risks to organizational operations and assets, individuals, other organizations, and the Nation). Special Publication 800-53A covers RMF Step 4, security control assessment, and RMF Step 6, continuous monitoring, and provides guidance on the security assessment process. This guidance includes how to build effective security assessment plans and how to analyze and manage assessment results.

Special Publication 800-53A allows organizations to tailor and supplement the basic assessment procedures provided. The concepts of tailoring and supplementation used in this document are similar to the concepts described in Special Publication 800-53. Tailoring involves scoping the assessment procedures to more closely match the characteristics of the information system and its environment of operation. The tailoring process gives organizations the flexibility needed to avoid assessment approaches that are unnecessarily complex or costly while simultaneously meeting the assessment requirements established by applying the fundamental concepts in the RMF. Supplementation involves adding assessment procedures or assessment details to adequately meet the risk management needs of the organization (e.g., adding organization-specific details such as system/platform-specific information for selected security controls). Supplementation decisions are left to the discretion of the organization in order to maximize

---

[5] Special Publication 800-37 provides guidance on applying the RMF to federal information systems.

flexibility in developing security assessment plans when applying the results of risk assessments in determining the extent, rigor, and level of intensity of the assessments.

While flexibility continues to be an important factor in developing security assessment plans, consistency of assessments is also an important consideration. A major design objective for Special Publication 800-53A is to provide an assessment framework and initial starting point for assessment procedures that are essential for achieving such consistency. In addition to the assessment framework and initial starting point for assessment procedures, NIST initiated an *Assessment Case Development Project.*[6] The purpose of the project is fourfold: (i) to actively engage experienced assessors from multiple organizations in the development of a representative set of assessment cases corresponding to the assessment procedures in Special Publication 800-53A; (ii) to provide organizations and the assessors supporting those organizations with an exemplary set of assessment cases for each assessment procedure in the catalog of procedures in this publication; (iii) to provide a vehicle for ongoing community-wide review of the assessment cases to promote continuous improvement in the assessment process for more consistent, cost-effective security assessments of federal information systems; and (iv) to serve as a basis for reciprocity among various communities of interest. The Assessment Case Development Project is described in Appendix H.

In addition to the assessment case project supporting this publication, NIST also initiated the Security Content Automation Protocol (SCAP)[7] project that supports and complements the approach for achieving consistent, cost-effective security control assessments. The primary purpose of the SCAP is to improve the automated application, verification, and reporting of information technology product-specific security configuration settings, enabling organizations to identify and reduce the vulnerabilities associated with products that are not configured properly. As part of this initiative, an Open Checklist Interactive Language (OCIL)[8] provides the capability to express the determination statements in the assessment procedures in Appendix F in a framework that will establish interoperability with the validated tool sets supporting SCAP.

---

[6] An *assessment case* represents a worked example of an assessment procedure that provides specific actions that an assessor might carry out during the assessment of a security control or control enhancement in an information system.

[7] Special Publication 800-126 provides guidance on the technical specification of the SCAP. Additional details on the SCAP initiative, as well as freely available SCAP reference data, can be found at http://nvd.nist.gov.

[8] OCIL is a framework for expressing security checks that cannot be evaluated without some human interaction or feedback. It is used to determine the state of a system by presenting one or more questionnaires to its intended users. The language includes constructs for questions, instructions for guiding users towards an answer, responses to questions, artifacts, and evaluation results.

CAUTIONARY NOTES

Organizations should carefully consider the potential impacts of employing the assessment procedures defined in this Special Publication when assessing the security controls in *operational* information systems. Certain assessment procedures, particularly those procedures that directly impact the operation of hardware, software, or firmware components of an information system, may inadvertently affect the routine processing, transmission, or storage of information supporting organizational missions or business functions. For example, a critical information system component may be taken offline for assessment purposes or a component may suffer a fault or failure during the assessment process. Organizations should also take necessary precautions during security assessment periods to ensure that organizational missions and business functions continue to be supported by the information system and that any potential impacts to operational effectiveness resulting from the assessment are considered in advance.

CHAPTER ONE

INTRODUCTION
THE NEED TO ASSESS SECURITY CONTROL EFFECTIVENESS IN INFORMATION SYSTEMS

Today's information systems[9] are complex assemblages of technology (i.e., hardware, software, and firmware), processes, and people, working together to provide organizations with the capability to process, store, and transmit information in a timely manner to support various missions and business functions. The degree to which organizations have come to depend upon these information systems to conduct routine, important, and critical missions and business functions means that the protection of the underlying systems is paramount to the success of the organization. The selection of appropriate security controls for an information system is an important task that can have major implications on the operations and assets of an organization as well as the welfare of individuals.[10] Security controls are the management, operational, and technical safeguards or countermeasures prescribed for an information system to protect the confidentiality, integrity (including non-repudiation and authenticity), and availability of the system and its information. Once employed within an information system, security controls are assessed to provide the information necessary to determine their overall effectiveness; that is, the extent to which the controls are implemented correctly, operating as intended, and producing the desired outcome with respect to meeting the security requirements for the system. Understanding the overall effectiveness of the security controls implemented in the information system and its environment of operation is essential in determining the risk to the organization's operations and assets, to individuals, to other organizations, and to the Nation resulting from the use of the system.

1.1 PURPOSE AND APPLICABILITY

The purpose of this publication is to provide guidelines for building effective security assessment plans and a comprehensive set of procedures for assessing the effectiveness of security controls employed in information systems supporting the executive agencies of the federal government. The guidelines apply to the security controls defined in Special Publication 800-53 (as amended), *Recommended Security Controls for Federal Information Systems and Organizations*. The guidelines have been developed to help achieve more secure information systems within the federal government by:

- Enabling more consistent, comparable, and repeatable assessments of security controls with reproducible results;

- Facilitating more cost-effective assessments of security controls contributing to the determination of overall control effectiveness;

- Promoting a better understanding of the risks to organizational operations, organizational assets, individuals, other organizations, and the Nation resulting from the operation and use of federal information systems; and

---

[9] An information system is a discrete set of information resources organized expressly for the collection, processing, maintenance, use, sharing, dissemination, or disposition of information.

[10] When selecting security controls for an information system, the organization also considers potential impacts to other organizations and, in accordance with the USA PATRIOT Act of 2001 and Homeland Security Presidential Directives, potential national-level impacts.

- Creating more complete, reliable, and trustworthy information for organizational officials to support risk management decisions, reciprocity of assessment results, information sharing, and FISMA compliance.

This publication satisfies the requirements of the Federal Information Security Management Act (FISMA) and meets or exceeds the information security requirements established for executive agencies[11] by the Office of Management and Budget (OMB) in Circular A-130, Appendix III, *Security of Federal Automated Information Resources.* The guidelines in this publication are applicable to all federal information systems other than those systems designated as national security systems as defined in 44 U.S.C., Section 3542. The guidelines have been broadly developed from a technical perspective to complement similar guidelines for national security systems and may be used for such systems with the approval of appropriate federal officials exercising policy authority over such systems. State, local, and tribal governments, as well as private sector organizations are encouraged to consider using these guidelines, as appropriate.[12]

Organizations use this publication in conjunction with an approved security plan in developing a viable security assessment plan for producing and compiling the information necessary to determine the effectiveness of the security controls employed in the information system. This publication has been developed with the intention of enabling organizations to tailor and supplement the basic assessment procedures provided. The assessment procedures are used as a starting point for and as input to the security assessment plan. In developing effective security assessment plans, organizations take into consideration existing information about the security controls to be assessed (e.g., results from organizational assessments of risk, platform-specific dependencies in the hardware, software, or firmware, and any assessment procedures needed as a result of organization-specific controls not included in Special Publication 800-53).[13]

The selection of appropriate assessment procedures and the rigor, intensity, and scope of the assessment depend on three factors:

- The security categorization of the information system;[14]

- The assurance requirements that the organization intends to meet in determining the overall effectiveness of the security controls; and

---

[11] An *executive agency* is: (i) an executive department specified in 5 U.S.C., Section 101; (ii) a military department specified in 5 U.S.C., Section 102; (iii) an independent establishment as defined in 5 U.S.C., Section 104(1); and (iv) a wholly owned government corporation fully subject to the provisions of 31 U.S.C., Chapter 91. In this publication, the term executive agency is synonymous with the term *federal agency.*

[12] In accordance with the provisions of FISMA and OMB policy, whenever the interconnection of federal information systems to information systems operated by state/local/tribal governments, contractors, or grantees involves the processing, storage, or transmission of federal information, the information security standards and guidelines described in this publication apply. Specific information security requirements and the terms and conditions of the system interconnections, are expressed in the Memorandums of Understanding and Interconnection Security Agreements established by participating organizations.

[13] For example, detailed test scripts may need to be developed for the specific operating system, network component, middleware, or application employed within the information system to adequately assess certain characteristics of a particular security control. Such test scripts are at a lower level of detail than provided by the assessment procedures contained in Appendix F (Assessment Procedures Catalog) and are therefore beyond the scope of this publication. Additional details for assessments are provided in the supporting assessment cases described in Appendix H.

[14] For national security systems, security categorization is accomplished in accordance with CNSS Instruction 1253. For other than national security systems, security categorization is accomplished in accordance with FIPS 199 and Special Publication 800-60.

- The selection of security controls from Special Publication 800-53 as identified in the approved security plan.[15]

The assessment process is an information-gathering activity, not a security-producing activity. Organizations determine the most cost-effective implementation of this key element in the organization's information security program by applying the results of risk assessments, considering the maturity and quality level of the organization's risk management processes, and taking advantage of the flexibility in the concepts described in this publication. The use of Special Publication 800-53A as a starting point in the process of defining procedures for assessing the security controls in information systems and organizations, promotes a consistent level of security and offers the needed flexibility to customize the assessment based on organizational policies and requirements, known threat and vulnerability information, operational considerations, information system and platform dependencies, and tolerance for risk.[16] The information produced during security control assessments can be used by an organization to:

- Identify potential problems or shortfalls in the organization's implementation of the Risk Management Framework;

- Identify information system weaknesses and deficiencies;

- Prioritize risk mitigation decisions and associated risk mitigation activities;

- Confirm that identified weaknesses and deficiencies in the information system have been addressed;

- Support continuous monitoring activities and information security situational awareness;

- Facilitate security authorization decisions; and

- Inform budgetary decisions and the capital investment process.

Organizations are not expected to employ *all* of the assessment methods and assessment objects contained within the assessment procedures identified in this publication for the associated security controls deployed within or inherited by organizational information systems. Rather, organizations have the inherent flexibility to determine the level of effort needed for a particular assessment (e.g., which assessment methods and assessment objects are deemed to be the most useful in obtaining the desired results). This determination is made on the basis of what will accomplish the assessment objectives in the most cost-effective manner and with sufficient confidence to support the subsequent determination of the resulting mission or business risk.

1.2 TARGET AUDIENCE

This publication is intended to serve a diverse group of information system and information security professionals including:

- Individuals with information system development and integration responsibilities (e.g., program managers, information technology product developers, information system developers, systems integrators, information security architects);

---

[15] The security controls for the information system are documented in the security plan after the initial selection, tailoring, and supplementation of the controls as described in NIST Special Publication 800-53 and CNSS Instruction 1253. The security plan is approved by the authorizing official with recommendations from other appropriate organizational officials prior to the start of the security control assessment.

[16] In this publication, the term *risk* is used to mean risk to organizational operations (i.e., mission, functions, image, and reputation), organizational assets, individuals, other organizations, and the Nation.

- Individuals with information security assessment and continuous monitoring responsibilities (e.g., system evaluators/testers, penetration testers, security control assessors, independent verifiers and validators, auditors, information system owners, common control providers);

- Individuals with information system and security management and oversight responsibilities (e.g., authorizing officials, senior information security officers,[17] information security managers); and

- Individuals with information security implementation and operational responsibilities (e.g., information system owners, common control providers, information owners/stewards, mission owners, systems administrators, information system security officers).

1.3 RELATED PUBLICATIONS AND ASSESSMENT PROCESSES

Special Publication 800-53A is designed to support Special Publication 800-37, *Guide for Applying the Risk Management Framework to Federal Information Systems: A Security Life Cycle Approach.* In particular, the assessment procedures contained in this publication and the guidelines provided for developing security assessment plans for organizational information systems directly support the security control assessment and continuous monitoring activities that are integral to the risk management process. This includes providing near real-time information to organizational officials regarding the ongoing security state of their information systems.

Organizations are encouraged, whenever possible, to take advantage of the assessment results and associated assessment-related documentation and evidence available on information system components from previous assessments including independent third-party testing, evaluation, and validation.[18] Product testing, evaluation, and validation may be conducted on cryptographic modules and general-purpose information technology products such as operating systems, database systems, firewalls, intrusion detection devices, Web browsers, Web applications, smart cards, biometrics devices, personal identity verification devices, network devices, and hardware platforms using national and international standards. If an information system component product is identified as providing support for the implementation of a particular security control in Special Publication 800-53, then evidence produced during the product testing, evaluation, and validation processes (e.g., security specifications, analyses and test results, validation reports, and validation certificates)[19] is used to the extent that it is applicable. This evidence is combined with the assessment-related evidence obtained from the application of the assessment procedures in this publication, to cost-effectively produce the information necessary to determine whether the security controls are effective in their application.

---

[17] At the *agency* level, this position is known as the Senior Agency Information Security Officer. Organizations may also refer to this position as the *Chief Information Security Officer.*

[18] Assessment results can be obtained from many activities that occur routinely during the system development life cycle. For example, assessment results are produced during the testing and evaluation of new information system components during system upgrades or system integration activities. Organizations can take advantage of previous assessment results whenever possible, to reduce the overall cost of assessments and to make the assessment process more efficient.

[19] Organizations review the available information from component information technology products to determine: (i) what security controls are implemented by the product; (ii) if those security controls meet the intended control requirements of the information system under assessment; (iii) if the configuration of the product and the environment in which the product operates are consistent with the environmental and product configuration stated by the vendor and/or developer; and (iv) if the assurance requirements stated in the developer/vendor specification satisfy the assurance requirements for assessing those controls. Meeting the above criteria provides a sound rationale that the product is suitable and meets the intended security control requirements of the information system under assessment.

1.4 ORGANIZATION OF THIS SPECIAL PUBLICATION

The remainder of this special publication is organized as follows:

- **Chapter Two** describes the fundamental concepts associated with security control assessments including: (i) the integration of assessments into the system development life cycle; (ii) the importance of an organization-wide strategy for conducting security control assessments; (iii) the development of effective assurance cases to help increase the grounds for confidence in the effectiveness of the security controls being assessed; and (iv) the format and content of assessment procedures.

- **Chapter Three** describes the process of assessing the security controls in organizational information systems and their environments of operation including: (i) the activities carried out by organizations and assessors to prepare for security control assessments; (ii) the development of security assessment plans; (iii) the conduct of security control assessments and the analysis, documentation, and reporting of assessment results; and (iv) the post-assessment report analysis and follow-on activities carried out by organizations.

- **Supporting appendices** provide detailed assessment-related information including: (i) general references; (ii) definitions and terms; (iii) acronyms; (iv) a description of assessment methods; (v) penetration testing guidelines; (vi) a master catalog of assessment procedures that can be used to develop plans for assessing security controls; (vii) content of security assessment reports; and (viii) the definition, format, and use of assessment cases.

CHAPTER TWO

THE FUNDAMENTALS

BASIC CONCEPTS ASSOCIATED WITH SECURITY CONTROL ASSESSMENTS

This chapter describes the basic concepts associated with assessing the security controls in organizational information systems including: (i) the integration of assessments into the system development life cycle; (ii) the importance of an organization-wide strategy for conducting security control assessments; (iii) the development of effective assurance cases to help increase the grounds for confidence in the effectiveness of the security controls; and (iv) the format and content of assessment procedures.

2.1 ASSESSMENTS WITHIN THE SYSTEM DEVELOPMENT LIFE CYCLE

Security assessments can be effectively carried out at various stages in the system development life cycle[20] to increase the grounds for confidence that the security controls employed within or inherited by an information system are effective in their application. This publication provides a comprehensive set of assessment procedures to support security assessment activities throughout the system development life cycle. For example, security assessments are routinely conducted by information system developers and system integrators during the development/acquisition and implementation phases of the life cycle to help ensure that the required security controls for the system are properly designed and developed, correctly implemented, and consistent with the established organizational information security architecture. Assessment activities in the initial system development life cycle phases include, for example, design and code reviews, application scanning, and regression testing. Security weaknesses and deficiencies identified early in the system development life cycle can be resolved more quickly and in a much more cost-effective manner before proceeding to subsequent phases in the life cycle. The objective is to identify the information security architecture and security controls up front and to ensure that the system design and testing validate the implementation of these controls. The assessment procedures described in Appendix F can support these types of assessments carried out during the initial stages of the system development life cycle.

Security assessments are also routinely conducted by information system owners, common control providers, information system security officers, independent assessors, auditors, and Inspectors General during the operations and maintenance phase of the life cycle to ensure that security controls are effective and continue to be effective in the operational environment where the system is deployed. For example, organizations assess all security controls employed within and inherited by the information system during the initial security authorization. Subsequent to the initial authorization, the organization assesses the security controls (including management, operational, and technical controls) on an ongoing basis. The frequency of such monitoring is based on the continuous monitoring strategy developed by the information system owner or common control provider and approved by the authorizing official.[21] Finally, at the end of the life cycle, security assessments are conducted as part of ensuring that important organizational information is purged from the information system prior to disposal.

---

[20] There are typically five phases in a generic system development life cycle: (i) initiation; (ii) development/acquisition; (iii) implementation; (iv) operations and maintenance; and (v) disposition (disposal).

[21] Special Publication 800-37 provides guidance on the continuous monitoring of security controls.

2.2 STRATEGY FOR CONDUCTING SECURITY CONTROL ASSESSMENTS

Organizations are encouraged to develop a broad-based, organization-wide strategy for conducting security assessments, facilitating more cost-effective and consistent assessments across the inventory of information systems. An organization-wide strategy begins by applying the initial steps of the Risk Management Framework to all information systems within the organization, with an organizational view of the security categorization process and the security control selection process (including the identification of common controls). Categorizing information systems as an organization-wide activity taking into consideration the enterprise architecture and the information security architecture helps to ensure that the individual systems are categorized based on the mission and business objectives of the organization. Maximizing the number of common controls employed within an organization: (i) significantly reduces the cost of development, implementation, and assessment of security controls; (ii) allows organizations to centralize security control assessments and to amortize the cost of those assessments across all information systems organization-wide; and (iii) increases overall security control consistency. An organization-wide approach to identifying common controls early in the application of the RMF facilitates a more global strategy for assessing those controls and sharing essential assessment results with information system owners and authorizing officials. The sharing of assessment results among key organizational officials across information system boundaries has many important benefits including:

- Providing the capability to review assessment results for all information systems and to make organization-wide, mission/business-related decisions on risk mitigation activities according to organizational priorities, the security categorization of the information systems supporting the organization, and risk assessments;

- Providing a more global view of systemic weaknesses and deficiencies occurring in information systems across the organization;

- Providing an opportunity to develop organization-wide solutions to information security problems; and

- Increasing the organization's knowledge base regarding threats, vulnerabilities, and strategies for more cost-effective solutions to common information security problems.

Organizations can also promote a more focused and cost-effective assessment process by: (i) developing more specific assessment procedures that are tailored for their specific organizational environments of operation and requirements (instead of relegating these tasks to each security control assessor or assessment team); and (ii) providing organization-wide tools, templates, and techniques to support more consistent assessments throughout the organization.

While the conduct of security control assessments is the primary responsibility of information system owners and common control providers with oversight by their respective authorizing officials, there is also significant involvement in the assessment process by other parties within the organization who have a vested interest in the outcome of assessments. Other interested parties include, for example, mission/business owners, information owners/stewards (when those roles are filled by someone other than the information system owner), information security officials, and the risk executive (function). It is imperative that information system owners and common control providers coordinate with the other parties in the organization having an interest in security control assessments to help ensure that the organization's core missions and business functions are adequately addressed in the selection of security controls to be assessed.

2.3 BUILDING AN EFFECTIVE ASSURANCE CASE

Building an effective assurance case[22] for security control effectiveness is a process that involves: (i) compiling evidence from a variety of activities conducted during the system development life cycle that the controls employed in the information system are implemented correctly, operating as intended, and producing the desired outcome with respect to meeting the security requirements of the system; and (ii) presenting this evidence in a manner that decision makers are able to use effectively in making risk-based decisions about the operation or use of the system. The evidence described above comes from the implementation of the security controls in the information system and inherited by the system (i.e., common controls) and from the assessments of that implementation. Ideally, the assessor is building on previously developed materials that started with the specification of the organization's information security needs and was further developed during the design, development, and implementation of the information system. These materials, developed while implementing security throughout the life cycle of the information system, provide the initial evidence for an assurance case.

Assessors obtain the required evidence during the assessment process to allow the appropriate organizational officials to make objective determinations about the effectiveness of the security controls and the overall security state of the information system. The assessment evidence needed to make such determinations can be obtained from a variety of sources including, but not limited to, information technology product and system assessments. Product assessments (also known as product testing, evaluation, and validation) are typically conducted by independent, third-party testing organizations. These assessments examine the security functions of products and established configuration settings. Assessments can be conducted against industry, national, or international information security standards as well as developer/vendor claims. Since many information technology products are assessed by commercial testing organizations and then subsequently deployed in millions of information systems, these types of assessments can be carried out at a greater level of depth and provide deeper insights into the security capabilities of the particular products.

System assessments are typically conducted by information systems developers, systems integrators, information system owners, common control providers, assessors, auditors, Inspectors General, and the information security staffs of organizations. The assessors or assessment teams bring together available information about the information system such as the results from individual component product assessments, if available, and conduct additional system-level assessments using a variety of methods and techniques. System assessments are used to compile and evaluate the evidence needed by organizational officials to determine how effective the security controls employed in the information system are likely to be in mitigating risks to organizational operations and assets, to individuals, to other organizations, and to the Nation. The results from assessments conducted using information system-specific and organization-specific assessment procedures derived from the guidelines in this publication contribute to compiling the necessary evidence to determine security control effectiveness in accordance with the assurance requirements documented in the security plan.

---

[22] An assurance case is a body of evidence organized into an argument demonstrating that some claim about an information system holds (i.e., is assured). An assurance case is needed when it is important to show that a system exhibits some complex property such as safety, security, or reliability. Additional information can be obtained at https://buildsecurityin.us-cert.gov/daisy/bsi/articles/knowledge/assurance/643.html.

2.4 ASSESSMENT PROCEDURES

An assessment procedure consists of a set of assessment *objectives*, each with an associated set of potential assessment *methods* and assessment *objects*. An assessment objective includes a set of *determination statements* related to the security control under assessment. The determination statements are linked to the content of the security control (i.e., the security control functionality) to ensure traceability of assessment results back to the fundamental control requirements. The application of an assessment procedure to a security control produces assessment *findings*. These assessment findings reflect, or are subsequently used, to help determine the overall effectiveness of the security control.

Assessment objects identify the specific items being assessed and include *specifications*, *mechanisms*, *activities*, and *individuals*. Specifications are the document-based artifacts (e.g., policies, procedures, plans, system security requirements, functional specifications, and architectural designs) associated with an information system. Mechanisms are the specific hardware, software, or firmware safeguards and countermeasures employed within an information system.[23] Activities are the specific protection-related pursuits or actions supporting an information system that involve people (e.g., conducting system backup operations, monitoring network traffic, exercising a contingency plan). Individuals, or groups of individuals, are people applying the specifications, mechanisms, or activities described above.

Assessment methods define the nature of the assessor actions and include *examine*, *interview*, and *test*. The *examine* method is the process of reviewing, inspecting, observing, studying, or analyzing one or more assessment objects (i.e., specifications, mechanisms, or activities). The purpose of the examine method is to facilitate assessor understanding, achieve clarification, or obtain evidence. The *interview* method is the process of holding discussions with individuals or groups of individuals within an organization to once again, facilitate assessor understanding, achieve clarification, or obtain evidence. The *test* method is the process of exercising one or more assessment objects (i.e., activities or mechanisms) under specified conditions to compare actual with expected behavior. In all three assessment methods, the results are used in making specific determinations called for in the determination statements and thereby achieving the objectives for the assessment procedure. A complete description of assessment methods and assessment objects is provided in Appendix D.

The assessment methods have a set of associated attributes, *depth* and *coverage*, which help define the level of effort for the assessment. These attributes are hierarchical in nature, providing the means to define the rigor and scope of the assessment for the increased assurances that may be needed for some information systems. The depth attribute addresses the rigor of and level of detail in the examination, interview, and testing processes. Values for the depth attribute include *basic*, *focused*, and *comprehensive*. The coverage attribute addresses the scope or breadth of the examination, interview, and testing processes including the number and type of specifications, mechanisms, and activities to be examined or tested and the number and types of individuals to be interviewed. Similar to the depth attribute, values for the coverage attribute include *basic*, *focused*, and *comprehensive*. The appropriate depth and coverage attribute values for a particular assessment method are based on the assurance requirements specified by the organization.[24] As assurance requirements increase with regard to the development, implementation, and operation

---

[23] Mechanisms also include physical protection devices associated with an information system (e.g., locks, keypads, security cameras, fire protection devices, fireproof safes, etc.).

[24] For other than national security systems, organizations meet minimum assurance requirements specified in Special Publication 800-53, Appendix E.

of security controls within or inherited by the information system, the rigor and scope of the assessment activities (as reflected in the selection of assessment methods and objects and the assignment of depth and coverage attribute values), tend to increase as well. Appendix D provides a detailed description of assessment method attributes and attribute values.

While flexibility continues to be an important factor in developing security assessment plans, consistency of assessments is also an important consideration. A major design objective for Special Publication 800-53A is to provide an assessment framework and initial starting point for assessment procedures that are essential for achieving such consistency. In addition to the assessment framework and initial starting point for assessment procedures, Appendix H describes the Assessment Case Development Project. The purpose of this project is fourfold: (i) to actively engage experienced assessors in the development of a representative set of assessment cases corresponding to the assessment procedures in Appendix F; (ii) to provide organizations and the assessors supporting those organizations with an exemplary set of assessment cases for each assessment procedure in the catalog of procedures in Appendix F; (iii) to provide a vehicle for ongoing community-wide review of the assessment cases to promote continuous improvement in the assessment process for more consistent, cost-effective security assessments of federal information systems; and (iv) to serve as a basis of reciprocity among various communities of interest. Appendix H contains several examples of assessment cases.

AN EXAMPLE ASSESSMENT PROCEDURE

SECURITY CONTROL	
CP-2	**CONTINGENCY PLAN**

Control:	The organization:
	 a. Develops a contingency plan for the information system that:
	   - Identifies essential missions and business functions and associated contingency requirements;
	   - Provides recovery objectives, restoration priorities, and metrics;
	   - Addresses contingency roles, responsibilities, assigned individuals with contact information;
	   - Addresses maintaining essential missions and business functions despite an information system disruption, compromise, or failure;
	   - Addresses eventual, full information system restoration without deterioration of the security measures originally planned and implemented; and
	   - Is reviewed and approved by designated officials within the organization;
	 b. Distributes copies of the contingency plan to [*Assignment: organization-defined list of key contingency personnel (identified by name and/or by role) and organizational elements*];
	 c. Coordinates contingency planning activities with incident handling activities;
	 d. Reviews the contingency plan for the information system [*Assignment: organization-defined frequency*];
	 e. Revises the contingency plan to address changes to the organization, information system, or environment of operation and problems encountered during contingency plan implementation, execution, or testing; and
	 f. Communicates contingency plan changes to [*Assignment: organization-defined list of key contingency personnel (identified by name and/or by role) and organizational elements*].

SECURITY CONTROL	
CP-2	**CONTINGENCY PLAN**
Supplemental Guidance:	Contingency planning for information systems is part of an overall organizational program for achieving continuity of operations for mission/business operations. Contingency planning addresses both information system restoration and implementation of alternative mission/business processes when systems are compromised. Information system recovery objectives are consistent with applicable laws, Executive Orders, directives, policies, standards, or regulations. In addition to information system availability, contingency plans also address other security-related events resulting in a reduction in mission/business effectiveness, such as malicious attacks compromising the confidentiality or integrity of the information system. Examples of actions to call out in contingency plans include, for example, graceful degradation, information system shutdown, fall back to a manual mode, alternate information flows, or operating in a mode that is reserved solely for when the system is under attack. Related controls: AC-14, CP-6, CP-7, CP-8, IR-4, PM-8, PM-11.

The first assessment objective for CP-2 is derived from the basic control statement. Potential assessment methods and objects are added to the assessment procedure.

ASSESSMENT PROCEDURE	
CP-2.1	**ASSESSMENT OBJECTIVE:** *Determine if:*
	(i) *the organization develops a contingency plan for the information system that:*
	- *identifies essential missions and business functions and associated contingency requirements;*
	- *provides recovery objectives, restoration priorities, and metrics;*
	- *addresses contingency roles, responsibilities, assigned individuals with contact information;*
	- *addresses maintaining essential missions and business functions despite an information system disruption, compromise, or failure; and*
	- *addresses eventual, full information system restoration without deterioration of the security measures originally planned and implemented; and*
	- *is reviewed and approved by designated officials within the organization;*
	(ii) *the organization defines key contingency personnel (identified by name and/or by role) and organizational elements designated to receive copies of the contingency plan; and*
	(iii) *the organization distributes copies of the contingency plan to organization-defined key contingency personnel and organizational elements.*
	POTENTIAL ASSESSMENT METHODS AND OBJECTS:
	Examine: [*SELECT FROM:* Contingency planning policy; procedures addressing contingency operations for the information system; contingency plan; security plan; other relevant documents or records].[25]
	Interview: [*SELECT FROM:* Organizational personnel with contingency planning and plan implementation responsibilities].

---

[25] Although not explicitly noted with each identified assessment method in the assessment procedure format in Appendix F, the attribute values of *depth* and *coverage* described in Appendix D are assigned by the organization and applied by the assessor/assessment team in the execution of the assessment method against an assessment object.

In a similar manner, the second assessment objective and potential assessment methods and objects for CP-2 are established.

ASSESSMENT PROCEDURE	
CP-2.2	*Determine if:* *(i) the organization coordinates contingency planning activities with incident handling activities:* *(ii) the organization defines the frequency of contingency plan reviews;* *(iii) the organization reviews the contingency plan for the information system in accordance with the organization-defined frequency;* *(iv) the organization revises the contingency plan to address changes to the organization, information system, or environment of operation and problems encountered during contingency plan implementation, execution or testing; and* *(v) the organization communicates contingency plan changes to the key contingency personnel and organizational elements as identified in CP-2.1 (ii).* **POTENTIAL ASSESSMENT METHODS AND OBJECTS:** **Examine**: [*SELECT FROM:* Contingency planning policy; procedures addressing contingency operations for the information system; contingency plan; security plan; other relevant documents or records]. **Interview**: [*SELECT FROM:* Organizational personnel with contingency planning and plan implementation responsibilities; organizational personnel with incident handling responsibilities].

The assessment objectives within a particular assessment procedure are numbered sequentially (e.g., CP-2.1,…, CP-2.n). If the security control has any enhancements, assessment objectives are developed for each enhancement using the same process as for the base control. The resulting assessment objectives within the assessment procedure are numbered sequentially (e.g., CP-2(1).1 indicating the first assessment objective for the first enhancement for security control CP-2).

CHAPTER THREE

THE PROCESS
CONDUCTING EFFECTIVE SECURITY CONTROL ASSESSMENTS

This chapter describes the process of assessing the security controls in organizational information systems including: (i) the activities carried out by organizations and assessors to prepare for security control assessments; (ii) the development of security assessment plans; (iii) the conduct of security control assessments and the analysis, documentation, and reporting of assessment results; and (iv) post-assessment report analysis and follow-on activities carried out by organizations.

3.1 PREPARING FOR SECURITY CONTROL ASSESSMENTS

Conducting security control assessments in today's complex environment of sophisticated information technology infrastructures and high-visibility, mission-critical applications can be difficult, challenging, and resource-intensive. Success requires the cooperation and collaboration among all parties having a vested interest in the organization's information security posture, including information system owners, common control providers, authorizing officials, chief information officers, senior information security officers, chief executive officers/heads of agencies, Inspectors General, and the OMB. Establishing an appropriate set of expectations before, during, and after the assessment is paramount to achieving an acceptable outcome—that is, producing information necessary to help the authorizing official make a credible, risk-based decision on whether to place the information system into operation or continue its operation.

Thorough preparation by the organization and the assessors is an important aspect of conducting effective security control assessments. Preparatory activities address a range of issues relating to the cost, schedule, and performance of the assessment. From the organizational perspective, preparing for a security control assessment includes the following key activities:

- Ensuring that appropriate policies covering security control assessments are in place and understood by all affected organizational elements;

- Ensuring that all steps in the RMF prior to the security control assessment step, have been successfully completed and received appropriate management oversight;[26]

- Ensuring that security controls identified as common controls (and the common portion of hybrid controls) have been assigned to appropriate organizational entities (i.e., common control providers) for development and implementation;[27]

- Establishing the objective and scope of the security control assessment (i.e., the purpose of the assessment and what is being assessed);

---

[26] Conducting security control assessments in parallel with the development/acquisition and implementation phases of the life cycle permits the identification of weaknesses and deficiencies early and provides the most cost-effective method for initiating corrective actions. Issues found during these assessments can be referred to authorizing officials for early resolution, as appropriate. The results of security control assessments carried out during system development and implementation can also be used (consistent with reuse criteria) during the security authorization process to avoid system fielding delays or costly repetition of assessments.

[27] Security control assessments include common controls that are the responsibility of organizational entities other than the information system owner inheriting the controls or hybrid controls where there is shared responsibility among the system owner and designated organizational entities.

- Notifying key organizational officials of the impending security control assessment and allocating necessary resources to carry out the assessment;

- Establishing appropriate communication channels among organizational officials having an interest in the security control assessment;[28]

- Establishing time frames for completing the security control assessment and key milestone decision points required by the organization to effectively manage the assessment;

- Identifying and selecting a competent assessor/assessment team that will be responsible for conducting the security control assessment, considering issues of assessor independence;

- Collecting artifacts to provide to the assessor/assessment team (e.g., policies, procedures, plans, specifications, designs, records, administrator/operator manuals, information system documentation, interconnection agreements, previous assessment results); and

- Establishing a mechanism between the organization and the assessor and/or assessment team to minimize ambiguities or misunderstandings about security control implementation or security control weaknesses/deficiencies identified during the assessment.

Security control assessors/assessment teams begin preparing for the assessment by:

- Obtaining a general understanding of the organization's operations (including mission, functions, and business processes) and how the information system that is the subject of the security control assessment supports those organizational operations;

- Obtaining an understanding of the structure of the information system (i.e., system architecture);

- Obtaining a thorough understanding of the security controls being assessed (including system-specific, hybrid, and common controls);

- Identifying the organizational entities responsible for the development and implementation of the common controls (or the common portion of hybrid controls) supporting the information system;

- Establishing appropriate organizational points of contact needed to carry out the security control assessment;

- Obtaining artifacts needed for the security control assessment (e.g., policies, procedures, plans, specifications, designs, records, administrator/operator manuals, information system documentation, interconnection agreements, previous assessment results);

- Obtaining previous assessment results that may be appropriately reused for the security control assessment (e.g., Inspector General reports, audits, vulnerability scans, physical security inspections, prior assessments, developmental testing and evaluation, vendor flaw remediation activities , ISO/IEC 15408 [Common Criteria] evaluations);

- Meeting with appropriate organizational officials to ensure common understanding for assessment objectives and the proposed rigor and scope of the assessment; and

- Developing a security assessment plan.

---

[28] Typically, these individuals include authorizing officials, information system owners, common control providers, mission and information owners/stewards (if other than the information system owner), chief information officers, senior information security officers, Inspectors General, information system security officers, users from organizations that the information system supports, and assessors.

In preparation for the assessment of security controls, the necessary background information is assembled and made available to the assessors or assessment team.[29] To the extent necessary to support the specific assessment, the organization identifies and arranges access to: (i) elements of the organization responsible for developing, documenting, disseminating, reviewing, and updating all security policies and associated procedures for implementing policy-compliant controls; (ii) the security policies for the information system and any associated implementing procedures; (iii) individuals or groups responsible for the development, implementation, operation, and maintenance of security controls; (iv) any materials (e.g., security plans, records, schedules, assessment reports, after-action reports, agreements, authorization packages) associated with the implementation and operation of security controls; and (v) the objects to be assessed.[30] The availability of essential documentation as well as access to key organizational personnel and the information system being assessed are paramount to a successful assessment of the security controls.

Organizations consider both the *technical expertise* and level of *independence* required in selecting security control assessors. Organizations ensure that security control assessors possess the required skills and technical expertise to successfully carry out assessments of system-specific, hybrid, and common controls. This includes knowledge of and experience with the specific hardware, software, and firmware components employed by the organization. An independent assessor is any individual or group capable of conducting an impartial assessment of security controls employed within or inherited by an information system. Impartiality implies that assessors are free from any perceived or actual conflicts of interest with respect to the development, operation, and/or management of the information system or the determination of security control effectiveness.[31] The authorizing official or designated representative determines the required level of independence for security control assessors based on the results of the security categorization process for the information system and the ultimate risk to organizational operations and assets, individuals, other organizations, and the Nation. The authorizing official determines if the level of assessor independence is sufficient to provide confidence that the assessment results produced are sound and can be used to make a risk-based decision on whether to place the information system into operation or continue its operation. Independent security control assessment services can be obtained from other elements within the organization or can be contracted to a public or private sector entity outside of the organization. In special situations, for example when the organization that owns the information system is small or the organizational structure requires that the security control assessment be accomplished by individuals that are in the developmental, operational, and/or management chain of the system owner, independence in the assessment process can be achieved by ensuring that the assessment results are carefully reviewed and analyzed by an independent team of experts to validate the completeness, consistency, and veracity of the results.[32]

---

[29] Information system owners and organizational entities developing, implementing, and/or administering common controls (i.e., common control providers) are responsible for providing needed information to assessors.

[30] In situations where there are multiple security assessments ongoing or planned within an organization, access to organizational elements, individuals, and artifacts supporting the assessments is centrally managed by the organization to ensure a cost-effective use of time and resources.

[31] Contracted assessment services are considered independent if the information system owner is not directly involved in the contracting process or cannot unduly influence the independence of the assessor(s) conducting the assessment of the security controls.

[32] The authorizing official consults with the Office of the Inspector General, the senior information security officer, and the chief information officer to discuss the implications of any decisions on assessor independence in the types of special circumstances described above.

3.2 DEVELOPING SECURITY ASSESSMENT PLANS

The *security assessment plan* provides the objectives for the security control assessment and a detailed roadmap of how to conduct such an assessment. The following steps are considered by assessors in developing plans to assess the security controls in organizational information systems or inherited by those systems:

- Determine which security controls/control enhancements are to be included in the assessment based upon the contents of the security plan and the purpose/scope of the assessment;

- Select the appropriate assessment procedures to be used during the assessment based on the security controls and control enhancements that are to be included in the assessment;

- Tailor the selected assessment procedures (e.g., select appropriate assessment methods and objects, assign depth and coverage attribute values);

- Develop additional assessment procedures to address any security requirements or controls that are not sufficiently covered by Special Publication 800-53;

- Optimize the assessment procedures to reduce duplication of effort (e.g., sequencing and consolidating assessment procedures) and provide cost-effective assessment solutions; and

- Finalize the assessment plan and obtain the necessary approvals to execute the plan.

3.2.1 Determine which security controls are to be assessed.

The security plan provides an overview of the security requirements for the information system and describes the security controls in place or planned for meeting those requirements. The assessor starts with the security controls described in the security plan and considers the purpose of the assessment. A security control assessment can be a *complete* assessment of all security controls in the information system or inherited by the system (e.g., during an initial security authorization process) or a *partial* assessment of the security controls in the information system or inherited by the system (e.g., during system development, during continuous monitoring where controls are assessed on an ongoing basis and as a result of changes affecting the controls, or where controls were previously assessed and the results accepted in the reciprocity process).[33]

For partial assessments, information system owners and common control providers collaborate with organizational officials having an interest in the assessment (e.g., senior information security officers, mission/information owners, Inspectors General, and authorizing officials) to determine which security controls are to be assessed. The selection of the security controls depends on the continuous monitoring strategy established by the information system owner or common control provider to ensure that: (i) all controls are assessed during the authorization period established by federal legislation, policies, directives, standards, and guidelines; (ii) items on the plan of action and milestones receive adequate oversight; (iii) controls with greater volatility or importance to the organization are assessed more frequently; and (iv) control implementations that have changed since the last assessment are reevaluated.[34]

---

[33] Partial assessments of security controls can be conducted in the initial phases of system development life cycle to promote early detection of weakness and deficiencies and a more cost-effective approach to risk mitigation.

[34] Special Publication 800-37 provides guidance on continuous monitoring as part of the risk management process.

3.2.2 Select appropriate procedures to assess the security controls.

Special Publication 800-53A, Appendix F, provides an assessment procedure for each security control and control enhancement in Special Publication 800-53. For each security control and control enhancement in the security plan to be included in the assessment, assessors select the corresponding assessment procedure from Appendix F. The selected assessment procedures vary from assessment to assessment based on the current content of the security plan and the purpose of the security assessment (e.g., complete security control assessment, partial security control assessment).

3.2.3 Tailor assessment procedures.

In a similar manner to how the security controls from Special Publication 800-53 are tailored for the organization's mission, business functions, characteristics of the information system and operating environment, organizations tailor the assessment procedures listed in Appendix F to meet specific organizational needs. Organizations have the flexibility to perform the tailoring process at the organization level for all information systems, at the individual information system level, or using a combination of organization-level and system-specific approaches. Security control assessors determine if the organization provides additional tailoring guidance prior to initiating the tailoring process. Assessment procedures are tailored by:

- Selecting the appropriate assessment methods and objects needed to satisfy the stated assessment objectives;

- Selecting the appropriate depth and coverage attribute values to define the rigor and scope of the assessment;

- Identifying common controls that have been assessed by a separately-documented security assessment plan, and do not require the repeated execution of the assessment procedures;

- Developing information system/platform-specific and organization-specific assessment procedures (which may be adaptations to those procedures in Appendix F);

- Incorporating assessment results from previous assessments where the results are deemed applicable; and

- Making appropriate adjustments in assessment procedures to be able to obtain the requisite assessment evidence from external providers.

Assessment method and object-related considerations—

It is recognized that organizations can specify, document, and configure their information systems in a variety of ways and that the content and applicability of existing assessment evidence will vary. This may result in the need to apply a variety of assessment methods to various assessment objects to generate the assessment evidence needed to determine whether the security controls are effective in their application. Therefore, the assessment methods and objects provided with each assessment procedure are termed *potential* to reflect the need to be able to choose the methods and objects most appropriate for a specific assessment. The assessment methods and objects chosen are those deemed as necessary to produce the evidence needed to make the determinations described in the determination statements. The potential methods and objects in the assessment procedure are provided as a resource to assist in the selection of appropriate methods and objects, and not with the intent to limit the selection. Organizations use their judgment in selecting from the potential assessment methods and the list of assessment objects associated with each selected method. Organizations select those methods and objects that most cost-effectively contribute to making the determinations associated with the assessment objective.[35] The measure of the quality of assessment results is based on the soundness of the rationale provided, not the specific set of methods and objects applied. It will not be necessary, in most cases, to apply every assessment method to every assessment object to obtain the desired assessment results. And for certain assessments, it may be appropriate to employ a method not currently listed in the set of potential methods.

Depth and coverage-related considerations—

In addition to selecting appropriate assessment methods and objects, each assessment method (i.e., examine, interview, and test) is associated with depth and coverage attributes that are described in Appendix D. The attribute values identify the rigor and scope of the assessment procedures executed by the assessor. The values selected by the organization are based on the characteristics of the information system being assessed (including assurance requirements) and the specific determinations to be made. The depth and coverage attribute values are associated with the assurance requirements specified by the organization (i.e., the rigor and scope of the assessment increases in direct relationship to the assurance requirements).

Common control-related considerations—

Assessors note which security controls (or parts of security controls) in the security plan are designated as *common controls*.[36] Since the assessment of common controls is the responsibility of the organizational entity that developed and implemented the controls (i.e., common control provider), the assessment procedures in Appendix F used to assess these controls incorporate assessment results from that organizational entity. Common controls may have been previously assessed as part of the organization's information security program or as part of an information system providing common controls inherited by other organizational systems. There may also be a separate plan to assess the common controls. In either situation, information system owners coordinate the assessment of common controls with appropriate organizational officials (e.g., chief information officer, senior information security officer, mission/information owners, authorizing officials) obtaining the results of common control assessments or, if the common controls have not been assessed or are due to be reassessed, making the necessary arrangements to include or reference the common control assessment results in the current assessment.[37]

Another consideration in assessing common controls is that there are occasionally system-specific aspects of a common control that are not covered by the organizational entities responsible for the common aspects of the control. These types of security controls are referred to as *hybrid controls*. For example, CP-2, the contingency planning security control, may be deemed a hybrid control by the organization if there is a master contingency plan developed by the organization for all organizational information systems. Following up on the initial master contingency plan,

---

[35] The selection of assessment methods and objects (including the number and type of assessment objects) can be a significant factor in cost-effectively meeting the assessment objectives.

[36] Common controls support multiple information systems within the organization and the protection measures provided by those controls are inherited by the individual systems. Therefore, the organization determines the appropriate set of common controls to ensure that both the strength of the controls (i.e., security capability) and level of rigor and intensity of the control assessments are commensurate with the criticality and/or sensitivity of the individual information systems inheriting those controls. Weaknesses or deficiencies in common controls have the potential to adversely affect large portions of the organization and thus require significant attention.

[37] If assessment results are not currently available for the common controls, the assessment plans for the information systems under assessment that depend on those controls are duly noted. The assessments cannot be considered complete until the assessment results for the common controls are made available to information system owners.

information system owners are expected to adjust, tailor, or supplement the contingency plan as necessary, when there are system-specific aspects of the plan that need to be defined for the particular system where the control is employed. For each hybrid control, assessors include in the assessment plan, the portions of the assessment procedures from Appendix F related to the parts of the control that are system-specific to ensure that, along with the results from common control assessments, all aspects of the security control are assessed.

System/platform and organization-related considerations—

The assessment procedures in Special Publication 800-53A may be adapted to address system/platform-specific or organization-specific dependencies. This situation arises frequently in the assessment procedures associated with the security controls from the technical families in Special Publication 800-53 (i.e., access control, audit and accountability, identification and authentication, system and communications protection). For example, the assessment of a UNIX implementation of the IA-2 control for identification and authentication of users might include an explicit examination of the *.rhosts* file for UNIX systems since improper entries in that file can result in bypassing user authentication. Recent test results may also be applicable to the current assessment if those test methods provide a high degree of transparency (e.g., what was tested, when was it tested, how was it tested). Standards-based testing protocols such as the Security Content Automation Protocol (SCAP) provide an example of how organizations can help achieve this level of transparency.

Reuse of assessment evidence-related considerations—

Reuse of assessment results from previously accepted or approved assessments are considered in the body of evidence for determining overall security control effectiveness. Previously accepted or approved assessments include: (i) those assessments of common controls that are managed by the organization and support multiple information systems; or (ii) assessments of security controls that are reviewed as part of the control implementation (e.g., CP-2 requires a review of the contingency plan). The acceptability of using previous assessment results in a security control assessment is coordinated with and approved by the users of the assessment results. It is essential that information system owners and common control providers collaborate with authorizing officials and other appropriate organizational officials in determining the acceptability of using previous assessment results. When considering the reuse of previous assessment results and the value of those results to the current assessment, assessors determine: (i) the credibility of the assessment evidence; (ii) the appropriateness of previous analysis; and (iii) the applicability of the assessment evidence to current information system operating conditions. If previous assessment results are reused, the date of the original assessment and type of assessment are documented in the security assessment plan and security assessment report. It may be necessary, in certain situations, to supplement previous assessment results under consideration for reuse with additional assessment activities to fully address the assessment objectives. For example, if an independent evaluation of an information technology product did not test a particular configuration setting that is employed by the organization in an information system, then the assessor may need to supplement the original test results with additional testing to cover that configuration setting for the current information system environment. The decision to reuse assessment results is documented in the security assessment plan and the final security assessment report and is consistent with federal legislation, policies, directives, standards, and guidelines with respect to the security control assessments.

The following items are considered in validating previous assessment results for reuse:

- Changing conditions associated with security controls over time.

Security controls that were deemed effective during previous assessments may have become ineffective due to changing conditions within the information system or its environment of operation. Assessment results that were found to be previously acceptable may no longer provide credible evidence for the determination of security control effectiveness, and therefore, a reassessment would be required. Applying previous assessment results to a current assessment necessitates the identification of any changes that have occurred since the previous assessment and the impact of these changes on the previous results. For example, reusing previous assessment results from examining an organization's security policies and procedures may be acceptable if it is determined that there have not been any significant changes to the identified policies and procedures. Reusing assessment results produced during the previous authorization of an information system is a cost-effective method for supporting continuous monitoring activities and annual FISMA reporting requirements when the related controls have not changed and there are adequate reasons for confidence in their continued application.

- Amount of time that has transpired since previous assessments.

In general, as the time period between current and previous assessments increases, the credibility/utility of the previous assessment results decreases. This is primarily due to the fact that the information system or the environment in which the information system operates is more likely to change with the passage of time, possibly invalidating the original conditions or assumptions on which the previous assessment was based.

- Degree of independence of previous assessments.

Assessor independence can be a critical factor in certain types of assessments. The degree of independence required from assessment to assessment is consistent. For example, it is not appropriate to reuse results from a previous self-assessment where no assessor independence was required, in a current assessment requiring a greater degree of independence.

External information system-related considerations—

The assessment procedures in Appendix F need to be adjusted as appropriate to accommodate the assessment of external information systems.[38] Because the organization does not always have direct control over the security controls used in external information systems, or sufficient visibility into the development, implementation, and assessment of those controls, alternative assessment approaches may need to be applied, resulting in the need to tailor the assessment procedures described in Appendix F. Where required assurances of agreed-upon security controls within an information system or inherited by the system are documented in contracts or service-level agreements, assessors review these contracts or agreements and where appropriate, tailor the assessment procedures to assess either the security controls or the security control assessment results provided through these agreements. In addition, assessors take into account any other assessments that have been conducted, or are in the process of being conducted, for external information systems that are relied upon with regard to protecting the information system under

---

[38] An *external information system* is an information system or component of an information system that is outside of the authorization boundary established by the organization and for which the organization typically has no direct control over the application of required security controls or the assessment of security control effectiveness. Special Publications 800-37 and 800-53 provide additional guidance on external information systems and the effect of employing security controls in those types of environments.

assessment. Applicable information from these assessments, if deemed reliable, is incorporated into the security assessment report.

3.2.4 Develop assessment procedures for organization-specific security controls.

Based on organizational policies, mission or business function requirements, and an assessment of risk, organizations may choose to develop and implement additional (organization-specific) security controls or control enhancements for their information systems that are beyond the scope of Special Publication 800-53. Such security controls are documented in the security plan for the information system as controls not found in Special Publication 800-53. To assess the security controls in this situation, assessors use the guidelines in Chapter Two to develop assessment procedures for those controls and control enhancements. The assessment procedures developed are subsequently integrated into the security assessment plan.

3.2.5 Optimize selected assessment procedures to ensure maximum efficiency.

Assessors have a great deal of flexibility in organizing a security assessment plan that meets the needs of the organization and that provides the best opportunity for obtaining the necessary evidence to determine security control effectiveness, while reducing overall assessment costs. Combining and consolidating assessment procedures is one area where this flexibility can be applied. During the assessment of an information system, assessment methods are applied numerous times to a variety of assessment objects within a particular family of security controls. To save time, reduce assessment costs, and maximize the usefulness of assessment results, assessors review the selected assessment procedures for the security control families and combine or consolidate the procedures (or parts of procedures) whenever possible or practicable. For example, assessors may wish to consolidate interviews with key organizational officials dealing with a variety of security-related topics. Assessors may have other opportunities for significant consolidations and cost savings by examining all security policies and procedures from the eighteen families of security controls at the same time or organizing groups of related policies and procedures that could be examined as a unified entity. Obtaining and examining configuration settings from similar hardware and software components within the information system is another example that can provide significant assessment efficiencies.

An additional area for consideration in optimizing the assessment process is the sequence in which security controls are assessed. The assessment of some security controls before others may provide information that facilitates understanding and assessment of other controls. For example, security controls such as CM-2 (Baseline Configuration), CM-8 (Information System Component Inventory), PL-2 (System Security Plan), RA-2 (Security Categorization), and RA-3 (Risk Assessment) produce general descriptions of the information system. Assessing these security controls early in the assessment process may provide a basic understanding of the information system that can aid in assessing other security controls. The supplemental guidance of many security controls also identifies related controls that can provide useful information in organizing the assessment procedures.[39] For example, AC-19 (Access Control for Portable and Mobile Devices) lists security controls MP-4 (Media Storage) and MP-5 (Media Transport) as being related to AC-19. Since AC-19 is related to MP-4 and MP-5, the sequence in which assessments are conducted for AC-19, MP-4, and MP-5 may facilitate the reuse of assessment information from one control in assessing other related controls.

---

[39] Security control assessment sequencing is also addressed in the assessment cases described in Appendix H.

3.2.6 Finalize security assessment plan and obtain approval to execute plan.

After selecting the assessment procedures (including developing necessary procedures not contained in the Special Publication 800-53A catalog of procedures), tailoring the procedures for information system/platform-specific and organization-specific conditions, optimizing the procedures for efficiency, and addressing the potential for unexpected events impacting the assessment, the assessment plan is finalized and the schedule is established including key milestones for the assessment process. Once the security assessment plan is completed, the plan is reviewed and approved by appropriate organizational officials[40] to ensure that the plan is complete, consistent with the security objectives of the organization and the organization's assessment of risk, and cost-effective with regard to the resources allocated for the assessment.

3.3 CONDUCTING SECURITY CONTROL ASSESSMENTS

After the security assessment plan is approved by the organization, the assessor or assessment team executes the plan in accordance with the agreed-upon schedule. Determining the size and organizational makeup of the security assessment team (i.e., skill sets, technical expertise, and assessment experience of the individuals composing the team) is part of the risk management decisions made by the organization requesting and initiating the assessment.

The output and end result of the security control assessment is the *security assessment report*, which documents the assurance case for the information system and is one of three key documents in the security authorization package developed by information system owners and common control providers for authorizing officials.[41] The security assessment report includes information from the assessor (in the form of assessment findings) necessary to determine the effectiveness of the security controls employed within or inherited by the information system. The security assessment report is an important factor in an authorizing official's determination of risk. Organizations may choose to develop an assessment *summary* from the detailed findings that are generated by the assessor during the security control assessment. An assessment summary can provide an authorizing official with an abbreviated version a of *Security Assessment Report* focusing on the highlights of the assessment, synopsis of key findings, and/or recommendations for addressing weaknesses and deficiencies in the security controls. Appendix G provides additional information on the recommended content of security assessment reports.

Assessment objectives are achieved by applying the designated assessment methods to selected assessment objects and compiling/producing the evidence necessary to make the determination associated with each assessment objective. Each determination statement contained within an assessment procedure executed by an assessor produces one of the following findings: (i) *satisfied (S)*; or (ii) *other than satisfied (O)*. A finding of satisfied indicates that for the portion of the security control addressed by the determination statement, the assessment information obtained (i.e., evidence collected) indicates that the assessment objective for the control has been met producing a fully acceptable result. A finding of other than satisfied indicates that for the portion of the security control addressed by the determination statement, the assessment information obtained indicates potential anomalies in the operation or implementation of the control that may need to be addressed by the organization. A finding of other than satisfied may

---

[40] Organizations establish a security assessment plan approval process with the specific organizational officials (e.g., information systems owners, common control providers, information system security officers, senior information security officers, authorizing officials) designated as approving authorities.

[41] In accordance with Special Publication 800-37, the security authorization package consists of the security plan (including the risk assessment), the security assessment report, and the plan of action and milestones (POAM).

also indicate that for reasons specified in the assessment report, the assessor was unable to obtain sufficient information to make the particular determination called for in the determination statement. For assessment findings that are *other than satisfied*, organizations may choose to define *subcategories* of findings indicating the severity and/or criticality of the weaknesses or deficiencies discovered and the potential adverse effects on organizational operations (i.e., mission, functions, image, or reputation), organizational assets, individuals, other organizations, and the Nation. Defining such subcategories can help to establish priorities for needed risk mitigation actions.

Assessor findings are an unbiased, factual reporting of what was found concerning the security control assessed. For each finding of other than satisfied, assessors indicate which parts of the security control are affected by the finding (i.e., aspects of the control that were deemed not satisfied or were not able to be assessed) and describe how the control differs from the planned or expected state. The potential for compromises to confidentiality, integrity, and availability due to *other than satisfied* findings are also noted by the assessor in the security assessment report. This notation reflects the lack of a specified protection and the exploitation that could occur as a result (i.e. workstation, dataset, root level access). Risk determination and acceptance activities are conducted by the organization post assessment as part of the risk management strategy established by the organization. These risk management activities involve the senior leadership of the organization including for example, heads of agencies, mission/business owners, information owners/stewards, risk executive (function), and authorizing officials, in consultation with appropriate organizational support staff (e.g., senior information security officers, chief information officers, information system owners, common control providers, and assessors). Security control assessment results are documented at the level of detail appropriate for the assessment in accordance with the reporting format prescribed by organizational policy, NIST guidelines, and OMB policy. The reporting format is appropriate for the type of security control assessment conducted (e.g., self-assessments by information system owners and common control providers, independent verification and validation, independent assessments supporting the security authorization process, or independent audits or inspections).

Information system owners and common control providers rely on the security expertise and the technical judgment of assessors to: (i) assess the security controls in the information system and inherited by the system; and (ii) provide recommendations on how to correct weaknesses or deficiencies in the controls and reduce or eliminate identified vulnerabilities. The assessment results produced by the assessor (i.e., findings of *satisfied* or *other than satisfied*, identification of the parts of the security control that did not produce a satisfactory result, and a description of resulting potential for compromises to the information system or its environment of operation) are provided to information system owners and common control providers in the initial security assessment report. System owners and common control providers may choose to act on selected recommendations of the assessor before the security assessment report is finalized if there are specific opportunities to correct weaknesses or deficiencies in security controls or to correct and/or clarify misunderstandings or interpretations of assessment results.[42] Security controls that

---

[42] The correction of weaknesses or deficiencies in security controls or carrying out of selected recommendations during the review of the initial security assessment report by information system owners or common control providers is not intended to replace the formal risk mitigation process by the organization which occurs after the delivery of the final report. Rather, it provides the information system owner or common control provider with an opportunity to address weaknesses or deficiencies that may be quickly corrected. However, in situations where limited resources exist for remediating weaknesses and deficiencies discovered during the security control assessment, organizations may decide without prejudice that waiting for the risk assessment to prioritize remediation efforts is the better course of action.

are modified, enhanced, or added during this process are reassessed by the assessor prior to the production of the final security assessment report.

3.4 ANALYZING SECURITY ASSESSMENT REPORT RESULTS

Since results of the security control assessment ultimately influence the content of the security plan and the plan of action and milestones, information system owners and common control providers review the security assessment report and the updated risk assessment and with the concurrence of designated organizational officials (e.g., authorizing officials, chief information officer, senior information security officer, mission/information owners), determine the appropriate steps required to correct weaknesses and deficiencies identified during the assessment. By using the labels of *satisfied* and *other than satisfied*, the reporting format for the assessment findings provides visibility for organizational officials into specific weaknesses and deficiencies in security controls within the information system or inherited by the system and facilitates a disciplined and structured approach to mitigating risks in accordance with organizational priorities. For example, information system owners or common control providers in consultation with designated organizational officials, may decide that certain assessment findings marked as other than satisfied are of an inconsequential nature and present no significant risk to the organization. Conversely, system owners or common control providers may decide that certain findings marked as other than satisfied are significant, requiring immediate remediation actions. In all cases, the organization reviews each assessor finding of other than satisfied and applies its judgment with regard to the severity or seriousness of the finding and whether the finding is significant enough to be worthy of further investigation or remedial action.

Senior leadership involvement in the mitigation process may be necessary in order to ensure that the organization's resources are effectively allocated in accordance with organizational priorities, providing resources first to the information systems that are supporting the most critical and sensitive missions for the organization or correcting the deficiencies that pose the greatest degree of risk. Ultimately, the security control assessment findings and any subsequent mitigation actions (informed by the updated risk assessment) initiated by information system owners or common control providers in collaboration with designated organizational officials trigger updates to the key documents used by authorizing officials to determine the security status of the information system and its suitability for authorization to operate. These documents include the security plan with updated risk assessment, security assessment report, and plan of action and milestones.

Figure 1 provides an overview of the security control assessment process including the activities carried out during pre-assessment, assessment, and post-assessment.

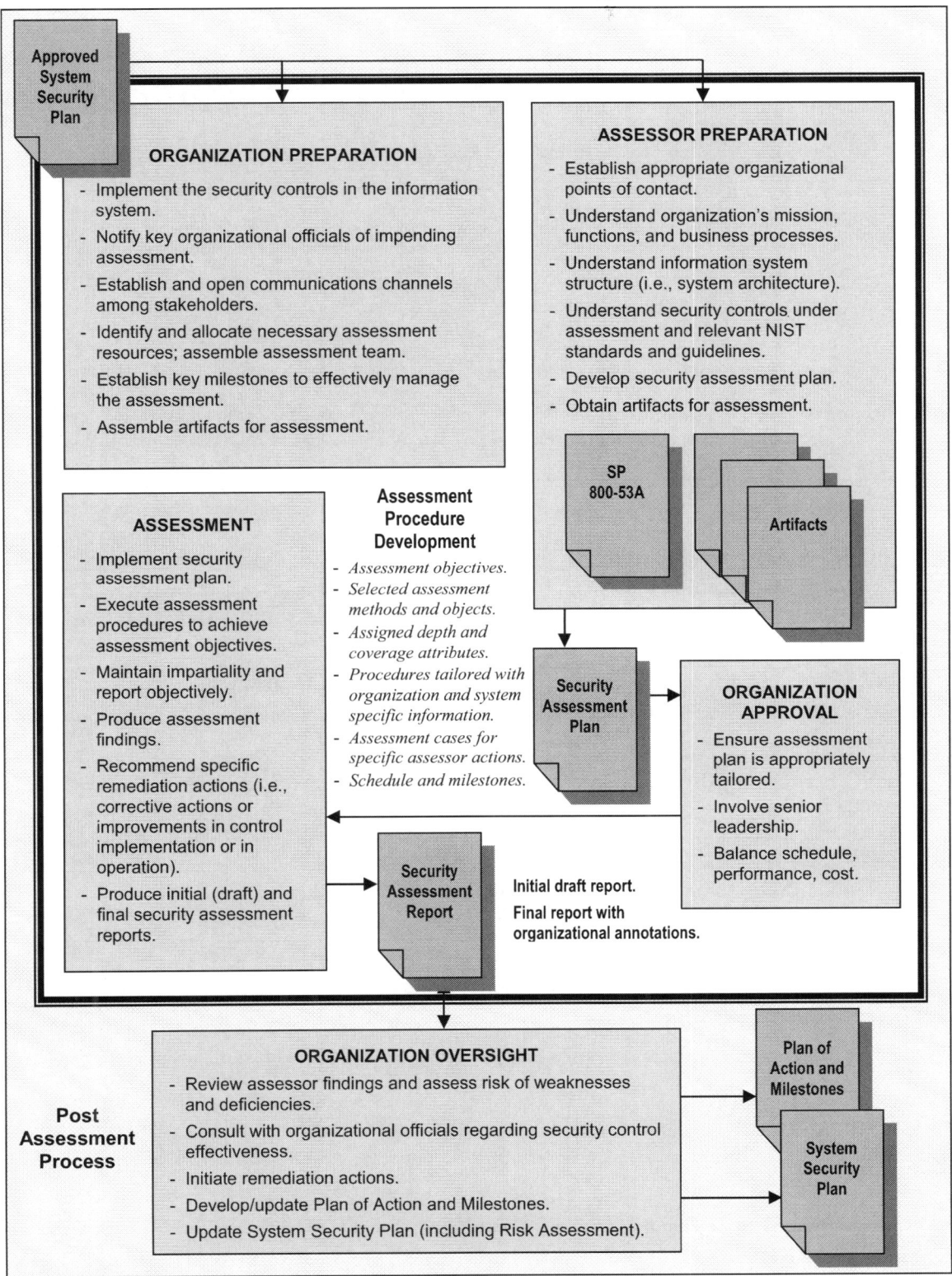

FIGURE 1: SECURITY CONTROL ASSESSMENT PROCESS OVERVIEW

APPENDIX A

REFERENCES

LAWS, POLICIES, DIRECTIVES, INSTRUCTIONS, STANDARDS, AND GUIDELINES

LEGISLATION

1. E-Government Act [includes FISMA] (P.L. 107-347), December 2002.

2. Federal Information Security Management Act (P.L. 107-347, Title III), December 2002.

POLICIES, DIRECTIVES, INSTRUCTIONS

1. Committee on National Security Systems (CNSS) Instruction 4009, *National Information Assurance Glossary*, April 2010.

2. Committee on National Security Systems (CNSS) Instruction 1253, *Security Categorization and Control Selection for National Security Systems*, October 2009.

3. Office of Management and Budget, Circular A-130, Appendix III, Transmittal Memorandum #4, *Management of Federal Information Resources*, November 2000.

4. Office of Management and Budget Memorandum M-02-01, *Guidance for Preparing and Submitting Security Plans of Action and Milestones*, October 2001.

STANDARDS

1. National Institute of Standards and Technology Federal Information Processing Standards Publication 199, *Standards for Security Categorization of Federal Information and Information Systems*, February 2004.

2. National Institute of Standards and Technology Federal Information Processing Standards Publication 200, *Minimum Security Requirements for Federal Information and Information Systems*, March 2006.

3. ISO/IEC 15408:2005, *Common Criteria for Information Technology Security Evaluation*, 2005.

GUIDELINES

1. National Institute of Standards and Technology Special Publication 800-18, Revision 1, *Guide for Developing Security Plans for Federal Information Systems*, February 2006.

2. National Institute of Standards and Technology Special Publication 800-30, *Risk Management Guide for Information Technology Systems*, July 2002.

3. National Institute of Standards and Technology Special Publication 800-37, Revision 1, *Guide for Applying the Risk Management Framework to Federal Information Systems: A Security Life Cycle Approach*, February 2010.

4. National Institute of Standards and Technology Special Publication 800-39 (Second Public Draft), *Managing Risk from Information Systems: An Organizational Perspective*, April 2008.

5. National Institute of Standards and Technology Special Publication 800-53, Revision 3, *Recommended Security Controls for Federal Information Systems and Organizations*, August 2009.

6. National Institute of Standards and Technology Special Publication 800-59, *Guideline for Identifying an Information System as a National Security System*, August 2003.

7. National Institute of Standards and Technology Special Publication 800-60, Revision 1, *Guide for Mapping Types of Information and Information Systems to Security Categories*, August 2008.

8. National Institute of Standards and Technology Special Publication 800-126, Revision 1 (Draft), *The Technical Specification for the Security Content Automation Protocol (SCAP): SCAP Version 1.0*, May 2010.

APPENDIX B

GLOSSARY

COMMON TERMS AND DEFINITIONS

This appendix provides definitions for security terminology used within Special Publication 800-53A. The terms in the glossary are consistent with the terms used in the suite of FISMA-related security standards and guidelines developed by NIST. Unless otherwise stated, all terms used in this publication are also consistent with the definitions contained in the CNSS Instruction 4009, *National Information Assurance Glossary*.

Activities	An assessment object that includes specific protection-related pursuits or actions supporting an information system that involve people (e.g., conducting system backup operations, monitoring network traffic).
Adequate Security [OMB Circular A-130, Appendix III]	Security commensurate with the risk and the magnitude of harm resulting from the loss, misuse, or unauthorized access to or modification of information.
Agency	See *Executive Agency*.
Assessment	See *Security Control Assessment*.
Assessment Findings	Assessment results produced by the application of an assessment procedure to a security control or control enhancement to achieve an assessment objective; the execution of a determination statement within an assessment procedure by an assessor that results in either a *satisfied* or *other than satisfied* condition.
Assessment Method	One of three types of actions (i.e., examine, interview, test) taken by assessors in obtaining evidence during an assessment.
Assessment Object	The item (i.e., specifications, mechanisms, activities, individuals) upon which an assessment method is applied during an assessment.
Assessment Objective	A set of determination statements that expresses the desired outcome for the assessment of a security control or control enhancement.
Assessment Procedure	A set of assessment *objectives* and an associated set of assessment *methods* and assessment *objects*.
Assessor	See *Security Control Assessor*.
Assurance	The grounds for confidence that the set of intended security controls in an information system are effective in their application.
Assurance Case [Software Engineering Institute, Carnegie Mellon University]	A structured set of arguments and a body of evidence showing that an information system satisfies specific claims with respect to a given quality attribute.

Authentication [FIPS 200]	Verifying the identity of a user, process, or device, often as a prerequisite to allowing access to resources in an information system.
Authenticity	The property of being genuine and being able to be verified and trusted; confidence in the validity of a transmission, a message, or message originator. See Authentication.
Authorization (to operate)	The official management decision given by a senior organizational official to authorize operation of an information system and to explicitly accept the risk to organizational operations (including mission, functions, image, or reputation), organizational assets, individuals, other organizations, and the Nation based on the implementation of an agreed-upon set of security controls.
Authorization Boundary [NIST SP 800-37]	All components of an information system to be authorized for operation by an authorizing official and excludes separately authorized systems, to which the information system is connected.
Authorizing Official [NIST SP 800-37]	A senior (federal) official or executive with the authority to formally assume responsibility for operating an information system at an acceptable level of risk to organizational operations (including mission, functions, image, or reputation), organizational assets, individuals, other organizations, and the Nation.
Authorizing Official Designated Representative [NIST SP 800-37]	An organizational official acting on behalf of an authorizing official in carrying out and coordinating the required activities associated with security authorization.
Availability [44 U.S.C., Sec. 3542]	Ensuring timely and reliable access to and use of information.
Basic Testing	A test methodology that assumes no knowledge of the internal structure and implementation detail of the assessment object. Also known as black box testing.
Black Box Testing	See *Basic Testing*.

Chief Information Officer [PL 104-106, Sec. 5125(b)]	Agency official responsible for: (i) Providing advice and other assistance to the head of the executive agency and other senior management personnel of the agency to ensure that information technology is acquired and information resources are managed in a manner that is consistent with laws, Executive Orders, directives, policies, regulations, and priorities established by the head of the agency; (ii) Developing, maintaining, and facilitating the implementation of a sound and integrated information technology architecture for the agency; and (iii) Promoting the effective and efficient design and operation of all major information resources management processes for the agency, including improvements to work processes of the agency.
Chief Information Security Officer	See *Senior Agency Information Security Officer*.
Common Control [NIST SP 800-37]	A security control that is inherited by one or more organizational information systems. See *Security Control Inheritance*.
Common Control Provider [NIST SP 800-37]	An organizational official responsible for the development, implementation, assessment, and monitoring of common controls (i.e., security controls inherited by information systems).
Compensating Security Controls [NIST SP 800-53]	The management, operational, and technical controls (i.e., safeguards or countermeasures) employed by an organization in lieu of the recommended controls in the baselines described in NIST Special Publication 800-53 and CNSS Instruction 1253, that provide equivalent or comparable protection for an information system.
Comprehensive Testing	A test methodology that assumes explicit and substantial knowledge of the internal structure and implementation detail of the assessment object. Also known as white box testing.
Confidentiality [44 U.S.C., Sec. 3542]	Preserving authorized restrictions on information access and disclosure, including means for protecting personal privacy and proprietary information.
Controlled Unclassified Information	A categorical designation that refers to unclassified information that does not meet the standards for National Security Classification under Executive Order 12958, as amended, but is (i) pertinent to the national interests of the United States or to the important interests of entities outside the federal government, and (ii) under law or policy requires protection from unauthorized disclosure, special handling safeguards, or prescribed limits on exchange or dissemination. Henceforth, the designation CUI replaces *Sensitive But Unclassified (SBU)*.

Coverage	An attribute associated with an assessment method that addresses the scope or breadth of the assessment objects included in the assessment (e.g., types of objects to be assessed and the number of objects to be assessed by type). The values for the coverage attribute, hierarchically from less coverage to more coverage, are basic, focused, and comprehensive.
Depth	An attribute associated with an assessment method that addresses the rigor and level of detail associated with the application of the method. The values for the depth attribute, hierarchically from less depth to more depth, are basic, focused, and comprehensive.
Environment of Operation [NIST SP 800-37]	The physical surroundings in which an information system processes, stores, and transmits information.
Examine	A type of assessment method that is characterized by the process of checking, inspecting, reviewing, observing, studying, or analyzing one or more assessment objects to facilitate understanding, achieve clarification, or obtain evidence, the results of which are used to support the determination of security control effectiveness over time.
Executive Agency [41 U.S.C., Sec. 403]	An executive department specified in 5 U.S.C., Sec. 101; a military department specified in 5 U.S.C., Sec. 102; an independent establishment as defined in 5 U.S.C., Sec. 104(1); and a wholly owned Government corporation fully subject to the provisions of 31 U.S.C., Chapter 91.
Federal Agency	See *Executive Agency*.
Federal Information System [40 U.S.C., Sec. 11331]	An information system used or operated by an executive agency, by a contractor of an executive agency, or by another organization on behalf of an executive agency.
Focused Testing	A test methodology that assumes some knowledge of the internal structure and implementation detail of the assessment object. Also known as gray box testing.
Gray Box Testing	See *Focused Testing*.
Hybrid Security Control [NIST SP 800-53]	A security control that is implemented in an information system in part as a common control and in part as a system-specific control. See *Common Control* and *System-Specific Security Control*.
Individuals	An assessment object that includes people applying specifications, mechanisms, or activities.

Industrial Control System	An information system used to control industrial processes such as manufacturing, product handling, production, and distribution. Industrial control systems include supervisory control and data acquisition systems used to control geographically dispersed assets, as well as distributed control systems and smaller control systems using programmable logic controllers to control localized processes.
Information [FIPS 199]	An instance of an information type.
Information Owner [CNSSI 4009]	Official with statutory or operational authority for specified information and responsibility for establishing the controls for its generation, collection, processing, dissemination, and disposal.
Information Resources [44 U.S.C., Sec. 3502]	Information and related resources, such as personnel, equipment, funds, and information technology.
Information Security [44 U.S.C., Sec. 3542]	The protection of information and information systems from unauthorized access, use, disclosure, disruption, modification, or destruction in order to provide confidentiality, integrity, and availability.
Information Security Program Plan [NIST SP 800-53]	Formal document that provides an overview of the security requirements for an organization-wide information security program and describes the program management controls and common controls in place or planned for meeting those requirements.
Information System [44 U.S.C., Sec. 3502]	A discrete set of information resources organized for the collection, processing, maintenance, use, sharing, dissemination, or disposition of information.
Information System Boundary	See *Authorization Boundary*.
Information System Owner (or Program Manager)	Official responsible for the overall procurement, development, integration, modification, or operation and maintenance of an information system.
Information System Security Officer	Individual assigned responsibility by the senior agency information security officer, authorizing official, management official, or information system owner for maintaining the appropriate operational security posture for an information system or program.
Information System-related Security Risks	Information system-related security risks are those risks that arise through the loss of confidentiality, integrity, or availability of information or information systems and consider impacts to the organization (including assets, mission, functions, image, or reputation), individuals, other organizations, and the Nation. See *Risk*.

Information Technology [40 U.S.C., Sec. 1401]	Any equipment or interconnected system or subsystem of equipment that is used in the automatic acquisition, storage, manipulation, management, movement, control, display, switching, interchange, transmission, or reception of data or information by the executive agency. For purposes of the preceding sentence, equipment is used by an executive agency if the equipment is used by the executive agency directly or is used by a contractor under a contract with the executive agency which: (i) requires the use of such equipment; or (ii) requires the use, to a significant extent, of such equipment in the performance of a service or the furnishing of a product. The term information technology includes computers, ancillary equipment, software, firmware, and similar procedures, services (including support services), and related resources.
Information Type [FIPS 199]	A specific category of information (e.g., privacy, medical, proprietary, financial, investigative, contractor sensitive, security management) defined by an organization or in some instances, by a specific law, Executive Order, directive, policy, or regulation.
Integrity [44 U.S.C., Sec. 3542]	Guarding against improper information modification or destruction, and includes ensuring information non-repudiation and authenticity.
Interview	A type of assessment method that is characterized by the process of conducting discussions with individuals or groups within an organization to facilitate understanding, achieve clarification, or lead to the location of evidence, the results of which are used to support the determination of security control effectiveness over time.
Management Controls [FIPS 200]	The security controls (i.e., safeguards or countermeasures) for an information system that focus on the management of risk and the management of information system security.
Mechanisms	An assessment object that includes specific protection-related items (e.g., hardware, software, or firmware) employed within or at the boundary of an information system.
National Security Information	Information that has been determined pursuant to Executive Order 12958 as amended by Executive Order 13292, or any predecessor order, or by the Atomic Energy Act of 1954, as amended, to require protection against unauthorized disclosure and is marked to indicate its classified status.

National Security System [44 U.S.C., Sec. 3542]	Any information system (including any telecommunications system) used or operated by an agency or by a contractor of an agency, or other organization on behalf of an agency—(i) the function, operation, or use of which involves intelligence activities; involves cryptologic activities related to national security; involves command and control of military forces; involves equipment that is an integral part of a weapon or weapons system; or is critical to the direct fulfillment of military or intelligence missions (excluding a system that is to be used for routine administrative and business applications, for example, payroll, finance, logistics, and personnel management applications); or (ii) is protected at all times by procedures established for information that have been specifically authorized under criteria established by an Executive Order or an Act of Congress to be kept classified in the interest of national defense or foreign policy.
Operational Controls [FIPS 200]	The security controls (i.e., safeguards or countermeasures) for an information system that are primarily implemented and executed by people (as opposed to systems).
Organization [FIPS 200, Adapted]	An entity of any size, complexity, or positioning within an organizational structure (e.g., a federal agency or, as appropriate, any of its operational elements).
Penetration Testing	A test methodology in which assessors, using all available documentation (e.g., system design, source code, manuals) and working under specific constraints, attempt to circumvent the security features of an information system.
Plan of Action and Milestones [OMB Memorandum 02-01]	A document that identifies tasks needing to be accomplished. It details resources required to accomplish the elements of the plan, any milestones in meeting the tasks, and scheduled completion dates for the milestones.
Reciprocity	Mutual agreement among participating organizations to accept each other's security assessments in order to reuse information system resources and/or to accept each other's assessed security posture in order to share information.
Records	The recordings (automated and/or manual) of evidence of activities performed or results achieved (e.g., forms, reports, test results), which serve as a basis for verifying that the organization and the information system are performing as intended. Also used to refer to units of related data fields (i.e., groups of data fields that can be accessed by a program and that contain the complete set of information on particular items).

Risk
[CNSSI 4009]

A measure of the extent to which an entity is threatened by a potential circumstance or event, and typically a function of: (i) the adverse impacts that would arise if the circumstance or event occurs; and (ii) the likelihood of occurrence.

[Note: Information system-related security risks are those risks that arise from the loss of confidentiality, integrity, or availability of information or information systems and reflect the potential adverse impacts to organizational operations (including mission, functions, image, or reputation), organizational assets, individuals, other organizations, and the Nation. Adverse impacts to the Nation include, for example, compromises to information systems that support critical infrastructure applications or are paramount to government continuity of operations as defined by the Department of Homeland Security.]

Risk Assessment

The process of identifying risks to organizational operations (including mission, functions, image, reputation), organizational assets, individuals, other organizations, and the Nation, resulting from the operation of an information system.

Part of risk management, incorporates threat and vulnerability analyses, and considers mitigations provided by security controls planned or in place. Synonymous with risk analysis.

Risk Executive (Function)
[NIST SP 800-37]

An individual or group within an organization that helps to ensure that: (i) security risk-related considerations for individual information systems, to include the authorization decisions, are viewed from an organization-wide perspective with regard to the overall strategic goals and objectives of the organization in carrying out its missions and business functions; and (ii) managing information system-related security risks is consistent across the organization, reflects organizational risk tolerance, and is considered along with other organizational risks affecting mission/business success.

Risk Management
[CNSSI 4009]

The process of managing risks to organizational operations (including mission, functions, image, reputation), organizational assets, individuals, other organizations, and the Nation, resulting from the operation of an information system, and includes: (i) the conduct of a risk assessment; (ii) the implementation of a risk mitigation strategy; and (iii) employment of techniques and procedures for the continuous monitoring of the security state of the information system.

Security Authorization

See *Authorization*.

Security Categorization	The process of determining the security category for information or an information system. Security categorization methodologies are described in CNSS Instruction 1253 for national security systems and in FIPS 199 for other than national security systems.
Security Control Assessment	The testing and/or evaluation of the management, operational, and technical security controls in an information system to determine the extent to which the controls are implemented correctly, operating as intended, and producing the desired outcome with respect to meeting the security requirements for the system.
Security Control Assessor	The individual, group, or organization responsible for conducting a security control assessment.
Security Control Baseline [FIPS 200, Adapted]	One of the sets of minimum security controls defined for federal information systems in NIST Special Publication 800-53 and CNSS Instruction 1253.
Security Control Enhancements	Statements of security capability to: (i) build in additional, but related, functionality to a basic control; and/or (ii) increase the strength of a basic control.
Security Control Inheritance	A situation in which an information system or application receives protection from security controls (or portions of security controls) that are developed, implemented, assessed, authorized, and monitored by entities other than those responsible for the system or application; entities either internal or external to the organization where the system or application resides. See *Common Control*.
Security Controls [FIPS 199, CNSSI 4009]	The management, operational, and technical controls (i.e., safeguards or countermeasures) prescribed for an information system to protect the confidentiality, integrity, and availability of the system and its information.
Security Impact Analysis [NIST SP 800-37]	The analysis conducted by an organizational official to determine the extent to which changes to the information system have affected the security state of the system.
Security Objective [FIPS 199]	Confidentiality, integrity, or availability.
Security Plan [NIST SP 800-18]	Formal document that provides an overview of the security requirements for an information system or an information security program and describes the security controls in place or planned for meeting those requirements. See *System Security Plan* or *Information Security Program Plan*.

Security Requirements [FIPS 200]	Requirements levied on an information system that are derived from applicable laws, Executive Orders, directives, policies, standards, instructions, regulations, procedures, or organizational mission/business case needs to ensure the confidentiality, integrity, and availability of the information being processed, stored, or transmitted.
Senior Agency Information Security Officer [44 U.S.C., Sec. 3544]	Official responsible for carrying out the Chief Information Officer responsibilities under FISMA and serving as the Chief Information Officer's primary liaison to the agency's authorizing officials, information system owners, and information system security officers.
	[Note: Organizations subordinate to federal agencies may use the term *Senior Information Security Officer* or *Chief Information Security Officer* to denote individuals filling positions with similar responsibilities to Senior Agency Information Security Officers.]
Senior Information Security Officer	See *Senior Agency Information Security Officer*.
Specification	An assessment object that includes document-based artifacts (e.g., policies, procedures, plans, system security requirements, functional specifications, and architectural designs) associated with an information system.
Subsystem	A major subdivision or component of an information system consisting of information, information technology, and personnel that performs one or more specific functions.
Supplementation (Assessment Procedures)	The process of adding assessment procedures or assessment details to assessment procedures in order to adequately meet the organization's risk management needs.
Supplementation (Security Controls)	The process of adding security controls or control enhancements to a security control baseline from NIST Special Publication 800-53 or CNSS Instruction 1253 in order to adequately meet the organization's risk management needs.
System	See *Information System*.
System Security Plan [NIST SP 800-18]	Formal document that provides an overview of the security requirements for an information system and describes the security controls in place or planned for meeting those requirements.
System-Specific Security Control [NIST SP 800-37]	A security control for an information system that has not been designated as a common control or the portion of a hybrid control that is to be implemented within an information system.

Tailoring [NIST SP 800-53, CNSSI 4009]	The process by which a security control baseline is modified based on: (i) the application of scoping guidance; (ii) the specification of compensating security controls, if needed; and (iii) the specification of organization-defined parameters in the security controls via explicit assignment and selection statements.
Tailoring (Assessment Procedures)	The process by which assessment procedures defined in Special Publication 800-53A are adjusted, or scoped, to match the characteristics of the information system under assessment, providing organizations with the flexibility needed to meet specific organizational requirements and to avoid overly-constrained assessment approaches.
Tailored Security Control Baseline	A set of security controls resulting from the application of tailoring guidance to the security control baseline. See *Tailoring*.
Technical Controls [FIPS 200]	The security controls (i.e., safeguards or countermeasures) for an information system that are primarily implemented and executed by the information system through mechanisms contained in the hardware, software, or firmware components of the system.
Test	A type of assessment method that is characterized by the process of exercising one or more assessment objects under specified conditions to compare actual with expected behavior, the results of which are used to support the determination of security control effectiveness over time.
Threat [CNSSI 4009]	Any circumstance or event with the potential to adversely impact organizational operations (including mission, functions, image, or reputation), organizational assets, individuals, other organizations, or the Nation through an information system via unauthorized access, destruction, disclosure, modification of information, and/or denial of service.
Threat Assessment [CNSSI 4009]	Process of formally evaluating the degree of threat to an information system or enterprise and describing the nature of the threat.
Threat Source [FIPS 200]	The intent and method targeted at the intentional exploitation of a vulnerability or a situation and method that may accidentally trigger a vulnerability. Synonymous with threat agent.
Vulnerability [CNSSI 4009]	Weakness in an information system, system security procedures, internal controls, or implementation that could be exploited or triggered by a threat source.

Vulnerability Assessment [CNSSI 4009]	Systematic examination of an information system or product to determine the adequacy of security measures, identify security deficiencies, provide data from which to predict the effectiveness of proposed security measures, and confirm the adequacy of such measures after implementation.
White Box Testing	See *Comprehensive Testing*.

APPENDIX C

ACRONYMS

COMMON ABBREVIATIONS

CIO	Chief Information Officer
CNSS	Committee on National Security Systems
CUI	Controlled Unclassified Information
COTS	Commercial Off-The-Shelf
DoD	Department of Defense
FIPS	Federal Information Processing Standards
FISMA	Federal Information Security Management Act
ICS	Industrial Control System
IEC	International Electrotechnical Commission
ISO	International Organization for Standardization
NIST	National Institute of Standards and Technology
NSA	National Security Agency
ODNI	Office of the Director of National Intelligence
OMB	Office of Management and Budget
PKI	Public Key Infrastructure
POAM	Plan of Action and Milestones
RMF	Risk Management Framework
SCAP	Security Content Automation Protocol
SP	Special Publication
U.S.C.	United States Code
VoIP	Voice over Internet Protocol

APPENDIX D

ASSESSMENT METHOD DESCRIPTIONS
ASSESSMENT METHOD DEFINITIONS, APPLICABLE OBJECTS, AND ATTRIBUTES

This appendix defines the three assessment methods that can be used by assessors during security control assessments: (i) *examine*; (ii) *interview*; and (iii) *test*. Included in the definition of each assessment method are types of objects to which the method can be applied. The application of each method is described in terms of the attributes of *depth* and *coverage*, progressing from *basic* to *focused* to *comprehensive*. The attribute values correlate to the assurance requirements specified by the organization.[43] The depth attribute addresses the rigor and level of detail of the assessment. For the depth attribute, the *focused* attribute value includes and builds upon the assessment rigor and level of detail defined for the *basic* attribute value; the *comprehensive* attribute value includes and builds upon the assessment rigor and level of detail defined for the *focused* attribute value. The coverage attribute addresses the scope or breadth of the assessment. For the coverage attribute, the *focused* attribute value includes and builds upon the number and type of assessment objects defined for the *basic* attribute value; the *comprehensive* attribute value includes and builds upon the number and type of assessment objects defined for the *focused* attribute value. The use of **bolded text** in the assessment method description indicates the content that was added to and appears for the first time, in the description indicating greater rigor and detail for the attribute value.

---

[43] For other than national security systems, organizations meet minimum assurance requirements specified in Special Publication 800-53, Appendix E.

ASSESSMENT METHOD: Examine

ASSESSMENT OBJECTS: Specifications (e.g., policies, plans, procedures, system requirements, designs)
Mechanisms (e.g., functionality implemented in hardware, software, firmware)
Activities (e.g., system operations, administration, management; exercises)

DEFINITION: The process of checking, inspecting, reviewing, observing, studying, or analyzing one or more assessment objects to facilitate understanding, achieve clarification, or obtain evidence, the results of which are used to support the determination of security control existence, functionality, correctness, completeness, and potential for improvement over time.

SUPPLEMENTAL GUIDANCE: Typical assessor actions may include, for example: reviewing information security policies, plans, and procedures; analyzing system design documentation and interface specifications; observing system backup operations, reviewing the results of contingency plan exercises; observing incident response activities; studying technical manuals and user/administrator guides; checking, studying, or observing the operation of an information technology mechanism in the information system hardware/software; or checking, studying, or observing physical security measures related to the operation of an information system.

ATTRIBUTES: Depth, Coverage

- The *depth* attribute addresses the rigor of and level of detail in the examination process. There are three possible values for the depth attribute: (i) *basic*; (ii) *focused*; and (iii) *comprehensive*.

  - Basic examination: Examination that consists of high-level reviews, checks, observations, or inspections of the assessment object. This type of examination is conducted using a limited body of evidence or documentation (e.g., functional-level descriptions for mechanisms; high-level process descriptions for activities; and actual documents for specifications). Basic examinations provide a level of understanding of the security control necessary for determining whether the control is implemented and free of obvious errors.

  - Focused examination: Examination that consists of high-level reviews, checks, observations, or inspections **and more in depth studies/analyses** of the assessment object. This type of examination is conducted using a **substantial** body of evidence or documentation (e.g., functional-level descriptions **and where appropriate and available, high-level design information** for mechanisms; high-level process descriptions **and implementation procedures** for activities; and the actual documents **and related documents** for specifications). **Focused** examinations provide a level of understanding of the security control necessary for determining whether the control is implemented and free of obvious errors **and whether there are increased grounds for confidence that the control is implemented correctly and operating as intended**.

  - Comprehensive examination: Examination that consists of high-level reviews, checks, observations, or inspections and more in depth, **detailed, and thorough** studies/analyses of the assessment object. This type of examination is conducted using an **extensive** body of evidence or documentation (e.g., functional-level descriptions and where appropriate and available, high-level design information, **low-level design information, and implementation information** for mechanisms; high-level process descriptions and **detailed** implementation procedures for activities; and the actual documents and related documents for specifications[44]). **Comprehensive** examinations provide a level of understanding of the security control necessary for determining whether the control is implemented and free of obvious errors and whether there are **further** increased grounds for confidence that the control is implemented correctly and operating as intended **on an ongoing and consistent basis, and that there is support for continuous improvement in the effectiveness of the control**.

---

[44] While additional documentation is likely for mechanisms when moving from basic to focused to comprehensive examinations, the documentation associated with specifications and activities may be the same or similar for focused and comprehensive examinations, with the rigor of the examinations of these documents being increased at the comprehensive level.

- The *coverage* attribute addresses the scope or breadth of the examination process and includes the types of assessment objects to be examined, the number of objects to be examined (by type), and specific objects to be examined.[45] There are three possible values for the coverage attribute: (i) *basic*, (ii) *focused*, and (iii) *comprehensive*.

    - <u>Basic examination</u>: Examination that uses a representative sample of assessment objects (by type and number within type) to provide a level of coverage necessary for determining whether the security control is implemented and free of obvious errors.

    - <u>Focused examination</u>: Examination that uses a representative sample of assessment objects (by type and number within type) **and other specific assessment objects deemed particularly important to achieving the assessment objective** to provide a level of coverage necessary for determining whether the security control is implemented and free of obvious errors **and whether there are increased grounds for confidence that the control is implemented correctly and operating as intended**.

    - <u>Comprehensive examination</u>: Examination that uses a **sufficiently large** sample of assessment objects (by type and number within type) and other specific assessment objects deemed particularly important to achieving the assessment objective to provide a level of coverage necessary for determining whether the security control is implemented and free of obvious errors and whether there are **further** increased grounds for confidence that the control is implemented correctly and operating as intended **on an ongoing and consistent basis, and that there is support for continuous improvement in the effectiveness of the control**.

---

[45] The organization, considering a variety of factors (e.g., available resources, importance of the assessment, the organization's overall assessment goals and objectives), confers with assessors and provides direction on the type, number, and specific objects to be examined for the particular attribute value described.

ASSESSMENT METHOD: Interview

ASSESSMENT OBJECTS: Individuals or groups of individuals.

DEFINITION: The process of conducting discussions with individuals or groups within an organization to facilitate understanding, achieve clarification, or lead to the location of evidence, the results of which are used to support the determination of security control existence, functionality, correctness, completeness, and potential for improvement over time.

SUPPLEMENTAL GUIDANCE: Typical assessor actions may include, for example, interviewing agency heads, chief information officers, senior agency information security officers, authorizing officials, information owners, information system and mission owners, information system security officers, information system security managers, personnel officers, human resource managers, facilities managers, training officers, information system operators, network and system administrators, site managers, physical security officers, and users.

ATTRIBUTES: Depth, Coverage

- The *depth* attribute addresses the rigor of and level of detail in the interview process. There are three possible values for the depth attribute: (i) *basic*; (ii) *focused*; and (iii) *comprehensive*.

    - Basic interview: Interview that consists of broad-based, high-level discussions with individuals or groups of individuals. This type of interview is conducted using a set of generalized, high-level questions. Basic interviews provide a level of understanding of the security control necessary for determining whether the control is implemented and free of obvious errors.

    - Focused interview: Interview that consists of broad-based, high-level discussions **and more in depth discussions in specific areas** with individuals or groups of individuals. This type of interview is conducted using a set of generalized, high-level questions **and more in depth questions in specific areas where responses indicate a need for more in depth investigation. Focused** interviews provide a level of understanding of the security control necessary for determining whether the control is implemented and free of obvious errors **and whether there are increased grounds for confidence that the control is implemented correctly and operating as intended**.

    - Comprehensive interview: Interview that consists of broad-based, high-level discussions and more in depth, **probing** discussions in specific areas with individuals or groups of individuals. This type of interview is conducted using a set of generalized, high-level questions and more in depth, **probing** questions in specific areas where responses indicate a need for more in depth investigation. **Comprehensive** interviews provide a level of understanding of the security control necessary for determining whether the control is implemented and free of obvious errors and whether there are **further** increased grounds for confidence that the control is implemented correctly and operating as intended **on an ongoing and consistent basis, and that there is support for continuous improvement in the effectiveness of the control**.

- The *coverage* attribute addresses the scope or breadth of the interview process and includes the types of individuals to be interviewed (by organizational role and associated responsibility), the number of individuals to be interviewed (by type), and specific individuals to be interviewed.[46] There are three possible values for the coverage attribute: (i) *basic*, (ii) *focused*; and (iii) *comprehensive*.

    - Basic interview: Interview that uses a representative sample of individuals in key organizational roles to provide a level of coverage necessary for determining whether the security control is implemented and free of obvious errors.

    - Focused interview: Interview that uses a representative sample of individuals in key organizational roles **and other specific individuals deemed particularly important to achieving the assessment objective** to provide a level of coverage necessary for determining whether the security control is implemented and free of obvious errors **and whether there are increased grounds for confidence that the control is implemented correctly and operating as intended**.

---

[46] The organization, considering a variety of factors (e.g., available resources, importance of the assessment, the organization's overall assessment goals and objectives), confers with assessors and provides direction on the type, number, and specific individuals to be interviewed for the particular attribute value described.

- Comprehensive interview: Interview that uses a **sufficiently large** sample of individuals in key organizational roles and other specific individuals deemed particularly important to achieving the assessment objective to provide a level of coverage necessary for determining whether the security control is implemented and free of obvious errors and whether there are **further** increased grounds for confidence that the control is implemented correctly and operating as intended **on an ongoing and consistent basis, and that there is support for continuous improvement in the effectiveness of the control**.

ASSESSMENT METHOD: Test

ASSESSMENT OBJECTS: Mechanisms (e.g., hardware, software, firmware)
Activities (e.g., system operations, administration, management; exercises)

DEFINITION: The process of exercising one or more assessment objects under specified conditions to compare actual with expected behavior, the results of which are used to support the determination of security control existence, functionality, correctness, completeness, and potential for improvement over time.[47]

SUPPLEMENTAL GUIDANCE: Typical assessor actions may include, for example: testing access control, identification and authentication, and audit mechanisms; testing security configuration settings; testing physical access control devices; conducting penetration testing of key information system components; testing information system backup operations; testing incident response capability; and exercising contingency planning capability.

ATTRIBUTES: Depth, Coverage

- The *depth* attribute addresses the types of testing to be conducted. There are three possible values for the depth attribute: (i) *basic* testing; (ii) *focused* testing; and (iii) *comprehensive* testing.

  - Basic testing: Test methodology (also known as *black box* testing) that assumes no knowledge of the internal structure and implementation detail of the assessment object. This type of testing is conducted using a functional specification for mechanisms and a high-level process description for activities. Basic testing provides a level of understanding of the security control necessary for determining whether the control is implemented and free of obvious errors.

  - Focused testing: Test methodology (also known as *gray box* testing) that assumes **some** knowledge of the internal structure and implementation detail of the assessment object. This type of testing is conducted using a functional specification **and limited system architectural information (e.g., high-level design)** for mechanisms and a high-level process description **and high-level description of integration into the operational environment** for activities. Focused testing provides a level of understanding of the security control necessary for determining whether the control is implemented and free of obvious errors **and whether there are increased grounds for confidence that the control is implemented correctly and operating as intended**.

  - Comprehensive testing: Test methodology (also known as *white box* testing) that assumes **explicit and substantial** knowledge of the internal structure and implementation detail of the assessment object. This type of testing is conducted using a functional specification, **extensive** system architectural information (e.g., high-level design, **low-level design) and implementation representation (e.g., source code, schematics)** for mechanisms and a high-level process description and **detailed** description of integration into the operational environment for activities. Comprehensive testing provides a level of understanding of the security control necessary for determining whether the control is implemented and free of obvious errors and whether there are **further** increased grounds for confidence that the control is implemented correctly and operating as intended **on an ongoing and consistent basis, and that there is support for continuous improvement in the effectiveness of the control**.

- The *coverage* attribute addresses the scope or breadth of the testing process and includes the types of assessment objects to be tested, the number of objects to be tested (by type), and specific objects to be tested.[48] There are three possible values for the coverage attribute: (i) *basic*; (ii) *focused*; and (iii) *comprehensive*.

---

[47] Testing is typically used to determine if mechanisms or activities meet a set of predefined specifications. Testing can also be performed to determine characteristics of a security control that are not commonly associated with predefined specifications, with an example of such testing being penetration testing. Guidelines for conducting penetration testing are provided in Appendix E.

[48] The organization, considering a variety of factors (e.g., available resources, importance of the assessment, the organization's overall assessment goals and objectives), confers with assessors and provides direction on the type, number, and specific objects to be tested for the particular attribute value described. For mechanism-related testing, the coverage attribute also addresses the extent of the testing conducted (e.g., for software, the number of test cases and modules tested; for hardware, the range of inputs, number of components tested, and range of environmental factors over which the testing is conducted).

- <u>Basic testing</u>: Testing that uses a representative sample of assessment objects (by type and number within type) to provide a level of coverage necessary for determining whether the security control is implemented and free of obvious errors.

- <u>Focused testing</u>: Testing that uses a representative sample of assessment objects (by type and number within type) **and other specific assessment objects deemed particularly important to achieving the assessment objective** to provide a level of coverage necessary for determining whether the security control is implemented and free of obvious errors **and whether there are increased grounds for confidence that the control is implemented correctly and operating as intended**.

- <u>Comprehensive testing</u>: Testing that uses a **sufficiently large** sample of assessment objects (by type and number within type) and other specific assessment objects deemed particularly important to achieving the assessment objective to provide a level of coverage necessary for determining whether the security control is implemented and free of obvious errors and whether there are **further** increased grounds for confidence that the control is implemented correctly and operating as intended **on an ongoing and consistent basis, and that there is support for continuous improvement in the effectiveness of the control**.

APPENDIX E

PENETRATION TESTING

ASSESSMENT TOOLS AND TECHNIQUES TO IDENTIFY INFORMATION SYSTEM WEAKNESSES

Organizations should consider adding controlled penetration testing to their arsenal of tools and techniques used to assess the security controls in organizational information systems. Penetration testing is a specific type of assessment in which assessors simulate the actions of a given class of attacker by using a defined set of documentation (that is, the documentation representative of what that class of attacker is likely to possess) and working under other specific constraints to attempt to circumvent the security features of an information system. Penetration testing is conducted as a controlled attempt to breach the security controls employed within the information system using the attacker's techniques and appropriate hardware and software tools. Penetration testing represents the results of a specific assessor or group of assessors at a specific point in time using agreed-upon *rules of engagement*. Considering the complexity of the information technologies commonly employed by organizations today, penetration testing should be viewed not as a means to verify the security of an information system, but rather as a means to: (i) enhance the organization's understanding of the system; (ii) uncover weaknesses or deficiencies in the system; and (iii) indicate the level of effort required on the part of adversaries to breach the system safeguards.

Penetration testing exercises can be scheduled and/or random in accordance with organizational policy and organizational assessments of risk. Consideration should be given to performing penetration tests: (i) on any newly developed information system (or legacy system undergoing a major upgrade) before the system is authorized for operation; (ii) after important changes are made to the environment in which the information system operates; and (iii) when a new type of attack is discovered that may impact the system. Organizations actively monitor the information systems environment and the threat landscape (e.g., new vulnerabilities, attack techniques, new technology deployments, user security awareness and training) to identify changes that require out-of-cycle penetration testing.

Organizations specify which components within the information system are subject to penetration testing and the attacker's profile to be adopted throughout the penetration testing exercises. Organizations train selected personnel in the use and maintenance of penetration testing tools and techniques. Effective penetration testing tools should have the capability to readily update the list of attack techniques and exploitable vulnerabilities used during the exercises. Organizations should update the list of attack techniques and exploitable vulnerabilities used in penetration testing in accordance with an organizational assessment of risk or when significant new vulnerabilities or threats are identified and reported. Whenever possible, organizations should employ tools and attack techniques that include the capability to perform penetration testing exercises on information systems and security controls in an automated manner.

The information obtained from the penetration testing process should be shared with appropriate personnel throughout the organization to help prioritize the vulnerabilities in the information system that are demonstrably subject to compromise by attackers of a profile equivalent to the ones used in the penetration testing exercises. The prioritization helps to determine effective strategies for eliminating the identified vulnerabilities and mitigating associated risks to the organization's operations and assets, to individuals, to other organizations, and to the Nation resulting from the operation and use of the information system. Penetration testing should be integrated into the network security testing process and the patch and vulnerability management process. Special Publication 800-40 provides guidance on patch and vulnerability management. Special Publication 800-42 provides guidance on network security testing. Special Publication 800-115 provides guidance on information security testing.

Penetration Testing Considerations

Organizations consider the following criteria in developing and implementing a controlled penetration testing program. An effective penetration test:

- Goes beyond vulnerability scanning, to provide an explicit and often dramatic proof of mission risks and an indicator of the level of effort an adversary would need to expend in order to cause harm to the organization's operations and assets, to individuals, to other organizations, or to the Nation;

- Approaches the information system as the adversary would, considering vulnerabilities, incorrect system configurations, trust relationships between organizations, and architectural weaknesses in the environment under test;

- Has a clearly defined scope and contains as a minimum:

  - A definition of the environment subject to test (e.g., facilities, users, organizational groups, etc.);

  - A definition of the attack surface to be tested (e.g., servers, desktop systems, wireless networks, Web applications, intrusion detection and prevention systems, firewalls, email accounts, user security awareness and training posture, incident response posture, etc.);

  - A definition of the threat sources to simulate (e.g., an enumeration of attacker's profiles to be used: internal attacker, casual attacker, single or group of external targeted attackers, criminal organization, etc.);

  - A definition of level of effort (time and resources) to be expended; and

  - A definition of the rules of engagement.

- Thoroughly documents all activities performed during the test, including all exploited vulnerabilities, and how the vulnerabilities were combined into attacks;

- Produces results indicating a likelihood of occurrence for a given attacker by using the level of effort the team needed to expend in penetrating the information system as an indicator of the penetration resistance of the system;

- Validates existing security controls (including risk mitigation mechanisms such as firewalls, intrusion detection and prevention systems);

- Provides a verifiable and reproducible log of all the activities performed during the test; and

- Provides actionable results with information about possible remediation measures for the successful attacks performed.

APPENDIX F

ASSESSMENT PROCEDURE CATALOG
OBJECTIVES, METHODS, AND OBJECTS FOR ASSESSING SECURITY CONTROLS

This appendix provides a catalog of procedures to assess the security controls and control enhancements in Special Publication 800-53.[49] Assessors select assessment procedures from the catalog in accordance with the guidance provided in Section 3.2. Since the contents of the security plan affect the development of the security assessment plan and the assessment, there will likely be assessment procedures in the catalog that assessors will not use because: (i) the associated security controls or control enhancements are not contained in the security plan for the information system;[50] or (ii) the security controls or control enhancements are not being assessed at this particular time (e.g., during an assessment of a subset of the controls as part of continuous monitoring activities).

The same assessment object may appear in multiple object lists in a variety of assessment procedures. The same object may be used in multiple contexts to obtain needed information or evidence for a particular aspect of an assessment. Assessors use the general references as appropriate to obtain the necessary information to make the specified determinations required by the assessment objective. For example, a reference to access control policy appears in the assessment procedures for AC-2 and AC-7. For assessment procedure AC-2, assessors use the access control policy to find information about that portion of the policy that addresses account management for the information system. For assessment procedure AC-7, assessors use the access control policy to find information about that portion of the policy that addresses unsuccessful login attempts for the information system.

Assessors are responsible for combining and consolidating the assessment procedures whenever possible or practical. Optimizing assessment procedures can save time, reduce assessment costs, and maximize the usefulness of assessment results. Assessors optimize assessment procedures by determining the best sequencing of the procedures. The assessment of some security controls before others may provide information that facilitates understanding and assessment of other controls.

---

[49] In the event of any differences between the assessment objectives identified for assessing the security controls and the underlining intent expressed by the security control statements defined in the most recent version of Special Publication 800-53, Special Publication 800-53 remains the definitive expression of the control or enhancement.

[50] The execution of the RMF includes the selection of an initial set of security controls employed within or inherited by an organizational information system followed by a control *tailoring* and *supplementation* process. The tailoring and supplementation process will likely change the set of security controls that will be contained in the final security plan. Therefore, the selection of assessment procedures from the catalog of available procedures is based solely on the content of the security plan after the tailoring and supplementation activities are completed.

Implementation Tips

TIP #1: Select only those assessment procedures from Appendix F that correspond to the security controls and control enhancements in the *approved security plan* and that are to be included in the assessment.

TIP #2: The assessment procedures selected from Appendix F are simply *example* procedures that serve as a starting point for organizations preparing for assessments. These assessment procedures are tailored and supplemented as necessary, in accordance with the guidance in Section 3.2 to adapt the procedures to specific organizational requirements and operating environments.

TIP #3: With respect to the *assessment procedures* in Appendix F, assessors need apply only those procedures, methods, and objects necessary for making a final determination that a particular security control objective is satisfied or not satisfied (see Section 3.3).

TIP #4: Assessors apply to each assessment method, values for depth and coverage (described in Appendix D) that are commensurate with the characteristics of the information system (including assurance requirements) and the specific assessment activity that supports making a determination of the effectiveness of the security controls under review. The values selected for the depth and coverage attributes indicate the relative effort required in applying an assessment method to an assessment object (i.e., the rigor and scope of the activities associated with the assessment). The depth and coverage attributes, while not repeated in every assessment procedure in this appendix, can be represented as follows:

Interview: [*ASSIGN ATTRIBUTE VALUES:* <depth>, <coverage>].
   [*SELECT FROM:* Organizational personnel with contingency planning and plan implementation responsibilities].

TIP #5: Assessors may find useful assessment-related information in the Supplemental Guidance section of each security control described in Special Publication 800-53. This information can be used to carry out more effective assessments with regard to the application of assessment procedures.

Note: When assessing agency compliance with NIST guidance, auditors, Inspectors General, evaluators, and/or assessors consider the intent of the security concepts and principles articulated within the particular guidance document and how the agency applied the guidance in the context of its specific mission responsibilities, operational environments, and unique organizational conditions.

REMINDER

Whereas a set of potential assessment methods have been included in the following catalog of assessment procedures, these are not intended to be mandatory or exclusive and, depending on the particular circumstances of the information system to be assessed, not all methods may be required or other assessment methods may also be used. In addition, the potential assessment objects listed are not intended to be a mandatory set, but rather a set from which the necessary and sufficient set of objects for a given assessment can be selected to make the appropriate determinations. For specific recommendations regarding current best practices for security control assessments, organizations can consult the assessment case development project described in Appendix H and the assessment cases listed on the NIST Web site.

FAMILY: ACCESS CONTROL   **CLASS:** TECHNICAL

ASSESSMENT PROCEDURE	
AC-1	**ACCESS CONTROL POLICY AND PROCEDURES**

AC-1.1	**ASSESSMENT OBJECTIVE:**
	Determine if:
	(i) the organization develops and formally documents access control policy;
	(ii) the organization access control policy addresses:
	    - *purpose;*
	    - *scope;*
	    - *roles and responsibilities;*
	    - *management commitment;*
	    - *coordination among organizational entities; and*
	    - *compliance;*
	(iii) the organization disseminates formal documented access control policy to elements within the organization having associated access control roles and responsibilities;
	(iv) the organization develops and formally documents access control procedures;
	(v) the organization access control procedures facilitate implementation of the access control policy and associated access controls; and
	(vi) the organization disseminates formal documented access control procedures to elements within the organization having associated access control roles and responsibilities.
	
	POTENTIAL ASSESSMENT METHODS AND OBJECTS:
	Examine: [*SELECT FROM:* Access control policy and procedures; other relevant documents or records].
	Interview: [*SELECT FROM:* Organizational personnel with access control responsibilities].

AC-1.2	**ASSESSMENT OBJECTIVE:** *Determine if:* *(i) the organization defines the frequency of access control policy reviews/updates;* *(ii) the organization reviews/updates access control policy in accordance with organization-defined frequency;* *(iii) the organization defines the frequency of access control procedure reviews/updates; and* *(iv) the organization reviews/updates access control procedures in accordance with organization-defined frequency.* **POTENTIAL ASSESSMENT METHODS AND OBJECTS:** **Examine**: [*SELECT FROM:* Access control policy and procedures; other relevant documents or records]. **Interview**: [*SELECT FROM:* Organizational personnel with access control responsibilities].

FAMILY: ACCESS CONTROL   **CLASS:** TECHNICAL

ASSESSMENT PROCEDURE	
AC-2	**ACCOUNT MANAGEMENT**

AC-2.1	**ASSESSMENT OBJECTIVE:**
	Determine if:
	(i) the organization manages information system accounts, including;
	  - *identifying account types (i.e., individual, group, system, application, guest/anonymous, and temporary);*
	  - *establishing conditions for group membership;*
	  - *identifying authorized users of the information system and specifying access privileges;*
	  - *requiring appropriate approvals for requests to establish accounts;*
	  - *establishing, activating, modifying, disabling, and removing accounts;*
	  - *specifically authorizing and monitoring the use of guest/anonymous and temporary accounts;*
	  - *notifying account managers when temporary accounts are no longer required and when information system users are terminated, transferred, or information system usage or need-to-know/need-to-share changes;*
	  - *deactivating: i) temporary accounts that are no longer required; and ii) accounts of terminated or transferred users; and*
	  - *granting access to the system based on:*
	    - *a valid access authorization;*
	    - *intended system usage; and*
	    - *other attributes as required by the organization or associated missions/business functions; and*
	(ii) the organization defines the frequency of information system account reviews; and
	(iii) the organization reviews information system accounts in accordance with organization-defined frequency.
	
	POTENTIAL ASSESSMENT METHODS AND OBJECTS:
	Examine: [*SELECT FROM:* Access control policy; procedures addressing account management; security plan; list of active system accounts along with the name of the individual associated with each account; list of guest/anonymous and temporary accounts along with the name of the individual associated with each account and the date the account expires; lists of recently transferred, separated, or terminated employees; list of recently disabled information system accounts along with the name of the individual associated with each account; system-generated records with user IDs and last login date; other relevant documents or records].
	Interview: [*SELECT FROM:* Organizational personnel with account management responsibilities].

AC-2(1)	ACCOUNT MANAGEMENT
AC-2(1).1	**ASSESSMENT OBJECTIVE:** *Determine if the organization employs automated mechanisms to support information system account management functions.* **POTENTIAL ASSESSMENT METHODS AND OBJECTS:** **Examine**: [*SELECT FROM:* Procedures addressing account management; information system design documentation; information system configuration settings and associated documentation; other relevant documents or records]. **Test**: [*SELECT FROM:* Automated mechanisms implementing account management functions].

AC-2(2)	ACCOUNT MANAGEMENT
AC-2(2).1	**ASSESSMENT OBJECTIVE:** *Determine if:* (i) *the organization defines a time period for each type of account after which the information system terminates temporary and emergency accounts; and* (ii) *the information system automatically terminates temporary and emergency accounts after organization-defined time period for each type of account.* **POTENTIAL ASSESSMENT METHODS AND OBJECTS:** **Examine**: [*SELECT FROM:* Security plan; information system design documentation; information system configuration settings and associated documentation; information system-generated list of active accounts; information system audit records; other relevant documents or records]. **Test**: [*SELECT FROM:* Automated mechanisms implementing account management functions].

AC-2(3)	ACCOUNT MANAGEMENT
AC-2(3).1	**ASSESSMENT OBJECTIVE:** *Determine if:* (i) *the organization defines in a time period after which the information system disables inactive accounts; and* (ii) *the information system automatically disables inactive accounts after organization-defined time period.* **POTENTIAL ASSESSMENT METHODS AND OBJECTS:** **Examine**: [*SELECT FROM:* Procedures addressing account management; security plan; information system design documentation; information system configuration settings and associated documentation; information system-generated list of last login dates; information system-generated list of active accounts; information system audit records; other relevant documents or records]. **Test**: [*SELECT FROM:* Automated mechanisms implementing account management functions].

AC-2(4)	ACCOUNT MANAGEMENT

AC-2(4).1	**ASSESSMENT OBJECTIVE:**
	Determine if:
	
	(i) *the information system automatically audits:*
	
	  - *account creation;*
	  - *modification;*
	  - *disabling; and*
	  - *termination actions; and*
	
	(ii) *the information system notifies, as required, appropriate individuals.*
	
	POTENTIAL ASSESSMENT METHODS AND OBJECTS:
	
	Examine: [*SELECT FROM:* Procedures addressing account management; information system design documentation; information system configuration settings and associated documentation; information system audit records; other relevant documents or records].
	
	Test: [*SELECT FROM:* Automated mechanisms implementing account management functions].

AC-2(5)	ACCOUNT MANAGEMENT
AC-2(5).1	**ASSESSMENT OBJECTIVE:** *Determine if:* (i) *the organization defines the time period of expected inactivity and/or description of when users log out;* (ii) *the organization requires that users log out in accordance with the organization-defined time-period of inactivity and/or description of when to log out;* (iii) *the organization determines normal time-of-day and duration usage for information system accounts;* (iv) *the organization monitors for atypical usage of information system accounts; and* (v) *the organization reports atypical usage to designated organizational officials.* **POTENTIAL ASSESSMENT METHODS AND OBJECTS:** **Examine:** [*SELECT FROM:* Procedures addressing account management; security plan; information system design documentation; information system configuration settings and associated documentation; security violation reports; information system audit records; other relevant documents or records]. **Interview:** [*SELECT FROM:* Organizational personnel with account management responsibilities].

AC-2(6)	ACCOUNT MANAGEMENT
AC-2(6).1	**ASSESSMENT OBJECTIVE:** *Determine if the information system dynamically manages user privileges and associated access authorizations.* **POTENTIAL ASSESSMENT METHODS AND OBJECTS:** **Examine:** [*SELECT FROM:* Procedures addressing account management; information system design documentation; information system configuration settings and associated documentation; information system audit records; other relevant documents or records]. **Interview:** [*SELECT FROM:* Organizational personnel with account management responsibilities]. **Test:** [*SELECT FROM:* Automated mechanisms implementing account management functions].

AC-2(7)	ACCOUNT MANAGEMENT
AC-2(7).1	**ASSESSMENT OBJECTIVE:** *Determine if:* (i) *the organization establishes and administers privileged user accounts in accordance with a role-based access scheme that organizes information system and network privileges into roles; and* (ii) *the organization tracks and monitors privileged role assignments.* **POTENTIAL ASSESSMENT METHODS AND OBJECTS:** **Examine**: [*SELECT FROM:* Procedures addressing account management; information system design documentation; information system configuration settings and associated documentation; information system-generated list of privileged user accounts and associated role; information system audit records; audit tracking and monitoring reports; other relevant documents or records]. **Interview**: [*SELECT FROM:* Organizational personnel with account management responsibilities].

FAMILY: ACCESS CONTROL   **CLASS:** TECHNICAL

ASSESSMENT PROCEDURE	
AC-3	**ACCESS ENFORCEMENT**
AC-3.1	**ASSESSMENT OBJECTIVE:** *Determine if the information system enforces approved authorizations for logical access to the system in accordance with applicable policy.* **POTENTIAL ASSESSMENT METHODS AND OBJECTS:** **Examine:** [*SELECT FROM:* Access control policy; procedures addressing access enforcement; information system configuration settings and associated documentation; list of approved authorizations (user privileges); information system audit records; other relevant documents or records]. **Test:** [*SELECT FROM:* Automated mechanisms implementing access enforcement policy].

AC-3(1)	**ACCESS ENFORCEMENT** [Withdrawn: Incorporated into AC-6].
AC-3(1).1	**ASSESSMENT OBJECTIVE:** [Withdrawn: Incorporated into AC-6]. **POTENTIAL ASSESSMENT METHODS AND OBJECTS:** [Withdrawn: Incorporated into AC-6].

AC-3(2)	**ACCESS ENFORCEMENT**
AC-3(2).1	**ASSESSMENT OBJECTIVE:** *Determine if:* *(i) the organization defines, in organizational policies and procedures, the privileged commands for which dual authorization is to be enforced; and* *(ii) the information system enforces dual authorization based on organizational policies and procedures for organization-defined privileged commands.* **POTENTIAL ASSESSMENT METHODS AND OBJECTS:** **Examine:** [*SELECT FROM:* Access control policy; procedures addressing access enforcement and dual authorization; security plan; information system design documentation; information system configuration settings and associated documentation; list of privileged commands requiring dual authorization; list of approved authorizations (user privileges); other relevant documents or records]. **Interview:** [*SELECT FROM:* Organizational personnel with access enforcement responsibilities]. **Test:** [*SELECT FROM:* Dual authorization mechanisms implementing access control policy].

AC-3(3)	ACCESS ENFORCEMENT
AC-3(3).1	**ASSESSMENT OBJECTIVE:** *Determine if:* *(i) the organization defines the users and resources over which the information system is to enforce nondiscretionary access control policies;* *(ii) the organization defines nondiscretionary access control policies to be enforced over the organization-defined set of users and resources, where the rule set for each policy specifies:* – *access control information (i.e., attributes) employed by the policy rule set (e.g., position, nationality, age, project, time of day); and* – *required relationships among the access control information to permit access; and* *(iii) the information system enforces organization-defined nondiscretionary access control policies over the organization-defined set of users and resources.* **POTENTIAL ASSESSMENT METHODS AND OBJECTS:** **Examine**: [*SELECT FROM:* Access control policy; nondiscretionary access control policies; procedures addressing access enforcement; security plan; information system design documentation; information system configuration settings and associated documentation; list of users and resources requiring enforcement of nondiscretionary access control policies; other relevant documents or records]. **Interview**: [*SELECT FROM:* Organizational personnel with access enforcement responsibilities]. **Test**: [*SELECT FROM:* Automated mechanisms implementing nondiscretionary access control policy].

AC-3(4)	ACCESS ENFORCEMENT
AC-3(4).1	**ASSESSMENT OBJECTIVE:** *Determine if the information system enforces a Discretionary Access Control (DAC) policy that:* – *allows users to specify and control sharing by named individuals or groups of individuals, or by both;* – *limits propagation of access rights; and* – *includes or excludes access to the granularity of a single user.* **POTENTIAL ASSESSMENT METHODS AND OBJECTS:** **Examine**: [*SELECT FROM:* Access control policy; discretionary access control policy; procedures addressing access enforcement; security plan; information system design documentation; information system configuration settings and associated documentation; other relevant documents or records]. **Test**: [*SELECT FROM:* Automated mechanisms implementing discretionary access control policy].

AC-3(5)	ACCESS ENFORCEMENT
AC-3(5).1	**ASSESSMENT OBJECTIVE:** *Determine if:* *(i) the organization defines the security-relevant information to which the information system prevents access except during secure, nonoperable system states; and* *(ii) the information system prevents access to organization-defined security-relevant information except during secure, nonoperable system states.* **POTENTIAL ASSESSMENT METHODS AND OBJECTS:** **Examine**: [*SELECT FROM:* Access control policy; procedures addressing access enforcement; security plan; information system design documentation; information system configuration settings and associated documentation; information system audit records; other relevant documents or records]. **Interview**: [*SELECT FROM:* Organizational personnel with access enforcement responsibilities]. **Test**: [*SELECT FROM:* Automated mechanisms preventing access to security-relevant information within the information system].

AC-3(6)	ACCESS ENFORCEMENT
AC-3(6).1	**ASSESSMENT OBJECTIVE:** *Determine if:* *(i) the organization defines the user and/or system information to be encrypted or stored off-line in a secure location; and* *(ii) the organization encrypts, or stores off-line in a secure location, organization-defined user and/or system information.* **POTENTIAL ASSESSMENT METHODS AND OBJECTS:** **Examine**: [*SELECT FROM:* Access control policy; procedures addressing access enforcement; information system design documentation; information system configuration settings and associated documentation; information system audit records; other relevant documents or records]. **Interview**: [*SELECT FROM:* Organizational personnel with access enforcement responsibilities]. **Test**: [*SELECT FROM:* Automated mechanisms implementing access enforcement functions].

FAMILY: ACCESS CONTROL   **CLASS:** TECHNICAL

ASSESSMENT PROCEDURE

AC-4	INFORMATION FLOW ENFORCEMENT
AC-4.1	**ASSESSMENT OBJECTIVE:** *Determine if:* (i) the organization defines applicable policy for controlling the flow of information within the system and between interconnected systems; (ii) the organization defines approved authorizations for controlling the flow of information within the system and between interconnected systems in accordance with applicable policy; and (iii) the information system enforces approved authorizations for controlling the flow of information within the system and between interconnected systems in accordance with applicable policy. **POTENTIAL ASSESSMENT METHODS AND OBJECTS:** **Examine:** [*SELECT FROM:* Access control policy; procedures addressing information flow enforcement; information system design documentation; information system configuration settings and associated documentation; information system baseline configuration; list of information flow authorizations; information system audit records; other relevant documents or records]. **Test:** [*SELECT FROM:* Automated mechanisms implementing information flow enforcement policy].

AC-4(1)	INFORMATION FLOW ENFORCEMENT
AC-4(1).1	**ASSESSMENT OBJECTIVE:** *Determine if the information system enforces information flow control using explicit security attributes on information, source, and destination objects as a basis for flow control decisions.* **POTENTIAL ASSESSMENT METHODS AND OBJECTS:** **Examine:** [*SELECT FROM:* Access control policy; procedures addressing information flow enforcement; information system design documentation; information system configuration settings and associated documentation; information system audit records; other relevant documents or records]. **Test:** [*SELECT FROM:* Automated mechanisms implementing information flow enforcement policy].

AC-4(2)	INFORMATION FLOW ENFORCEMENT
AC-4(2).1	**ASSESSMENT OBJECTIVE:** *Determine if the information system enforces information flow control using protected processing domains (e.g., domain type-enforcement) as a basis for flow control decisions.* **POTENTIAL ASSESSMENT METHODS AND OBJECTS:** **Examine:** [*SELECT FROM:* Access control policy; procedures addressing information flow enforcement; information system design documentation; information system configuration settings and associated documentation; information system audit records; other relevant documents or records]. **Test:** [*SELECT FROM:* Automated mechanisms implementing information flow enforcement policy].

AC-4(3)	INFORMATION FLOW ENFORCEMENT
AC-4(3).1	**ASSESSMENT OBJECTIVE:** *Determine if:* (i) *the organization defines policy that allows or disallows information flows based on changing conditions or operational consideration; and* (ii) *the information system enforces dynamic information flow control based on policy that allows or disallows information flows based on changing conditions or operational considerations.* **POTENTIAL ASSESSMENT METHODS AND OBJECTS:** **Examine**: [*SELECT FROM:* Access control policy; procedures addressing information flow enforcement; information system design documentation; information system configuration settings and associated documentation; information system audit records; other relevant documents or records]. **Test**: [*SELECT FROM:* Automated mechanisms implementing information flow enforcement policy].

AC-4(4)	INFORMATION FLOW ENFORCEMENT
AC-4(4).1	**ASSESSMENT OBJECTIVE:** *Determine if the information system prevents encrypted data from bypassing content-checking mechanisms.* **POTENTIAL ASSESSMENT METHODS AND OBJECTS:** **Examine**: [*SELECT FROM:* Access control policy; procedures addressing information flow enforcement; information system design documentation; information system configuration settings and associated documentation; information system audit records; other relevant documents or records]. **Test**: [*SELECT FROM:* Automated mechanisms implementing information flow enforcement policy].

AC-4(5)	INFORMATION FLOW ENFORCEMENT
AC-4(5).1	**ASSESSMENT OBJECTIVE:** *Determine if:* (i) *the organization defines the limitations on the embedding of data types with other data types; and* (ii) *the information system enforces organization-defined limitations on the embedding of data types within other data types.* **POTENTIAL ASSESSMENT METHODS AND OBJECTS:** **Examine**: [*SELECT FROM:* Access control policy; procedures addressing information flow enforcement; information system design documentation; information system configuration settings and associated documentation; information system audit records; other relevant documents or records]. **Test**: [*SELECT FROM:* Automated mechanisms implementing information flow enforcement policy].

AC-4(6)	INFORMATION FLOW ENFORCEMENT
AC-4(6).1	**ASSESSMENT OBJECTIVE:** *Determine if the information system enforces information flow control on metadata.* **POTENTIAL ASSESSMENT METHODS AND OBJECTS:** **Examine**: [*SELECT FROM:* Access control policy; procedures addressing information flow enforcement; information system design documentation; information system configuration settings and associated documentation; information system audit records; other relevant documents or records]. **Test**: [*SELECT FROM:* Automated mechanisms implementing information flow enforcement policy].

AC-4(7)	INFORMATION FLOW ENFORCEMENT
AC-4(7).1	**ASSESSMENT OBJECTIVE:** *Determine if:* (i) *the organization defines the one-way information flows to be enforced by the information system; and* (ii) *the information system enforces organization-defined one-way information flows using hardware mechanisms.* **POTENTIAL ASSESSMENT METHODS AND OBJECTS:** **Examine**: [*SELECT FROM:* Access control policy; procedures addressing information flow enforcement; information system design documentation; information system configuration settings and associated documentation; information system audit records; other relevant documents or records]. **Test**: [*SELECT FROM:* Hardware mechanisms implementing information flow enforcement policy].

AC-4(8)	INFORMATION FLOW ENFORCEMENT
AC-4(8).1	**ASSESSMENT OBJECTIVE:** *Determine if:* (i) *the organization defines the security policy filters to be enforced by the information system; and* (ii) *the information system enforces information flow control using organization-defined security policy filters as a basis for flow control decisions.* **POTENTIAL ASSESSMENT METHODS AND OBJECTS:** **Examine**: [*SELECT FROM:* Access control policy; procedures addressing information flow enforcement; information system design documentation; information system configuration settings and associated documentation; list of security policy filters; information system audit records; other relevant documents or records]. **Test**: [*SELECT FROM:* Automated mechanisms implementing information flow enforcement policy].

AC-4(9)	INFORMATION FLOW ENFORCEMENT
AC-4(9).1	**ASSESSMENT OBJECTIVE:** *Determine if:* (i) *the organization defines the security policy filters that the information system enforces for the use of human review; and* (ii) *the information system enforces the use of human review for the organization-defined security policy filters, when the system is not capable of making an information flow control decision.* **POTENTIAL ASSESSMENT METHODS AND OBJECTS:** **Examine:** [*SELECT FROM:* Access control policy; procedures addressing information flow enforcement; information system design documentation; information system configuration settings and associated documentation; information system audit records; other relevant documents or records]. **Interview:** [*SELECT FROM:* Organizational personnel with responsibilities for making information flow control decisions when the information system is not capable of doing so].

AC-4(10)	INFORMATION FLOW ENFORCEMENT
AC-4(10).1	**ASSESSMENT OBJECTIVE:** *Determine if:* (i) *the organization defines the security policy filters that privileged administrators have the capability to enable/disable; and* (ii) *the information system provides the capability for a privileged administrator to enable/disable organization-defined security policy filters.* **POTENTIAL ASSESSMENT METHODS AND OBJECTS:** **Examine:** [*SELECT FROM:* Access control policy; procedures addressing information flow enforcement; information system design documentation; information system configuration settings and associated documentation; information system audit records; other relevant documents or records]. **Interview:** [*SELECT FROM:* Organizational personnel with responsibilities for enabling/disabling security policy filters]. **Test:** [*SELECT FROM:* Automated mechanisms implementing information flow enforcement policy].

AC-4(11)	INFORMATION FLOW ENFORCEMENT
AC-4(11).1	**ASSESSMENT OBJECTIVE:** *Determine if:* (i) *the organization defines the security policy filters that privileged administrators have the capability to configure; and* (ii) *the information system provides the capability for a privileged administrator to configure organization-defined security policy filters to support different security policies.* **POTENTIAL ASSESSMENT METHODS AND OBJECTS:** **Examine:** [*SELECT FROM:* Access control policy; procedures addressing information flow enforcement; information system design documentation; information system configuration settings and associated documentation; information system audit records; other relevant documents or records]. **Interview:** [*SELECT FROM:* Organizational personnel with responsibilities for configuring security policy filters]. **Test:** [*SELECT FROM:* Automated mechanisms implementing information flow enforcement policy].

AC-4(12)	INFORMATION FLOW ENFORCEMENT
AC-4(12).1	**ASSESSMENT OBJECTIVE:** *Determine if the information system, when transferring information between different security domains, identifies information flows by data type specification and usage.* **POTENTIAL ASSESSMENT METHODS AND OBJECTS:** **Examine:** [*SELECT FROM:* Access control policy; procedures addressing information flow enforcement; information system design documentation; information system configuration settings and associated documentation; information system audit records; other relevant documents or records]. **Test:** [*SELECT FROM:* Automated mechanisms implementing information flow enforcement policy].

AC-4(13)	INFORMATION FLOW ENFORCEMENT
AC-4(13).1	**ASSESSMENT OBJECTIVE:** *Determine if the information system, when transferring information between different security domains, decomposes information into policy-relevant subcomponents for submission to policy enforcement mechanisms.* **POTENTIAL ASSESSMENT METHODS AND OBJECTS:** **Examine:** [*SELECT FROM:* Access control policy; procedures addressing information flow enforcement; information system design documentation; information system configuration settings and associated documentation; information system audit records; other relevant documents or records]. **Test:** [*SELECT FROM:* Automated mechanisms implementing information flow enforcement policy].

AC-4(14)	INFORMATION FLOW ENFORCEMENT
AC-4(14).1	**ASSESSMENT OBJECTIVE:** *Determine if:* (i) *the organization defines the security policy requirements for constraining data structure and content; and* (ii) *the information system, when transferring information between different security domains, implements policy filters that constrain data structure and content in accordance with organization-defined information security policy requirements.* **POTENTIAL ASSESSMENT METHODS AND OBJECTS:** **Examine:** [*SELECT FROM:* Access control policy; procedures addressing information flow enforcement; information system design documentation; information system configuration settings and associated documentation; list of policy filters; information system audit records; other relevant documents or records]. **Test:** [*SELECT FROM:* Automated mechanisms implementing information flow enforcement policy].

AC-4(15)	INFORMATION FLOW ENFORCEMENT
AC-4(15).1	**ASSESSMENT OBJECTIVE:** *Determine if:* (i) *the information system, when transferring information between different security domains, detects unsanctioned information; and* (ii) *the information system prohibits the transfer of unsanctioned information in accordance with the security policy.* **POTENTIAL ASSESSMENT METHODS AND OBJECTS:** **Examine:** [*SELECT FROM:* Access control policy; procedures addressing information flow enforcement; information system design documentation; information system configuration settings and associated documentation; information system audit records; other relevant documents or records]. **Test:** [*SELECT FROM:* Automated mechanisms implementing information flow enforcement policy].

AC-4(16)	INFORMATION FLOW ENFORCEMENT
AC-4(16).1	**ASSESSMENT OBJECTIVE:** *Determine if the information system enforces security policies regarding information on interconnected systems.* **POTENTIAL ASSESSMENT METHODS AND OBJECTS:** **Examine:** [*SELECT FROM:* Access control policy; procedures addressing information flow enforcement; information system design documentation; information system configuration settings and associated documentation; information system audit records; other relevant documents or records]. **Test:** [*SELECT FROM:* Automated mechanisms implementing information flow enforcement policy].

AC-4(17)	INFORMATION FLOW ENFORCEMENT
AC-4(17).1	**ASSESSMENT OBJECTIVE:** *Determine if:* *(i) the information system uniquely identifies source domains for information transfer;* *(ii) the information system uniquely authenticates source domains for information transfer;* *(iii) the information system uniquely identifies destination domains for information transfer;* *(iv) the information system uniquely authenticates destination domains for information transfer;* *(v) the information system binds security attributes to information to facilitate information flow policy enforcement;* *(vi) the information system tracks problems associated with the security attribute binding; and* *(vii) the information system tracks problems associated with the information transfer.* **POTENTIAL ASSESSMENT METHODS AND OBJECTS:** **Examine:** [*SELECT FROM:* Access control policy; procedures addressing information flow enforcement; procedures addressing source and destination domain identification and authentication, and information transfer error handling; information system design documentation; information system configuration settings and associated documentation; information system audit records; other relevant documents or records]. **Test:** [*SELECT FROM:* Automated mechanisms implementing information flow enforcement policy].

FAMILY: ACCESS CONTROL　　　　　　　　　　　　　　**CLASS:** TECHNICAL

ASSESSMENT PROCEDURE	
AC-5	**SEPARATION OF DUTIES**
AC-5.1	**ASSESSMENT OBJECTIVE:** *Determine if:* *(i)　the organization separates duties of individuals as necessary, to prevent malevolent activity without collusion;* *(ii)　the organization documents separation of duties; and* *(iii)　the organization implements separation of duties through assigned information system access authorizations.* **POTENTIAL ASSESSMENT METHODS AND OBJECTS:** **Examine:** [*SELECT FROM:* Access control policy; procedures addressing divisions of responsibility and separation of duties; information system configuration settings and associated documentation; list of divisions of responsibility and separation of duties; information system audit records; other relevant documents or records]. **Interview:** [*SELECT FROM:* Organizational personnel with responsibilities for defining appropriate divisions of responsibility and separation of duties]. **Test:** [*SELECT FROM:* Automated mechanisms implementing separation of duties policy].

FAMILY: ACCESS CONTROL   **CLASS:** TECHNICAL

ASSESSMENT PROCEDURE

AC-6	LEAST PRIVILEGE
AC-6.1	**ASSESSMENT OBJECTIVE:**
	Determine if the organization employs the concept of least privilege, allowing only authorized accesses for users (and processes acting on behalf of users) which are necessary to accomplish assigned tasks in accordance with organizational missions and business functions.
	POTENTIAL ASSESSMENT METHODS AND OBJECTS:
	Examine: [*SELECT FROM:* Access control policy; procedures addressing least privilege; list of assigned access authorizations (user privileges); information system configuration settings and associated documentation; information system audit records; other relevant documents or records].
	Interview: [*SELECT FROM:* Organizational personnel with responsibilities for defining least privileges necessary to accomplish specified tasks].

AC-6(1)	LEAST PRIVILEGE
AC-6(1).1	**ASSESSMENT OBJECTIVE:**
	Determine if:
	(i) *the organization defines the security functions (deployed in hardware, software, and firmware) and security-relevant information for which access must be explicitly authorized; and*
	(ii) *the organization explicitly authorizes access to the organization-defined security functions and security-relevant information.*
	POTENTIAL ASSESSMENT METHODS AND OBJECTS:
	Examine: [*SELECT FROM:* Access control policy; procedures addressing least privilege; list of security functions and security-relevant information for which access must be explicitly authorized; information system configuration settings and associated documentation; information system audit records; other relevant documents or records].
	Interview: [*SELECT FROM:* Organizational personnel with responsibilities for defining least privileges necessary to accomplish specified tasks].

AC-6(2)	LEAST PRIVILEGE
AC-6(2).1	**ASSESSMENT OBJECTIVE:** *Determine if:* (i) *the organization defines the security functions or security-relevant information to which users of information system accounts, or roles, have access; and* (ii) *the organization requires that users of information system accounts, or roles, with access to organization-defined security functions or security-relevant information, use non-privileged accounts, or roles, when accessing other system functions; and* (iii) *the organization, if deemed feasible, audits any use of privileged accounts, or roles, with access to organization-defined security functions or security-relevant information, when accessing other system functions.* **POTENTIAL ASSESSMENT METHODS AND OBJECTS:** **Examine:** [*SELECT FROM:* Access control policy; procedures addressing least privilege; list of system-generated security functions or security-relevant information assigned to information system accounts or roles; information system configuration settings and associated documentation; information system audit records; other relevant documents or records]. **Interview:** [*SELECT FROM:* Organizational personnel with responsibilities for defining least privileges necessary to accomplish specified tasks].

AC-6(3)	LEAST PRIVILEGE
AC-6(3).1	**ASSESSMENT OBJECTIVE:** *Determine if:* (i) *the organization defines the privileged commands to which network access is to be authorized only for compelling operational needs;* (ii) *the organization authorizes network access to organization-defined privileged commands only for compelling operational needs; and* (iii) *the organization documents the rationale for authorized network access to organization-defined privileged commands in the security plan for the information system.* **POTENTIAL ASSESSMENT METHODS AND OBJECTS:** **Examine:** [*SELECT FROM:* Access control policy; procedures addressing least privilege; security plan; information system configuration settings and associated documentation; information system audit records; other relevant documents or records]. **Interview:** [*SELECT FROM:* Organizational personnel with responsibilities for defining least privileges necessary to accomplish specified tasks].

AC-6(4)	LEAST PRIVILEGE
AC-6(4).1	**ASSESSMENT OBJECTIVE:** *Determine if the information system provides separate processing domains to enable finer-grained allocation of user privileges.* **POTENTIAL ASSESSMENT METHODS AND OBJECTS:** **Examine:** [*SELECT FROM:* Access control policy; procedures addressing least privilege; information system design documentation; information system configuration settings and associated documentation; information system audit records; other relevant documents or records]. **Interview:** [*SELECT FROM:* Organizational personnel with responsibilities for defining least privileges necessary to accomplish specified tasks].

AC-6(5)	LEAST PRIVILEGE
AC-6(5).1	**ASSESSMENT OBJECTIVE:** *Determine if the organization limits authorization to super user accounts on the information system to designated system administration personnel.* **POTENTIAL ASSESSMENT METHODS AND OBJECTS:** **Examine**: [*SELECT FROM:* Access control policy; procedures addressing least privilege; list of system-generated super user accounts; list of system administration personnel; information system configuration settings and associated documentation; information system audit records; other relevant documents or records]. **Interview**: [*SELECT FROM:* Organizational personnel with responsibilities for defining least privileges necessary to accomplish specified tasks].

AC-6(6)	LEAST PRIVILEGE
AC-6(6).1	**ASSESSMENT OBJECTIVE:** *Determine if the organization prohibits privileged access to the information system by non-organizational users.* **POTENTIAL ASSESSMENT METHODS AND OBJECTS:** **Examine**: [*SELECT FROM:* Access control policy; procedures addressing least privilege; list of system-generated privileged accounts; list of non-organizational users; information system configuration settings and associated documentation; information system audit records; other relevant documents or records]. **Interview**: [*SELECT FROM:* Organizational personnel with responsibilities for defining least privileges necessary to accomplish specified tasks].

FAMILY: ACCESS CONTROL   **CLASS:** TECHNICAL

ASSESSMENT PROCEDURE	
AC-7	**UNSUCCESSFUL LOGIN ATTEMPTS**

AC-7.1	**ASSESSMENT OBJECTIVE:**
	Determine if:
	
	(i) the organization defines the maximum number of consecutive invalid login attempts to the information system by a user and the time period in which the consecutive invalid attempts occur;
	
	(ii) the information system enforces the organization-defined limit of consecutive invalid login attempts by a user during the organization-defined time period;
	
	(iii) the organization defines action to be taken by the system when the maximum number of unsuccessful login attempts is exceeded as:
	
	   – *lock out the account/node for a specified time period;*
	
	   – *lock out the account/note until released by an administrator; or*
	
	   – *delay the next login prompt according to organization-defined delay algorithm;*
	
	(iv) the information system either automatically locks the account/node for the organization-defined time period, locks the account/node until released by an administrator, or delays next login prompt for the organization-defined delay period when the maximum number of unsuccessful login attempts is exceeded; and
	
	(v) the information system performs the organization-defined actions when the maximum number of unsuccessful login attempts is exceeded regardless of whether the login occurs via a local or network connection.
	
	POTENTIAL ASSESSMENT METHODS AND OBJECTS:
	Examine: [*SELECT FROM:* Access control policy; procedures addressing unsuccessful login attempts; security plan; information system configuration settings and associated documentation; information system audit records; other relevant documents or records].
	
	Test: [*SELECT FROM:* Automated mechanisms implementing the access control policy for unsuccessful login attempts].

AC-7(1)	**UNSUCCESSFUL LOGIN ATTEMPTS**
AC-7(1).1	**ASSESSMENT OBJECTIVE:** *Determine if the information system automatically locks the account/node until released by an administrator when the maximum number of unsuccessful login attempts is exceeded.* **POTENTIAL ASSESSMENT METHODS AND OBJECTS:** **Examine:** [*SELECT FROM:* Access control policy; procedures addressing unsuccessful login attempts; information system design documentation; information system configuration settings and associated documentation; list of information system accounts; information system audit records; other relevant documents or records]. **Test:** [*SELECT FROM:* Automated mechanisms implementing the access control policy for unsuccessful login attempts].

AC-7(2)	UNSUCCESSFUL LOGIN ATTEMPTS
AC-7(2).1	**ASSESSMENT OBJECTIVE:** *Determine if:* *(i) the organization defines the number of consecutive, unsuccessful login attempts allowed for accessing a mobile device before the information system purges information from the device; and* *(ii) the information system provides protection for mobile devices accessed via login by purging information from such devices after the organization-defined number of consecutive, unsuccessful login attempts to the device is exceeded.* **POTENTIAL ASSESSMENT METHODS AND OBJECTS:** **Examine**: [*SELECT FROM:* Access control policy; procedures addressing unsuccessful login attempts on mobile devices; information system design documentation; information system configuration settings and associated documentation; information system audit records; other relevant documents or records]. **Test**: [*SELECT FROM:* Automated mechanisms implementing the access control policy for unsuccessful login attempts].

FAMILY: ACCESS CONTROL   **CLASS:** TECHNICAL

ASSESSMENT PROCEDURE	
AC-8	**SYSTEM USE NOTIFICATION**
AC-8.1	**ASSESSMENT OBJECTIVE:** *Determine if:* (i) *the organization approves the information system use notification message or banner to be displayed by the information system before granting access to the system;* (ii) *the information system displays the approved system use notification message or banner before granting access to the system that provides privacy and security notices consistent with applicable federal laws, Executive Orders, directives, policies, regulations, standards, and guidance and states that:* - *users are accessing a U.S. Government information system;* - *system usage may be monitored, recorded, and subject to audit;* - *unauthorized use of the system is prohibited and subject to criminal and civil penalties; and* - *use of the system indicates consent to monitoring and recording; and* (iii) *the information system retains the notification message or banner on the screen until the user takes explicit actions to log on to or further access the information system.* **POTENTIAL ASSESSMENT METHODS AND OBJECTS:** **Examine:** [*SELECT FROM:* Access control policy; privacy and security policies; procedures addressing system use notification; documented approval of information system use notification messages or banners; information system notification messages; information system configuration settings and associated documentation; information system audit records for user acceptance of notification message or banner; other relevant documents or records]. **Test:** [*SELECT FROM:* Automated mechanisms implementing the access control policy for system use notification].
AC-8.2	**ASSESSMENT OBJECTIVE:** *Determine if:* (i) *the information system (for publicly accessible systems) displays the system use information when appropriate, before granting further access;* (ii) *the information system (for publicly accessible systems) displays references, if any, to monitoring, recording, or auditing that are consistent with privacy accommodations for such systems that generally prohibit those activities; and* (iii) *the information system (for publicly accessible systems) includes in the notice given to public users of the information system, a description of the authorized uses of the information system.* **POTENTIAL ASSESSMENT METHODS AND OBJECTS:** **Examine:** [*SELECT FROM:* Access control policy; privacy and security policies; procedures addressing system use notification; documented approval of information system use notification messages or banners; information system notification messages; information system configuration settings and associated documentation; other relevant documents or records]. **Test:** [*SELECT FROM:* Automated mechanisms implementing the access control policy for system use notification].

FAMILY: ACCESS CONTROL   **CLASS:** TECHNICAL

ASSESSMENT PROCEDURE	
AC-9	**PREVIOUS LOGON (ACCESS) NOTIFICATION**
AC-9.1	**ASSESSMENT OBJECTIVE:** *Determine if the information system, upon successful user logon (access), displays to the user the date and time of the last logon (access).* **POTENTIAL ASSESSMENT METHODS AND OBJECTS:** **Examine:** [*SELECT FROM:* Access control policy; procedures addressing previous logon notification; information system configuration settings and associated documentation; information system notification messages; information system design documentation; other relevant documents or records]. **Test:** [*SELECT FROM:* Automated mechanisms implementing the access control policy for previous logon notification].

AC-9(1)	**PREVIOUS LOGON (ACCESS) NOTIFICATION**
AC-9(1).1	**ASSESSMENT OBJECTIVE:** *Determine if the information system, upon successful user logon/access, displays to the user the number of unsuccessful logon/access attempts since the last successful logon/access.* **POTENTIAL ASSESSMENT METHODS AND OBJECTS:** **Examine:** [*SELECT FROM:* Access control policy; procedures addressing previous logon notification; information system design documentation; information system configuration settings and associated documentation; information system audit records; other relevant documents or records]. **Test:** [*SELECT FROM:* Automated mechanisms implementing the access control policy for previous logon notification].

AC-9(2)	**PREVIOUS LOGON (ACCESS) NOTIFICATION**
AC-9(2).1	**ASSESSMENT OBJECTIVE:** *Determine if:* (i) *the organization defines the time period during which the number of successful logins/accesses and/or unsuccessful user login/access attempts occurs; and* (ii) *the information system notifies the user of the number of successful logins/accesses and/or unsuccessful login/access attempts that occur during the organization-defined time period.* **POTENTIAL ASSESSMENT METHODS AND OBJECTS:** **Examine:** [*SELECT FROM:* Access control policy; procedures addressing previous logon notification; information system design documentation; information system configuration settings and associated documentation; information system audit records; other relevant documents or records]. **Test:** [*SELECT FROM:* Automated mechanisms implementing the access control policy for previous logon notification].

AC-9(3)	PREVIOUS LOGON (ACCESS) NOTIFICATION
AC-9(3).1	**ASSESSMENT OBJECTIVE:** *Determine if:* (i) *the organization defines the time period for which security-related changes to the user's account occur; and* (ii) *the information system notifies the user of the organization-defined security-related changes to the user's account that occur during the organization-defined time period.* **POTENTIAL ASSESSMENT METHODS AND OBJECTS:** **Examine:** [*SELECT FROM:* Access control policy; procedures addressing previous logon notification; information system design documentation; information system configuration settings and associated documentation; information system audit records; other relevant documents or records]. **Test**: [*SELECT FROM:* Automated mechanisms implementing the access control policy for previous logon notification].

FAMILY: ACCESS CONTROL   **CLASS:** TECHNICAL

ASSESSMENT PROCEDURE
AC-10   **CONCURRENT SESSION CONTROL**

| AC-10.1 | **ASSESSMENT OBJECTIVE:**

Determine if:

(i)   *the organization defines the maximum number of concurrent sessions to be allowed for each system account; and*

(ii)   *the information system limits the number of concurrent sessions for each system account to the organization-defined number of sessions.*

POTENTIAL ASSESSMENT METHODS AND OBJECTS:

Examine: [*SELECT FROM:* Access control policy; procedures addressing concurrent session control; information system design documentation; information system configuration settings and associated documentation; security plan; other relevant documents or records].

Test: [*SELECT FROM:* Automated mechanisms implementing the access control policy for concurrent session control]. |

FAMILY: ACCESS CONTROL   **CLASS:** TECHNICAL

ASSESSMENT PROCEDURE
AC-11	**SESSION LOCK**
AC-11.1	**ASSESSMENT OBJECTIVE:** _Determine if:_ _(i) the organization defines the time period of user inactivity after which the information system initiates a session lock;_ _(ii) the information system initiates a session lock after the organization-defined time period of inactivity or upon receiving a request from a user;_ _(iii) the information system retains the session lock until the user reestablishes access using established identification and authentication procedures._ **POTENTIAL ASSESSMENT METHODS AND OBJECTS:** **Examine:** [_SELECT FROM:_ Access control policy; procedures addressing session lock; information system design documentation; information system configuration settings and associated documentation; security plan; other relevant documents or records]. **Test:** [_SELECT FROM:_ Automated mechanisms implementing the access control policy for session lock].

AC-11(1)	**SESSION LOCK**
AC-11(1).1	**ASSESSMENT OBJECTIVE:** _Determine if the information system session lock mechanism, when activated on a device with a display screen, places a publicly viewable pattern onto the associated display, hiding what was previously visible on the screen._ **POTENTIAL ASSESSMENT METHODS AND OBJECTS:** **Examine:** [_SELECT FROM:_ Access control policy; procedures addressing session lock; display screen with session lock activated; information system design documentation; information system configuration settings and associated documentation; other relevant documents or records]. **Test:** [_SELECT FROM:_ Information system session lock mechanisms].

FAMILY: ACCESS CONTROL   **CLASS:** TECHNICAL

ASSESSMENT PROCEDURE	
AC-12	**SESSION TERMINATION** [Withdrawn: Incorporated into SC-10].
AC-12.1	**ASSESSMENT OBJECTIVE:** [Withdrawn: Incorporated into SC-10]. **POTENTIAL ASSESSMENT METHODS AND OBJECTS:** [Withdrawn: Incorporated into SC-10].

FAMILY: ACCESS CONTROL　　　　　　　　　　　　　　　　**CLASS:** TECHNICAL

ASSESSMENT PROCEDURE	
AC-13	**SUPERVISION AND REVIEW — ACCESS CONTROL** [Withdrawn: Incorporated into AC-2 and AU-6].
AC-13.1	**ASSESSMENT OBJECTIVE:** [Withdrawn: Incorporated into AC-2 and AU-6]. **POTENTIAL ASSESSMENT METHODS AND OBJECTS:** [Withdrawn: Incorporated into AC-2 and AU-6].

FAMILY: ACCESS CONTROL   **CLASS:** TECHNICAL

ASSESSMENT PROCEDURE	
AC-14	**PERMITTED ACTIONS WITHOUT IDENTIFICATION OR AUTHENTICATION**
AC-14.1	**ASSESSMENT OBJECTIVE:** *Determine if:* (i) *the organization identifies specific user actions that can be performed on the information system without identification or authentication; and* (ii) *the organization documents and provides supporting rationale in the security plan for the information system, user actions not requiring identification and authentication.* **POTENTIAL ASSESSMENT METHODS AND OBJECTS:** **Examine:** [*SELECT FROM:* Access control policy; procedures addressing permitted actions without identification and authentication; information system configuration settings and associated documentation; security plan; list of information system actions that can be performed without identification and authentication; information system audit records; other relevant documents or records].

AC-14(1)	**PERMITTED ACTIONS WITHOUT IDENTIFICATION OR AUTHENTICATION**
AC-14(1).1	**ASSESSMENT OBJECTIVE:** *Determine if the organization permits actions to be performed without identification and authentication only to the extent necessary to accomplish mission/business objectives.* **POTENTIAL ASSESSMENT METHODS AND OBJECTS:** **Examine:** [*SELECT FROM:* Access control policy; procedures addressing permitted actions without identification and authentication; information system configuration settings and associated documentation; security plan; list of information system actions that can be performed without identification and authentication; information system audit records; other relevant documents or records].

FAMILY: ACCESS CONTROL   **CLASS:** TECHNICAL

ASSESSMENT PROCEDURE	
AC-15	**AUTOMATED MARKING** [Withdrawn: Incorporated into MP-3].
AC-15.1	**ASSESSMENT OBJECTIVE:** [Withdrawn: Incorporated into MP-3]. **POTENTIAL ASSESSMENT METHODS AND OBJECTS:** [Withdrawn: Incorporated into MP-3].

FAMILY: ACCESS CONTROL   **CLASS:** TECHNICAL

ASSESSMENT PROCEDURE

AC-16	SECURITY ATTRIBUTES

AC-16.1	**ASSESSMENT OBJECTIVE:**
	Determine if:
	(i) *the organization defines the security attributes the information system binds to information:*
	     - *in storage;*
	     - *in process; and*
	     - *in transmission; and*
	(ii) *the information system supports and maintains the binding of the organization-defined security attributes to information in storage, in process, and in transmission.*
	
	POTENTIAL ASSESSMENT METHODS AND OBJECTS:
	Examine: [*SELECT FROM:* Access control policy; procedures addressing the binding of security attributes to information in storage, in process, and in transmission; information system design documentation; information system configuration settings and associated documentation; other relevant documents or records].
	Test: [*SELECT FROM:* Automated mechanisms supporting and maintaining the binding of security attributes to information in storage, in process, and in transmission].

AC-16(1)	SECURITY ATTRIBUTES
AC-16(1).1	**ASSESSMENT OBJECTIVE:** *Determine if the information system dynamically reconfigures security attributes in accordance with an identified security policy as information is created and combined.* **POTENTIAL ASSESSMENT METHODS AND OBJECTS:** **Examine**: [*SELECT FROM:* Access control policy; procedures addressing the dynamic reconfiguration of security attributes; information system design documentation; information system configuration settings and associated documentation; other relevant documents or records]. **Test**: [*SELECT FROM:* Automated mechanisms implementing the dynamic reconfiguration of security attributes to information].

AC-16(2)	SECURITY ATTRIBUTES
AC-16(2).1	**ASSESSMENT OBJECTIVE:** *Determine if:* *(i) the organization identifies the entities authorized to change security attributes; and* *(ii) the information system allows authorized entities to change security attributes.* **POTENTIAL ASSESSMENT METHODS AND OBJECTS:** **Examine:** [*SELECT FROM:* Access control policy; procedures addressing the change of security attributes; information system design documentation; information system configuration settings and associated documentation; list of entities authorized to change security attributes; information system audit records; other relevant documents or records]. **Interview:** [*SELECT FROM:* Organizational personnel with responsibilities for changing security attributes]. **Test:** [*SELECT FROM:* Automated mechanisms allowing the change of security attributes].

AC-16(3)	SECURITY ATTRIBUTES
AC-16(3).1	**ASSESSMENT OBJECTIVE:** *Determine if the information system maintains the binding of security attributes to information with sufficient assurance that the information-attribute association can be used as the basis for automated policy actions.* **POTENTIAL ASSESSMENT METHODS AND OBJECTS:** **Examine:** [*SELECT FROM:* Access control policy; procedures addressing the binding of security attributes to information; information system design documentation; information system configuration settings and associated documentation; other relevant documents or records]. **Test:** [*SELECT FROM:* Automated mechanisms maintaining the binding of security attributes to information].

AC-16(4)	SECURITY ATTRIBUTES
AC-16(4).1	**ASSESSMENT OBJECTIVE:** *Determine if:* *(i) the organization identifies users authorized to associate security attributes with information; and* *(ii) the information system allows authorized users to associate security attributes with information.* **POTENTIAL ASSESSMENT METHODS AND OBJECTS:** **Examine:** [*SELECT FROM:* Access control policy; procedures addressing the association of security attributes to information; information system design documentation; information system configuration settings and associated documentation; list of users authorized to associate security attributes with information; information system audit records; other relevant documents or records]. **Interview:** [*SELECT FROM:* Organizational personnel with responsibilities for associating security attributes with information]. **Test:** [*SELECT FROM:* Automated mechanisms allowing users to associate security attributes with information].

AC-16(5)	SECURITY ATTRIBUTES
AC-16(5).1	**ASSESSMENT OBJECTIVE:** *Determine if:* *(i) the organization defines the set of special dissemination, handling, or distribution instructions to be used for each object output from the information system;* *(ii) the organization defines standard naming conventions for the security attributes to be displayed in human-readable form on each object output from the system to system output devices; and* *(iii) the information system displays security attributes in human-readable form on each object output from the system to system output devices to identify the organization-defined set of special dissemination, handling, or distribution instructions using organization-defined human readable, standard naming conventions.* **POTENTIAL ASSESSMENT METHODS AND OBJECTS:** **Examine**: [*SELECT FROM:* Access control policy; procedures addressing display of security attributes in human-readable form; special instructions for the dissemination, handling, or distribution of object output from the information system; information system design documentation; information system configuration settings and associated documentation; information system audit records; other relevant documents or records]. **Test**: [*SELECT FROM:* System output devices displaying security attributes in human-readable form on each object].

FAMILY: ACCESS CONTROL   **CLASS:** TECHNICAL

ASSESSMENT PROCEDURE	
AC-17	**REMOTE ACCESS**
AC-17.1	**ASSESSMENT OBJECTIVE:** *Determine if:* *(i) the organization documents allowed methods of remote access to the information system;* *(ii) the organization establishes usage restrictions and implementation guidance for each allowed remote access method;* *(iii) the organization monitors for unauthorized remote access to the information system;* *(iv) the organization authorizes remote access to the information system prior to connection; and* *(v) the organization enforces requirements for remote connections to the information system.* **POTENTIAL ASSESSMENT METHODS AND OBJECTS:** **Examine:** [*SELECT FROM:* Access control policy; procedures addressing remote access to the information system; information system configuration settings and associated documentation; information system audit records; other relevant documents or records]. **Interview:** [*SELECT FROM:* Organizational personnel with remote access authorization, monitoring, and control responsibilities]. **Test:** [*SELECT FROM:* Remote access methods for the information system].

AC-17(1)	**REMOTE ACCESS**
AC-17(1).1	**ASSESSMENT OBJECTIVE:** *Determine if the organization employs automated mechanisms to facilitate the monitoring and control of remote access methods.* **POTENTIAL ASSESSMENT METHODS AND OBJECTS:** **Examine:** [*SELECT FROM:* Access control policy; procedures addressing remote access to the information system; information system configuration settings and associated documentation; other relevant documents or records]. **Test:** [*SELECT FROM:* Automated mechanisms implementing the access control policy for remote access].

AC-17(2)	REMOTE ACCESS
AC-17(2).1	**ASSESSMENT OBJECTIVE:** *Determine if the organization uses cryptography to protect the confidentiality and integrity of remote access sessions.* **POTENTIAL ASSESSMENT METHODS AND OBJECTS:** **Examine**: [*SELECT FROM:* Access control policy; procedures addressing remote access to the information system; information system design documentation; information system configuration settings and associated documentation; other relevant documents or records]. **Test**: [*SELECT FROM:* Automated mechanisms implementing cryptographic protections for remote access].

AC-17(3)	REMOTE ACCESS
AC-17(3).1	**ASSESSMENT OBJECTIVE:** *Determine if:* *(i) the organization defines a limited number of managed access control points for remote access to the information system; and* *(ii) the information system routes all remote accesses through managed access control points.* **POTENTIAL ASSESSMENT METHODS AND OBJECTS:** **Examine**: [*SELECT FROM:* Access control policy; procedures addressing remote access to the information system; information system design documentation; list of managed access control points; information system configuration settings and associated documentation; information system audit records; other relevant documents or records]. **Test**: [*SELECT FROM:* Automated mechanisms implementing the access control policy for remote access].

AC-17(4)	REMOTE ACCESS
AC-17(4).1	**ASSESSMENT OBJECTIVE:** *Determine if:* *(i) the organization authorizes the execution of privileged commands and access to security-relevant information via remote access only for compelling operational needs; and* *(ii) the organization documents the rationale for such access in the security plan for the information system.* **POTENTIAL ASSESSMENT METHODS AND OBJECTS:** **Examine**: [*SELECT FROM:* Access control policy; procedures addressing remote access to the information system; information system configuration settings and associated documentation; security plan; information system audit records; other relevant documents or records].

AC-17(5)	REMOTE ACCESS
AC-17(5).1	**ASSESSMENT OBJECTIVE:** *Determine if:* (i) *the organization defines the frequency of monitoring for unauthorized remote connections to the information system;* (ii) *the organization monitors for unauthorized remote connections to the information system in accordance with the organization-defined frequency;* (iii) *the organization defines the appropriate action(s) to be taken if an unauthorized connection is discovered; and* (iv) *the organization takes organization-defined appropriate action(s) if an unauthorized connection is discovered.* **POTENTIAL ASSESSMENT METHODS AND OBJECTS:** **Examine:** [*SELECT FROM:* Access control policy; procedures addressing remote access to the information system; information system design documentation; information system configuration settings and associated documentation; information system audit records; other relevant documents or records]. **Interview:** [*SELECT FROM:* Organizational personnel with responsibilities for monitoring remote connections to the information system].

AC-17(6)	REMOTE ACCESS
AC-17(6).1	**ASSESSMENT OBJECTIVE:** *Determine if the organization ensures that users protect information about remote access mechanisms from unauthorized use and disclosure.* **POTENTIAL ASSESSMENT METHODS AND OBJECTS:** **Examine:** [*SELECT FROM:* Access control policy; procedures addressing remote access to the information system; other relevant documents or records]. **Interview:** [*SELECT FROM:* Organizational personnel with responsibilities for implementing or monitoring remote access to the information system; information system users with knowledge of information about remote access mechanisms].

AC-17(7)	REMOTE ACCESS
AC-17(7).1	**ASSESSMENT OBJECTIVE:** *Determine if:* *(i) the organization defines the security functions and security-relevant information that can be accessed using remote sessions;* *(ii) the organization defines the additional security measures to be employed for remote sessions used to access organization-defined security functions and security-relevant information;* *(iii) the organization employs organization-defined additional security measures for remote sessions used to access organization-defined security functions and security-relevant information; and* *(iv) the organization audits remote sessions for accessing organization-defined security functions and security-relevant information.* **POTENTIAL ASSESSMENT METHODS AND OBJECTS:** **Examine**: [*SELECT FROM:* Access control policy; procedures addressing remote access to the information system; information system design documentation; information system configuration settings and associated documentation; information system audit records; other relevant documents or records]. **Test**: [*SELECT FROM:* Automated mechanisms implementing the access control policy for remote access].

AC-17(8)	REMOTE ACCESS
AC-17(8).1	**ASSESSMENT OBJECTIVE:** *Determine if:* *(i) the organization defines the networking protocols within the information system deemed to be nonsecure; and* *(ii) the organization disables the organization-defined networking protocols within the information system deemed to be nonsecure except for explicitly identified components in support of specific operational requirements.* **POTENTIAL ASSESSMENT METHODS AND OBJECTS:** **Examine**: [*SELECT FROM:* Access control policy; procedures addressing remote access to the information system; information system design documentation; information system configuration settings and associated documentation; security plan; list of networking protocols deemed to be non-secure; other relevant documents or records]. **Test**: [*SELECT FROM:* Automated mechanisms disabling networking protocols deemed to be non-secure].

FAMILY: ACCESS CONTROL   **CLASS:** TECHNICAL

ASSESSMENT PROCEDURE

AC-18	WIRELESS ACCESS
AC-18.1	**ASSESSMENT OBJECTIVE:** *Determine if:* (i) *the organization establishes usage restrictions and implementation guidance for wireless access;* (ii) *the organization monitors for unauthorized wireless access to the information system;* (iii) *the organization authorizes wireless access to the information system prior to connection; and* (iv) *the organization enforces requirements for wireless connections to the information system.* **POTENTIAL ASSESSMENT METHODS AND OBJECTS:** **Examine:** [*SELECT FROM:* Access control policy; procedures addressing wireless implementation and usage (including restrictions); activities related to wireless monitoring, authorization, and enforcement; information system audit records; other relevant documents or records]. **Interview:** [*SELECT FROM:* Organizational personnel responsible for authorizing, monitoring or controlling the use of wireless technologies in the information system]. **Test:** [*SELECT FROM:* Wireless access usage and restrictions].

AC-18(1)	WIRELESS ACCESS
AC-18(1).1	**ASSESSMENT OBJECTIVE:** *Determine if the information system protects wireless access to the system using authentication and encryption.* **POTENTIAL ASSESSMENT METHODS AND OBJECTS:** **Examine:** [*SELECT FROM:* Access control policy; procedures addressing wireless implementation and usage (including restrictions); information system design documentation; information system configuration settings and associated documentation; information system audit records; other relevant documents or records]. **Test:** [*SELECT FROM:* Automated mechanisms implementing the access control policy for wireless access to the information system].

AC-18(2)	WIRELESS ACCESS
AC-18(2).1	**ASSESSMENT OBJECTIVE:** *Determine if:* (i) *the organization defines the frequency of monitoring for unauthorized wireless connections to the information system, including scans for unauthorized wireless access points;* (ii) *the organization monitors for unauthorized wireless connections to the information system, including scanning for unauthorized wireless access points, in accordance with organization-defined frequency;* (iii) *the organization defines the appropriate action(s) to be taken if an unauthorized connection is discovered; and* (iv) *the organization takes appropriate action(s) if an unauthorized connection discovered.* **POTENTIAL ASSESSMENT METHODS AND OBJECTS:** **Examine**: [*SELECT FROM:* Access control policy; procedures addressing wireless implementation and usage (including restrictions); wireless scanning reports; other relevant documents or records]. **Interview**: [*SELECT FROM:* Organizational personnel responsible for monitoring wireless connections to the information system]. **Test**: [*SELECT FROM:* Scanning procedures for detecting unauthorized wireless connections and access points].

AC-18(3)	WIRELESS ACCESS
AC-18(3).1	**ASSESSMENT OBJECTIVE:** *Determine if the organization disables, when not intended for use, wireless networking capabilities internally embedded within the information system components prior to issuance and deployment.* **POTENTIAL ASSESSMENT METHODS AND OBJECTS:** **Examine**: [*SELECT FROM:* Access control policy; procedures addressing wireless implementation and usage (including restrictions); information system design documentation; information system configuration settings and associated documentation; information system audit records; other relevant documents or records]. **Test**: [*SELECT FROM:* Automated mechanisms controlling the disabling of wireless networking capabilities internally embedded within the information system components].

AC-18(4)	WIRELESS ACCESS
AC-18(4).1	**ASSESSMENT OBJECTIVE:** *Determine if the organization does not allow users to independently configure wireless networking capabilities.* **POTENTIAL ASSESSMENT METHODS AND OBJECTS:** **Examine**: [*SELECT FROM:* Access control policy; procedures addressing wireless implementation and usage (including restrictions); information system design documentation; information system configuration settings and associated documentation; information system audit records; other relevant documents or records]. **Test**: [*SELECT FROM:* Automated mechanisms preventing independent configuration of wireless networking capabilities].

AC-18(5)	WIRELESS ACCESS
AC-18(5).1	**ASSESSMENT OBJECTIVE:** *Determine if the organization confines wireless communications to organization-controlled boundaries.* **POTENTIAL ASSESSMENT METHODS AND OBJECTS:** **Examine:** [*SELECT FROM:* Access control policy; procedures addressing wireless implementation and usage (including restrictions); information system design documentation; information system configuration settings and associated documentation; information system audit records; other relevant documents or records]. **Test:** [*SELECT FROM:* Automated mechanisms implementing the access control policy for wireless access to the information system; Wireless connections and access points outside of organizational boundaries using scanning devices.].

FAMILY: ACCESS CONTROL   **CLASS:** TECHNICAL

ASSESSMENT PROCEDURE	
AC-19	**ACCESS CONTROL FOR MOBILE DEVICES**
AC-19.1	**ASSESSMENT OBJECTIVE:** *Determine if:* (i) *the organization establishes usage restrictions and implementation guidance for organization-controlled portable and mobile devices;* (ii) *the organization authorizes connection of mobile devices meeting organizational usage restrictions and implementation guidance to organizational information systems;* (iii) *the organization monitors for unauthorized connections of mobile devices to organizational information systems;* (iv) *the organization enforces requirements for the connection of mobile devices to organizational information systems;* (v) *the organization disables information system functionality that provides the capability for automatic execution of code on mobile devices without user direction;* (vi) *the organization issues specially configured mobile devices to individuals traveling to locations that the organization deems to be of significant risk in accordance with organizational policies and procedures;* (vii) *the organization defines the inspection and preventative measures to be applied to mobile devices returning from locations that the organization deems to be of significant risk; and* (viii) *the organization applies organization-defined inspection and preventative measures to mobile devices returning from locations that the organization deems to be of significant risk in accordance with organizational policies and procedures.* **POTENTIAL ASSESSMENT METHODS AND OBJECTS:** **Examine:** [*SELECT FROM:* Access control policy; procedures addressing access control for portable and mobile devices; information system design documentation; information system configuration settings and associated documentation; information system audit records; other relevant documents or records]. **Interview:** [*SELECT FROM:* Organizational personnel who use portable and mobile devices to access the information system]. **Test:** [*SELECT FROM:* Automated mechanisms implementing access control policy for portable and mobile devices].

AC-19(1)	ACCESS CONTROL FOR MOBILE DEVICES
AC-19(1).1	**ASSESSMENT OBJECTIVE:** *Determine if the organization restricts the use of writable, removable media in organizational information systems.* **POTENTIAL ASSESSMENT METHODS AND OBJECTS:** **Examine:** [*SELECT FROM:* Access control policy; procedures addressing access control for portable and mobile devices; information system design documentation; information system configuration settings and associated documentation; information system audit records; other relevant documents or records]. **Interview:** [*SELECT FROM:* Organizational personnel who use portable and mobile devices to access the information system]. **Test:** [*SELECT FROM:* Automated mechanisms implementing access control policy for portable and mobile devices].

AC-19(2)	ACCESS CONTROL FOR MOBILE DEVICES
AC-19(2).1	**ASSESSMENT OBJECTIVE:** *Determine if the organization prohibits the use of personally owned, removable media in organizational information systems.* **POTENTIAL ASSESSMENT METHODS AND OBJECTS:** **Examine:** [*SELECT FROM:* Access control policy; procedures addressing access control for portable and mobile devices; information system design documentation; information system configuration settings and associated documentation; information system audit records; other relevant documents or records]. **Test:** [*SELECT FROM:* Automated mechanisms implementing access control policy for portable and mobile devices].

AC-19(3)	ACCESS CONTROL FOR MOBILE DEVICES
AC-19(3).1	**ASSESSMENT OBJECTIVE:** *Determine if the organization prohibits the use of removable media in organizational information systems when the media has no identifiable owner.* **POTENTIAL ASSESSMENT METHODS AND OBJECTS:** **Examine:** [*SELECT FROM:* Access control policy; procedures addressing access control for portable and mobile devices; information system design documentation; information system configuration settings and associated documentation; information system audit records; other relevant documents or records]. **Test:** [*SELECT FROM:* Automated mechanisms implementing access control policy for portable and mobile devices].

AC-19(4)	ACCESS CONTROL FOR MOBILE DEVICES

AC-19(4).1	**ASSESSMENT OBJECTIVE:**
	Determine if:
	
	(i) *the organization prohibits the use of unclassified mobile devices in facilities containing information systems processing, storing, or transmitting classified information unless specifically permitted by the appropriate authorizing official(s);*
	
	(ii) *the organization defines the security officials authorized to randomly review/inspect mobile devices and the information stored on those devices for classified information; and*
	
	(iii) *the organization enforces the following restrictions on individuals permitted to use mobile devices in facilities containing information systems processing, storing, or transmitting classified information:*
	
	  - *connection of unclassified mobile devices to classified information systems is prohibited;*
	
	  - *connection of unclassified mobile devices to unclassified information systems requires approval from the appropriate authorizing official(s);*
	
	  - *use of internal or external modems or wireless interfaces within the mobile devices is prohibited; and*
	
	  - *mobile devices and the information stored on those devices are subject to random reviews/inspections by organization-defined security officials, and if classified information is found, the incident handling policy is enforced.*
	
	POTENTIAL ASSESSMENT METHODS AND OBJECTS:
	
	Examine: [*SELECT FROM:* Access control policy; procedures addressing access control for portable and mobile devices; evidentiary documentation for random inspections of mobile devices; information system audit records; other relevant documents or records].
	
	Interview: [*SELECT FROM:* Organizational personnel responsible for randomly reviewing/inspecting mobile devices; Organizational personnel using mobile devices in facilities containing information systems processing, storing, or transmitting classified information].
	
	Test: [*SELECT FROM:* Test automated mechanisms prohibiting the use of internal or external modems or wireless interfaces with mobile devices].

FAMILY: ACCESS CONTROL   **CLASS:** TECHNICAL

ASSESSMENT PROCEDURE
AC-20	**USE OF EXTERNAL INFORMATION SYSTEMS**
AC-20.1	**ASSESSMENT OBJECTIVE:**

Determine if:

(i)   *the organization identifies individuals authorized to:*

-   *access the information system from the external information systems; and*

-   *process, store, and/or transmit organization-controlled information using the external information systems; and*

(ii) *the organization establishes terms and conditions, consistent with any trust relationships established with other organizations owning, operating, and/or maintaining external information systems, allowing authorized individuals to:*

-   *access the information system from the external information systems; and*

-   *process, store, and/or transmit organization-controlled information using the external information system.*

POTENTIAL ASSESSMENT METHODS AND OBJECTS:

Examine: [*SELECT FROM:* Access control policy; procedures addressing the use of external information systems; external information systems terms and conditions; list of types of applications accessible from external information systems; maximum security categorization for information processed, stored, or transmitted on external information systems; information system configuration settings and associated documentation; other relevant documents or records].

Interview: [*SELECT FROM:* Organizational personnel with responsibilities for defining terms and conditions for use of external information systems to access organizational systems].

AC-20(1)	**USE OF EXTERNAL INFORMATION SYSTEMS**
AC-20(1).1	**ASSESSMENT OBJECTIVE:**

Determine if the organization permits authorized individuals to use an external information system to access the information system or to process, store, or transmit organization-controlled information only when the organization:

-   *can verify the implementation of required security controls on the external system as specified in the organization's information security policy and security plan; or*

-   *has approved information system connection or processing agreements with the organizational entity hosting the external information system.*

POTENTIAL ASSESSMENT METHODS AND OBJECTS:

Examine: [*SELECT FROM:* Access control policy; procedures addressing the use of external information systems; security plan; information system connection or processing agreements; account management documents; other relevant documents or records].

AC-20(2)	USE OF EXTERNAL INFORMATION SYSTEMS
AC-20(2).1	**ASSESSMENT OBJECTIVE:** *Determine if the organization limits the use of organization-controlled portable storage media by authorized individuals on external information systems.* **POTENTIAL ASSESSMENT METHODS AND OBJECTS:** **Examine:** [*SELECT FROM:* Access control policy; procedures addressing the use of external information systems; security plan; information system configuration settings and associated documentation; information system connection or processing agreements; account management documents; other relevant documents or records].

FAMILY: ACCESS CONTROL   **CLASS:** TECHNICAL

ASSESSMENT PROCEDURE
AC-21	**USER-BASED COLLABORATION AND INFORMATION SHARING**

| AC-21.1 | **ASSESSMENT OBJECTIVE:**
Determine if:

(i)   the organization defines the circumstances where user discretion is required to facilitate information sharing;

(ii) the organization facilitates information sharing by enabling authorized users to determine whether access authorizations assigned to the sharing partner match the access restrictions on the information for the organization-defined circumstances;

(iii) the organization defines the information sharing circumstances and automated mechanisms or manual processes required to assist users in making information sharing/collaboration decisions; and

(iv) the organization employs organization-defined circumstances and automated mechanisms or manual processes to assist users in making information sharing/collaboration decisions.

POTENTIAL ASSESSMENT METHODS AND OBJECTS:
Examine: [*SELECT FROM:* Access control policy; procedures addressing user-based collaboration and information sharing (including restrictions); information system design documentation; information system configuration settings and associated documentation; list of users authorized to make information sharing/collaboration decisions; list of information sharing circumstances requiring user discretion; other relevant documents or records].

Interview: [*SELECT FROM:* Organizational personnel responsible for making information sharing/collaboration decisions].

Test: [*SELECT FROM:* Automated mechanisms or manual process implementing access authorizations supporting information sharing/user collaboration decisions]. |

| **AC-21(1)** | **USER-BASED COLLABORATION AND INFORMATION SHARING** |

| AC-21(1).1 | **ASSESSMENT OBJECTIVE:**
Determine if the information system employs automated mechanisms to enable authorized users to make information-sharing decisions based on access authorizations of sharing partners and access restrictions on information to be shared.

POTENTIAL ASSESSMENT METHODS AND OBJECTS:
Examine: [*SELECT FROM:* Access control policy; procedures addressing user-based collaboration and information sharing (including restrictions); information system design documentation; information system configuration settings and associated documentation; system-generated list of users authorized to make information sharing/collaboration decisions; system-generated list of sharing partners and access authorizations; system-generated list of access restrictions regarding information to be shared; other relevant documents or records].

Test: [*SELECT FROM:* Automated mechanisms implementing access authorizations supporting information sharing/user collaboration decisions]. |

FAMILY: ACCESS CONTROL   **CLASS:** TECHNICAL

ASSESSMENT PROCEDURE
AC-22	**PUBLICLY ACCESSIBLE CONTENT**

AC-22.1	**ASSESSMENT OBJECTIVE:**
	Determine if:
	(i) *the organization designates individuals authorized to post information onto an organizational information system that is publicly accessible;*
	(ii) *the organization trains authorized individuals to ensure that publicly accessible information does not contain nonpublic information;*
	(iii) *the organization reviews the proposed content of publicly accessible information for nonpublic information prior to posting onto the organizational information system;*
	(iv) *the organization defines the frequency of reviews of the content on the publicly accessible organizational information system for nonpublic information;*
	(v) *the organization reviews the content on the publicly accessible organizational information system for nonpublic information in accordance with the organization-defined frequency; and*
	(vi) *the organization removes nonpublic information from the publicly accessible organizational information system, if discovered.*
	POTENTIAL ASSESSMENT METHODS AND OBJECTS:
	Examine: [*SELECT FROM:* Access control policy; procedures addressing publicly accessible content; list of users authorized to post publicly accessible content on organizational information systems; training materials and/or records; records of publicly accessible information reviews; records of response to nonpublic information on public Web sites; system audit logs; security awareness training records; other relevant documents or records].
	Interview: [*SELECT FROM:* Organizational personnel responsible for managing publicly accessible information posted on organizational information systems].

FAMILY: AWARENESS AND TRAINING   **CLASS:** OPERATIONAL

ASSESSMENT PROCEDURE
AT-1   **SECURITY AWARENESS AND TRAINING POLICY AND PROCEDURES**

AT-1.1	**ASSESSMENT OBJECTIVE:**
	 Determine if:
	
	 (i) *the organization develops and formally documents security awareness and training policy;*
	
	 (ii) *the organization security awareness and training policy addresses:*
	     - *purpose;*
	     - *scope;*
	     - *roles and responsibilities;*
	     - *management commitment; and*
	     - *coordination among organizational entities, and compliance;*
	
	 (iii) *the organization disseminates formal documented security awareness and training policy to elements within the organization having associated security awareness and training roles and responsibilities;*
	
	 (iv) *the organization develops and formally documents security awareness and training procedures;*
	
	 (v) *the organization security awareness and training procedures facilitate implementation of the security awareness and training policy and associated security awareness and training controls; and*
	
	 (vi) *the organization disseminates formal documented security awareness and training procedures to elements within the organization having associated security awareness and training roles and responsibilities.*
	
	 POTENTIAL ASSESSMENT METHODS AND OBJECTS:
	 Examine: [*SELECT FROM:* Security awareness and training policy and procedures; other relevant documents or records].
	 Interview: [*SELECT FROM:* Organizational personnel with security awareness and training responsibilities].

AT-1.2	**ASSESSMENT OBJECTIVE:** *Determine if:* (i) *the organization defines the frequency of security awareness and training policy reviews/updates;* (ii) *the organization reviews/updates security awareness and training policy in accordance with organization-defined frequency;* (iii) *the organization defines the frequency of security awareness and training procedure reviews/updates; and* (iv) *the organization reviews/updates security awareness and training procedures in accordance with organization-defined frequency.* **POTENTIAL ASSESSMENT METHODS AND OBJECTS:** **Examine:** [*SELECT FROM:* Security awareness and training policy and procedures; other relevant documents or records]. **Interview:** [*SELECT FROM:* Organizational personnel with security awareness and training responsibilities].

FAMILY: AWARENESS AND TRAINING   **CLASS:** OPERATIONAL

ASSESSMENT PROCEDURE

AT-2	SECURITY AWARENESS
AT-2.1	**ASSESSMENT OBJECTIVE:** *Determine if:* (i) *the organization provides basic security awareness training to all information system users (including managers, senior executives, and contractors) as part of initial training for new users and when required by system changes;* (ii) *the organization defines the frequency of refresher security awareness training;* (iii) *the organization provides refresher security awareness training in accordance with the organization-defined frequency;* **POTENTIAL ASSESSMENT METHODS AND OBJECTS:** **Examine:** [*SELECT FROM:* Security awareness and training policy; procedures addressing security awareness training implementation; appropriate codes of federal regulations; security awareness training curriculum; security awareness training materials; security plan; training records; other relevant documents or records]. **Interview:** [*SELECT FROM:* Organizational personnel comprising the general information system user community].

AT-2(1)	SECURITY AWARENESS
AT-2(1).1	**ASSESSMENT OBJECTIVE:** *Determine if the organization includes practical exercises in security awareness training that simulate actual cyber attacks.* **POTENTIAL ASSESSMENT METHODS AND OBJECTS:** **Examine:** [*SELECT FROM:* Security awareness and training policy; procedures addressing security awareness training implementation; security awareness training curriculum; security awareness training materials; other relevant documents or records]. **Interview:** [*SELECT FROM:* Organizational personnel that participate in security awareness training].

FAMILY: AWARENESS AND TRAINING   **CLASS:** OPERATIONAL

ASSESSMENT PROCEDURE

AT-3	SECURITY TRAINING
AT-3.1	**ASSESSMENT OBJECTIVE:** *Determine if:* (i) *the organization provides role-based security-related training before authorizing access to the system or performing assigned duties, and when required by system changes;* (ii) *the organization defines the frequency of refresher role-based security-related training;* (iii) *the organization provides refresher role-based security-related training in accordance with the organization-defined frequency.* **POTENTIAL ASSESSMENT METHODS AND OBJECTS:** **Examine:** [*SELECT FROM:* Security awareness and training policy; procedures addressing security training implementation; codes of federal regulations; security training curriculum; security training materials; security plan; training records; other relevant documents or records]. **Interview:** [*SELECT FROM:* Organizational personnel with responsibilities for role-based, security-related training; organizational personnel with significant information system security responsibilities].

AT-3(1)	SECURITY TRAINING
AT-3(1).1	**ASSESSMENT OBJECTIVE:** *Determine if:* (i) *the organization provides employees with initial training in the employment and operation of environment controls;* (ii) *the organization defines the frequency of refresher training in the employment and operation of environmental controls; and* (iii) *the organization provides refresher training in the employment and operation of environmental controls in accordance with the organization-defined frequency.* **POTENTIAL ASSESSMENT METHODS AND OBJECTS:** **Examine:** [*SELECT FROM:* Security awareness and training policy; procedures addressing security training implementation; security training curriculum; security training materials; security plan; training records; other relevant documents or records]. **Interview:** [*SELECT FROM:* Organization personnel with security training responsibilities; organizational personnel with significant information system security responsibilities].

AT-3(2)	SECURITY TRAINING
AT-3(2).1	**ASSESSMENT OBJECTIVE:** *Determine if:* *(i) the organization provides employees with initial training in the employment and operation of physical security controls;* *(ii) the organization defines the frequency of refresher training in the employment and operation of physical security controls; and* *(iii) the organization provides refresher training in the employment and operation of physical security controls in accordance with the organization-defined frequency.* **POTENTIAL ASSESSMENT METHODS AND OBJECTS:** **Examine:** [*SELECT FROM:* Security awareness and training policy; procedures addressing security training implementation; codes of federal regulations; security training curriculum; security training materials; security plan; training records; other relevant documents or records]. **Interview:** [*SELECT FROM:* Organizational personnel with security training responsibilities; organizational personnel with significant information system security responsibilities].

FAMILY: AWARENESS AND TRAINING   **CLASS:** OPERATIONAL

ASSESSMENT PROCEDURE	
AT-4	**SECURITY TRAINING RECORDS**
AT-4.1	**ASSESSMENT OBJECTIVE:** *Determine if:* (i) the organization documents and monitors individual information system security training activities including basic security awareness training and specific information system security training; (ii) the organization defines the time period for retaining individual training records; and (iii) the organization retains individual training records in accordance with the organization-defined time period. **POTENTIAL ASSESSMENT METHODS AND OBJECTS:** **Examine:** [*SELECT FROM:* Security awareness and training policy; procedures addressing security training records; security awareness and training records; other relevant documents or records]. **Interview:** [*SELECT FROM:* Organizational personnel with security training record retention responsibilities].

FAMILY: AWARENESS AND TRAINING

CLASS: OPERATIONAL

ASSESSMENT PROCEDURE	
AT-5	**CONTACTS WITH SECURITY GROUPS AND ASSOCIATION**
AT-5.1	**ASSESSMENT OBJECTIVE:** *Determine if the organization establishes and institutionalizes contact with selected groups and associations within the security community:* – *to facilitate ongoing security education and training for organizational personnel;* – *to stay up to date with the latest recommended security practices, techniques, and technologies; and* – *to share current security-related information including threats, vulnerabilities, and incidents.* **POTENTIAL ASSESSMENT METHODS AND OBJECTS:** **Examine:** [*SELECT FROM:* Security awareness and training policy; procedures addressing contacts with security groups and associations; list of organization-defined key contacts to obtain ongoing information system security knowledge, expertise, and general information; other relevant documents or records]. **Interview:** [*SELECT FROM:* Organizational personnel with security responsibilities (e.g., individuals that have contacts with selected groups and associations within the security community)].

FAMILY: AUDIT AND ACCOUNTABILITY   **CLASS:** TECHNICAL

ASSESSMENT PROCEDURE
AU-1   **AUDIT AND ACCOUNTABILITY POLICY AND PROCEDURES**

| AU-1.1 | **ASSESSMENT OBJECTIVE:**
Determine if:

(i)   *the organization develops and formally documents audit and accountability policy;*

(ii)   *the organization audit and accountability policy addresses:*
     -   *purpose;*
     -   *scope;*
     -   *roles and responsibilities;*
     -   *management commitment;*
     -   *coordination among organizational entities; and*
     -   *compliance;*

(iii)   *the organization disseminates formal documented audit and accountability policy to elements within the organization having associated audit and accountability roles and responsibilities;*

(iv)   *the organization develops and formally documents audit and accountability procedures;*

(v)   *the organization audit and accountability procedures facilitate implementation of the audit and accountability policy and associated audit and accountability controls; and*

(vi)   *the organization disseminates formal documented audit and accountability procedures to elements within the organization having associated audit and accountability roles and responsibilities.*

POTENTIAL ASSESSMENT METHODS AND OBJECTS:
Examine: [*SELECT FROM:* Audit and accountability policy and procedures; other relevant documents or records].
Interview: [*SELECT FROM:* Organizational personnel with audit and accountability responsibilities]. |
| AU-1.2 | **ASSESSMENT OBJECTIVE:**
Determine if:

(i)   *the organization defines the frequency of audit and accountability policy reviews/updates;*

(ii)   *the organization reviews/updates audit and accountability policy in accordance with organization-defined frequency;*

(iii)   *the organization defines the frequency of audit and accountability procedure reviews/updates; and*

(iv)   *the organization reviews/updates audit and accountability procedures in accordance with organization-defined frequency.*

POTENTIAL ASSESSMENT METHODS AND OBJECTS:
Examine: [*SELECT FROM:* Audit and accountability policy and procedures; other relevant documents or records].
Interview: [*SELECT FROM:* Organizational personnel with audit and accountability responsibilities]. |

FAMILY: AUDIT AND ACCOUNTABILITY   **CLASS:** TECHNICAL

ASSESSMENT PROCEDURE

AU-2	AUDITABLE EVENTS

AU-2.1	**ASSESSMENT OBJECTIVE:** *Determine if:* (i) *the organization defines the list of events the information system must be capable of auditing based on a risk assessment and mission/business needs;* (ii) *the organization coordinates the security audit function with other organizational entities requiring audit-related information to enhance mutual support and help guide the selection of auditable events;* (iii) *the organization provides a rationale for why the list of auditable events are deemed to be adequate to support after-the-fact investigations of security incidents;* (iv) *the organization defines the subset of auditable events defined in (i) that are to be audited within the information system and the frequency of (or situation requiring) auditing for each identified event; and* (v) *the organization determines, based on current threat information and ongoing assessment of risk, the subset of auditable events defined in (i) to be audited within the information system, and the frequency of (or situation requiring) auditing for each identified event .* **POTENTIAL ASSESSMENT METHODS AND OBJECTS:** **Examine**: [*SELECT FROM:* Audit and accountability policy; procedures addressing auditable events; security plan; information system configuration settings and associated documentation; information system audit records; list of information system auditable events; other relevant documents or records]. **Interview**: [*SELECT FROM:* Organizational personnel with auditing and accountability responsibilities]. **Test**: [*SELECT FROM:* Automated mechanisms implementing information system auditing of organization-defined auditable events].

AU-2(1)	AUDITABLE EVENTS [Withdrawn: Incorporated into AU-12].
AU-2(1).1	**ASSESSMENT OBJECTIVE:** [Withdrawn: Incorporated into AU-12]. **POTENTIAL ASSESSMENT METHODS AND OBJECTS:** [Withdrawn: Incorporated into AU-12].

AU-2(2)	AUDITABLE EVENTS
	[Withdrawn: Incorporated into AU-12].
AU-2(2).1	ASSESSMENT OBJECTIVE:
	[Withdrawn: Incorporated into AU-12].
	POTENTIAL ASSESSMENT METHODS AND OBJECTS:
	[Withdrawn: Incorporated into AU-12].

AU-2(3)	AUDITABLE EVENTS
AU-2(3).1	ASSESSMENT OBJECTIVE:
	Determine if:
	(i) *the organization defines the frequency of reviews and updates to the list of organization-defined auditable events; and*
	(ii) *the organization reviews and updates the list of organization-defined auditable events in accordance with the organization-defined frequency.*
	POTENTIAL ASSESSMENT METHODS AND OBJECTS:
	Examine: [*SELECT FROM:* Audit and accountability policy; procedures addressing auditable events; security plan; list of organization-defined auditable events; auditable events review and update records; information system audit records; information system incident reports; other relevant documents or records].
	Interview: [*SELECT FROM:* Organizational personnel with auditing and accountability responsibilities].

AU-2(4)	AUDITABLE EVENTS
AU-2(4).1	ASSESSMENT OBJECTIVE:
	Determine if the organization includes execution of privileged functions in the list of events to be audited by the information system.
	POTENTIAL ASSESSMENT METHODS AND OBJECTS:
	Examine: [*SELECT FROM:* Audit and accountability policy; procedures addressing auditable events; information system configuration settings and associated documentation; list of organization-defined auditable events; list of privileged security functions; other relevant documents or records].

FAMILY: AUDIT AND ACCOUNTABILITY   **CLASS:** TECHNICAL

ASSESSMENT PROCEDURE

AU-3	CONTENT OF AUDIT RECORDS
AU-3.1	**ASSESSMENT OBJECTIVE:** *Determine if the information system produces audit records that contain sufficient information to, at a minimum, establish:* − *what type of event occurred;* − *when (date and time) the event occurred;* − *where the event occurred;* − *the source of the event;* − *the outcome (success or failure) of the event; and* − *the identity of any user/subject associated with the event.* **POTENTIAL ASSESSMENT METHODS AND OBJECTS:** **Examine:** [*SELECT FROM:* Audit and accountability policy; procedures addressing content of audit records; list of organization-defined auditable events; information system audit records; information system incident reports; other relevant documents or records]. **Test:** [*SELECT FROM:* Automated mechanisms implementing information system auditing of auditable events].

AU-3(1)	CONTENT OF AUDIT RECORDS
AU-3(1).1	**ASSESSMENT OBJECTIVE:** *Determine if:* (i) *the organization defines the additional, more detailed information to be included in audit records for audit events identified by type, location, or subject; and* (ii) *the information system includes the organization-defined additional, more detailed information in the audit records for audit events identified by type, location, or subject.* **POTENTIAL ASSESSMENT METHODS AND OBJECTS:** **Examine:** [*SELECT FROM:* Audit and accountability policy; procedures addressing content of audit records; list of organization-defined auditable events; information system design documentation; security plan; information system configuration settings and associated documentation; other relevant documents or records]. **Test:** [*SELECT FROM:* Information system audit capability to include more detailed information in audit records for audit events identified by type, location, or subject].

AU-3(2)	CONTENT OF AUDIT RECORDS
AU-3(2).1	**ASSESSMENT OBJECTIVE:** *Determine if:* *(i) the organization defines the information system components for which the content of audit records generated is centrally managed; and* *(ii) the organization centrally manages the content of audit records generated by organization-defined information system components.* **POTENTIAL ASSESSMENT METHODS AND OBJECTS:** **Examine**: [*SELECT FROM:* Audit and accountability policy; procedures addressing content of audit records; information system design documentation; list of organization-defined auditable events; information system configuration settings and associated documentation; information system audit records; other relevant documents or records]. **Test**: [*SELECT FROM:* Automated mechanisms implementing centralized management of audit record content].

FAMILY: AUDIT AND ACCOUNTABILITY   **CLASS:** TECHNICAL

ASSESSMENT PROCEDURE	
AU-4	**AUDIT STORAGE CAPACITY**
AU-4.1	**ASSESSMENT OBJECTIVE:** *Determine if:* *(i) the organization allocates audit record storage capacity; and* *(ii) the organization configures auditing to reduce the likelihood of audit record storage capacity being exceeded.* **POTENTIAL ASSESSMENT METHODS AND OBJECTS:** **Examine:** [*SELECT FROM:* Audit and accountability policy; procedures addressing audit storage capacity; information system design documentation; organization-defined audit record storage capacity for information system components that store audit records; list of organization-defined auditable events; information system configuration settings and associated documentation; information system audit records; other relevant documents or records]. **Test:** [*SELECT FROM:* Audit record storage capacity and related configuration settings].

FAMILY: AUDIT AND ACCOUNTABILITY   **CLASS:** TECHNICAL

ASSESSMENT PROCEDURE

AU-5	**RESPONSE TO AUDIT PROCESSING FAILURES**
AU-5.1	**ASSESSMENT OBJECTIVE:** *Determine if:* (i) the organization defines designated organizational officials to be alerted in the event of an audit processing failure; (ii) the information system alerts designated organizational officials in the event of an audit processing failure; (iii) the organization defines additional actions to be taken in the event of an audit processing failure; and (iv) the information system takes the additional organization-defined actions in the event of an audit processing failure. **POTENTIAL ASSESSMENT METHODS AND OBJECTS:** **Examine**: [*SELECT FROM:* Audit and accountability policy; procedures addressing response to audit processing failures; information system design documentation; security plan; information system configuration settings and associated documentation; list of personnel to be notified in case of an audit processing failure; information system audit records; other relevant documents or records]. **Test**: [*SELECT FROM:* Automated mechanisms implementing information system response to audit processing failures].

AU-5(1)	**RESPONSE TO AUDIT PROCESSING FAILURES**
AU-5(1).1	**ASSESSMENT OBJECTIVE:** *Determine if:* (i) the organization defines the percentage of maximum audit record storage capacity that, if reached, requires a warning to be provided; and (ii) the information system provides a warning when the allocated audit record storage volume reaches the organization-defined percentage of maximum audit record storage capacity. **POTENTIAL ASSESSMENT METHODS AND OBJECTS:** **Examine**: [*SELECT FROM:* Audit and accountability policy; procedures addressing response to audit processing failures; information system design documentation; security plan; information system configuration settings and associated documentation; information system audit records; other relevant documents or records]. **Test**: [*SELECT FROM:* Automated mechanisms implementing audit storage limit warnings].

AU-5(2)	RESPONSE TO AUDIT PROCESSING FAILURES
AU-5(2).1	**ASSESSMENT OBJECTIVE:** *Determine if:* *(i) the organization defines audit failure events requiring real-time alerts; and* *(ii) the information system provides a real-time alert when organization-defined audit failure events occur.* **POTENTIAL ASSESSMENT METHODS AND OBJECTS:** **Examine:** [*SELECT FROM:* Audit and accountability policy; procedures addressing response to audit processing failures; information system design documentation; security plan; information system configuration settings and associated documentation; information system audit records; other relevant documents or records]. **Test:** [*SELECT FROM:* Automated mechanisms implementing real time audit alerts when organization-defined audit failure events occur].

AU-5(3)	RESPONSE TO AUDIT PROCESSING FAILURES
AU-5(3).1	**ASSESSMENT OBJECTIVE:** *Determine if:* *(i) the information system enforces configurable traffic volume thresholds representing auditing capacity for network traffic;* *(ii) the organization defines if the network traffic above configurable traffic volume thresholds are rejected or delayed; and* *(iii) the information system rejects or delays, as defined by the organization, network traffic generated above configurable traffic volume thresholds.* **POTENTIAL ASSESSMENT METHODS AND OBJECTS:** **Examine:** [*SELECT FROM:* Audit and accountability policy; procedures addressing response to audit processing failures; information system design documentation; security plan; information system configuration settings and associated documentation; information system audit records; other relevant documents or records]. **Test:** [*SELECT FROM:* Information system capability implementing configurable traffic volume thresholds].

AU-5(4)	RESPONSE TO AUDIT PROCESSING FAILURES
AU-5(4).1	**ASSESSMENT OBJECTIVE:** *Determine if the information system invokes a system shutdown in the event of an audit failure, unless an alternative audit capability exists.* **POTENTIAL ASSESSMENT METHODS AND OBJECTS:** **Examine:** [*SELECT FROM:* Audit and accountability policy; procedures addressing response to audit processing failures; information system design documentation; security plan; information system configuration settings and associated documentation; information system audit records; other relevant documents or records]. **Test:** [*SELECT FROM:* Information system capability invoking system shutdown in the event of an audit failure].

FAMILY: AUDIT AND ACCOUNTABILITY   **CLASS:** TECHNICAL

ASSESSMENT PROCEDURE	
AU-6	**AUDIT REVIEW, ANALYSIS, AND REPORTING**
AU-6.1	**ASSESSMENT OBJECTIVE:** *Determine if:* (i) *the organization defines the frequency of information system audit record reviews and analyses;* (ii) *the organization reviews and analyzes information system audit records for indications of inappropriate or unusual activity in accordance with the organization-defined frequency; and* (iii) *the organization reports findings of inappropriate/unusual activities, to designated organizational officials.* **POTENTIAL ASSESSMENT METHODS AND OBJECTS:** **Examine:** [*SELECT FROM:* Audit and accountability policy; procedures addressing audit review, analysis, and reporting; reports of audit findings; records of actions taken in response to reviews/analyses of audit records; other relevant documents or records]. **Interview:** [*SELECT FROM:* Organizational personnel with information system audit review, analysis, and reporting responsibilities]. **Test:** [*SELECT FROM:* Information system audit review, analysis, and reporting capability].
AU-6.2	**ASSESSMENT OBJECTIVE:** *Determine if the organization adjusts the level of audit review, analysis, and reporting within the information system when there is a change in risk to organizational operations, organizational assets, individuals, other organizations, or the Nation based on law enforcement information , intelligence information, or other credible sources of information.* **POTENTIAL ASSESSMENT METHODS AND OBJECTS:** **Examine:** [*SELECT FROM:* Audit and accountability policy; procedures addressing audit review, analysis, and reporting; threat information documentation from law enforcement, intelligence community, or other sources; information system configuration settings and associated documentation; information system audit records; other relevant documents or records]. **Interview:** [*SELECT FROM:* Organizational personnel with information system audit review, analysis, and reporting responsibilities].

AU-6(1)	AUDIT REVIEW, ANALYSIS, AND REPORTING
AU-6(1).1	**ASSESSMENT OBJECTIVE:** *Determine if the information system integrates audit review, analysis, and reporting processes to support organizational processes for investigation and response to suspicious activities.* **POTENTIAL ASSESSMENT METHODS AND OBJECTS:** **Examine**: [*SELECT FROM:* Audit and accountability policy; procedures addressing audit review, analysis, and reporting; information system design documentation; information system configuration settings and associated documentation; procedures for investigating and responding to suspicious activities; other relevant documents or records]. **Interview**: [*SELECT FROM:* Organizational personnel with information system audit review, analysis, and reporting responsibilities]. **Test**: [*SELECT FROM:* Information system capability integrating audit review, analysis, and reporting into an organizational process for investigation and response to suspicious activities].

AU-6(2)	AUDIT REVIEW, ANALYSIS, AND REPORTING [Withdrawn: Incorporated into SI-4].
AU-6(2).1	**ASSESSMENT OBJECTIVE:** [Withdrawn: Incorporated into SI-4]. **POTENTIAL ASSESSMENT METHODS AND OBJECTS:** [Withdrawn: Incorporated into SI-4].

AU-6(3)	AUDIT REVIEW, ANALYSIS, AND REPORTING
AU-6(3).1	**ASSESSMENT OBJECTIVE:** *Determine if the organization analyzes and correlates audit records across different repositories to gain organization-wide situational awareness.* **POTENTIAL ASSESSMENT METHODS AND OBJECTS:** **Examine**: [*SELECT FROM:* Audit and accountability policy; procedures addressing audit review, analysis, and reporting; information system design documentation; information system configuration settings and associated documentation; information system audit records across different repositories; other relevant documents or records]. **Interview**: [*SELECT FROM:* Organizational personnel with information system audit review, analysis, and reporting responsibilities].

AU-6(4)	AUDIT REVIEW, ANALYSIS, AND REPORTING
AU-6(4).1	**ASSESSMENT OBJECTIVE:** *Determine if the information system centralizes the review and analysis of audit records from multiple components within the system.* **POTENTIAL ASSESSMENT METHODS AND OBJECTS:** **Examine:** [*SELECT FROM:* Audit and accountability policy; procedures addressing audit review, analysis, and reporting; information system design documentation; information system configuration settings and associated documentation; security plan; information system audit records; other relevant documents or records]. **Interview:** [*SELECT FROM:* Organizational personnel with information system audit review, analysis, and reporting responsibilities]. **Test:** [*SELECT FROM:* Information system capability for centralizing review and analysis of audit records from multiple information system components].

AU-6(5)	AUDIT REVIEW, ANALYSIS, AND REPORTING
AU-6(5).1	**ASSESSMENT OBJECTIVE:** *Determine if the organization integrates analysis of audit records with analysis of vulnerability scanning information, performance data, and network monitoring information to enhance the ability to identify inappropriate or unusual activity.* **POTENTIAL ASSESSMENT METHODS AND OBJECTS:** **Examine:** [*SELECT FROM:* Audit and accountability policy; procedures addressing audit review, analysis, and reporting; information system design documentation; information system configuration settings and associated documentation; integrated analysis of audit records, vulnerability scanning information, performance data, network monitoring information and associated documentation; other relevant documents or records]. **Test:** [*SELECT FROM:* Information system capability for centralizing review and analysis of audit records from multiple information system components].

AU-6(6)	AUDIT REVIEW, ANALYSIS, AND REPORTING
AU-6(6).1	**ASSESSMENT OBJECTIVE:** *Determine if the organization correlates information from audit records with information obtained from monitoring physical access to enhance the ability to identify suspicious, inappropriate, unusual, or malevolent activity.* **POTENTIAL ASSESSMENT METHODS AND OBJECTS:** **Examine:** [*SELECT FROM:* Audit and accountability policy; procedures addressing audit review, analysis, and reporting; information system design documentation; information system configuration settings and associated documentation; documentation providing evidence of correlated information obtained from audit records and physical access monitoring records; security plan; other relevant documents or records]. **Test:** [*SELECT FROM:* Information system capability for centralizing review and analysis of audit records from multiple information system components].

AU-6(7)	AUDIT REVIEW, ANALYSIS, AND REPORTING
AU-6(7).1	**ASSESSMENT OBJECTIVE:** *Determine if the organization specifies the permitted actions for each authorized information system process, role, and/or user in the audit and accountability policy.* **POTENTIAL ASSESSMENT METHODS AND OBJECTS:** **Examine:** [*SELECT FROM:* Audit and accountability policy; procedures addressing audit review, analysis, and reporting; security plan; other relevant documents or records].

AU-6(8)	AUDIT REVIEW, ANALYSIS, AND REPORTING [Withdrawn: Incorporated into SI-4].
AU-6(8).1	**ASSESSMENT OBJECTIVE:** [Withdrawn: Incorporated into SI-4]. **POTENTIAL ASSESSMENT METHODS AND OBJECTS:** [Withdrawn: Incorporated into SI-4].

AU-6(9)	AUDIT REVIEW, ANALYSIS, AND REPORTING
AU-6(9).1	**ASSESSMENT OBJECTIVE:** *Determine if the organization performs full-text analysis of privileged functions executed in a physically dedicated information system.* **POTENTIAL ASSESSMENT METHODS AND OBJECTS:** **Examine:** [*SELECT FROM:* Audit and accountability policy; procedures addressing audit review, analysis, and reporting; information system design documentation; information system configuration settings and associated documentation; other relevant documents or records]. **Interview:** [*SELECT FROM:* Organizational personnel with information system audit review, analysis, and reporting responsibilities].

FAMILY: AUDIT AND ACCOUNTABILITY   **CLASS:** TECHNICAL

ASSESSMENT PROCEDURE

AU-7	AUDIT REDUCTION AND REPORT GENERATION
AU-7.1	**ASSESSMENT OBJECTIVE:** *Determine if the information system provides an audit reduction and report generation capability.* **POTENTIAL ASSESSMENT METHODS AND OBJECTS:** **Examine:** [*SELECT FROM:* Audit and accountability policy; procedures addressing audit reduction and report generation; information system design documentation; audit reduction, review, and reporting tools; information system audit records; other relevant documents or records]. **Interview:** [*SELECT FROM:* Organizational personnel with information system audit review, analysis, and reporting responsibilities]. **Test:** [*SELECT FROM:* Audit reduction and report generation capability].

AU-7(1)	AUDIT REDUCTION AND REPORT GENERATION
AU-7(1).1	**ASSESSMENT OBJECTIVE:** *Determine if the information system provides the capability to automatically process audit records for events of interest based on selectable event criteria.* **POTENTIAL ASSESSMENT METHODS AND OBJECTS:** **Examine:** [*SELECT FROM:* Audit and accountability policy; procedures addressing audit reduction and report generation; information system design documentation; information system configuration settings and associated documentation; documented criteria for selectable events to audit; audit reduction, review, and reporting tools; information system audit records; other relevant documents or records]. **Test:** [*SELECT FROM:* Audit reduction and report generation capability].

FAMILY: AUDIT AND ACCOUNTABILITY   **CLASS:** TECHNICAL

ASSESSMENT PROCEDURE	
AU-8	**TIME STAMPS**
AU-8.1	**ASSESSMENT OBJECTIVE:** *Determine if the information system uses internal system clocks to generate time stamps for audit records.* **POTENTIAL ASSESSMENT METHODS AND OBJECTS:** **Examine:** [*SELECT FROM:* Audit and accountability policy; procedures addressing time stamp generation; information system design documentation; information system configuration settings and associated documentation; information system audit records; other relevant documents or records]. **Test:** [*SELECT FROM:* Automated mechanisms implementing time stamp generation].

AU-8(1)	**TIME STAMPS**
AU-8(1).1	**ASSESSMENT OBJECTIVE:** *Determine if:* (i) *the organization defines the frequency of internal clock synchronization for the information system;* (ii) *the organization defines the authoritative time source for internal clock synchronization; and* (iii) *the organization synchronizes internal information system clocks with the organization-defined authoritative time source in accordance with the organization-defined frequency.* **POTENTIAL ASSESSMENT METHODS AND OBJECTS:** **Examine:** [*SELECT FROM:* Audit and accountability policy; procedures addressing time stamp generation; security plan; information system design documentation; information system configuration settings and associated documentation; other relevant documents or records]. **Test:** [*SELECT FROM:* Automated mechanisms implementing internal information system clock synchronization].

FAMILY: AUDIT AND ACCOUNTABILITY   **CLASS:** TECHNICAL

ASSESSMENT PROCEDURE	
AU-9	**PROTECTION OF AUDIT INFORMATION**
AU-9.1	**ASSESSMENT OBJECTIVE:** *Determine if the information system protects audit information and audit tools from unauthorized:* – *access;* – *modification; and* – *deletion.* **POTENTIAL ASSESSMENT METHODS AND OBJECTS:** **Examine:** [*SELECT FROM:* Audit and accountability policy; procedures addressing protection of audit information; access control policy and procedures; information system design documentation; information system configuration settings and associated documentation, information system audit records; audit tools; other relevant documents or records]. **Test:** [*SELECT FROM:* Automated mechanisms implementing audit information protection].

AU-9(1)	**PROTECTION OF AUDIT INFORMATION**
AU-9(1).1	**ASSESSMENT OBJECTIVE:** *Determine if the information system produces audit records on hardware-enforced, write-once media.* **POTENTIAL ASSESSMENT METHODS AND OBJECTS:** **Examine:** [*SELECT FROM:* Audit and accountability policy; procedures addressing protection of audit information; access control policy and procedures; information system design documentation; information system hardware settings; information system configuration settings and associated documentation, information system audit records; other relevant documents or records]. **Test:** [*SELECT FROM:* Media storage devices to hold audit records].

AU-9(2)	PROTECTION OF AUDIT INFORMATION
AU-9(2).1	**ASSESSMENT OBJECTIVE:** *Determine if:* (i) *the organization defines the system or media for storing back up audit records that is a different system or media than the system being audited;* (ii) *the organization defines the frequency of information system backups of audit records; and* (iii) *the information system backs up audit records, in accordance with the organization-defined frequency, onto organization-defined system or media.* **POTENTIAL ASSESSMENT METHODS AND OBJECTS:** **Examine:** [*SELECT FROM:* Audit and accountability policy; procedures addressing protection of audit information; security plan; information system design documentation; information system configuration settings and associated documentation, system or media storing backups of information system audit records; information system audit records; other relevant documents or records]. **Interview:** [*SELECT FROM:* Organizational personnel with auditing and accountability responsibilities].

AU-9(3)	PROTECTION OF AUDIT INFORMATION
AU-9(3).1	**ASSESSMENT OBJECTIVE:** *Determine if the information system uses cryptographic mechanisms to protect the integrity of audit information and audit tools.* **POTENTIAL ASSESSMENT METHODS AND OBJECTS:** **Examine:** [*SELECT FROM:* Audit and accountability policy; procedures addressing protection of audit information; access control policy and procedures; information system design documentation; information system hardware settings; information system configuration settings and associated documentation, information system audit records; other relevant documents or records]. **Interview:** [*SELECT FROM:* Organizational personnel with auditing and accountability responsibilities].

AU-9(4)	PROTECTION OF AUDIT INFORMATION
AU-9(4).1	**ASSESSMENT OBJECTIVE:** *Determine if :* (i) *the organization authorizes access to management of audit functionality to only a limited subset of privileged users; and* (ii) *the organization protects the audit records of non-local accesses to privileged accounts and the execution of privileged functions.* **POTENTIAL ASSESSMENT METHODS AND OBJECTS:** **Examine:** [*SELECT FROM:* Audit and accountability policy; procedures addressing protection of audit information; access control policy and procedures; information system design documentation; information system configuration settings and associated documentation, information system audit records; other relevant documents or records]. **Interview:** [*SELECT FROM:* Organizational personnel with auditing and accountability responsibilities].

FAMILY: AUDIT AND ACCOUNTABILITY   **CLASS:** TECHNICAL

ASSESSMENT PROCEDURE	
AU-10	**NON-REPUDIATION**
AU-10.1	**ASSESSMENT OBJECTIVE:** *Determine if the information system protects against an individual falsely denying having performed a particular action.* **POTENTIAL ASSESSMENT METHODS AND OBJECTS:** **Examine:** [*SELECT FROM:* Audit and accountability policy; procedures addressing non-repudiation; information system design documentation; information system configuration settings and associated documentation; information system audit records; other relevant documents or records]. **Test:** [*SELECT FROM:* Automated mechanisms implementing non-repudiation capability].

AU-10(1)	**NON-REPUDIATION**
AU-10(1).1	**ASSESSMENT OBJECTIVE:** *Determine if the information system associates the identity of the information producer with the information.* **POTENTIAL ASSESSMENT METHODS AND OBJECTS:** **Examine:** [*SELECT FROM:* Audit and accountability policy; procedures addressing non-repudiation; information system design documentation; information system configuration settings and associated documentation; information system audit records; other relevant documents or records]. **Test:** [*SELECT FROM:* Automated mechanisms implementing non-repudiation capability].

AU-10(2)	**NON-REPUDIATION**
AU-10(2).1	**ASSESSMENT OBJECTIVE:** *Determine if the information system validates the binding of the information producer's identity to the information.* **POTENTIAL ASSESSMENT METHODS AND OBJECTS:** **Examine:** [*SELECT FROM:* Audit and accountability policy; procedures addressing non-repudiation; information system design documentation; information system configuration settings and associated documentation; information system audit records; other relevant documents or records]. **Test:** [*SELECT FROM:* Automated mechanisms implementing non-repudiation capability].

AU-10(3)	NON-REPUDIATION
AU-10(3).1	**ASSESSMENT OBJECTIVE:** *Determine if the information system maintains reviewer/releaser identity and credentials within the established chain of custody for all information reviewed or released.* **POTENTIAL ASSESSMENT METHODS AND OBJECTS:** **Examine:** [*SELECT FROM:* Audit and accountability policy; procedures addressing non-repudiation; information system design documentation; information system configuration settings and associated documentation; information system audit records; other relevant documents or records]. **Test:** [*SELECT FROM:* Automated mechanisms implementing non-repudiation capability].

AU-10(4)	NON-REPUDIATION
AU-10(4).1	**ASSESSMENT OBJECTIVE:** *Determine if the information system validates the binding of the reviewer's identity to the information at the transfer/release point prior to release/transfer from one security domain to another security domain.* **POTENTIAL ASSESSMENT METHODS AND OBJECTS:** **Examine:** [*SELECT FROM:* Audit and accountability policy; procedures addressing non-repudiation; information system design documentation; information system configuration settings and associated documentation; information system audit records; other relevant documents or records]. **Test:** [*SELECT FROM:* Automated mechanisms implementing non-repudiation capability].

AU-10(5)	NON-REPUDIATION
AU-10(5).1	**ASSESSMENT OBJECTIVE:** *Determine if:* (i) *the organization defines whether FIPS-validated or NSA-approved cryptography is employed to implement digital signatures; and* (ii) *the organization employs the organization-defined cryptography to implement digital signatures.* **POTENTIAL ASSESSMENT METHODS AND OBJECTS:** **Examine:** [*SELECT FROM:* Audit and accountability policy; procedures addressing non-repudiation; information system design documentation; information system configuration settings and associated documentation; information system audit records; other relevant documents or records]. **Test:** [*SELECT FROM:* Cryptographic mechanisms implementing digital signature capability within the information system].

FAMILY: AUDIT AND ACCOUNTABILITY   **CLASS:** TECHNICAL

ASSESSMENT PROCEDURE
AU-11	**AUDIT RECORD RETENTION**
AU-11.1	**ASSESSMENT OBJECTIVE:** *Determine if:* (i) *the organization defines the retention period for audit records;* (ii) *the retention period for audit records is consistent with the records retention policy; and* (iii) *the organization retains audit records for the organization-defined time period consistent with the records retention policy to provide support for after-the-fact investigations of security incidents and to meet regulatory and organizational information retention requirements.* **POTENTIAL ASSESSMENT METHODS AND OBJECTS:** **Examine:** [*SELECT FROM:* Audit and accountability policy; procedures addressing audit record retention; security plan; organization-defined retention period for audit records; information system audit records; other relevant documents or records]. **Interview:** [*SELECT FROM:* Organizational personnel with information system audit record retention responsibilities].

FAMILY: AUDIT AND ACCOUNTABILITY   **CLASS:** TECHNICAL

ASSESSMENT PROCEDURE

AU-12	AUDIT GENERATION
AU-12.1	**ASSESSMENT OBJECTIVE:** *Determine if:* (i) *the organization defines the information system components that provide audit record generation capability for the list of auditable events defined in AU-2;* (ii) *the information system provides audit record generation capability, at organization-defined information system components, for the list of auditable events defined in AU-2;* (iii) *the information system allows designated organizational personnel to select which auditable events are to be audited by specific components of the system; and* (iv) *the information system generates audit records for the list of audited events defined in AU-2 with the content as defined in AU-3..* **POTENTIAL ASSESSMENT METHODS AND OBJECTS:** **Examine:** [*SELECT FROM:* Audit and accountability policy; procedures addressing audit record generation; security plan; information system design documentation; information system configuration settings and associated documentation; information system audit records; other relevant documents or records]. **Interview:** [*SELECT FROM:* Organizational personnel with information system audit record generation responsibilities]. **Test:** [*SELECT FROM:* Automated mechanisms implementing audit record generation capability].

AU-12(1)	AUDIT GENERATION
AU-12(1).1	**ASSESSMENT OBJECTIVE:** *Determine if:* (i) *the information system produces a system-wide (logical or physical) audit trail of information system audit records;* (ii) *the organization defines the information system components from which audit records are to be compiled into the system-wide audit trail;* (iii) *the information system compiles audit records from organization-defined information system components into the system-wide audit trail;* (iv) *the organization defines the acceptable level of tolerance for relationship between time stamps of individual records in the system-wide audit trail; and* (v) *the system-wide audit trail is time-correlated to within the organization-defined level of tolerance to achieve a time ordering of audit records.* **POTENTIAL ASSESSMENT METHODS AND OBJECTS:** **Examine:** [*SELECT FROM:* Audit and accountability policy; procedures addressing audit record generation; information system design documentation; information system configuration settings and associated documentation; information system audit records; other relevant documents or records]. **Test:** [*SELECT FROM:* Automated mechanisms implementing audit record generation capability].

AU-12(2)	AUDIT GENERATION
AU-12(2).1	**ASSESSMENT OBJECTIVE:** *Determine if the information system produces a system-wide (logical or physical) audit trail composed of audit records in a standardized format.* **POTENTIAL ASSESSMENT METHODS AND OBJECTS:** **Examine:** [*SELECT FROM:* Audit and accountability policy; procedures addressing audit record generation; information system design documentation; information system configuration settings and associated documentation; information system audit records; other relevant documents or records]. **Test:** [*SELECT FROM:* Automated mechanisms implementing audit record generation capability].

FAMILY: AUDIT AND ACCOUNTABILITY   **CLASS:** TECHNICAL

ASSESSMENT PROCEDURE	
AU-13	**MONITORING FOR INFORMATION DISCLOSURE**
AU-13.1	**ASSESSMENT OBJECTIVE:** *Determine if:* (i) *the organization defines the frequency of monitoring open source information for evidence of unauthorized exfiltration or disclosure of organization information; and* (ii) *the organization monitors open source information for evidence of unauthorized exfiltration or disclosure of organizational information in accordance with the organization-defined frequency.* **POTENTIAL ASSESSMENT METHODS AND OBJECTS:** **Examine:** [*SELECT FROM:* Audit and accountability policy; procedures addressing information disclosure monitoring; information system design documentation; information system configuration settings and associated documentation; information system audit records; other relevant documents or records]. **Interview:** [*SELECT FROM:* Organizational personnel with responsibilities for monitoring open source information for evidence of unauthorized exfiltration or disclosure].

FAMILY: AUDIT AND ACCOUNTABILITY   **CLASS:** TECHNICAL

ASSESSMENT PROCEDURE	
AU-14	**SESSION AUDIT**
AU-14.1	**ASSESSMENT OBJECTIVE:** *Determine if:* (i) the information system provides the capability to capture/record and log all content related to a user session; and (ii) the information system provides the capability to remotely view/hear all content related to an established user session in real time. **POTENTIAL ASSESSMENT METHODS AND OBJECTS:** **Examine:** [*SELECT FROM:* Audit and accountability policy; procedures addressing user session auditing; information system design documentation; information system configuration settings and associated documentation; information system audit records; other relevant documents or records]. **Test:** [*SELECT FROM:* Automated mechanisms implementing user session auditing capability].

AU-14(1)	**SESSION AUDIT**
AU-14(1).1	**ASSESSMENT OBJECTIVE:** *Determine if the information system initiates session audits at system start-up* **POTENTIAL ASSESSMENT METHODS AND OBJECTS:** **Examine:** [*SELECT FROM:* Audit and accountability policy; procedures addressing user session auditing; information system design documentation; information system configuration settings and associated documentation; information system audit records; other relevant documents or records]. **Test:** [*SELECT FROM:* Automated mechanisms implementing user session auditing capability].

FAMILY: SECURITY ASSESSMENT AND AUTHORIZATION   **CLASS:** MANAGEMENT

ASSESSMENT PROCEDURE	
CA-1	**SECURITY ASSESSMENT AND AUTHORIZATION POLICIES AND PROCEDURES**

CA-1.1	**ASSESSMENT OBJECTIVE:**
	Determine if:
	
	(i) the organization develops and formally documents security assessment and authorization policy;
	
	(ii) the organization security assessment and authorization policy addresses:
	  - *purpose;*
	  - *scope;*
	  - *roles and responsibilities;*
	  - *management commitment;*
	  - *coordination among organizational entities; and*
	  - *compliance;*
	
	(iii) the organization disseminates formal documented security assessment and authorization policy to elements within the organization having associated security assessment and authorization roles and responsibilities;
	
	(iv) the organization develops and formally documents security assessment and authorization procedures;
	
	(v) the organization security assessment and authorization procedures facilitate implementation of the security assessment and authorization policy and associated security assessment and authorization controls; and
	
	(vi) the organization disseminates formal documented security assessment and authorization procedures to elements within the organization having associated security assessment and authorization roles and responsibilities.
	
	POTENTIAL ASSESSMENT METHODS AND OBJECTS:
	Examine: [*SELECT FROM:* Security assessment and authorization policies and procedures; other relevant documents or records].
	Interview: [*SELECT FROM:* Organizational personnel with security assessment and authorization responsibilities].

CA-1.2	**ASSESSMENT OBJECTIVE:** *Determine if:* (i) the organization defines the frequency of security assessment and authorization policy reviews/updates; (ii) the organization reviews/updates security assessment and authorization policy in accordance with organization-defined frequency; (iii) the organization defines the frequency of security assessment and authorization procedure reviews/updates; and (iv) the organization reviews/updates security assessment and authorization procedures in accordance with organization-defined frequency. **POTENTIAL ASSESSMENT METHODS AND OBJECTS:** **Examine:** [*SELECT FROM:* Security assessment and authorization policies and procedures; other relevant documents or records]. **Interview:** [*SELECT FROM:* Organizational personnel with security assessment and authorization responsibilities].

FAMILY: SECURITY ASSESSMENT AND AUTHORIZATION   **CLASS:** MANAGEMENT

ASSESSMENT PROCEDURE	
CA-2	**SECURITY ASSESSMENTS**
CA-2.1	**ASSESSMENT OBJECTIVE:** *Determine if:* (i) *the organization develops a security assessment plan for the information system; and* (ii) *the security assessment plan describes the scope of the assessment including:* - *security controls and control enhancements under assessment;* - *assessment procedures to be used to determine security control effectiveness; and* - *assessment environment, assessment team, and assessment roles and responsibilities.* **POTENTIAL ASSESSMENT METHODS AND OBJECTS:** **Examine**: [*SELECT FROM:* Security assessment and authorization policy; procedures addressing security assessments; security assessment plan; other relevant documents or records].
CA-2.2	**ASSESSMENT OBJECTIVE:** *Determine if:* (i) *the organization defines the frequency of assessing the security controls in the information system to determine the extent to which the controls are implemented correctly, operating as intended, and producing the desired outcome with respect to meeting the security requirements for the system;* (ii) *the organization assesses the security controls in the information system at the organization-defined frequency;* (iii) *the organization produces a security assessment report that documents the results of the security control assessment; and* (iv) *the results of the security control assessment are provided, in writing, to the authorizing official or authorizing official designated representative.* **POTENTIAL ASSESSMENT METHODS AND OBJECTS:** **Examine**: [*SELECT FROM:* Security assessment and authorization policy; procedures addressing security assessments; security plan; security assessment plan; security assessment report; security assessment evidence; plan of action and milestones; other relevant documents or records]. **Interview**: [*SELECT FROM:* Organizational personnel with security assessment responsibilities].

CA-2(1)	SECURITY ASSESSMENTS
CA-2(1).1	**ASSESSMENT OBJECTIVE:** *Determine if the organization employs an independent assessor or assessment team to conduct an assessment of the security controls in the information system.* **POTENTIAL ASSESSMENT METHODS AND OBJECTS:** **Examine:** [*SELECT FROM:* Security assessment and authorization policy; procedures addressing security assessments; security authorization package (including security plan, security assessment report, plan of action and milestones, authorization statement); other relevant documents or records]. **Interview:** [*SELECT FROM:* Organizational personnel with security assessment responsibilities].

CA-2(2)	SECURITY ASSESSMENTS

CA-2(2).1	**ASSESSMENT OBJECTIVE:**
	
	 Determine if:
	
	 (i) the organization defines:
	
	    - *the forms of security testing to be included in security control assessments, selecting from in-depth monitoring, malicious user testing, penetration testing, red team exercises, or an organization-defined form of security testing;*
	
	    - *the frequency for conducting each form of security testing;*
	
	    - *whether the security testing will be announced or unannounced; and*
	
	 (ii) the organization conducts security control assessments using organization-defined forms of testing in accordance with organization-defined frequency and assessment techniques established for each form of testing.
	
	 POTENTIAL ASSESSMENT METHODS AND OBJECTS:
	
	 Examine: [*SELECT FROM:* Security assessment and authorization policy; procedures addressing security assessments; security plan; security assessment plan; security assessment report; assessment evidence; other relevant documents or records].
	
	 Interview: [*SELECT FROM:* Organizational personnel with security assessment responsibilities].

FAMILY: SECURITY ASSESSMENT AND AUTHORIZATION   **CLASS:** MANAGEMENT

ASSESSMENT PROCEDURE

CA-3	INFORMATION SYSTEM CONNECTIONS
CA-3.1	**ASSESSMENT OBJECTIVE:** *Determine if:* (i) *the organization identifies connections to external information systems (i.e., information systems outside of the authorization boundary);* (ii) *the organization authorizes connections from the information system to external information systems through the use of Interconnection Security Agreements;* (iii) *the organization documents, for each connection, the interface characteristics, security requirements, and the nature of the information communicated; and* (iv) *the organization monitors the information system connections on an ongoing basis to verify enforcement of security requirements.* **POTENTIAL ASSESSMENT METHODS AND OBJECTS:** **Examine:** [*SELECT FROM:* Access control policy; procedures addressing information system connections; system and communications protection policy; information system interconnection security agreements; security plan; information system design documentation; security assessment report; plan of action and milestones; other relevant documents or records]. **Interview:** [*SELECT FROM:* Organizational personnel with responsibility for developing, implementing, or approving information system interconnection agreements].

CA-3(1)	INFORMATION SYSTEM CONNECTIONS
CA-3(1).1	**ASSESSMENT OBJECTIVE:** *Determine if the organization prohibits the direct connection of an unclassified, national security system to an external network.* **POTENTIAL ASSESSMENT METHODS AND OBJECTS:** **Examine:** [*SELECT FROM:* Access control policy; procedures addressing information system connections; system and communications protection policy; information system interconnection security agreements; security plan; information system design documentation; security assessment report; plan of action and milestones; other relevant documents or records].

CA-3(2)	INFORMATION SYSTEM CONNECTIONS
CA-3(2).1	**ASSESSMENT OBJECTIVE:** *Determine if the organization prohibits the direct connection of a classified, national security system to an external network.* **POTENTIAL ASSESSMENT METHODS AND OBJECTS:** **Examine:** [*SELECT FROM:* Access control policy; procedures addressing information system connections; system and communications protection policy; information system interconnection agreements; security plan; information system design documentation;; security assessment report; plan of action and milestones; other relevant documents or records].

FAMILY: SECURITY ASSESSMENT AND AUTHORIZATION   **CLASS:** MANAGEMENT

ASSESSMENT PROCEDURE	
CA-4	**SECURITY CERTIFICATION**
	[Withdrawn: Incorporated into CA-2].
CA-4.1	**ASSESSMENT OBJECTIVE:**
	[Withdrawn: Incorporated into CA-2].
	POTENTIAL ASSESSMENT METHODS AND OBJECTS:
	[Withdrawn: Incorporated into CA-2].

CA-4(1)	**SECURITY CERTIFICATION**
	[Withdrawn: Incorporated into CA-2].
CA-4(1).1	**ASSESSMENT OBJECTIVE:**
	[Withdrawn: Incorporated into CA-2].
	POTENTIAL ASSESSMENT METHODS AND OBJECTS:
	[Withdrawn: Incorporated into CA-2].

FAMILY: SECURITY ASSESSMENT AND AUTHORIZATION   **CLASS:** MANAGEMENT

ASSESSMENT PROCEDURE

CA-5	PLAN OF ACTION AND MILESTONES
CA-5.1	**ASSESSMENT OBJECTIVE:** *Determine if:* (i) *the organization develops a plan of action and milestones for the information system;* (ii) *the plan of action and milestones documents the organization's planned remedial actions to correct weaknesses or deficiencies noted during the assessment of the security controls and to reduce or eliminate known vulnerabilities in the system;* (iii) *the organization defines the frequency of plan of action and milestone updates; and* (iv) *the organization updates the plan of action and milestones at an organization-defined frequency with findings from:* - *security controls assessments;* - *security impact analyses; and* - *continuous monitoring activities.* **POTENTIAL ASSESSMENT METHODS AND OBJECTS:** **Examine:** [*SELECT FROM:* Security assessment and authorization policy; procedures addressing plan of action and milestones; security plan; security assessment plan; security assessment report; assessment evidence; plan of action and milestones; other relevant documents or records]. **Interview:** [*SELECT FROM:* Organizational personnel with plan of action and milestones development and implementation responsibilities].

CA-5(1)	PLAN OF ACTION AND MILESTONES
CA-5(1).1	**ASSESSMENT OBJECTIVE:** *Determine if the organization employs automated mechanisms to help ensure that the plan of action and milestones for the information system is:* - *accurate;* - *up to date; and* - *readily available.* **POTENTIAL ASSESSMENT METHODS AND OBJECTS:** **Examine:** [*SELECT FROM:* Security assessment and authorization policy; procedures addressing plan of action and milestones; information system design documentation, information system configuration settings and associated documentation; plan of action and milestones; other relevant documents or records]. **Interview:** [*SELECT FROM:* Organizational personnel with plan of action and milestones development and implementation responsibilities]. **Test:** [*SELECT FROM:* Automated mechanisms for developing, implementing and maintaining plan of action and milestones].

FAMILY: SECURITY ASSESSMENT AND AUTHORIZATION   **CLASS:** MANAGEMENT

ASSESSMENT PROCEDURE	
CA-6	**SECURITY AUTHORIZATION**
CA-6.1	**ASSESSMENT OBJECTIVE:** *Determine if:* (i) *the organization assigns a senior-level executive or manager to the role of authorizing official for the information system;* (ii) *the authorizing official authorizes the information system for processing before commencing operations;* (iii) *the organization defines the frequency of security authorization updates; and* (iv) *the organization updates the security authorization in accordance with an organization-defined frequency.* **POTENTIAL ASSESSMENT METHODS AND OBJECTS:** **Examine**: [*SELECT FROM:* Security assessment and authorization policy; procedures addressing security authorization; security authorization package (including security plan; security assessment report; plan of action and milestones; authorization statement); other relevant documents or records]. **Interview**: [*SELECT FROM:* Organizational personnel with security authorization responsibilities].

FAMILY: SECURITY ASSESSMENT AND AUTHORIZATION   **CLASS:** MANAGEMENT

ASSESSMENT PROCEDURE

CA-7	CONTINUOUS MONITORING
CA-7.1	**ASSESSMENT OBJECTIVE:** *Determine if:* (i) *the organization establishes a continuous monitoring strategy and program;* (ii) *the organization defines the frequency for reporting the security state of the information system to appropriate organizational officials;* (iii) *the organization defines organizational officials to whom the security state of the information system should be reported; and* (iv) *the organization implements a continuous monitoring program that includes:* - *a configuration management process for the information system and its constituent components;* - *a determination of the security impact of changes to the information system and environment of operation;* - *ongoing security control assessments in accordance with the organizational continuous monitoring strategy; and* - *reporting the security state of the information system to appropriate organizational officials in accordance with organization-defined frequency.* **POTENTIAL ASSESSMENT METHODS AND OBJECTS:** **Examine:** [*SELECT FROM:* Security assessment and authorization policy; procedures addressing continuous monitoring of information system security controls; procedures addressing configuration management; security plan; security assessment report; plan of action and milestones; information system monitoring records; configuration management records, security impact analyses; status reports; other relevant documents or records]. **Interview:** [*SELECT FROM:* Organizational personnel with continuous monitoring responsibilities; organizational personnel with configuration management responsibilities].

CA-7(1)	CONTINUOUS MONITORING
CA-7(1).1	**ASSESSMENT OBJECTIVE:** *Determine if the organization employs an independent assessor or assessment team to monitor the security controls in the information system on an ongoing basis.* **POTENTIAL ASSESSMENT METHODS AND OBJECTS:** **Examine:** [*SELECT FROM:* Security assessment and authorization policy; procedures addressing continuous monitoring of information system security controls; security plan; security assessment report; plan of action and milestones; information system monitoring records; security impact analyses; status reports; other relevant documents or records]. **Interview:** [*SELECT FROM:* Organizational personnel with continuous monitoring responsibilities].

CA-7(2)	CONTINUOUS MONITORING
CA-7(2).1	**ASSESSMENT OBJECTIVE:** *Determine if:* (i) *the organization defines:* - *the forms of security testing to be included in planning, scheduling, and security control assessments selecting from in-depth monitoring, malicious user testing, penetration testing, red team exercises, or an organization-defined form of security testing to ensure compliance with all vulnerability mitigation procedures;* - *the frequency for conducting each form of security testing;* - *whether the security testing will be announced or unannounced; and* (ii) *the organization plans, schedules, and conducts assessments using organization-defined forms of security testing in accordance with the organization-defined frequency and assessment techniques established for each form of testing to ensure compliance with all vulnerability mitigation procedures.* **POTENTIAL ASSESSMENT METHODS AND OBJECTS:** **Examine:** [*SELECT FROM:* Security assessment and authorization policy; procedures addressing continuous monitoring of information system security controls; procedures addressing vulnerability mitigation; security plan; security assessment report; plan of action and milestones; information system monitoring records; security impact analyses; status reports; other relevant documents or records]. **Interview:** [*SELECT FROM:* Organizational personnel with continuous monitoring responsibilities].

FAMILY: CONFIGURATION MANAGEMENT   **CLASS:** OPERATIONAL

ASSESSMENT PROCEDURE	
CM-1	**CONFIGURATION MANAGEMENT POLICY AND PROCEDURES**

CM-1.1	**ASSESSMENT OBJECTIVE:**
	Determine if:
	(i) *the organization develops and formally documents configuration management policy;*
	(ii) *the organization configuration management policy addresses:*
	   - *purpose;*
	   - *scope;*
	   - *roles and responsibilities;*
	   - *management commitment;*
	   - *coordination among organizational entities; and*
	   - *compliance;*
	(iii) *the organization disseminates formal documented configuration management policy to elements within the organization having associated configuration management roles and responsibilities;*
	(iv) *the organization develops and formally documents configuration management procedures;*
	(v) *the organization configuration management procedures facilitate implementation of the configuration management policy and associated configuration management controls; and*
	(vi) *the organization disseminates formal documented configuration management procedures to elements within the organization having associated configuration management roles and responsibilities.*
	
	POTENTIAL ASSESSMENT METHODS AND OBJECTS:
	Examine: [*SELECT FROM:* Configuration management policy and procedures; other relevant documents or records].
	Interview: [*SELECT FROM:* Organizational personnel with configuration management and control responsibilities].

CM-1.2	**ASSESSMENT OBJECTIVE:** *Determine if:* (i) *the organization defines the frequency of configuration management policy reviews/updates;* (ii) *the organization reviews/updates configuration management policy in accordance with organization-defined frequency;* (iii) *the organization defines the frequency of configuration management procedure reviews/updates; and* (iv) *the organization reviews/updates configuration management procedures in accordance with organization-defined frequency.* **POTENTIAL ASSESSMENT METHODS AND OBJECTS:** **Examine**: [*SELECT FROM:* Configuration management policy and procedures; other relevant documents or records]. **Interview**: [*SELECT FROM:* Organizational personnel with configuration management and control responsibilities].

FAMILY: CONFIGURATION MANAGEMENT   **CLASS:** OPERATIONAL

ASSESSMENT PROCEDURE

CM-2	BASELINE CONFIGURATION
CM-2.1	**ASSESSMENT OBJECTIVE:** *Determine if:* *(i) the organization develops and documents a baseline configuration of the information system and* *(ii) the organization maintains, under configuration control, a current baseline configuration of the information system.* **POTENTIAL ASSESSMENT METHODS AND OBJECTS:** **Examine:** [*SELECT FROM:* Configuration management policy; configuration management plan; procedures addressing the baseline configuration of the information system; enterprise architecture documentation; information system design documentation; information system architecture and configuration documentation; other relevant documents or records].

CM-2(1)	BASELINE CONFIGURATION
CM-2(1).1	**ASSESSMENT OBJECTIVE:** *Determine if:* *(i) the organization defines:* - *the frequency of reviews and updates to the baseline configuration of the information system; and* - *the circumstances that require reviews and updates to the baseline configuration of the information system; and* *(ii) the organization reviews and updates the baseline configuration of the information system* - *in accordance with the organization-defined frequency;* - *when required due to organization-defined circumstances; and* - *as an integral part of information system component installations and upgrades.* **POTENTIAL ASSESSMENT METHODS AND OBJECTS:** **Examine:** [*SELECT FROM:* Configuration management policy; configuration management plan; procedures addressing the baseline configuration of the information system; information system architecture and configuration documentation; other relevant documents or records]. **Interview:** [*SELECT FROM:* Organizational personnel with configuration change control responsibilities].

CM-2(2)	BASELINE CONFIGURATION
CM-2(2).1	**ASSESSMENT OBJECTIVE:** *Determine if the organization employs automated mechanisms to maintain an up-to-date, complete, accurate, and readily available baseline configuration of the information system.* **POTENTIAL ASSESSMENT METHODS AND OBJECTS:** **Examine:** [*SELECT FROM:* Configuration management policy; configuration management plan; procedures addressing the baseline configuration of the information system; information system design documentation; information system architecture and configuration documentation; other relevant documents or records]. **Test:** [*SELECT FROM:* Automated mechanisms implementing baseline configuration maintenance].

CM-2(3)	BASELINE CONFIGURATION
CM-2(3).1	**ASSESSMENT OBJECTIVE:** *Determine if the organization retains older versions of baseline configurations as deemed necessary to support rollback.* **POTENTIAL ASSESSMENT METHODS AND OBJECTS:** **Examine:** [*SELECT FROM:* Configuration management policy; configuration management plan; procedures addressing the baseline configuration of the information system; information system architecture and configuration documentation; historical copies of baseline configurations; other relevant documents or records].

CM-2(4)	BASELINE CONFIGURATION
CM-2(4).1	**ASSESSMENT OBJECTIVE:** *Determine if:* *(i) the organization develops and maintains a list of software programs not authorized to execute on the information system; and* *(ii) the organization employs an allow-all, deny-by-exception authorization policy to identify software allowed to execute on the information system.* **POTENTIAL ASSESSMENT METHODS AND OBJECTS:** **Examine:** [*SELECT FROM:* Configuration management policy; configuration management plan; procedures addressing the baseline configuration of the information system; list of software programs not authorized to execute on the information system; information system architecture and configuration documentation; security plan; other relevant documents or records].

CM-2(5)	BASELINE CONFIGURATION
CM-2(5).1	**ASSESSMENT OBJECTIVE:** *Determine if:* *(i) the organization develops and maintains a list of software programs authorized to execute on the information system; and* *(ii) the organization employs a deny-all, permit-by-exception authorization policy to identify software allowed to execute on the information system.* **POTENTIAL ASSESSMENT METHODS AND OBJECTS:** **Examine**: [*SELECT FROM:* Configuration management policy; configuration management plan; procedures addressing the baseline configuration of the information system; list of software authorized to execute on the information system; information system architecture and configuration documentation; security plan; other relevant documents or records].

CM-2(6)	BASELINE CONFIGURATION
CM-2(6).1	**ASSESSMENT OBJECTIVE:** *Determine if the organization maintains a baseline configuration for development and test environments that is managed separately from the operational baseline configuration.* **POTENTIAL ASSESSMENT METHODS AND OBJECTS:** **Examine**: [*SELECT FROM:* Configuration management policy; configuration management plan; procedures addressing the baseline configuration of the information system; information system design documentation; information system architecture and configuration documentation; other relevant documents or records]. **Test**: [*SELECT FROM:* Automated mechanisms implementing baseline configuration environments].

FAMILY: CONFIGURATION MANAGEMENT   **CLASS:** OPERATIONAL

ASSESSMENT PROCEDURE

CM-3	CONFIGURATION CHANGE CONTROL

CM-3.1	**ASSESSMENT OBJECTIVE:**
	
	Determine if:
	
	(i) *the organization determines the types of changes to the information system that are configuration controlled;*
	
	(ii) *the organization approves configuration-controlled changes to the system with explicit consideration for security impact analyses;*
	
	(iii) *the organization documents approved configuration-controlled changes to the system;*
	
	(iv) *the organization retains and reviews records of configuration-controlled changes to the system;*
	
	(v) *the organization audits activities associated with configuration-controlled changes to the system;*
	
	(vi) *the organization defines:*
	
	   - *the configuration change control element (e.g., committee, board) responsible for coordinating and providing oversight for configuration change control activities;*
	
	   - *the frequency with which the configuration change control element convenes; and/or;*
	
	   - *configuration change conditions that prompt the configuration change control element to convene.*
	
	(vii) *the organization coordinates and provides oversight for configuration change control activities through the organization-defined configuration change control element that convenes at the organization-defined frequency and/or for any organization-defined configuration change conditions.*
	
	POTENTIAL ASSESSMENT METHODS AND OBJECTS:
	
	Examine: [*SELECT FROM:* Configuration management policy; configuration management plan; procedures addressing information system configuration change control; information system architecture and configuration documentation; security plan; change control records; information system audit records; other relevant documents or records].
	
	Interview: [*SELECT FROM:* Organizational personnel with configuration change control responsibilities].

CM-3(1)	CONFIGURATION CHANGE CONTROL
CM-3(1).1	**ASSESSMENT OBJECTIVE:** *Determine if:* (i) *the organization defines the time period after which approvals that have not been received for proposed changes to the information system are highlighted; and* (ii) *the organization employs automated mechanisms to:* - *document proposed changes to the information system;* - *notify designated approval authorities;* - *highlight approvals that have not been received by the organization-defined time period;* - *inhibit change until designated approvals are received; and* - *document completed changes to the information system.* **POTENTIAL ASSESSMENT METHODS AND OBJECTS:** **Examine:** [*SELECT FROM:* Configuration management policy; configuration management plan; procedures addressing information system configuration change control; information system design documentation; information system architecture and configuration documentation; automated configuration control mechanisms; change control records; information system audit records; other relevant documents or records]. **Test:** [*SELECT FROM:* Automated mechanisms implementing configuration change control].

CM-3(2)	CONFIGURATION CHANGE CONTROL
CM-3(2).1	**ASSESSMENT OBJECTIVE:** *Determine if the organization tests, validates, and documents changes to the information system before implementing the changes on the operational system.* **POTENTIAL ASSESSMENT METHODS AND OBJECTS:** **Examine:** [*SELECT FROM:* Configuration management policy; configuration management plan; procedures addressing information system configuration change control; information system design documentation; information system architecture and configuration documentation; change control records; information system audit records; other relevant documents or records]. **Interview:** [*SELECT FROM:* Organizational personnel with configuration change control responsibilities].

CM-3(3)	CONFIGURATION CHANGE CONTROL
CM-3(3).1	**ASSESSMENT OBJECTIVE:** *Determine if:* (i) *the organization employs automated mechanisms to implement changes to the current information system baseline; and* (ii) *the organization deploys the updated baseline across the installed base.* **POTENTIAL ASSESSMENT METHODS AND OBJECTS:** **Examine:** [*SELECT FROM:* Configuration management policy; configuration management plan; procedures addressing information system configuration change control; information system design documentation; information system architecture and configuration documentation; automated configuration control mechanisms; change control records; information system audit records; other relevant documents or records]. **Test:** [*SELECT FROM:* Automated mechanisms implementing changes to the information system baseline].

CM-3(4)	CONFIGURATION CHANGE CONTROL
CM-3(4).1	**ASSESSMENT OBJECTIVE:** *Determine if the organization requires an information security representative to be a member of the configuration change control element as defined by the organization in CM-3.1 (vi).* **POTENTIAL ASSESSMENT METHODS AND OBJECTS:** **Examine:** [*SELECT FROM:* Configuration management policy; configuration management plan; procedures addressing information system configuration change control; security plan; other relevant documents or records]. **Interview:** [*SELECT FROM:* Organizational personnel with configuration change control responsibilities].

FAMILY: CONFIGURATION MANAGEMENT   **CLASS:** OPERATIONAL

ASSESSMENT PROCEDURE	
CM-4	**SECURITY IMPACT ANALYSIS**
CM-4.1	**ASSESSMENT OBJECTIVE:** *Determine if the organization analyzes changes to the information system to determine potential security impacts prior to change implementation.* **POTENTIAL ASSESSMENT METHODS AND OBJECTS:** **Examine:** [*SELECT FROM:* Configuration management policy; configuration management plan; procedures addressing security impact analysis for changes to the information system; security impact analysis documentation; information system architecture and configuration documentation; change control records; information system audit records; other relevant documents or records]. **Interview:** [*SELECT FROM:* Organizational personnel with responsibilities for determining security impacts prior to implementation of information system changes].

CM-4(1)	SECURITY IMPACT ANALYSIS
CM-4(1).1	**ASSESSMENT OBJECTIVE:** *Determine if:* *(i) the organization analyzes new software in a separate test environment before installation in an operational environment; and* *(ii) the organization, when analyzing new software in a separate test environment, looks for security impacts due to flaws, weaknesses, incompatibility, or intentional malice.* **POTENTIAL ASSESSMENT METHODS AND OBJECTS:** **Examine:** [*SELECT FROM:* Configuration management policy; configuration management plan; procedures addressing security impact analysis for changes to the information system; security impact analysis documentation; information system design documentation; information system architecture and configuration documentation; change control records; information system audit records; information system test and operational environments; other relevant documents or records]. **Interview:** [*SELECT FROM:* Organizational personnel with responsibilities for determining security impacts prior to implementation of information system changes].

CM-4(2)	SECURITY IMPACT ANALYSIS
CM-4(2).1	**ASSESSMENT OBJECTIVE:** *Determine if the organization, after the information system is changed, checks the security functions to verify that the functions are:* – *implemented correctly;* – *operating as intended; and* – *producing the desired outcome with regard to meeting the security requirements for the system.* **POTENTIAL ASSESSMENT METHODS AND OBJECTS:** **Examine**: [*SELECT FROM:* Configuration management policy; configuration management plan; procedures addressing security impact analysis for changes to the information system; security impact analysis documentation; change control records; information system audit records; other relevant documents or records]. **Interview**: [*SELECT FROM:* Organizational personnel with responsibilities for determining security impacts prior to implementation of information system changes].

FAMILY: CONFIGURATION MANAGEMENT   **CLASS:** OPERATIONAL

ASSESSMENT PROCEDURE

CM-5	ACCESS RESTRICTIONS FOR CHANGE
CM-5.1	**ASSESSMENT OBJECTIVE:** *Determine if the organization defines, documents, approves, and enforces physical and logical access restrictions associated with changes to the information system.* **POTENTIAL ASSESSMENT METHODS AND OBJECTS:** **Examine:** [*SELECT FROM:* Configuration management policy; configuration management plan; procedures addressing access restrictions for changes to the information system; information system architecture and configuration documentation; change control records; information system audit records; other relevant documents or records]. **Interview:** [*SELECT FROM:* Organizational personnel with logical access control responsibilities; organizational personnel with physical access control responsibilities]. **Test:** [*SELECT FROM:* Change control process and associated restrictions for changes to the information system].

CM-5(1)	ACCESS RESTRICTIONS FOR CHANGE
CM-5(1).1	**ASSESSMENT OBJECTIVE:** *Determine if the organization employs automated mechanisms to enforce access restrictions and support auditing of the enforcement actions.* **POTENTIAL ASSESSMENT METHODS AND OBJECTS:** **Examine:** [*SELECT FROM:* Configuration management policy; configuration management plan; procedures addressing access restrictions for changes to the information system; information system design documentation; information system architecture and configuration documentation; change control records; information system audit records; other relevant documents or records]. **Test:** [*SELECT FROM:* Automated mechanisms implementing access restrictions for changes to the information system].

CM-5(2)	ACCESS RESTRICTIONS FOR CHANGE
CM-5(2).1	**ASSESSMENT OBJECTIVE:** *Determine if:* (i) *the organization defines the frequency for conducting audits of information system changes; and* (ii) *the organization conducts audits of information system changes in accordance with the organization-defined frequency and when indications so warrant to determine whether unauthorized changes have occurred.* **POTENTIAL ASSESSMENT METHODS AND OBJECTS:** **Examine:** [*SELECT FROM:* Configuration management policy; configuration management plan; procedures addressing access restrictions for changes to the information system; information system design documentation; information system architecture and configuration documentation; security plan; change control records; information system audit records; other relevant documents or records].

CM-5(3)	ACCESS RESTRICTIONS FOR CHANGE
CM-5(3).1	**ASSESSMENT OBJECTIVE:** *Determine if:* *(i) the organization defines critical software programs that the information system will prevent from being installed if such software programs are not signed with a recognized and approved certificate; and* *(ii) the information system prevents the installation of organization-defined critical software programs that are not signed with a certificate that is recognized and approved by the organization.* **POTENTIAL ASSESSMENT METHODS AND OBJECTS:** **Examine:** [*SELECT FROM:* Configuration management policy; configuration management plan; procedures addressing access restrictions for changes to the information system; list of critical software programs to be prohibited from installation without an approved certificate; information system design documentation; information system architecture and configuration documentation; security plan; change control records; information system audit records; other relevant documents or records]. **Test:** [*SELECT FROM:* Information system mechanisms preventing installation of software programs not signed with an organization-approved certificate].

CM-5(4)	ACCESS RESTRICTIONS FOR CHANGE
CM-5(4).1	**ASSESSMENT OBJECTIVE:** *Determine if:* *(i) the organization defines information system components and system-level information requiring enforcement of a two-person rule for information system changes; and* *(ii) the organization enforces a two-person rule for changes to organization-defined information system components and system-level information.* **POTENTIAL ASSESSMENT METHODS AND OBJECTS:** **Examine:** [*SELECT FROM:* Configuration management policy; configuration management plan; procedures addressing access restrictions for changes to the information system; security plan; information system design documentation; information system architecture and configuration documentation; change control records; information system audit records; other relevant documents or records]. **Interview:** [*SELECT FROM:* Organizational personnel responsible for enforcing a two-person rule for system changes].

CM-5(5)	ACCESS RESTRICTIONS FOR CHANGE
CM-5(5).1	**ASSESSMENT OBJECTIVE:** *Determine if:* (i) *the organization limits information system developer/integrator privileges to change hardware, software, and firmware components and system information directly within a production environment;* (ii) *the organization defines the frequency for reviews and reevaluations of information system developer/integrator privileges; and* (iii) *the organization reviews and reevaluates information system developer/integrator privileges in accordance with the organization-defined frequency.* **.POTENTIAL ASSESSMENT METHODS AND OBJECTS:** **Examine**: [*SELECT FROM:* Configuration management policy; configuration management plan; procedures addressing access restrictions for changes to the information system; security plan; information system design documentation; information system architecture and configuration documentation; change control records; information system audit records; other relevant documents or records]. **Interview**: [*SELECT FROM:* Organizational personnel with logical access control responsibilities; organizational personnel with physical access control responsibilities].

CM-5(6)	ACCESS RESTRICTIONS FOR CHANGE
CM-5(6).1	**ASSESSMENT OBJECTIVE:** *Determine if the organization limits privileges to change software resident within software libraries (including privileged programs).* **POTENTIAL ASSESSMENT METHODS AND OBJECTS:** **Examine**: [*SELECT FROM:* Configuration management policy; configuration management plan; procedures addressing access restrictions for changes to the information system; information system design documentation; information system architecture and configuration documentation; change control records; information system audit records; other relevant documents or records].

CM-5(7)	ACCESS RESTRICTIONS FOR CHANGE
CM-5(7).1	**ASSESSMENT OBJECTIVE:** *Determine if:* (i) *the organization defines safeguards and countermeasures to be employed by the information system if security functions (or mechanisms) are changed inappropriately; and* (ii) *the information system automatically implements organization-defined safeguards and countermeasures if security functions (or mechanisms) are changed inappropriately.* **POTENTIAL ASSESSMENT METHODS AND OBJECTS:** **Examine**: [*SELECT FROM:* Configuration management policy; configuration management plan; procedures addressing access restrictions for changes to the information system; information system design documentation; information system architecture and configuration documentation; change control records; information system audit records; other relevant documents or records]. **Test**: [*SELECT FROM:* Information system implementing safeguards and countermeasures for inappropriate changes to security functions].

FAMILY: CONFIGURATION MANAGEMENT　　　　　　　　　　　　**CLASS:** OPERATIONAL

ASSESSMENT PROCEDURE

CM-6	CONFIGURATION SETTINGS
CM-6.1	**ASSESSMENT OBJECTIVE:** *Determine if:* *(i)　the organization defines security configuration checklists to be used to establish and document mandatory configuration settings for the information system technology products employed;* *(ii)　the organization-defined security configuration checklists reflect the most restrictive mode consistent with operational requirements;* *(iii)　the organization establishes and documents mandatory configuration settings for information technology products employed within the information system using organization-defined security configuration checklists;* *(iv)　the organization implements the security configuration settings;* *(v)　the organization identifies, documents, and approves exceptions from the mandatory configuration settings for individual components within the information system based on explicit operational requirements; and* *(vi)　the organization monitors and controls changes to the configuration settings in accordance with organizational policies and procedures.* **POTENTIAL ASSESSMENT METHODS AND OBJECTS:** **Examine:** [*SELECT FROM:* Configuration management policy; configuration management plan; procedures addressing configuration settings for the information system; security plan; information system configuration settings and associated documentation; security configuration checklists; other relevant documents or records]. **Interview:** [*SELECT FROM:* Organizational personnel with security configuration responsibilities].

CM-6(1)	CONFIGURATION SETTINGS
CM-6(1).1	**ASSESSMENT OBJECTIVE:** *Determine if the organization employs automated mechanisms to centrally manage, apply, and verify configuration settings.* **POTENTIAL ASSESSMENT METHODS AND OBJECTS:** **Examine:** [*SELECT FROM:* Configuration management policy; configuration management plan; procedures addressing configuration settings for the information system; information system design documentation; information system configuration settings and associated documentation; security configuration checklists; other relevant documents or records]. **Test:** [*SELECT FROM:* Automated mechanisms implementing the centralized management, application, and verification of configuration settings].

CM-6(2)	CONFIGURATION SETTINGS
CM-6(2).1	**ASSESSMENT OBJECTIVE:** *Determine if:* (i) *the organization defines configuration settings that, if modified by unauthorized changes, initiate the automated mechanisms to be employed to respond to such changes; and* (ii) *the organization employs automated mechanisms to respond to unauthorized changes to organization-defined configuration settings.* **POTENTIAL ASSESSMENT METHODS AND OBJECTS:** **Examine**: [*SELECT FROM*: Configuration management policy; configuration management plan; procedures addressing configuration settings for the information system; security plan; information system design documentation; information system configuration settings and associated documentation; security configuration checklists; other relevant documents or records]. **Test**: [*SELECT FROM*: Automated mechanisms implementing responses to unauthorized changes to configuration settings].

CM-6(3)	CONFIGURATION SETTINGS
CM-6(3).1	**ASSESSMENT OBJECTIVE:** *Determine if:* (i) *the organization incorporates detection of unauthorized, security-relevant configuration changes into the organization's incident response capability; and* (ii) *the organization ensures that such detected events are tracked, monitored, corrected, and available for historical purposes.* **POTENTIAL ASSESSMENT METHODS AND OBJECTS:** **Examine**: [*SELECT FROM*: Configuration management policy; configuration management plan; procedures addressing configuration settings for the information system; procedures addressing incident response planning; information system design documentation; information system configuration settings and associated documentation; incident response plan; other relevant documents or records]. **Interview**: [*SELECT FROM*: Organizational personnel with security configuration responsibilities; organization personnel with incident response planning responsibilities].

CM-6(4)	CONFIGURATION SETTINGS
CM-6(4).1	**ASSESSMENT OBJECTIVE:** *Determine if the information system (including modifications to the baseline configuration) demonstrates conformance to security configuration guidance (i.e., security checklists), prior to being introduced into a production environment.* **POTENTIAL ASSESSMENT METHODS AND OBJECTS:** **Examine**: [*SELECT FROM*: Configuration management policy; configuration management plan; procedures addressing configuration settings for the information system; information system design documentation; information system configuration settings and associated documentation; security configuration checklists; other relevant documents or records]. **Interview**: [*SELECT FROM*: Organizational personnel with security configuration responsibilities].

FAMILY: CONFIGURATION MANAGEMENT　　　　　　　　　　**CLASS:** OPERATIONAL

ASSESSMENT PROCEDURE	
CM-7	**LEAST FUNCTIONALITY**
CM-7.1	**ASSESSMENT OBJECTIVE:** *Determine if:* *(i)　the organization defines for the information system prohibited or restricted:* 　　- *functions;* 　　- *ports;* 　　- *protocols; and* 　　- *services;* *(ii)　the organization configures the information system to provide only essential capabilities; and* *(iii)　the organization configures the information system to specifically prohibit or restrict the use of organization-defined:* 　　- *functions;* 　　- *ports;* 　　- *protocols; and/or* 　　- *services.* **POTENTIAL ASSESSMENT METHODS AND OBJECTS:** **Examine:** [*SELECT FROM:* Configuration management policy; configuration management plan; procedures addressing least functionality in the information system; security plan; information system configuration settings and associated documentation; security configuration checklists; other relevant documents or records]. **Test:** [*SELECT FROM:* Information system for disabling or restricting functions, ports, protocols, and services].

CM-7(1)	LEAST FUNCTIONALITY

CM-7(1).1	**ASSESSMENT OBJECTIVE:**
	Determine if:
	
	(i) *the organization defines the frequency of information system reviews to identify and eliminate unnecessary:*
	   - *functions;*
	   - *ports;*
	   - *protocols; and/or*
	   - *services; and*
	
	(ii) *the organization reviews the information system in accordance with organization-defined frequency to identify and eliminate unnecessary:*
	   - *functions;*
	   - *ports;*
	   - *protocols; and/or*
	   - *services.*
	
	POTENTIAL ASSESSMENT METHODS AND OBJECTS:
	
	Examine: [*SELECT FROM:* Configuration management policy; configuration management plan; procedures addressing least functionality in the information system; security plan; information system configuration settings and associated documentation; security configuration checklists; other relevant documents or records].
	
	Interview: [*SELECT FROM:* Organizational personnel with responsibilities for identifying and eliminating unnecessary functions, ports, protocols, and services on the information system].

CM-7(2)	LEAST FUNCTIONALITY

CM-7(2).1	**ASSESSMENT OBJECTIVE:**
	Determine if:
	
	(i) *the organization develops and maintains one or more of the following specifications to prevent software program execution on the information system:*
	   - *a list of software programs authorized to execute on the information system;*
	   - *a list of software programs not authorized to execute on the information system; and/or*
	   - *rules authorizing the terms and conditions of software program usage on the information system; and*
	
	(ii) *the organization employs automated mechanisms to prevent software program execution on the information system in accordance with the organization-defined specifications.*
	
	POTENTIAL ASSESSMENT METHODS AND OBJECTS:
	
	Examine: [*SELECT FROM:* Configuration management policy; configuration management plan; procedures addressing least functionality in the information system; security plan; information system design documentation; specification of preventing software program execution; information system configuration settings and associated documentation; other relevant documents or records].
	
	Test: [*SELECT FROM:* Automated mechanisms preventing software program execution on the information system].

CM-7(3)	LEAST FUNCTIONALITY
CM-7(3).1	**ASSESSMENT OBJECTIVE:** *Determine if:* *(i) the organization defines registration requirements for:* - *ports;* - *protocols; and* - *services; and* *(ii) the organization ensures compliance with organization-defined registration requirements for:* - *ports;* - *protocols; and* - *services.* **POTENTIAL ASSESSMENT METHODS AND OBJECTS:** **Examine:** [*SELECT FROM:* Configuration management policy; configuration management plan; procedures addressing least functionality in the information system; security plan; information system configuration settings and associated documentation; other relevant documents or records].

FAMILY: CONFIGURATION MANAGEMENT   **CLASS:** OPERATIONAL

ASSESSMENT PROCEDURE

CM-8	INFORMATION SYSTEM COMPONENT INVENTORY

CM-8.1	**ASSESSMENT OBJECTIVE:**
	Determine if:
	
	(i) the organization defines information deemed necessary to achieve effective property accountability; and
	
	(ii) the organization develops, documents, and maintains an inventory of information system components that:
	
	    - *accurately reflects the current information system;*
	
	    - *is consistent with the authorization boundary of the information system;*
	
	    - *is at the level of granularity deemed necessary for tracking and reporting;*
	
	    - *includes organization-defined information deemed necessary to achieve effective property accountability; and*
	
	    - *is available for review and audit by designated organizational officials.*
	
	POTENTIAL ASSESSMENT METHODS AND OBJECTS:
	Examine: [*SELECT FROM:* Configuration management policy; configuration management plan; procedures addressing information system component inventory; security plan; information system inventory records; other relevant documents or records].

CM-8(1)	INFORMATION SYSTEM COMPONENT INVENTORY
CM-8(1).1	**ASSESSMENT OBJECTIVE:** *Determine if the organization updates the inventory of information system components as an integral part of component:* – *installations;* – *removals; and* – *information system updates.* **POTENTIAL ASSESSMENT METHODS AND OBJECTS:** **Examine:** [*SELECT FROM:* Configuration management policy; configuration management plan; procedures addressing information system component inventory; information system inventory records; component installation records; other relevant documents or records]. **Interview:** [*SELECT FROM:* Organizational personnel with information system installation and inventory responsibilities].

CM-8(2)	INFORMATION SYSTEM COMPONENT INVENTORY
CM-8(2).1	**ASSESSMENT OBJECTIVE:** *Determine if the organization employs automated mechanisms to maintain an up-to-date, complete, accurate, and readily available inventory of information system components.* **POTENTIAL ASSESSMENT METHODS AND OBJECTS:** **Examine**: [*SELECT FROM:* Configuration management policy; configuration management plan; procedures addressing information system component inventory; information system design documentation; information system inventory records; component installation records; other relevant documents or records]. **Test**: [*SELECT FROM:* Automated mechanisms implementing information system component inventory management].

CM-8(3)	INFORMATION SYSTEM COMPONENT INVENTORY
CM-8(3).1	**ASSESSMENT OBJECTIVE:** *Determine if:* (i) *the organization defines the frequency of employing automated mechanisms to detect the addition of unauthorized components/devices into the information system;* (ii) *the organization employs automated mechanisms, in accordance with the organization-defined frequency, to detect the addition of unauthorized components/devices into the information system; and* (iii) *the organization disables network access by such components/devices or notifies designated organizational officials.* **POTENTIAL ASSESSMENT METHODS AND OBJECTS:** **Examine**: [*SELECT FROM:* Configuration management policy; configuration management plan; procedures addressing information system component inventory; security plan; information system design documentation; information system inventory records; component installation records; change control records; other relevant documents or records]. **Test**: [*SELECT FROM:* Automated mechanisms for detecting unauthorized components/devices on the information system].

CM-8(4)	INFORMATION SYSTEM COMPONENT INVENTORY
CM-8(4).1	**ASSESSMENT OBJECTIVE:** *Determine if the organization includes in property accountability information for information system components, a means for identifying by name, position, or role, individuals responsible for administering those components.* **POTENTIAL ASSESSMENT METHODS AND OBJECTS:** **Examine**: [*SELECT FROM:* Configuration management policy; configuration management plan; procedures addressing information system component inventory; information system inventory records; component installation records; other relevant documents or records].

CM-8(5)	INFORMATION SYSTEM COMPONENT INVENTORY
CM-8(5).1	**ASSESSMENT OBJECTIVE:** *Determine if the organization verifies that all components within the authorization boundary of the information system are either inventoried as a part of the system or recognized by another system as a component within that system.* **POTENTIAL ASSESSMENT METHODS AND OBJECTS:** **Examine:** [*SELECT FROM:* Configuration management policy; configuration management plan; procedures addressing information system component inventory; security plan; information system inventory records; component installation records; other relevant documents or records]. **Interview:** [*SELECT FROM:* Organizational personnel with information system inventory responsibilities; organizational personnel with responsibilities for defining information system components within the authorization boundary of the system].

CM-8(6)	INFORMATION SYSTEM COMPONENT INVENTORY
CM-8(6).1	**ASSESSMENT OBJECTIVE:** *Determine if the organization includes assessed component configurations and any approved deviations to current deployed configurations in the information system component inventory.* **POTENTIAL ASSESSMENT METHODS AND OBJECTS:** **Examine:** [*SELECT FROM:* Configuration management policy; configuration management plan; procedures addressing information system component inventory; information system design documentation; information system inventory records; component installation records; other relevant documents or records]. **Interview:** [*SELECT FROM:* Organizational personnel with inventory management and assessment responsibilities for information system components].

FAMILY: CONFIGURATION MANAGEMENT

CLASS: OPERATIONAL

ASSESSMENT PROCEDURE

CM-9	CONFIGURATION MANAGEMENT PLAN
CM-9.1	**ASSESSMENT OBJECTIVE:** *Determine if the organization develops, documents, and implements a configuration management plan for the information system that:* – *addresses roles, responsibilities, and configuration management processes and procedures;* – *defines the configuration items for the information system and when in the system development life cycle the configuration items are placed under configuration management; and* – *establishes the means for identifying configuration items throughout the system development life cycle and a process for managing the configuration of the configuration items.* **POTENTIAL ASSESSMENT METHODS AND OBJECTS:** **Examine:** [*SELECT FROM:* Configuration management policy; configuration management plan; procedures addressing configuration management planning; security plan; other relevant documents or records].

CM-9(1)	CONFIGURATION MANAGEMENT PLAN
CM-9(1).1	**ASSESSMENT OBJECTIVE:** *Determine if the organization assigns responsibility for developing the configuration management process to organizational personnel that are not directly involved in system development.* **POTENTIAL ASSESSMENT METHODS AND OBJECTS:** **Examine:** [*SELECT FROM:* Configuration management policy; configuration management plan; procedures addressing responsibilities for configuration management process development; security plan other relevant documents or records]. **Interview:** [*SELECT FROM:* Organizational personnel with responsibilities for configuration management process development].

FAMILY: CONTINGENCY PLANNING   **CLASS:** OPERATIONAL

ASSESSMENT PROCEDURE	
CP-1	**CONTINGENCY PLANNING POLICY AND PROCEDURES**

CP-1.1	**ASSESSMENT OBJECTIVE:**
	Determine if:
	(i) the organization develops and formally documents contingency planning policy;
	(ii) the organization contingency planning policy addresses:
	    - *purpose;*
	    - *scope;*
	    - *roles and responsibilities;*
	    - *management commitment;*
	    - *coordination among organizational entities; and*
	    - *compliance;*
	(iii) the organization disseminates formal documented contingency planning policy to elements within the organization having associated contingency planning roles and responsibilities;
	(iv) the organization develops and formally documents contingency planning procedures;
	(v) the organization contingency planning procedures facilitate implementation of the contingency planning policy and associated contingency planning controls; and
	(vi) the organization disseminates formal documented contingency planning procedures to elements within the organization having associated contingency planning roles and responsibilities.
	
	POTENTIAL ASSESSMENT METHODS AND OBJECTS:
	Examine: [*SELECT FROM:* Contingency planning policy and procedures; other relevant documents or records].
	Interview: [*SELECT FROM:* Organizational personnel with contingency planning responsibilities].

CP-1.2	**ASSESSMENT OBJECTIVE:** *Determine if:* *(i) the organization defines the frequency of contingency planning policy reviews/updates;* *(ii) the organization reviews/updates contingency planning policy in accordance with organization-defined frequency;* *(iii) the organization defines the frequency of contingency planning procedure reviews/updates; and* *(iv) the organization reviews/updates contingency planning procedures in accordance with organization-defined frequency.* **POTENTIAL ASSESSMENT METHODS AND OBJECTS:** **Examine:** [*SELECT FROM:* Contingency planning policy and procedures; other relevant documents or records]. **Interview:** [*SELECT FROM:* Organizational personnel with contingency planning responsibilities].

FAMILY: CONTINGENCY PLANNING   **CLASS:** OPERATIONAL

ASSESSMENT PROCEDURE	
CP-2	**CONTINGENCY PLAN**

CP-2.1	**ASSESSMENT OBJECTIVE:**
	Determine if:
	
	(i) the organization develops a contingency plan for the information system that:
	  - identifies essential missions and business functions and associated contingency requirements;
	  - provides recovery objectives, restoration priorities, and metrics;
	  - addresses contingency roles, responsibilities, assigned individuals with contact information;
	  - addresses maintaining essential missions and business functions despite an information system disruption, compromise, or failure; and
	  - addresses eventual, full information system restoration without deterioration of the security measures originally planned and implemented; and
	  - is reviewed and approved by designated officials within the organization;
	
	(ii) the organization defines key contingency personnel (identified by name and/or by role) and organizational elements designated to receive copies of the contingency plan; and
	
	(iii) the organization distributes copies of the contingency plan to organization-defined key contingency personnel and organizational elements.
	
	POTENTIAL ASSESSMENT METHODS AND OBJECTS:
	
	Examine: [*SELECT FROM:* Contingency planning policy; procedures addressing contingency operations for the information system; contingency plan; security plan; other relevant documents or records].
	
	Interview: [*SELECT FROM:* Organizational personnel with contingency planning and plan implementation responsibilities].

CP-2.2	**ASSESSMENT OBJECTIVE:** *Determine if:* *(i) the organization coordinates contingency planning activities with incident handling activities:* *(ii) the organization defines the frequency of contingency plan reviews;* *(iii) the organization reviews the contingency plan for the information system in accordance with the organization-defined frequency;* *(iv) the organization revises the contingency plan to address changes to the organization, information system, or environment of operation and problems encountered during contingency plan implementation, execution or testing; and* *(v) the organization communicates contingency plan changes to the key contingency personnel and organizational elements as identified in CP-2.1 (ii).* **POTENTIAL ASSESSMENT METHODS AND OBJECTS:** **Examine**: [*SELECT FROM:* Contingency planning policy; procedures addressing contingency operations for the information system; contingency plan; security plan; other relevant documents or records]. **Interview**: [*SELECT FROM:* Organizational personnel with contingency planning and plan implementation responsibilities; organizational personnel with incident handling responsibilities].

CP-2(1)	CONTINGENCY PLAN
CP-2(1).1	**ASSESSMENT OBJECTIVE:** *Determine if the organization coordinates the contingency plan development with other organizational elements responsible for related plans.* **Examine:** [*SELECT FROM:* Contingency planning policy; procedures addressing contingency operations for the information system; contingency plan; other related plans; other relevant documents or records]. **Interview:** [*SELECT FROM:* Organizational personnel with contingency planning and plan implementation responsibilities and responsibilities in related plan areas].

CP-2(2)	CONTINGENCY PLAN
CP-2(2).1	**ASSESSMENT OBJECTIVE:** *Determine if the organization conducts capacity planning so that necessary capacity for information processing, telecommunications, and environmental support exists during contingency operations.* **POTENTIAL ASSESSMENT METHODS AND OBJECTS:** **Examine:** [*SELECT FROM:* Contingency planning policy; procedures addressing contingency operations for the information system; contingency plan; capacity planning documents; other relevant documents or records]. **Interview:** [*SELECT FROM:* Organizational personnel with contingency planning and plan implementation responsibilities].

CP-2(3)	CONTINGENCY PLAN
CP-2(3).1	**ASSESSMENT OBJECTIVE:** *Determine if:* *(i) the organization defines the time period for planning the resumption of essential missions and business functions as a result of contingency plan activation; and* *(ii) the organization plans for the resumption of essential missions and business function within organization-defined time period of contingency plan activation.* **POTENTIAL ASSESSMENT METHODS AND OBJECTS:** **Examine:** [*SELECT FROM:* Contingency planning policy; procedures addressing contingency operations for the information system; contingency plan; security plan; business impact assessment; other related plans; other relevant documents or records]. **Interview:** [*SELECT FROM:* Organizational personnel with contingency planning and plan implementation responsibilities].

CP-2(4)	CONTINGENCY PLAN
CP-2(4).1	**ASSESSMENT OBJECTIVE:** *Determine if:* (i) the organization defines the time period for planning the full resumption of affected missions and business functions as a result of contingency plan activation; and (ii) the organization plans for the full resumption of affected missions and business functions within organization-defined time period of contingency plan activation. **POTENTIAL ASSESSMENT METHODS AND OBJECTS:** **Examine:** [*SELECT FROM:* Contingency planning policy; procedures addressing contingency operations for the information system; contingency plan; security plan; business impact assessment; other relevant documents or records]. **Interview:** [*SELECT FROM:* Organizational personnel with contingency planning and plan implementation responsibilities].

CP-2(5)	CONTINGENCY PLAN
CP-2(5).1	**ASSESSMENT OBJECTIVE:** *Determine if:* (i) the organization plans for the continuance of essential missions and business functions with little or no loss of operational continuity; and (ii) the organization sustains operational continuity until full information system restoration at primary processing and/or storage sites. **POTENTIAL ASSESSMENT METHODS AND OBJECTS:** **Examine:** [*SELECT FROM:* Contingency planning policy; procedures addressing contingency operations for the information system; contingency plan; business impact assessment; other relevant documents or records]. **Interview:** [*SELECT FROM:* Organizational personnel with contingency planning and plan implementation responsibilities].

CP-2(6)	CONTINGENCY PLAN
CP-2(6).1	**ASSESSMENT OBJECTIVE:** *Determine if:* (i) the organization provides for the transfer of all essential missions and business functions to alternate processing and/or storage sites with little or no loss of operational continuity; and (ii) the organization sustains operational continuity through restoration to primary processing and/or storage sites. **POTENTIAL ASSESSMENT METHODS AND OBJECTS:** **Examine:** [*SELECT FROM:* Contingency planning policy; procedures addressing contingency operations for the information system; contingency plan; alternate processing site agreements; alternate storage site agreements; contingency plan testing and/or exercise documentation; contingency plan test results; other relevant documents or records]. **Interview:** [*SELECT FROM:* Organizational personnel with contingency planning and plan implementation responsibilities].

FAMILY: CONTINGENCY PLANNING   **CLASS:** OPERATIONAL

ASSESSMENT PROCEDURE	
CP-3	**CONTINGENCY TRAINING**
CP-3.1	**ASSESSMENT OBJECTIVE:** *Determine if:* (i) *the organization provides initial contingency training to personnel with contingency roles and responsibilities with respect to the information system;* (ii) *the organization defines the frequency of refresher contingency training; and* (iii) *the organization provides refresher training in accordance with organization-defined frequency.* **POTENTIAL ASSESSMENT METHODS AND OBJECTS:** **Examine:** [*SELECT FROM:* Contingency planning policy; contingency plan; procedures addressing contingency training; contingency training curriculum; contingency training material; security plan; contingency training records; other relevant documents or records]. **Interview:** [*SELECT FROM:* Organizational personnel with contingency planning, plan implementation, and training responsibilities].

CP-3(1)	**CONTINGENCY TRAINING**
CP-3(1).1	**ASSESSMENT OBJECTIVE:** *Determine if:* (i) *the organization incorporates simulated events into contingency training; and* (ii) *the incorporation of simulated events into contingency training facilitates effective response by personnel in crisis situations.* **POTENTIAL ASSESSMENT METHODS AND OBJECTS:** **Examine:** [*SELECT FROM:* Contingency planning policy; contingency plan; procedures addressing contingency training; contingency training curriculum; contingency training material; other relevant documents or records]. **Interview:** [*SELECT FROM:* Organizational personnel with contingency planning, plan implementation, and training responsibilities].

CP-3(2)	**CONTINGENCY TRAINING**
CP-3(2).1	**ASSESSMENT OBJECTIVE:** *Determine if the organization employs automated mechanisms that provide a more thorough and realistic contingency training environment.* **POTENTIAL ASSESSMENT METHODS AND OBJECTS:** **Examine:** [*SELECT FROM:* Contingency planning policy; contingency plan; procedures addressing contingency training; automated mechanisms supporting contingency training; contingency training curriculum; contingency training material; other relevant documents or records]. **Interview:** [*SELECT FROM:* Organizational personnel with contingency planning, plan implementation, and training responsibilities].

FAMILY: CONTINGENCY PLANNING   **CLASS:** OPERATIONAL

ASSESSMENT PROCEDURE
CP-4	**CONTINGENCY PLAN TESTING AND EXERCISES**

| CP-4.1 | **ASSESSMENT OBJECTIVE:**
Determine if:

(i)   the organization defines the contingency plan tests and/or exercises to be conducted;

(ii) the organization defines the frequency of contingency plan tests and/or exercises;

(iii) the organization tests/exercises the contingency plan using organization-defined tests/exercises in accordance with organization-defined frequency; and

(iv) the organization reviews the contingency plan test/exercise results and takes corrective actions.

POTENTIAL ASSESSMENT METHODS AND OBJECTS:
Examine: [*SELECT FROM:* Contingency planning policy; contingency plan, procedures addressing contingency plan testing and exercises; security plan; contingency plan testing and/or exercise documentation; other relevant documents or records].
Interview: [*SELECT FROM:* Organizational personnel with responsibilities for reviewing or responding to contingency plan tests/exercises]. |

| **CP-4(1)** | **CONTINGENCY PLAN TESTING AND EXERCISES** |

| CP-4(1).1 | **ASSESSMENT OBJECTIVE:**
Determine if the organization coordinates contingency plan testing and/or exercises with organizational elements responsible for related plans.

POTENTIAL ASSESSMENT METHODS AND OBJECTS:
Examine: [*SELECT FROM:* Contingency planning policy; contingency plan; procedures addressing contingency plan testing and exercises; contingency plan testing and/or exercise documentation; other relevant documents or records].
Interview: [*SELECT FROM:* Organizational personnel with contingency planning, plan implementation, and testing responsibilities; organizational personnel with responsibilities for related plans]. |

| **CP-4(2)** | **CONTINGENCY PLAN TESTING AND EXERCISES** |

| CP-4(2).1 | **ASSESSMENT OBJECTIVE:**
Determine if the organization conducts contingency plan testing/exercises at the alternate processing site to familiarize contingency personnel with the facility and available resources and to evaluate the site's capabilities to support contingency operations.

POTENTIAL ASSESSMENT METHODS AND OBJECTS:
Examine: [*SELECT FROM:* Contingency planning policy; contingency plan, procedures addressing contingency plan testing and exercises; contingency plan testing and/or exercise documentation; contingency plan test results; other relevant documents or records]. |

CP-4(3)	CONTINGENCY PLAN TESTING AND EXERCISES
CP-4(3).1	**ASSESSMENT OBJECTIVE:** *Determine if the organization employs automated mechanisms to more thoroughly and effectively test/exercise the contingency plan by providing more complete coverage of contingency issues, selecting more realistic test/exercise scenarios and environments, and more effectively stressing the information system and supported missions.* **POTENTIAL ASSESSMENT METHODS AND OBJECTS:** **Examine:** [*SELECT FROM:* Contingency planning policy; contingency plan; procedures addressing contingency plan testing and exercises; automated mechanisms supporting contingency plan testing/exercises; contingency plan testing and/or exercise documentation; other relevant documents or records].

CP-4(4)	CONTINGENCY PLAN TESTING AND EXERCISES
CP-4(4).1	**ASSESSMENT OBJECTIVE:** *Determine if the organization includes a full recovery and reconstitution of the information system to a known state as part of contingency plan testing.* **POTENTIAL ASSESSMENT METHODS AND OBJECTS:** **Examine:** [*SELECT FROM:* Contingency planning policy; contingency plan; procedures addressing information system recovery and reconstitution; contingency plan testing and/or exercise documentation; contingency plan test results; other relevant documents or records]. **Interview:** [*SELECT FROM:* Organizational personnel with information system recovery and reconstitution responsibilities; organizational personnel with contingency plan testing and/or exercise responsibilities].

FAMILY: CONTINGENCY PLANNING   **CLASS:** OPERATIONAL

ASSESSMENT PROCEDURE	
CP-5	**CONTINGENCY PLAN UPDATE** [Withdrawn: Incorporated into CP-2].
CP-5.1	**ASSESSMENT OBJECTIVE:** [Withdrawn: Incorporated into CP-2]. **POTENTIAL ASSESSMENT METHODS AND OBJECTS:** [Withdrawn: Incorporated into CP-2].
CP-5.2	**ASSESSMENT OBJECTIVE:** [Withdrawn: Incorporated into CP-2]. **POTENTIAL ASSESSMENT METHODS AND OBJECTS:** [Withdrawn: Incorporated into CP-2].

FAMILY: CONTINGENCY PLANNING   **CLASS:** OPERATIONAL

ASSESSMENT PROCEDURE	
CP-6	**ALTERNATE STORAGE SITE**
CP-6.1	**ASSESSMENT OBJECTIVE:** *Determine if :* *(i) the organization establishes an alternate storage site; and* *(ii) the organization initiates necessary alternate storage site agreements to permit the storage and recovery of information system backup information.* **POTENTIAL ASSESSMENT METHODS AND OBJECTS:** **Examine:** [*SELECT FROM:* Contingency planning policy; contingency plan; procedures addressing alternate storage sites; alternate storage site agreements; other relevant documents or records].

CP-6(1)	**ALTERNATE STORAGE SITE**
CP-6(1).1	**ASSESSMENT OBJECTIVE:** *Determine if:* *(i) the contingency plan identifies the primary storage site hazards; and* *(ii) the alternate storage site is separated from the primary storage site so as not to be susceptible to the same hazards identified at the primary site.* **POTENTIAL ASSESSMENT METHODS AND OBJECTS:** **Examine:** [*SELECT FROM:* Contingency planning policy; contingency plan; procedures addressing alternate storage sites; alternate storage site; other relevant documents or records].

CP-6(2)	**ALTERNATE STORAGE SITE**
CP-6(2).1	**ASSESSMENT OBJECTIVE:** *Determine if the alternate storage site is configured to facilitate recovery operations in accordance with recovery time objectives and recovery point objectives.* **POTENTIAL ASSESSMENT METHODS AND OBJECTS:** **Examine:** [*SELECT FROM:* Contingency planning policy; contingency plan; procedures addressing alternate storage sites; alternate storage site agreements; alternate storage site; other relevant documents or records].

CP-6(3)	ALTERNATE STORAGE SITE
CP-6(3).1	**ASSESSMENT OBJECTIVE:** *Determine if:* (i) *the organization identifies potential accessibility problems to the alternate storage site in the event of an area-wide disruption or disaster; and* (ii) *the organization outlines explicit mitigation actions for organization identified accessibility problems to the alternate storage site in the event of an area-wide disruption or disaster.* **POTENTIAL ASSESSMENT METHODS AND OBJECTS:** **Examine:** [*SELECT FROM:* Contingency planning policy; contingency plan; procedures addressing alternate storage sites; alternate storage site; mitigation actions for accessibility problems to the alternate storage site; other relevant documents or records].

FAMILY: CONTINGENCY PLANNING   **CLASS:** OPERATIONAL

ASSESSMENT PROCEDURE	
CP-7	**ALTERNATE PROCESSING SITE**
CP-7.1	**ASSESSMENT OBJECTIVE:** *Determine if:* (i) *the organization establishes an alternate processing site;* (ii) *the organization defines the time period for achieving the recovery time objectives within which processing must be resumed at the alternate processing site;* (iii) *the organization includes necessary alternate processing site agreements to permit the resumption of information system operations for essential missions and business functions within organization-defined time period; and* (iv) *the equipment and supplies required to resume operations are available at the alternate site or contracts are in place to support delivery to the site in time to support the organization-defined time period for resumption.* **POTENTIAL ASSESSMENT METHODS AND OBJECTS:** **Examine:** [*SELECT FROM:* Contingency planning policy; contingency plan; procedures addressing alternate processing sites; alternate processing site agreements; security plan; spare equipment and supplies at alternate processing site; equipment and supply contracts; service level agreements; other relevant documents or records].

CP-7(1)	**ALTERNATE PROCESSING SITE**
CP-7(1).1	**ASSESSMENT OBJECTIVE:** *Determine if:* (i) *the contingency plan identifies the primary processing site hazards; and* (ii) *the alternate processing site is separated from the primary processing site so as not to be susceptible to the same hazards identified at the primary site.* **POTENTIAL ASSESSMENT METHODS AND OBJECTS:** **Examine:** [*SELECT FROM:* Contingency planning policy; contingency plan; procedures addressing alternate processing sites; alternate processing site; other relevant documents or records].

CP-7(2)	**ALTERNATE PROCESSING SITE**
CP-7(2).1	**ASSESSMENT OBJECTIVE:** *Determine if:* (i) *the organization identifies potential accessibility problems to the alternate processing site in the event of an area-wide disruption or disaster; and* (ii) *the organization outlines explicit mitigation actions for organization identified accessibility problems to the alternate processing site in the event of an area-wide disruption or disaster.* **POTENTIAL ASSESSMENT METHODS AND OBJECTS:** **Examine:** [*SELECT FROM:* Contingency planning policy; contingency plan; procedures addressing alternate processing sites; alternate processing site; other relevant documents or records].

CP-7(3)	ALTERNATE PROCESSING SITE
CP-7(3).1	**ASSESSMENT OBJECTIVE:** *Determine if the organization develops alternate processing site agreements that contain priority-of-service provisions in accordance with the organization's availability requirements.* **POTENTIAL ASSESSMENT METHODS AND OBJECTS:** **Examine:** [*SELECT FROM:* Contingency planning policy; contingency plan; procedures addressing alternate processing sites; alternate processing site agreements; other relevant documents or records].

CP-7(4)	ALTERNATE PROCESSING SITE
CP-7(4).1	**ASSESSMENT OBJECTIVE:** *Determine if the alternate processing site is configured so that it is ready to be used as the operational site to support essential missions and business functions.* **POTENTIAL ASSESSMENT METHODS AND OBJECTS:** **Examine:** [*SELECT FROM:* Contingency planning policy; contingency plan; procedures addressing alternate processing sites; alternate processing site; alternate processing site agreements; other relevant documents or records]. **Test:** [*SELECT FROM:* Information system at the alternate processing site].

CP-7(5)	ALTERNATE PROCESSING SITE
CP-7(5).1	**ASSESSMENT OBJECTIVE:** *Determine if the alternate processing site provides information security measures equivalent to that of the primary site.* **POTENTIAL ASSESSMENT METHODS AND OBJECTS:** **Examine:** [*SELECT FROM:* Contingency planning policy; contingency plan; procedures addressing alternate processing sites; alternate processing site; other relevant documents or records].

FAMILY: CONTINGENCY PLANNING   **CLASS:** OPERATIONAL

ASSESSMENT PROCEDURE	
CP-8	**TELECOMMUNICATIONS SERVICES**
CP-8.1	**ASSESSMENT OBJECTIVE:** *Determine if:* *(i) the organization establishes alternate telecommunications services to support the information system;* *(ii) the organization defines in the time period within which resumption of information system operations must take place; and* *(iii) the organization establishes necessary alternate telecommunications service agreements to permit the resumption of telecommunications services for essential missions and business functions within the organization-defined time period when the primary telecommunications capabilities are unavailable.* **POTENTIAL ASSESSMENT METHODS AND OBJECTS:** **Examine:** [*SELECT FROM:* Contingency planning policy; contingency plan; procedures addressing alternate telecommunications services; security plan; primary and alternate telecommunications service agreements; list of essential missions and business functions; other relevant documents or records].

CP-8(1)	**TELECOMMUNICATIONS SERVICES**
CP-8(1).1	**ASSESSMENT OBJECTIVE:** *Determine if:* *(i) the organization develops primary and alternate telecommunications service agreements that contain priority-of-service provisions in accordance with organizational availability requirements; and* *(ii) the organization requests Telecommunications Service Priority for all telecommunications services used for national security emergency preparedness in the event that the primary and/or alternate telecommunications services are provided by a common carrier.* **POTENTIAL ASSESSMENT METHODS AND OBJECTS:** **Examine:** [*SELECT FROM:* Contingency planning policy; contingency plan; procedures addressing alternate telecommunications services; primary and alternate telecommunications service agreements; Telecommunications Service Priority documentation; other relevant documents or records].

CP-8(2)	TELECOMMUNICATIONS SERVICES
CP-8(2).1	**ASSESSMENT OBJECTIVE:** *Determine if the organization obtains alternate telecommunications services with consideration for reducing the likelihood of sharing a single point of failure with primary telecommunications services.* **POTENTIAL ASSESSMENT METHODS AND OBJECTS:** **Examine:** [*SELECT FROM:* Contingency planning policy; contingency plan; procedures addressing alternate telecommunications services; primary and alternate telecommunications service agreements; other relevant documents or records]. **Interview:** [*SELECT FROM:* Organizational personnel with contingency planning and plan implementation responsibilities; telecommunications service providers].

CP-8(3)	TELECOMMUNICATIONS SERVICES
CP-8(3).1	**ASSESSMENT OBJECTIVE:** *Determine if:* (i) *the organization identifies the primary provider's telecommunications service hazards; and* (ii) *the alternate telecommunications service providers are separated from the primary telecommunications service providers so as not to be susceptible to the same hazards.* **POTENTIAL ASSESSMENT METHODS AND OBJECTS:** **Examine:** [*SELECT FROM:* Contingency planning policy; contingency plan; procedures addressing alternate telecommunications services; primary and alternate telecommunications service agreements; alternate telecommunications service provider's site; primary telecommunications service provider's site; other relevant documents or records]. **Interview:** [*SELECT FROM:* Organizational personnel with contingency planning and plan implementation responsibilities; telecommunications service providers].

CP-8(4)	TELECOMMUNICATIONS SERVICES
CP-8(4).1	**ASSESSMENT OBJECTIVE:** *Determine if the organization requires primary and alternate telecommunications service providers to have contingency plans.* **POTENTIAL ASSESSMENT METHODS AND OBJECTS:** **Examine:** [*SELECT FROM:* Contingency planning policy; contingency plan; procedures addressing alternate telecommunications services; primary and alternate telecommunications service agreements; other relevant documents or records]. **Interview:** [*SELECT FROM:* Organizational personnel with contingency planning, plan implementation, and testing responsibilities; telecommunications service providers].

FAMILY: CONTINGENCY PLANNING   **CLASS:** OPERATIONAL

ASSESSMENT PROCEDURE	
CP-9	**INFORMATION SYSTEM BACKUP**
CP-9.1	**ASSESSMENT OBJECTIVE:** *Determine if:* (i) *the organization defines the frequency of conducting user-level information backups to support recovery time objectives and recovery point objectives;* (ii) *the organization defines the frequency of conducting system-level information backups to support recovery time objectives and recovery point objectives;* (iii) *the organization defines the frequency of conducting information system documentation backups (including security-related information) to support recovery time objectives and recovery point objectives;* (iv) *the organization backs up user-level information in accordance with the organization-defined frequency;* (v) *the organization backs up system-level information in accordance with the organization-defined frequency; and* (vi) *the organization backs up information system documentation in accordance with the organization-defined frequency.* **POTENTIAL ASSESSMENT METHODS AND OBJECTS:** **Examine:** [*SELECT FROM:* Contingency planning policy; contingency plan; procedures addressing information system backup; security plan; backup storage location(s); information system backup logs or records; other relevant documents or records]. **Interview:** [*SELECT FROM:* Organizational personnel with information system backup responsibilities].
CP-9.2	**ASSESSMENT OBJECTIVE:** *Determine if the organization protects the confidentiality and integrity of backup information at the storage location.* **POTENTIAL ASSESSMENT METHODS AND OBJECTS:** **Examine:** [*SELECT FROM:* Contingency planning policy; contingency plan; procedures addressing information system backup; information system design documentation; information system configuration settings and associated documentation; backup storage location(s); other relevant documents or records]. **Interview:** [*SELECT FROM:* Organizational personnel with information system backup responsibilities].

CP-9(1)	INFORMATION SYSTEM BACKUP
CP-9(1).1	**ASSESSMENT OBJECTIVE:** *Determine if:* *(i) the organization defines the frequency of information system backup testing; and* *(ii) the organization conducts information system backup testing in accordance with organization-defined frequency to verify backup media reliability and information integrity.* **POTENTIAL ASSESSMENT METHODS AND OBJECTS:** **Examine:** [*SELECT FROM:* Contingency planning policy; contingency plan; procedures addressing information system backup; security plan; information system backup test results; backup storage location(s); other relevant documents or records].

CP-9(2)	INFORMATION SYSTEM BACKUP
CP-9(2).1	**ASSESSMENT OBJECTIVE:** *Determine if the organization uses a sample of backup information in the restoration of selected information system functions as part of contingency plan testing.* **POTENTIAL ASSESSMENT METHODS AND OBJECTS:** **Examine:** [*SELECT FROM:* Contingency planning policy; contingency plan; procedures addressing information system backup; information system backup test results; contingency plan testing and/or exercise documentation; contingency plan test results; other relevant documents or records].

CP-9(3)	INFORMATION SYSTEM BACKUP
CP-9(3).1	**ASSESSMENT OBJECTIVE:** *Determine if the organization stores backup copies of operating system and other critical information system software, as well as copies of the information system inventory (including hardware, software, and firmware components) in a separate facility or in a fire-rated container that is not collocated with the operational system.* **POTENTIAL ASSESSMENT METHODS AND OBJECTS:** **Examine:** [*SELECT FROM:* Contingency planning policy; contingency plan; procedures addressing information system backup; backup storage location(s); other relevant documents or records]. **Interview:** [*SELECT FROM:* Organizational personnel with contingency planning and plan implementation responsibilities; organizational personnel with information system backup responsibilities].

CP-9(4)	INFORMATION SYSTEM BACKUP [Withdrawn: Incorporated into CP-9].
CP-9(4).1	**ASSESSMENT OBJECTIVE:** [Withdrawn: Incorporated into CP-9]. **POTENTIAL ASSESSMENT METHODS AND OBJECTS:** [Withdrawn: Incorporated into CP-9].

CP-9(5)	INFORMATION SYSTEM BACKUP
CP-9(5).1	**ASSESSMENT OBJECTIVE:** *Determine if:* (i) *the organization defines the time period and rate of transferring information system backup information to the alternate storage site to support recovery time objectives and recovery point objectives; and* (ii) *the organization transfers information system backup information to the alternate storage site in accordance with the organization-defined frequency and transfer rate.* **POTENTIAL ASSESSMENT METHODS AND OBJECTS:** **Examine:** [*SELECT FROM:* Contingency planning policy; contingency plan; procedures addressing information system backup; security plan; information system backup test results; alternate site service agreements; backup storage location(s); other relevant documents or records].

CP-9(6)	INFORMATION SYSTEM BACKUP
CP-9(6).1	**ASSESSMENT OBJECTIVE:** *Determine if:* (i) *the organization maintains a redundant, secondary backup system that is not collocated with the primary backup system for the information system; and* (ii) *the redundant, secondary backup system can be activated to accomplish information system backups without causing loss of information or disruption to the operation.* **POTENTIAL ASSESSMENT METHODS AND OBJECTS:** **Examine:** [*SELECT FROM:* Contingency planning policy; contingency plan; procedures addressing information system backup; information system backup test results; contingency plan test results; contingency plan testing and/or exercise documentation; secondary backup storage location(s); redundant secondary system for information system backups; other relevant documents or records].

FAMILY: CONTINGENCY PLANNING   **CLASS:** OPERATIONAL

ASSESSMENT PROCEDURE
CP-10	**INFORMATION SYSTEM RECOVERY AND RECONSTITUTION**

| CP-10.1 | **ASSESSMENT OBJECTIVE:**
Determine if the organization provides automated mechanisms and/or manual procedures for the recovery and reconstitution of the information system to known state after a disruption, compromise, or failure.

POTENTIAL ASSESSMENT METHODS AND OBJECTS:
Examine: [*SELECT FROM:* Contingency planning policy; contingency plan; procedures addressing information system recovery and reconstitution; information system configuration settings and associated documentation; information system design documentation; other relevant documents or records].

Test: [*SELECT FROM:* Automated mechanisms and/or manual procedures for implementing information system recovery and reconstitution operations]. |

| **CP-10(1)** | **INFORMATION SYSTEM RECOVERY AND RECONSTITUTION**
[Withdrawn: Incorporated into CP-4(4)]. |

| CP-10(1).1 | **ASSESSMENT OBJECTIVE:**
[Withdrawn: Incorporated into CP-4(4)].

POTENTIAL ASSESSMENT METHODS AND OBJECTS:
[Withdrawn: Incorporated into CP-4(4)]. |

| **CP-10(2)** | **INFORMATION SYSTEM RECOVERY AND RECONSTITUTION** |

| CP-10(2).1 | **ASSESSMENT OBJECTIVE:**
Determine if the information system implements transaction recovery for systems that are transaction-based.

POTENTIAL ASSESSMENT METHODS AND OBJECTS:
Examine: [*SELECT FROM:* Contingency planning policy; contingency plan; procedures addressing information system recovery and reconstitution; information system design documentation; information system configuration settings and associated documentation; contingency plan test results; other relevant documents or records].

Test: [*SELECT FROM:* Automated mechanisms implementing transaction recovery capability]. |

CP-10(3)	INFORMATION SYSTEM RECOVERY AND RECONSTITUTION
CP-10(3).1	**ASSESSMENT OBJECTIVE:** *Determine if:* (i) *the organization defines in the security plan, explicitly or by reference, the circumstances that can inhibit recovery and reconstitution of the information system to a known state; and* (ii) *the organization provides compensating security controls for organization-defined circumstances that can inhibit recovery and reconstitution of the information system to a known state.* **POTENTIAL ASSESSMENT METHODS AND OBJECTS:** **Examine**: [*SELECT FROM:* Contingency planning policy; contingency plan; procedures addressing information system recovery and reconstitution; contingency plan test procedures; security plan; other relevant documents or records]. **Interview**: [*SELECT FROM:* Organizational personnel with information system recovery and reconstitution responsibilities].

CP-10(4)	INFORMATION SYSTEM RECOVERY AND RECONSTITUTION
CP-10(4).1	**ASSESSMENT OBJECTIVE:** *Determine if:* (i) *the organization defines the time-periods within which information system components must be reimaged from configuration-controlled and integrity-protected disk images representing a secure, operational state for the components; and* (ii) *the organization provides the capability to reimage information system components, within organization-defined time-periods, from configuration-controlled and integrity-protected disk images representing a secure, operational state for the components.* **POTENTIAL ASSESSMENT METHODS AND OBJECTS:** **Examine**: [*SELECT FROM:* Contingency planning policy; contingency plan; procedures addressing information system recovery and reconstitution; information system design documentation; information system configuration settings and associated documentation; other relevant documents or records]. **Interview**: [*SELECT FROM:* Organizational personnel with information system recovery and reconstitution responsibilities].

CP-10(5)	INFORMATION SYSTEM RECOVERY AND RECONSTITUTION
CP-10(5).1	**ASSESSMENT OBJECTIVE:** *Determine if:* (i) *the organization defines the type of failover capability for the information system (including whether the capability will be real-time or near real-time); and* (ii) *the organization provides the organization-defined failover capability for the information system.* **POTENTIAL ASSESSMENT METHODS AND OBJECTS:** **Examine:** [*SELECT FROM:* Contingency planning policy; contingency plan; procedures addressing information system recovery and reconstitution; security plan; other relevant documents or records]. **Interview:** [*SELECT FROM:* Organizational personnel with information system recovery and reconstitution responsibilities]. **Test:** [*SELECT FROM:* Failover capability for the information system].

CP-10(6)	INFORMATION SYSTEM RECOVERY AND RECONSTITUTION
CP-10(6).1	**ASSESSMENT OBJECTIVE:** *Determine if the organization protects backup and restoration hardware, firmware, and software.* **POTENTIAL ASSESSMENT METHODS AND OBJECTS:** **Examine:** [*SELECT FROM:* Contingency planning policy; contingency plan; procedures addressing information system recovery and reconstitution; location(s) of backup and restoration hardware, firmware, and software; other relevant documents or records]. **Interview:** [*SELECT FROM:* Organizational personnel with information system recovery and reconstitution responsibilities].

FAMILY: IDENTIFICATION AND AUTHENTICATION   **CLASS:** TECHNICAL

ASSESSMENT PROCEDURE	
IA-1	**IDENTIFICATION AND AUTHENTICATION POLICY AND PROCEDURES**

IA-1.1	**ASSESSMENT OBJECTIVE:**
	Determine if:
	(i) *the organization develops and formally documents identification and authentication policy;*
	(ii) *the organization identification and authentication policy addresses:*
	    - *purpose;*
	    - *scope;*
	    - *roles and responsibilities;*
	    - *management commitment;*
	    - *coordination among organizational entities; and*
	    - *compliance;*
	(iii) *the organization disseminates formal documented identification and authentication policy to elements within the organization having associated identification and authentication roles and responsibilities;*
	(iv) *the organization develops and formally documents identification and authentication procedures;*
	(v) *the organization identification and authentication procedures facilitate implementation of the identification and authentication policy and associated identification and authentication controls; and*
	(vi) *the organization disseminates formal documented identification and authentication procedures to elements within the organization having associated identification and authentication roles and responsibilities.*
	
	POTENTIAL ASSESSMENT METHODS AND OBJECTS:
	Examine: [*SELECT FROM:* Identification and authentication policy and procedures; other relevant documents or records].
	Interview: [*SELECT FROM:* Organizational personnel with identification and authentication responsibilities].

IA-1.2	**ASSESSMENT OBJECTIVE:** *Determine if:* (i) *the organization defines the frequency of identification and authentication policy reviews/updates;* (ii) *the organization reviews/updates identification and authentication policy in accordance with organization-defined frequency; and* (iii) *the organization defines the frequency of identification and authentication procedure reviews/updates;* (iv) *the organization reviews/updates identification and authentication procedures in accordance with organization-defined frequency.* **POTENTIAL ASSESSMENT METHODS AND OBJECTS:** **Examine**: [*SELECT FROM:* Identification and authentication policy and procedures; other relevant documents or records]. **Interview**: [*SELECT FROM:* Organizational personnel with identification and authentication responsibilities].

FAMILY: IDENTIFICATION AND AUTHENTICATION   **CLASS:** TECHNICAL

ASSESSMENT PROCEDURE

IA-2	IDENTIFICATION AND AUTHENTICATION (ORGANIZATIONAL USERS)
IA-2.1	**ASSESSMENT OBJECTIVE:** *Determine if the information system uniquely identifies and authenticates organizational users (or processes acting on behalf of organizational users).* **POTENTIAL ASSESSMENT METHODS AND OBJECTS:** **Examine:** [*SELECT FROM:* Identification and authentication policy; procedures addressing user identification and authentication; information system design documentation; information system configuration settings and associated documentation; information system audit records; list of information system accounts; other relevant documents or records]. **Test:** [*SELECT FROM:* Automated mechanisms implementing identification and authentication capability for the information system].

IA-2(1)	IDENTIFICATION AND AUTHENTICATION (ORGANIZATIONAL USERS)
IA-2(1).1	**ASSESSMENT OBJECTIVE:** *Determine if the information system uses multifactor authentication for network access to privileged accounts.* **POTENTIAL ASSESSMENT METHODS AND OBJECTS:** **Examine:** [*SELECT FROM:* Identification and authentication policy; procedures addressing user identification and authentication; information system design documentation; information system configuration settings and associated documentation; list of privileged information system accounts; other relevant documents or records]. **Test:** [*SELECT FROM:* Automated mechanisms implementing identification and authentication capability for the information system].

IA-2(2)	IDENTIFICATION AND AUTHENTICATION (ORGANIZATIONAL USERS)
IA-2(2).1	**ASSESSMENT OBJECTIVE:** *Determine if the information system uses multifactor authentication for network access to non-privileged accounts.* **POTENTIAL ASSESSMENT METHODS AND OBJECTS:** **Examine:** [*SELECT FROM:* Identification and authentication policy; procedures addressing user identification and authentication; information system design documentation; information system configuration settings and associated documentation; list of non-privileged information system accounts; other relevant documents or records]. **Test:** [*SELECT FROM:* Automated mechanisms implementing identification and authentication capability for the information system].

IA-2(3)	IDENTIFICATION AND AUTHENTICATION (ORGANIZATIONAL USERS)
IA-2(3).1	**ASSESSMENT OBJECTIVE:** *Determine if the information system uses multifactor authentication for local access to privileged accounts.* **POTENTIAL ASSESSMENT METHODS AND OBJECTS:** **Examine**: [*SELECT FROM:* Identification and authentication policy; procedures addressing user identification and authentication; information system design documentation; information system configuration settings and associated documentation; list of privileged information system accounts; other relevant documents or records]. **Test**: [*SELECT FROM:* Automated mechanisms implementing identification and authentication capability for the information system].

IA-2(4)	IDENTIFICATION AND AUTHENTICATION (ORGANIZATIONAL USERS)
IA-2(4).1	**ASSESSMENT OBJECTIVE:** *Determine if the information system uses multifactor authentication for local access to non-privileged accounts.* **POTENTIAL ASSESSMENT METHODS AND OBJECTS:** **Examine**: [*SELECT FROM:* Identification and authentication policy; procedures addressing user identification and authentication; information system design documentation; information system configuration settings and associated documentation; list of non-privileged information system accounts; other relevant documents or records]. **Test**: [*SELECT FROM:* Automated mechanisms implementing identification and authentication capability for the information system].

IA-2(5)	IDENTIFICATION AND AUTHENTICATION (ORGANIZATIONAL USERS)
IA-2(5).1	**ASSESSMENT OBJECTIVE:** *Determine if:* *(i) the organization allows the use of group authenticators only when used in conjunction with an individual/unique authenticator; and* *(ii) the organization requires individuals to be authenticated with an individual authenticator prior to using a group authenticator.* **POTENTIAL ASSESSMENT METHODS AND OBJECTS:** **Examine**: [*SELECT FROM:* Identification and authentication policy; procedures addressing user identification and authentication; information system design documentation; information system configuration settings and associated documentation; other relevant documents or records]. **Test**: [*SELECT FROM:* Automated mechanisms implementing identification and authentication capability for the information system].

IA-2(6)	IDENTIFICATION AND AUTHENTICATION (ORGANIZATIONAL USERS)
IA-2(6).1	**ASSESSMENT OBJECTIVE:** *Determine if the information system uses multifactor authentication for network access to privileged accounts where one of the factors is provided by a device separate from the information system being accessed.* **POTENTIAL ASSESSMENT METHODS AND OBJECTS:** **Examine**: [*SELECT FROM:* Identification and authentication policy; procedures addressing user identification and authentication; information system design documentation; information system configuration settings and associated documentation; list of privileged information system accounts; other relevant documents or records]. **Test**: [*SELECT FROM:* Automated mechanisms implementing identification and authentication capability for the information system].

IA-2(7)	IDENTIFICATION AND AUTHENTICATION (ORGANIZATIONAL USERS)
IA-2(7).1	**ASSESSMENT OBJECTIVE:** *Determine if the information system uses multifactor authentication for network access to non-privileged accounts where one of the factors is provided by a device separate from the information system being accessed.* **POTENTIAL ASSESSMENT METHODS AND OBJECTS:** **Examine**: [*SELECT FROM:* Identification and authentication policy; procedures addressing user identification and authentication; information system design documentation; information system configuration settings and associated documentation; list of non-privileged information system accounts; other relevant documents or records]. **Test**: [*SELECT FROM:* Automated mechanisms implementing identification and authentication capability for the information system].

IA-2(8)	IDENTIFICATION AND AUTHENTICATION (ORGANIZATIONAL USERS)
IA-2(8).1	**ASSESSMENT OBJECTIVE:** *Determine if:* (i) *the organization defines the replay-resistant authentication mechanisms to be used for network access to privileged accounts; and* (ii) *the information system uses the organization-defined replay-resistant authentication mechanisms for network access to privileged accounts.* **POTENTIAL ASSESSMENT METHODS AND OBJECTS:** **Examine**: [*SELECT FROM:* Identification and authentication policy; procedures addressing user identification and authentication; information system design documentation; information system configuration settings and associated documentation; list of privileged information system accounts; other relevant documents or records]. **Test**: [*SELECT FROM:* Automated mechanisms implementing identification and authentication capability for the information system].

IA-2(9)	IDENTIFICATION AND AUTHENTICATION (ORGANIZATIONAL USERS)
IA-2(9).1	**ASSESSMENT OBJECTIVE:** *Determine if:* (i) *the organization defines the replay-resistant authentication mechanisms to be used for network access to non-privileged accounts; and* (ii) *the information system uses the organization-defined replay-resistant authentication mechanisms for network access to non-privileged accounts.* **POTENTIAL ASSESSMENT METHODS AND OBJECTS:** **Examine:** [*SELECT FROM:* Identification and authentication policy; procedures addressing user identification and authentication; information system design documentation; information system configuration settings and associated documentation; other relevant documents or records]. **Test:** [*SELECT FROM:* Automated mechanisms implementing identification and authentication capability for the information system].

FAMILY: IDENTIFICATION AND AUTHENTICATION   **CLASS:** TECHNICAL

ASSESSMENT PROCEDURE	
IA-3	**DEVICE IDENTIFICATION AND AUTHENTICATION**
IA-3.1	**ASSESSMENT OBJECTIVE:** *Determine if:* (i) *the organization defines the specific and/or types of devices for which identification and authentication is required before establishing a connection to the information system; and* (ii) *the information system uniquely identifies and authenticates the organization-defined devices before establishing a connection to the information system.* **POTENTIAL ASSESSMENT METHODS AND OBJECTS:** **Examine**: [*SELECT FROM:* Identification and authentication policy; procedures addressing device identification and authentication; information system design documentation; list of devices requiring unique identification and authentication; device connection reports; information system configuration settings and associated documentation; other relevant documents or records]. **Test**: [*SELECT FROM:* Automated mechanisms implementing device identification and authentication].

IA-3(1)	**DEVICE IDENTIFICATION AND AUTHENTICATION**
IA-3(1).1	**ASSESSMENT OBJECTIVE:** *Determine if:* (i) *the information system authenticates devices before establishing remote network connections using bi-directional authentication between devices that is cryptographically based; and* (ii) *the information system authenticates devices before establishing wireless network connections using bi-directional authentication between devices that is cryptographically based.* **POTENTIAL ASSESSMENT METHODS AND OBJECTS:** **Examine**: [*SELECT FROM:* Identification and authentication policy; procedures addressing device identification and authentication; information system design documentation; device connection reports; information system configuration settings and associated documentation; other relevant documents or records]. **Test**: [*SELECT FROM:* Automated mechanisms implementing device identification and authentication].

IA-3(2)	DEVICE IDENTIFICATION AND AUTHENTICATION
IA-3(2).1	**ASSESSMENT OBJECTIVE:** *Determine if the information system authenticates devices before establishing network connections using bidirectional authentication between devices that is cryptographically based.* **POTENTIAL ASSESSMENT METHODS AND OBJECTS:** **Examine**: [*SELECT FROM:* Identification and authentication policy; procedures addressing device identification and authentication; information system design documentation; device connection reports; information system configuration settings and associated documentation; other relevant documents or records]. **Test**: [*SELECT FROM:* Automated mechanisms implementing device identification and authentication].

IA-3(3)	DEVICE IDENTIFICATION AND AUTHENTICATION
IA-3(3).1	**ASSESSMENT OBJECTIVE:** *Determine if:* (i) *the organization standardizes, with regard to dynamic address allocation, Dynamic Host Control Protocol (DHCP) lease information and the time assigned to DHCP-enabled devices; and* (ii) *the organization audits DHCP lease information (including IP addresses) when assigned to a DHCP-enabled devices.* **POTENTIAL ASSESSMENT METHODS AND OBJECTS:** **Examine**: [*SELECT FROM:* Identification and authentication policy; procedures addressing device identification and authentication; information system design documentation; information system configuration settings and associated documentation; DHCP lease information; device connection reports; other relevant documents or records].

FAMILY: IDENTIFICATION AND AUTHENTICATION

CLASS: TECHNICAL

ASSESSMENT PROCEDURE	
IA-4	**IDENTIFIER MANAGEMENT**
IA-4.1	**ASSESSMENT OBJECTIVE:** *Determine if:* *(i) the organization defines the time period for preventing reuse of user or device identifiers;* *(ii) the organization defines the time period of inactivity after which a user identifier is to be disabled; and* *(iii) the organization manages information system identifiers for users and devices by:* 　　- *receiving authorization from a designated organizational official to assign a user or device identifier;* 　　- *selecting an identifier that uniquely identifies an individual or device;* 　　- *assigning the user identifier to the intended party or the device identifier to the intended device;* 　　- *preventing reuse of user or device identifiers for the organization-defined time period; and* 　　- *disabling the user identifier after the organization-defined time period of inactivity.* **POTENTIAL ASSESSMENT METHODS AND OBJECTS:** **Examine:** [*SELECT FROM:* Identification and authentication policy; procedures addressing identifier management; procedures addressing account management; security plan; information system design documentation; information system configuration settings and associated documentation; list of information system accounts; list of identifiers generated from physical access control devices; other relevant documents or records]. **Interview:** [*SELECT FROM:* Organizational personnel with identifier management responsibilities].

IA-4(1)	**IDENTIFIER MANAGEMENT**
IA-4(1).1	**ASSESSMENT OBJECTIVE:** *Determine if organization prohibits the use of information system account identifiers as public identifiers for user electronic mail accounts (i.e., user identifier portion of the electronic mail address).* **POTENTIAL ASSESSMENT METHODS AND OBJECTS:** **Examine:** [*SELECT FROM:* Identification and authentication policy; procedures addressing identifier management; procedures addressing account management; information system design documentation; information system configuration settings and associated documentation; other relevant documents or records].

IA-4(2)	IDENTIFIER MANAGEMENT
IA-4(2).1	**ASSESSMENT OBJECTIVE:** *Determine if:* *(i) the organization requires that registration to receive a user ID and password include authorization by a supervisor; and* *(ii) the organization requires that registration to receive a user ID and password be done in person before a designated registration authority.* **POTENTIAL ASSESSMENT METHODS AND OBJECTS:** **Examine:** [*SELECT FROM:* Identification and authentication policy; procedures addressing identifier management; procedures addressing account management; user ID and password registration documentation; ID and password authorization records; registration authority records; other relevant documents or records]. **Interview:** [*SELECT FROM:* Organizational personnel with identifier management responsibilities].

IA-4(3)	IDENTIFIER MANAGEMENT
IA-4(3).1	**ASSESSMENT OBJECTIVE:** *Determine if the organization requires multiple forms of certification of individual identification such as documentary evidence or a combination of documents and biometrics be presented to the registration authority.* **POTENTIAL ASSESSMENT METHODS AND OBJECTS:** **Examine:** [*SELECT FROM:* Identification and authentication policy; procedures addressing identifier management; procedures addressing account management; identifier certification documentation; organizational personnel biometrics records; other relevant documents or records]. **Interview:** [*SELECT FROM:* Organizational personnel with identifier management responsibilities].

IA-4(4)	IDENTIFIER MANAGEMENT
IA-4(4).1	**ASSESSMENT OBJECTIVE:** *Determine if:* *(i) the organization defines the characteristic to be used to identify user status; and* *(ii) the organization manages user identifiers by uniquely identifying the user with the organization-defined characteristic identifying user status.* **POTENTIAL ASSESSMENT METHODS AND OBJECTS:** **Examine:** [*SELECT FROM:* Identification and authentication policy; procedures addressing identifier management; procedures addressing account management; list of characteristics identifying user status; other relevant documents or records].

IA-4(5)	IDENTIFIER MANAGEMENT
IA-4(5).1	**ASSESSMENT OBJECTIVE:** *Determine if the information system dynamically manages:* – *identifiers;* – *attributes; and* – *associated access authorizations.* **POTENTIAL ASSESSMENT METHODS AND OBJECTS:** **Examine**: [*SELECT FROM:* Identification and authentication policy; procedures addressing identifier management; information system design documentation; information system configuration settings and associated documentation; other relevant documents or records]. **Test**: [*SELECT FROM:* Automated mechanisms implementing identifier management functions].

FAMILY: IDENTIFICATION AND AUTHENTICATION   **CLASS:** TECHNICAL

ASSESSMENT PROCEDURE	
IA-5	**AUTHENTICATOR MANAGEMENT**
IA-5.1	**ASSESSMENT OBJECTIVE:** *Determine if:* *(i) the organization defines the time period (by authenticator type) for changing/refreshing authenticators; and* *(ii) the organization manages information system authenticators for users and devices by:* - *verifying, as part of the initial authenticator distribution, the identity of the individual and/or device receiving the authenticator;* - *establishing initial authenticator content for authenticators defined by the organization;* - *ensuring that authenticators have sufficient strength of mechanism for their intended use;* - *establishing and implementing administrative procedures for initial authenticator distribution;* - *establishing and implementing administrative procedures for lost/compromised or damaged authenticators;* - *establishing and implementing administrative procedures for revoking authenticators;* - *changing default content of authenticators upon information system installation;* - *establishing minimum and maximum lifetime restrictions and reuse conditions for authenticators (if deemed to be appropriate by the organization);* - *changing/refreshing authenticators in accordance with the organization-defined time period by authenticator type;* - *protecting authenticator content from unauthorized disclosure and modification; and* - *requiring users to take, and having devices implement, specific measures to safeguard authenticators.* **POTENTIAL ASSESSMENT METHODS AND OBJECTS:** **Examine:** [*SELECT FROM:* Identification and authentication policy; procedures addressing authenticator management; information system design documentation; information system configuration settings and associated documentation; list of information system accounts; other relevant documents or records]. **Interview:** [*SELECT FROM:* Organizational personnel with responsibilities for determining initial authenticator content]. **Test:** [*SELECT FROM:* Automated mechanisms implementing authenticator management functions].

IA-5(1)	AUTHENTICATOR MANAGEMENT

IA-5(1).1	**ASSESSMENT OBJECTIVE:**
	Determine if:
	
	(i) *the organization defines the minimum password complexity requirements to be enforced for case sensitivity, the number of characters, and the mix of upper-case letters, lower-case letters, numbers, and special characters including minimum requirements for each type;*
	
	(ii) *the organization defines the minimum number of characters that must be changed when new passwords are created;*
	
	(iii) *the organization defines the restrictions to be enforced for password minimum lifetime and password maximum lifetime parameters;*
	
	(iv) *the organization defines the number of generations for which password reuse is prohibited; and*
	
	(v) *the information system, for password-based authentication:*
	   - *enforces the minimum password complexity standards that meet the organization-defined requirements;*
	   - *enforces the organization-defined minimum number of characters that must be changed when new passwords are created;*
	   - *encrypts passwords in storage and in transmission;*
	   - *enforces the organization-defined restrictions for password minimum lifetime and password maximum lifetime parameters; and*
	   - *prohibits password reuse for the organization-defined number of generations.*
	
	POTENTIAL ASSESSMENT METHODS AND OBJECTS:
	Examine: [*SELECT FROM:* Identification and authentication policy; password policy; procedures addressing authenticator management; security plan; information system design documentation; information system configuration settings and associated documentation; other relevant documents or records].
	
	Test: [*SELECT FROM:* Automated mechanisms implementing authenticator management functions].

IA-5(2)	AUTHENTICATOR MANAGEMENT
IA-5(2).1	**ASSESSMENT OBJECTIVE:** *Determine if the information system, for PKI-based authentication:* – *validates certificates by constructing a certification path with status information to an accepted trust anchor;* – *enforces authorized access to the corresponding private key; and* – *maps the authenticated identity to the user account.* **POTENTIAL ASSESSMENT METHODS AND OBJECTS:** **Examine:** [*SELECT FROM:* Identification and authentication policy; procedures addressing authenticator management; security plan; information system design documentation; information system configuration settings and associated documentation; PKI certification revocation lists; other relevant documents or records]. **Interview:** [*SELECT FROM:* Organizational personnel with responsibilities for PKI-based authentication management]. **Test:** [*SELECT FROM:* Automated mechanisms implementing PKI-based authenticator management functions].

IA-5(3)	AUTHENTICATOR MANAGEMENT
IA-5(3).1	**ASSESSMENT OBJECTIVE:** *Determine if:* (i) *the organization defines the types of and/or specific authenticators for which the registration process must be carried out in person before a designated registration authority with authorization by a designated organizational official; and* (ii) *the organization requires that the registration process to receive organization-defined types of and/or specific authenticators be carried out in person before a designated registration authority with authorization by a designated organizational official (e.g., a supervisor).* **POTENTIAL ASSESSMENT METHODS AND OBJECTS:** **Examine:** [*SELECT FROM:* Identification and authentication policy; procedures addressing authenticator management; list of authenticators that require in-person registration; authenticator registration documentation; other relevant documents or records]. **Interview:** [*SELECT FROM:* Organizational personnel with authenticator management responsibilities].

IA-5(4)	AUTHENTICATOR MANAGEMENT

IA-5(4).1	**ASSESSMENT OBJECTIVE:** *Determine if the organization employs automated tools to determine if authenticators are sufficiently strong to resist attacks intended to discover or otherwise compromise the authenticators.* **POTENTIAL ASSESSMENT METHODS AND OBJECTS:** **Examine**: [*SELECT FROM:* Identification and authentication policy; procedures addressing authenticator management; information system design documentation; information system configuration settings and associated documentation; automated tools for testing authenticators; other relevant documents or records]. **Interview**: [*SELECT FROM:* Organizational personnel with authenticator management responsibilities]. **Test**: [*SELECT FROM:* Automated mechanisms for authenticator strength].

IA-5(5)	AUTHENTICATOR MANAGEMENT

IA-5(5).1	**ASSESSMENT OBJECTIVE:** *Determine if the organization requires vendors and/or manufacturers of information system components to provide unique authenticators or change default authenticators prior to delivery.* **POTENTIAL ASSESSMENT METHODS AND OBJECTS:** **Examine**: [*SELECT FROM:* Identification and authentication policy; system and services acquisition policy; procedures addressing authenticator management; procedures addressing the integration of security requirements into the acquisition process; acquisition documentation; acquisition contracts for information system procurements or services; other relevant documents or records]. **Interview**: [*SELECT FROM:* Organizational personnel with authenticator management responsibilities; organizational personnel with information system security, acquisition, and contracting responsibilities].

IA-5(6)	AUTHENTICATOR MANAGEMENT

IA-5(6).1	**ASSESSMENT OBJECTIVE:** *Determine if the organization protects authenticators commensurate with the classification or sensitivity of the information accessed.* **POTENTIAL ASSESSMENT METHODS AND OBJECTS:** **Examine**: [*SELECT FROM:* Identification and authentication policy; procedures addressing authenticator management; information classification or sensitivity documentation; security categorization documentation for the information system; security assessments of authenticator protections; risk assessment results; security plan; other relevant documents or records]. **Interview**: [*SELECT FROM:* Organizational personnel with authenticator management responsibilities; organizational personnel implementing and/or maintaining authenticator protections].

IA-5(7)	AUTHENTICATOR MANAGEMENT
IA-5(7).1	**ASSESSMENT OBJECTIVE:** *Determine if the organization ensures that unencrypted static authenticators are not embedded in applications or access scripts or stored on function keys.* **POTENTIAL ASSESSMENT METHODS AND OBJECTS:** **Examine:** [*SELECT FROM:* Identification and authentication policy; procedures addressing authenticator management; information system design documentation; information system configuration settings and associated documentation; logical access scripts; application code reviews for detecting unencrypted static authenticators; other relevant documents or records].

IA-5(8)	AUTHENTICATOR MANAGEMENT
IA-5(8).1	**ASSESSMENT OBJECTIVE:** *Determine if:* *(i) the organization defines measures taken to manage the risk of compromise due to individuals having accounts on multiple information systems; and* *(ii) the organization takes organization-defined measures to manage the risk of compromise due to individuals having accounts on multiple information systems.* **POTENTIAL ASSESSMENT METHODS AND OBJECTS:** **Examine:** [*SELECT FROM:* Identification and authentication policy; procedures addressing authenticator management; security plan; list of individuals having accounts on multiple information systems; list of measures intended to manage risk of compromise due to individuals having accounts on multiple information systems ; other relevant documents or records].

FAMILY: IDENTIFICATION AND AUTHENTICATION   **CLASS:** TECHNICAL

ASSESSMENT PROCEDURE	
IA-6	**AUTHENTICATOR FEEDBACK**
IA-6.1	**ASSESSMENT OBJECTIVE:** *Determine if the information system obscures feedback of authentication information during the authentication process to protect the information from possible exploitation/use by unauthorized individuals.* **POTENTIAL ASSESSMENT METHODS AND OBJECTS:** **Examine**: [*SELECT FROM:* Identification and authentication policy; procedures addressing authenticator feedback; information system design documentation; information system configuration settings and associated documentation; other relevant documents or records]. **Test**: [*SELECT FROM:* Automated mechanisms implementing authenticator feedback].

FAMILY: IDENTIFICATION AND AUTHENTICATION   **CLASS:** TECHNICAL

ASSESSMENT PROCEDURE	
IA-7	**CRYPTOGRAPHIC MODULE AUTHENTICATION**
IA-7.1	**ASSESSMENT OBJECTIVE:** *Determine if the information system uses mechanisms for authentication to a cryptographic module that meet the requirements of applicable federal laws, Executive Orders, directives, policies, regulations, standards, and guidance for such authentication.* **POTENTIAL ASSESSMENT METHODS AND OBJECTS:** **Examine**: [*SELECT FROM:* Identification and authentication policy; procedures addressing cryptographic module authentication; information system design documentation; information system configuration settings and associated documentation; other relevant documents or records]. **Test**: [*SELECT FROM:* Automated mechanisms implementing cryptographic module authentication].

FAMILY: IDENTIFICATION AND AUTHENTICATION   **CLASS:** TECHNICAL

ASSESSMENT PROCEDURE
IA-8	**IDENTIFICATION AND AUTHENTICATION (NON-ORGANIZATIONAL USERS)**
IA-8.1	**ASSESSMENT OBJECTIVE:** *Determine if the information system uniquely identifies and authenticates non-organizational users (or processes acting on behalf of non-organizational users).* **POTENTIAL ASSESSMENT METHODS AND OBJECTS:** **Examine**: [*SELECT FROM:* Identification and authentication policy; procedures addressing user identification and authentication; information system design documentation; information system configuration settings and associated documentation; information system audit records; list of information system accounts; other relevant documents or records]. **Test**: [*SELECT FROM:* Automated mechanisms implementing identification and authentication capability for the information system].

FAMILY: INCIDENT RESPONSE   **CLASS:** OPERATIONAL

ASSESSMENT PROCEDURE	
IR-1	**INCIDENT RESPONSE POLICY AND PROCEDURES**

IR-1.1	**ASSESSMENT OBJECTIVE:**
	Determine if:
	
	(i) *the organization develops and formally documents incident response policy;*
	
	(ii) *the organization incident response policy addresses:*
	
	  - *purpose;*
	  - *scope;*
	  - *roles and responsibilities;*
	  - *management commitment;*
	  - *coordination among organizational entities; and*
	  - *compliance;*
	
	(iii) *the organization disseminates formal documented incident response policy to elements within the organization having associated incident response roles and responsibilities;*
	
	(iv) *the organization develops and formally documents incident response procedures;*
	
	(v) *the organization incident response procedures facilitate implementation of the incident response policy and associated incident response controls; and*
	
	(vi) *the organization disseminates formal documented incident response procedures to elements within the organization having associated incident response roles and responsibilities.*
	
	POTENTIAL ASSESSMENT METHODS AND OBJECTS:
	Examine: [*SELECT FROM:* Incident response policy and procedures; other relevant documents or records].
	Interview: [*SELECT FROM:* Organizational personnel with incident response responsibilities].

IR-1.2	**ASSESSMENT OBJECTIVE:** *Determine if:* (i) *the organization defines the frequency of incident response policy reviews/updates;* (ii) *the organization reviews/updates incident response policy in accordance with organization-defined frequency;* (iii) *the organization defines the frequency of incident response procedure reviews/updates; and* (iv) *the organization reviews/updates incident response procedures in accordance with organization-defined frequency.* **POTENTIAL ASSESSMENT METHODS AND OBJECTS:** **Examine**: [*SELECT FROM:* Incident response policy and procedures; other relevant documents or records]. **Interview**: [*SELECT FROM:* Organizational personnel with incident response responsibilities].

FAMILY: INCIDENT RESPONSE   **CLASS:** OPERATIONAL

ASSESSMENT PROCEDURE

IR-2	INCIDENT RESPONSE TRAINING
IR-2.1	**ASSESSMENT OBJECTIVE:** *Determine if:* (i) *the organization identifies personnel with incident response roles and responsibilities with respect to the information system;* (ii) *the organization provides incident response training to personnel with incident response roles and responsibilities with respect to the information system;* (iii) *incident response training material addresses the procedures and activities necessary to fulfill identified organizational incident response roles and responsibilities;* (iv) *the organization defines the frequency of refresher incident response training; and* (v) *the organization provides refresher incident response training in accordance with the organization-defined frequency.* **POTENTIAL ASSESSMENT METHODS AND OBJECTS:** **Examine**: [*SELECT FROM:* Incident response policy; procedures addressing incident response training; incident response training material; security plan; incident response plan; incident response training records; other relevant documents or records]. **Interview**: [*SELECT FROM:* Organizational personnel with incident response training and operational responsibilities].

IR-2(1)	INCIDENT RESPONSE TRAINING
IR-2(1).1	**ASSESSMENT OBJECTIVE:** *Determine if the organization incorporates simulated events into incident response training to facilitate effective response by personnel in crisis situations.* **POTENTIAL ASSESSMENT METHODS AND OBJECTS:** **Examine**: [*SELECT FROM:* Incident response policy; procedures addressing incident response training; incident response training material; other relevant documents or records]. **Interview**: [*SELECT FROM:* Organizational personnel with incident response training and operational responsibilities].

IR-2(2)	INCIDENT RESPONSE TRAINING
IR-2(2).1	**ASSESSMENT OBJECTIVE:** *Determine if the organization employs automated mechanisms to provide a more thorough and realistic incident response training environment.* **POTENTIAL ASSESSMENT METHODS AND OBJECTS:** **Examine**: [*SELECT FROM:* Incident response policy; procedures addressing incident response training; incident response training material; automated mechanisms supporting incident response training; other relevant documents or records]. **Interview**: [*SELECT FROM:* Organizational personnel with incident response training and operational responsibilities].

FAMILY: INCIDENT RESPONSE   **CLASS:** OPERATIONAL

ASSESSMENT PROCEDURE	
IR-3	**INCIDENT RESPONSE TESTING AND EXERCISES**
IR-3.1	**ASSESSMENT OBJECTIVE:** *Determine if:* (i) *the organization defines incident response tests/exercises;* (ii) *the organization defines the frequency of incident response tests/exercises;* (iii) *the organization tests/exercises the incident response capability for the information system using organization-defined tests/exercises in accordance with organization-defined frequency;* (iv) *the organization documents the results of incident response tests/exercises; and* (v) *the organization determines the effectiveness of the incident response capability.* **POTENTIAL ASSESSMENT METHODS AND OBJECTS:** **Examine**: [*SELECT FROM:* Incident response policy; procedures addressing incident response testing and exercises; security plan; incident response testing material; incident response test results; incident response plan; other relevant documents or records]. **Interview**: [*SELECT FROM:* Organizational personnel with incident response testing responsibilities].

IR-3(1)	**INCIDENT RESPONSE TESTING AND EXERCISES**
IR-3(1).1	**ASSESSMENT OBJECTIVE:** *Determine if the organization employs automated mechanisms to more thoroughly and effectively test/exercise the incident response capability for the information system.* **POTENTIAL ASSESSMENT METHODS AND OBJECTS:** **Examine**: [*SELECT FROM:* Incident response policy; procedures addressing incident response testing and exercises; security plan; incident response testing documentation; automated mechanisms supporting incident response tests/exercises; incident response plan; other relevant documents or records]. **Interview**: [*SELECT FROM:* Organizational personnel with incident response testing responsibilities].

FAMILY: INCIDENT RESPONSE   **CLASS:** OPERATIONAL

ASSESSMENT PROCEDURE	
IR-4	**INCIDENT HANDLING**

IR-4.1	**ASSESSMENT OBJECTIVE:**
	Determine if:
	
	(i) the organization implements an incident handling capability for security incidents that includes:
	
	  - *preparation;*
	  - *detection and analysis;*
	  - *containment;*
	  - *eradication; and*
	  - *recovery;*
	
	(ii) the organization coordinates incident handling activities with contingency planning activities; and
	
	(iii) the organization incorporates lessons learned from ongoing incident handling activities into:
	
	  - *incident response procedures;*
	  - *training; and*
	  - *testing/exercises; and*
	
	(iv) the organization implements the resulting changes to incident response procedures, training and testing/exercise accordingly.
	
	POTENTIAL ASSESSMENT METHODS AND OBJECTS:
	Examine: [*SELECT FROM:* Incident response policy; procedures addressing incident handling; incident response plan; other relevant documents or records].
	Interview: [*SELECT FROM:* Organizational personnel with incident handling responsibilities; organizational personnel with contingency planning responsibilities].
	Test: [*SELECT FROM:* Incident handling capability for the organization].

IR-4(1)	INCIDENT HANDLING	
IR-4(1).1	**ASSESSMENT OBJECTIVE:** *Determine if the organization employs automated mechanisms to support the incident handling process.* **POTENTIAL ASSESSMENT METHODS AND OBJECTS:** **Examine**: [*SELECT FROM:* Incident response policy; procedures addressing incident handling; automated mechanisms supporting incident handling; other relevant documents or records]. **Interview**: [*SELECT FROM:* Organizational personnel with incident handling responsibilities].	

IR-4(2)	INCIDENT HANDLING
IR-4(2).1	**ASSESSMENT OBJECTIVE:** *Determine if the organization includes dynamic reconfiguration of the information system as part of the incident response capability.* **POTENTIAL ASSESSMENT METHODS AND OBJECTS:** **Examine**: [*SELECT FROM:* Incident response policy; procedures addressing incident handling; automated mechanisms supporting incident handling; other relevant documents or records]. **Interview**: [*SELECT FROM:* Organizational personnel with incident handling responsibilities].

IR-4(3)	INCIDENT HANDLING
IR-4(3).1	**ASSESSMENT OBJECTIVE:** *Determine if:* (i) *the organization identifies classes of incidents; and* (ii) *the organization defines the appropriate actions to take in response to each class of incidents to ensure continuation of organizational missions and business functions.* **POTENTIAL ASSESSMENT METHODS AND OBJECTS:** **Examine**: [*SELECT FROM:* Incident response policy; procedures addressing incident handling; automated mechanisms supporting incident handling; security plan; incident response plan; other relevant documents or records]. **Interview**: [*SELECT FROM:* Organizational personnel with incident handling responsibilities].

IR-4(4)	INCIDENT HANDLING
IR-4(4).1	**ASSESSMENT OBJECTIVE:** *Determine if the organization correlates incident information and individual incident responses to achieve an organization-wide perspective on incident awareness and response.* **POTENTIAL ASSESSMENT METHODS AND OBJECTS:** **Examine**: [*SELECT FROM:* Incident response policy; procedures addressing incident handling; incident response plan; automated mechanisms supporting incident handling; other relevant documents or records]. **Interview**: [*SELECT FROM:* Organizational personnel with incident handling responsibilities].

IR-4(5)	INCIDENT HANDLING
IR-4(5).1	**ASSESSMENT OBJECTIVE:** *Determine if:* (i) *the organization defines a list of security violations that, if detected, initiate a configurable capability to automatically disable the information system; and* (ii) *the organization implements a configurable capability to automatically disable the information system if any of the organization-defined security violations are detected.* **POTENTIAL ASSESSMENT METHODS AND OBJECTS:** **Examine**: [*SELECT FROM:* Incident response policy; procedures addressing incident handling; automated mechanisms supporting incident handling; security plan; incident response plan; other relevant documents or records]. **Interview**: [*SELECT FROM:* Organizational personnel with incident handling responsibilities].

FAMILY: INCIDENT RESPONSE   **CLASS:** OPERATIONAL

ASSESSMENT PROCEDURE	
IR-5	**INCIDENT MONITORING**
IR-5.1	**ASSESSMENT OBJECTIVE:** *Determine if the organization tracks and documents information system security incidents.* **POTENTIAL ASSESSMENT METHODS AND OBJECTS:** **Examine**: [*SELECT FROM:* Incident response policy; procedures addressing incident monitoring; incident response records and documentation; incident response plan; other relevant documents or records]. **Interview**: [*SELECT FROM:* Organizational personnel with incident monitoring responsibilities]. **Test**: [*SELECT FROM:* Incident monitoring capability for the organization].

IR-5(1)	INCIDENT MONITORING
IR-5(1).1	**ASSESSMENT OBJECTIVE:** *Determine if:* (i) *the organization employs automated mechanisms to assist in the tracking of security incidents;* (ii) *the organization employs automated mechanisms to assist in the collection of security incident information; and* (iii) *the organization employs automated mechanisms to assist in the analysis of security incident information.* **POTENTIAL ASSESSMENT METHODS AND OBJECTS:** **Examine**: [*SELECT FROM:* Incident response policy; procedures addressing incident monitoring; information system design documentation; information system configuration settings and associated documentation; automated mechanisms supporting incident monitoring; incident response plan; other relevant documents or records]. **Interview**: [*SELECT FROM:* Organizational personnel with incident monitoring responsibilities]. **Test**: [*SELECT FROM:* Automated mechanisms assisting in tracking of security incidents and in the collection and analysis of incident information].

FAMILY: INCIDENT RESPONSE   **CLASS:** OPERATIONAL

ASSESSMENT PROCEDURE

IR-6	INCIDENT REPORTING

IR-6.1	**ASSESSMENT OBJECTIVE:** *Determine if:* (i) *the organization defines in the time period required to report suspected security incidents to the organizational incident response capability;* (ii) *the organization requires personnel to report suspected security incidents to the organizational incident response capability within the organization-defined time period; and* (iii) *the organization reports security incident information to designated authorities.* **POTENTIAL ASSESSMENT METHODS AND OBJECTS:** **Examine**: [*SELECT FROM:* Incident response policy; procedures addressing incident reporting; incident reporting records and documentation; security plan; incident response plan; other relevant documents or records]. **Interview**: [*SELECT FROM:* Organizational personnel with incident reporting responsibilities].

IR-6(1)	INCIDENT REPORTING

IR-6(1).1	**ASSESSMENT OBJECTIVE:** *Determine if the organization employs automated mechanisms to assist in the reporting of security incidents.* **POTENTIAL ASSESSMENT METHODS AND OBJECTS:** **Examine**: [*SELECT FROM:* Incident response policy; procedures addressing incident reporting; automated mechanisms supporting incident reporting; incident response plan; other relevant documents or records]. **Interview**: [*SELECT FROM:* Organizational personnel with incident reporting responsibilities].

IR-6(2)	INCIDENT REPORTING

IR-6(2).1	**ASSESSMENT OBJECTIVE:** *Determine if the organization reports information system weaknesses, deficiencies, and/or vulnerabilities associated with reported security incidents to appropriate organizational officials.* **POTENTIAL ASSESSMENT METHODS AND OBJECTS:** **Examine**: [*SELECT FROM:* Incident response policy; procedures addressing incident reporting; automated mechanisms supporting incident reporting; incident response plan; other relevant documents or records]. **Interview**: [*SELECT FROM:* Organizational personnel with incident reporting responsibilities].

FAMILY: INCIDENT RESPONSE   **CLASS:** OPERATIONAL

ASSESSMENT PROCEDURE

IR-7	INCIDENT RESPONSE ASSISTANCE
IR-7.1	**ASSESSMENT OBJECTIVE:** *Determine if:* (i) *the organization provides an incident response support resource that offers advice and assistance to users of the information system for the handling and reporting of security incidents; and* (ii) *the incident response support resource is an integral part of the organization's incident response capability.* **POTENTIAL ASSESSMENT METHODS AND OBJECTS:** **Examine:** [*SELECT FROM:* Incident response policy; procedures addressing incident response assistance; incident response plan; other relevant documents or records]. **Interview:** [*SELECT FROM:* Organizational personnel with incident response assistance and support responsibilities].

IR-7(1)	INCIDENT RESPONSE ASSISTANCE
IR-7(1).1	**ASSESSMENT OBJECTIVE:** *Determine if the organization employs automated mechanisms to increase the availability of incident response-related information and support.* **POTENTIAL ASSESSMENT METHODS AND OBJECTS:** **Examine:** [*SELECT FROM:* Incident response policy; procedures addressing incident response assistance; automated mechanisms supporting incident response support and assistance; incident response plan; other relevant documents or records]. **Interview:** [*SELECT FROM:* Organizational personnel with incident response support and assistance responsibilities; organizational personnel that require incident response support and assistance].

IR-7(2)	INCIDENT RESPONSE ASSISTANCE
IR-7(2).1	**ASSESSMENT OBJECTIVE:** *Determine if:* (i) *the organization establishes a direct, cooperative relationship between its incident response capability and external providers of information system protection capability; and* (ii) *the organization identifies organizational incident response team members to the external providers.* **POTENTIAL ASSESSMENT METHODS AND OBJECTS:** **Examine:** [*SELECT FROM:* Incident response policy; procedures addressing incident response assistance; automated mechanisms supporting incident response support and assistance; incident response plan; other relevant documents or records]. **Interview:** [*SELECT FROM:* Organizational personnel with incident response support and assistance responsibilities; external providers of information system protection capability].

FAMILY: INCIDENT RESPONSE   **CLASS:** OPERATIONAL

ASSESSMENT PROCEDURE	
IR-8	**INCIDENT RESPONSE PLAN**
IR-8.1	**ASSESSMENT OBJECTIVE:** *Determine if the organization develops an incident response plan that:* – *provides the organization with a roadmap for implementing its incident response capability;* – *describes the structure and organization of the incident response capability;* – *provides a high-level approach for how the incident response capability fits into the overall organization;* – *meets the unique requirements of the organization, which relate to mission, size, structure, and functions;* – *defines reportable incidents;* – *provides metrics for measuring the incident response capability within the organization;* – *defines the resources and management support needed to effectively maintain and mature an incident response capability; and* – *is reviewed and approved by designated officials within the organization.* **POTENTIAL ASSESSMENT METHODS AND OBJECTS:** **Examine:** [*SELECT FROM:* Incident response policy; procedures addressing incident response assistance; incident response plan; other relevant documents or records]. **Interview:** [*SELECT FROM:* Organizational personnel with incident response planning responsibilities].
IR-8.2	**ASSESSMENT OBJECTIVE:** *Determine if:* (i) *the organization defines, in the incident response plan, incident response personnel (identified by name and/or role) and organizational elements;* (ii) *the organization distributes copies of the incident response plan to incident response personnel and organizational elements identified in the plan;* (iii) *the organization defines, in the incident response plan, the frequency to review the plan;* (iv) *the organization reviews the incident response plan in accordance with the organization-defined frequency;* (v) *the organization revises the incident response plan to address system/organizational changes or problems encountered during plan implementation, execution, or testing; and* (vi) *the organization communicates incident response plan changes to incident response personnel and organizational elements identified in the plan.* **POTENTIAL ASSESSMENT METHODS AND OBJECTS:** **Examine:** [*SELECT FROM:* Incident response policy; procedures addressing incident response assistance; incident response plan; other relevant documents or records]. **Interview:** [*SELECT FROM:* Organizational personnel with incident response planning responsibilities].

FAMILY: MAINTENANCE   **CLASS:** OPERATIONAL

ASSESSMENT PROCEDURE	
MA-1	**SYSTEM MAINTENANCE POLICY AND PROCEDURES**

MA-1.1	**ASSESSMENT OBJECTIVE:**
	Determine if:
	
	(i) *the organization develops and formally documents system maintenance policy;*
	
	(ii) *the organization system maintenance policy addresses:*
	
	   - *purpose;*
	   - *scope;*
	   - *roles and responsibilities;*
	   - *management commitment;*
	   - *coordination among organizational entities; and*
	   - *compliance;*
	
	(iii) *the organization disseminates formal documented system maintenance policy to elements within the organization having associated system maintenance roles and responsibilities;*
	
	(iv) *the organization develops and formally documents system maintenance procedures;*
	
	(v) *the organization system maintenance procedures facilitate implementation of the system maintenance policy and associated system maintenance controls; and*
	
	(vi) *the organization disseminates formal documented system maintenance procedures to elements within the organization having associated system maintenance roles and responsibilities.*
	
	POTENTIAL ASSESSMENT METHODS AND OBJECTS:
	Examine: [*SELECT FROM:* Information system maintenance policy and procedures; other relevant documents or records].
	Interview: [*SELECT FROM:* Organizational personnel with information system maintenance responsibilities].

MA-1.2	**ASSESSMENT OBJECTIVE:** *Determine if:* (i) *the organization defines the frequency of system maintenance policy reviews/updates;* (ii) *the organization reviews/updates system maintenance policy in accordance with organization-defined frequency; and* (iii) *the organization defines the frequency of system maintenance procedure reviews/updates;* (iv) *the organization reviews/updates system maintenance procedures in accordance with organization-defined frequency.* **POTENTIAL ASSESSMENT METHODS AND OBJECTS:** **Examine:** [*SELECT FROM:* Information system maintenance policy and procedures; other relevant documents or records]. **Interview:** [*SELECT FROM:* Organizational personnel with information system maintenance responsibilities].

FAMILY: MAINTENANCE   **CLASS:** OPERATIONAL

ASSESSMENT PROCEDURE
MA-2	**CONTROLLED MAINTENANCE**

| MA-2.1 | **ASSESSMENT OBJECTIVE:**
Determine if:
(i) the organization schedules, performs, documents, and reviews records of maintenance and repairs on information system components in accordance with manufacturer or vendor specifications and/or organizational requirements;
(ii) the organization controls all maintenance activities, whether performed on site or remotely and whether the equipment is serviced on site or removed to another location;
(iii) the organization requires that a designated official explicitly approve the removal of the information system or system components from organizational facilities for off-site maintenance or repairs;
(iv) the organization sanitizes equipment to remove all information from associated media prior to removal from organizational facilities for off-site maintenance or repairs; and
(v) the organization checks all potentially impacted security controls to verify that the controls are still functioning properly following maintenance or repair actions.

POTENTIAL ASSESSMENT METHODS AND OBJECTS:
Examine: [*SELECT FROM:* Information system maintenance policy; procedures addressing controlled maintenance for the information system; maintenance records; manufacturer/vendor maintenance specifications; equipment sanitization records; media sanitization records; other relevant documents or records].
Interview: [*SELECT FROM:* Organizational personnel with information system maintenance responsibilities]. |

| **MA-2(1)** | **CONTROLLED MAINTENANCE** |

| MA-2(1).1 | **ASSESSMENT OBJECTIVE:**
Determine if the organization maintains maintenance records for the information system that include:
– *date and time of maintenance;*
– *name of the individual performing the maintenance;*
– *name of escort, if necessary;*
– *a description of the maintenance performed; and*
– *a list of equipment removed or replaced (including identification numbers, if applicable).*

POTENTIAL ASSESSMENT METHODS AND OBJECTS:
Examine: [*SELECT FROM:* Information system maintenance policy; procedures addressing controlled maintenance for the information system; maintenance records; other relevant documents or records]. |

MA-2(2)	CONTROLLED MAINTENANCE
MA-2(2).1	**ASSESSMENT OBJECTIVE:** *Determine if:* (i) *the organization employs automated mechanisms to schedule, conduct, and document maintenance and repairs as required; and* (ii) *the organization employs automated mechanisms to produce up-to-date, accurate, complete, and available records of all maintenance and repair actions needed, in process and complete.* **POTENTIAL ASSESSMENT METHODS AND OBJECTS:** **Examine**: [*SELECT FROM:* Information system maintenance policy; procedures addressing controlled maintenance for the information system; automated mechanisms supporting information system maintenance activities; information system configuration settings and associated documentation; maintenance records; other relevant documents or records].

FAMILY: MAINTENANCE

CLASS: OPERATIONAL

ASSESSMENT PROCEDURE	
MA-3	**MAINTENANCE TOOLS**
MA-3.1	**ASSESSMENT OBJECTIVE:** *Determine if:* *(i) the organization approves, controls, and monitors the use of information system maintenance tools; and* *(ii) the organization maintains information system maintenance tools on an ongoing basis.* **POTENTIAL ASSESSMENT METHODS AND OBJECTS:** **Examine**: [*SELECT FROM:* Information system maintenance policy; information system maintenance tools and associated documentation; procedures addressing information system maintenance tools; maintenance records; other relevant documents or records].

MA-3(1)	**MAINTENANCE TOOLS**
MA-3(1).1	**ASSESSMENT OBJECTIVE:** *Determine if the organization inspects all maintenance tools carried into a facility by maintenance personnel for obvious improper modifications.* **POTENTIAL ASSESSMENT METHODS AND OBJECTS:** **Examine**: [*SELECT FROM:* Information system maintenance policy; information system maintenance tools and associated documentation; procedures addressing information system maintenance tools; maintenance records; other relevant documents or records]. **Interview**: [*SELECT FROM:* Organizational personnel with information system maintenance responsibilities].

MA-3(2)	**MAINTENANCE TOOLS**
MA-3(2).1	**ASSESSMENT OBJECTIVE:** *Determine if the organization checks all media containing diagnostic and test programs (e.g., software or firmware used for information system maintenance or diagnostics) for malicious code before the media are used in the information system.* **POTENTIAL ASSESSMENT METHODS AND OBJECTS:** **Examine**: [*SELECT FROM:* Information system maintenance policy; information system maintenance tools and associated documentation; procedures addressing information system maintenance tools; information system media containing maintenance programs (including diagnostic and test programs); maintenance records; other relevant documents or records]. **Interview**: [*SELECT FROM:* Organizational personnel with information system maintenance responsibilities]. **Test**: [*SELECT FROM:* Media checking process for malicious code detection].

MA-3(3)	MAINTENANCE TOOLS
MA-3(3).1	**ASSESSMENT OBJECTIVE:** *Determine if the organization prevents the unauthorized removal of maintenance equipment by one of the following:* – *verifying that there is no organizational information contained on the equipment;* – *sanitizing or destroying the equipment;* – *retaining the equipment within the facility; or* – *obtaining an exemption from a designated organization official explicitly authorizing removal of the equipment from the facility.* **POTENTIAL ASSESSMENT METHODS AND OBJECTS:** **Examine:** [*SELECT FROM:* Information system maintenance policy; information system maintenance tools and associated documentation; procedures addressing information system maintenance tools; information system media containing maintenance programs (including diagnostic and test programs); maintenance records; equipment sanitization records; media sanitization records; exemptions for equipment removal; other relevant documents or records]. **Interview:** [*SELECT FROM:* Organizational personnel with information system maintenance responsibilities].

MA-3(4)	MAINTENANCE TOOLS
MA-3(4).1	**ASSESSMENT OBJECTIVE:** *Determine if the organization employs automated mechanisms to restrict the use of maintenance tools to authorized personnel only.* **POTENTIAL ASSESSMENT METHODS AND OBJECTS:** **Examine:** [*SELECT FROM:* Information system maintenance policy; information system maintenance tools and associated documentation; procedures addressing information system maintenance tools; automated mechanisms supporting information system maintenance activities; information system design documentation; information system configuration settings and associated documentation; maintenance records; other relevant documents or records]. **Test:** [*SELECT FROM:* Automated mechanisms supporting information system maintenance activities].

FAMILY: MAINTENANCE   **CLASS:** OPERATIONAL

ASSESSMENT PROCEDURE	
MA-4	**NON-LOCAL MAINTENANCE**
MA-4.1	**ASSESSMENT OBJECTIVE:** *Determine if:* (i) the organization authorizes, monitors, and controls non-local maintenance and diagnostic activities; (ii) the organization documents, in the organizational policy and security plan for the information system, the acceptable conditions for allowing the use of non-local maintenance and diagnostic tools; (iii) the organization allows the use of non-local maintenance and diagnostic tools only as consistent with organizational policy and as documented in the security plan; (iv) the organization employs strong identification and authentication techniques in the establishment of non-local maintenance and diagnostic sessions; (v) the organization maintains records for non-local maintenance and diagnostic activities; and (vi) the organization (or information system in certain cases) terminates all sessions and network connections when non-local maintenance or diagnostics is completed. **POTENTIAL ASSESSMENT METHODS AND OBJECTS:** **Examine**: [*SELECT FROM:* Information system maintenance policy; procedures addressing non-local maintenance for the information system; security plan; information system design documentation; information system configuration settings and associated documentation; maintenance records; other relevant documents or records]. **Interview**: [*SELECT FROM:* Organizational personnel with information system maintenance responsibilities].

MA-4(1)	**NON-LOCAL MAINTENANCE**
MA-4(1).1	**ASSESSMENT OBJECTIVE:** *Determine if:* (i) the organization audits non-local maintenance and diagnostic sessions; and (ii) designated organizational personnel review the maintenance records of the sessions. **POTENTIAL ASSESSMENT METHODS AND OBJECTS:** **Examine**: [*SELECT FROM:* Information system maintenance policy; procedures addressing non-local maintenance for the information system; maintenance records; audit records; other relevant documents or records]. **Interview**: [*SELECT FROM:* Organizational personnel with information system maintenance responsibilities].

MA-4(2)	NON-LOCAL MAINTENANCE
MA-4(2).1	**ASSESSMENT OBJECTIVE:** *Determine if the organization documents the installation and use of non-local maintenance and diagnostic connections in the security plan for the information system.* **POTENTIAL ASSESSMENT METHODS AND OBJECTS:** **Examine**: [*SELECT FROM:* Information system maintenance policy; procedures addressing non-local maintenance for the information system; security plan; maintenance records; audit records; other relevant documents or records].

MA-4(3)	NON-LOCAL MAINTENANCE
MA-4(3).1	**ASSESSMENT OBJECTIVE:** *Determine if:* (i) *the organization requires and ensures non-local maintenance and diagnostic services are performed from an information system that implements a level of security at least as high as the level of security implemented on the information system being serviced; or* (ii) *the organization removes the component to be serviced from the information system and prior to non-local maintenance or diagnostic services, sanitizes the component (with regard to organizational information) before removal from organizational facilities; and* (iii) *the organization after the removed component service is performed, inspects and sanitizes the component (with regard to potentially malicious software and surreptitious implants) before reconnecting to the information system.* **POTENTIAL ASSESSMENT METHODS AND OBJECTS:** **Examine**: [*SELECT FROM:* Information system maintenance policy; procedures addressing non-local maintenance for the information system; service provider contracts and/or service level agreements; maintenance records; audit records; other relevant documents or records]. **Interview**: [*SELECT FROM:* Organizational personnel with information system maintenance responsibilities; information system maintenance provider].

MA-4(4)	NON-LOCAL MAINTENANCE
MA-4(4).1	**ASSESSMENT OBJECTIVE:** *Determine if:* (i) *the organization protects non-local maintenance sessions through the use of a strong authenticator tightly bound to the user; and* (ii) *the organization protects non-local maintenance sessions by separating the maintenance session from other network sessions with the information system by:* - *either physically separated communications paths; or* - *logically separated communications paths based upon encryption.* **POTENTIAL ASSESSMENT METHODS AND OBJECTS:** **Examine**: [*SELECT FROM:* Information system maintenance policy; procedures addressing non-local maintenance for the information system; information system design documentation; information system configuration settings and associated documentation; maintenance records; audit records; other relevant documents or records]. **Interview**: [*SELECT FROM:* Organizational personnel with information system maintenance responsibilities].

MA-4(5)	NON-LOCAL MAINTENANCE

MA-4(5).1	**ASSESSMENT OBJECTIVE:** *Determine if:* *(i) the organization defines the organizational personnel to be notified when non-local maintenance is planned;* *(ii) the organization requires that maintenance personnel notify organization-defined personnel when non-local maintenance is planned (i.e., date/time); and* *(iii) the organization requires that a designated organizational official with specific information security/information system knowledge approves the non-local maintenance.* **POTENTIAL ASSESSMENT METHODS AND OBJECTS:** **Examine**: [*SELECT FROM:* Information system maintenance policy; procedures addressing non-local maintenance for the information system; security plan; maintenance records; audit records; other relevant documents or records]. **Interview**: [*SELECT FROM:* Organizational personnel with information system maintenance responsibilities].

MA-4(6)	NON-LOCAL MAINTENANCE

MA-4(6).1	**ASSESSMENT OBJECTIVE:** *Determine if the organization employs cryptographic mechanisms to protect the integrity and confidentiality of non-local maintenance and diagnostic communications.* **POTENTIAL ASSESSMENT METHODS AND OBJECTS:** **Examine**: [*SELECT FROM:* Information system maintenance policy; procedures addressing non-local maintenance for the information system; cryptographic mechanisms supporting information system maintenance activities; information system design documentation; information system configuration settings and associated documentation; maintenance records; audit records; other relevant documents or records]. **Test**: [*SELECT FROM:* Cryptographic mechanisms supporting information system maintenance activities].

MA-4(7)	NON-LOCAL MAINTENANCE

MA-4(7).1	**ASSESSMENT OBJECTIVE:** *Determine if the organization employs remote disconnect verification at the termination of non-local maintenance and diagnostic sessions.* **POTENTIAL ASSESSMENT METHODS AND OBJECTS:** **Examine**: [*SELECT FROM:* Information system maintenance policy; procedures addressing non-local maintenance for the information system; information system design documentation; information system configuration settings and associated documentation; maintenance records; audit records; other relevant documents or records].

FAMILY: MAINTENANCE   **CLASS:** OPERATIONAL

ASSESSMENT PROCEDURE	
MA-5	**MAINTENANCE PERSONNEL**
MA-5.1	**ASSESSMENT OBJECTIVE:** *Determine if:* (i) *the organization establishes a process for maintenance personnel authorization;* (ii) *the organization maintains a current list of authorized maintenance organizations or personnel; and* (iii) *personnel performing maintenance on the information system either have the required access authorizations or are supervised by designated organizational personnel with the required access authorizations and technical competence deemed necessary to supervise information system maintenance.* **POTENTIAL ASSESSMENT METHODS AND OBJECTS:** **Examine:** [*SELECT FROM:* Information system maintenance policy; procedures addressing maintenance personnel; service provider contracts and/or service level agreements; list of authorized personnel; maintenance records; access control records; other relevant documents or records]. **Interview:** [*SELECT FROM:* Organizational personnel with information system maintenance responsibilities].

MA-5(1)	MAINTENANCE PERSONNEL	
MA-5(1).1	**ASSESSMENT OBJECTIVE:** *Determine if the organization maintains procedures for the use of maintenance personnel that lack appropriate security clearances or are not U.S. citizens, that include the following requirements:* – *maintenance personnel who do not have needed access authorizations, clearances, or formal access approvals are escorted and supervised during the performance of maintenance and diagnostic activities on the information system by approved organizational personnel who are fully cleared, have appropriate access authorizations, and are technically qualified;* – *prior to initiating maintenance or diagnostic activities by personnel who do not have needed access authorizations, clearances, or formal access approvals, all volatile information storage components within the information system are sanitized and all nonvolatile storage media are removed or physically disconnected from the system and secured; and* – *in the event an information system component cannot be sanitized, the procedures contained in the security plan for the system are enforced.* **POTENTIAL ASSESSMENT METHODS AND OBJECTS:** **Examine:** [*SELECT FROM:* Information system maintenance policy; procedures addressing maintenance personnel; information system media protection policy; physical and environmental protection policy; security plan; list of maintenance personnel requiring escort/supervision; maintenance records; access control records; other relevant documents or records]. **Interview:** [*SELECT FROM:* Organizational personnel with information system maintenance responsibilities; organizational personnel with personnel security responsibilities; organizational personnel with physical access control responsibilities].	

MA-5(2)	MAINTENANCE PERSONNEL
MA-5(2).1	**ASSESSMENT OBJECTIVE:** *Determine if personnel performing maintenance and diagnostic activities on an information system processing, storing, or transmitting classified information are cleared for the highest level of information on the system.* **POTENTIAL ASSESSMENT METHODS AND OBJECTS:** **Examine:** [*SELECT FROM:* Information system maintenance policy; procedures addressing maintenance personnel; maintenance records; access control records; access authorizations; access credentials; other relevant documents or records]. **Interview:** [*SELECT FROM:* Organizational personnel with information system maintenance responsibilities; organizational personnel with personnel security responsibilities].

MA-5(3)	MAINTENANCE PERSONNEL
MA-5(3).1	**ASSESSMENT OBJECTIVE:** *Determine if personnel performing maintenance and diagnostic activities on the information system processing, storing, or transmitting classified information are U.S. citizens.* **POTENTIAL ASSESSMENT METHODS AND OBJECTS:** **Examine:** [*SELECT FROM:* Information system maintenance policy; procedures addressing maintenance personnel; maintenance records; access control records; other relevant documents or records]. **Interview:** [*SELECT FROM:* Organizational personnel with information system maintenance responsibilities, organizational personnel with personnel security responsibilities].

MA-5(4)	MAINTENANCE PERSONNEL
MA-5(4).1	**ASSESSMENT OBJECTIVE:** *Determine if:* (i) *cleared foreign nationals are used to conduct maintenance and diagnostic activities on an information system only when the system is jointly owned and operated by the United States and foreign allied governments, or owned and operated solely by foreign allied governments; and* (ii) *the organization documents in a Memorandum of Agreement the approvals, consents, and detailed operational conditions under which foreign nationals are allowed to conduct maintenance and diagnostic activities on an information system.* **POTENTIAL ASSESSMENT METHODS AND OBJECTS:** **Examine:** [*SELECT FROM:* Information system maintenance policy; procedures addressing maintenance personnel; information system media protection policy; access control policy and procedures; physical and environmental protection policy and procedures; memorandum of agreement; maintenance records; access control records; other relevant documents or records]. **Interview:** [*SELECT FROM:* Organizational personnel with information system maintenance responsibilities, organizational personnel with personnel security responsibilities].

FAMILY: MAINTENANCE

CLASS: OPERATIONAL

ASSESSMENT PROCEDURE	
MA-6	**TIMELY MAINTENANCE**
MA-6.1	**ASSESSMENT OBJECTIVE:** *Determine if:* (i) *the organization defines security-critical information system components and/or key information technology components for which it will obtain maintenance support and/or spare parts;* (ii) *the organization defines the time period within which support and/or spare parts must be obtained after a failure; and* (iii) *the organization obtains maintenance support and/or spare parts for the organization-defined list of security-critical information system components and/or key information technology components within the organization-defined time period of failure.* **POTENTIAL ASSESSMENT METHODS AND OBJECTS:** **Examine:** [*SELECT FROM:* Information system maintenance policy; procedures addressing timely maintenance for the information system; service provider contracts and/or service level agreements; inventory and availability of spare parts; security plan; other relevant documents or records]. **Interview:** [*SELECT FROM:* Organizational personnel with information system maintenance responsibilities].

FAMILY: MEDIA PROTECTION   **CLASS:** OPERATIONAL

ASSESSMENT PROCEDURE	
MP-1	**MEDIA PROTECTION POLICY AND PROCEDURES**
MP-1.1	**ASSESSMENT OBJECTIVE:** *Determine if:* (i) *the organization develops and formally documents media protection policy;* (ii) *the organization media protection policy addresses:* 　　　- *purpose;* 　　　- *scope;* 　　　- *roles and responsibilities;* 　　　- *management commitment;* 　　　- *coordination among organizational entities; and* 　　　- *compliance;* (iii) *the organization disseminates formal documented media protection policy to elements within the organization having associated media protection roles and responsibilities;* (iv) *the organization develops and formally documents media protection procedures;* (v) *the organization media protection procedures facilitate implementation of the media protection policy and associated media protection controls; and* (vi) *the organization disseminates formal documented media protection procedures to elements within the organization having associated media protection roles and responsibilities.* **POTENTIAL ASSESSMENT METHODS AND OBJECTS:** **Examine:** [*SELECT FROM:* Media protection policy and procedures; other relevant documents or records]. **Interview:** [*SELECT FROM:* Organizational personnel with information system media protection responsibilities].
MP-1.2	**ASSESSMENT OBJECTIVE:** *Determine if:* (i) *the organization defines the frequency of media protection policy reviews/updates;* (ii) *the organization reviews/updates media protection policy in accordance with organization-defined frequency; and* (iii) *the organization defines the frequency of media protection procedure reviews/updates;* (iv) *the organization reviews/updates media protection procedures in accordance with organization-defined frequency.* **POTENTIAL ASSESSMENT METHODS AND OBJECTS:** **Examine:** [*SELECT FROM:* Media protection policy and procedures; other relevant documents or records]. **Interview:** [*SELECT FROM:* Organizational personnel with information system media protection responsibilities].

FAMILY: MEDIA PROTECTION   **CLASS:** OPERATIONAL

ASSESSMENT PROCEDURE	
MP-2	**MEDIA ACCESS**

MP-2.1	**ASSESSMENT OBJECTIVE:**
	Determine if:
	
	(i) the organization defines:
	
	    - *digital and non-digital media requiring restricted access;*
	
	    - *individuals authorized to access the media;*
	
	    - *security measures taken to restrict access; and*
	
	(ii) the organization restricts access to organization-defined information system media to organization-defined authorized individuals using organization-defined security measures.
	
	POTENTIAL ASSESSMENT METHODS AND OBJECTS:
	
	Examine: [*SELECT FROM:* Information system media protection policy; procedures addressing media access; access control policy and procedures; physical and environmental protection policy and procedures; media storage facilities; access control records; other relevant documents or records].
	
	Interview: [*SELECT FROM:* Organizational personnel with information system media protection responsibilities].

MP-2(1)	MEDIA ACCESS	
MP-2(1).1	**ASSESSMENT OBJECTIVE:** *Determine if:* *(i) the organization employs automated mechanisms to restrict access to media storage areas; and* *(ii) the organization employs automated mechanisms to audit access attempts and access granted to media storage areas.* **POTENTIAL ASSESSMENT METHODS AND OBJECTS:** **Examine**: [*SELECT FROM:* Information system media protection policy; procedures addressing media access; access control policy and procedures; physical and environmental protection policy and procedures; media storage facilities; access control devices; access control records; audit records; other relevant documents or records]. **Test**: [*SELECT FROM:* Automated mechanisms implementing access restrictions to media storage areas].	

MP-2(2)	MEDIA ACCESS	
MP-2(2).1	**ASSESSMENT OBJECTIVE:** *Determine if the information system uses cryptographic mechanisms to protect and restrict access to information on portable digital media.* **POTENTIAL ASSESSMENT METHODS AND OBJECTS:** **Examine**: [*SELECT FROM:* Information system media protection policy; procedures addressing media access; other relevant documents or records]. **Test**: [*SELECT FROM:* Cryptographic mechanisms protecting and restricting access to information system information on portable digital media].	

FAMILY: MEDIA PROTECTION   **CLASS:** OPERATIONAL

ASSESSMENT PROCEDURE

MP-3	MEDIA MARKING
MP-3.1	**ASSESSMENT OBJECTIVE:** *Determine if:* (i) *the organization defines removable media types and information system output that require marking;* (ii) *the organization marks removable media and information system output in accordance with organizational policies and procedures, indicating the distribution limitations, handling caveats, and applicable security markings (if any) of the information;* (iii) *the organization defines:* - *removable media types and information system output exempt from marking;* - *controlled areas designated for retaining removable media and information output exempt from marking; and* (iv) *removable media and information system output exempt from marking remain within designated controlled areas.* **POTENTIAL ASSESSMENT METHODS AND OBJECTS:** **Examine:** [*SELECT FROM:* Information system media protection policy; procedures addressing media labeling; physical and environmental protection policy and procedures; security plan; removable storage media and information system output; other relevant documents or records]. **Interview:** [*SELECT FROM:* Organizational personnel with information system media protection and marking responsibilities].

FAMILY: MEDIA PROTECTION   **CLASS:** OPERATIONAL

ASSESSMENT PROCEDURE	
MP-4	**MEDIA STORAGE**

MP-4.1	**ASSESSMENT OBJECTIVE:**
	Determine if:
	
	(i) the organization defines:
	
	    - *types of digital and non-digital media physically controlled and securely stored within designated controlled areas;*
	
	    - *controlled areas designated to physically control and securely store the media;*
	
	    - *security measures to physically control and securely store the media within designated controlled areas;*
	
	(ii) the organization physically controls and securely stores organization-defined information system media within organization-defined controlled areas using organization-defined security measures; and
	
	(iii) the organization protects information system media until the media are destroyed or sanitized using approved equipment, techniques, and procedures.
	
	POTENTIAL ASSESSMENT METHODS AND OBJECTS:
	
	Examine: [*SELECT FROM:* Information system media protection policy; procedures addressing media storage; physical and environmental protection policy and procedures; access control policy and procedures; security plan; information system media; other relevant documents or records].
	
	Interview: [*SELECT FROM:* Organizational personnel with information system media protection and storage responsibilities].

MP-4(1)	**MEDIA STORAGE**
MP-4(1).1	**ASSESSMENT OBJECTIVE:** *Determine if the organization employs cryptographic mechanisms to protect information in storage.* **POTENTIAL ASSESSMENT METHODS AND OBJECTS:** **Examine:** [*SELECT FROM:* Information system media protection policy; procedures addressing media access; access control policy and procedures; physical and environmental protection policy and procedures; media storage facilities; access control devices; access control records; audit records; other relevant documents or records]. **Test:** [*SELECT FROM:* Cryptographic mechanisms protecting information in storage].

FAMILY: MEDIA PROTECTION   **CLASS:** OPERATIONAL

ASSESSMENT PROCEDURE	
MP-5	**MEDIA TRANSPORT**

MP-5.1	**ASSESSMENT OBJECTIVE:**
	Determine if:
	(i) *the organization defines:*
	    - *types of digital and non-digital media protected and controlled during transport outside of controlled areas;*
	    - *security measures (e.g., locked container, encryption) for such media transported outside of controlled areas;*
	(ii) *the organization protects and controls organization-defined information system media during transport outside of controlled areas using organization-defined security measures;*
	(iii) *the organization maintains accountability for information system media during transport outside of controlled areas;*
	(iv) *the organization identifies personnel authorized to transport information system media outside of controlled areas; and*
	(v) *the organization restricts the activities associated with transport of information system media to authorized personnel.*
	
	POTENTIAL ASSESSMENT METHODS AND OBJECTS:
	Examine: [*SELECT FROM:* Information system media protection policy; procedures addressing media transport; physical and environmental protection policy and procedures; access control policy and procedures; security plan; list of organization-defined personnel authorized to transport information system media outside of controlled areas; information system media; information system media transport records; information system audit records; other relevant documents or records].
	
	Interview: [*SELECT FROM:* Organizational personnel with information system media transport responsibilities].

MP-5(1)	**MEDIA TRANSPORT** [Withdrawn: Incorporated into MP-5].
MP-5(1).1	**ASSESSMENT OBJECTIVE:** [Withdrawn: Incorporated into MP-5]. **POTENTIAL ASSESSMENT METHODS AND OBJECTS:** [Withdrawn: Incorporated into MP-5].

MP-5(2)	MEDIA TRANSPORT
MP-5(2).1	**ASSESSMENT OBJECTIVE:** *Determine if the organization documents activities associated with the transport of information system media.* **POTENTIAL ASSESSMENT METHODS AND OBJECTS:** **Examine:** [*SELECT FROM:* Information system media protection policy; procedures addressing media transport; physical and environmental protection policy and procedures; access control policy and procedures; security plan; information system media transport records; audit records; other relevant documents or records].

MP-5(3)	MEDIA TRANSPORT
MP-5(3).1	**ASSESSMENT OBJECTIVE:** *Determine if the organization employs an identified custodian throughout the transport of information system media.* **POTENTIAL ASSESSMENT METHODS AND OBJECTS:** **Examine:** [*SELECT FROM:* Information system media protection policy; procedures addressing media transport; physical and environmental protection policy and procedures; information system media transport records; audit records; other relevant documents or records]. **Interview:** [*SELECT FROM:* Organizational personnel with information system media transport responsibilities].

MP-5(4)	MEDIA TRANSPORT
MP-5(4).1	**ASSESSMENT OBJECTIVE:** *Determine if the organization employs cryptographic mechanisms to protect the confidentiality and integrity of information stored on digital media during transport outside of controlled areas.* **POTENTIAL ASSESSMENT METHODS AND OBJECTS:** **Examine:** [*SELECT FROM:* Information system media protection policy; procedures addressing media transport; information system media transport records; audit records; other relevant documents or records]. **Test:** [*SELECT FROM:* Cryptographic mechanisms protecting information during transportation outside controlled areas].

FAMILY: MEDIA PROTECTION

CLASS: OPERATIONAL

ASSESSMENT PROCEDURE
MP-6 — **MEDIA SANITIZATION**
MP-6.1 — **ASSESSMENT OBJECTIVE:** *Determine if:* (i)   *the organization sanitizes information system media both digital and non-digital prior to:* - *disposal;* - *release out of organizational control; or* - *release for reuse; and* (ii) *the organization employs sanitization mechanisms with strength and integrity commensurate with the classification or sensitivity of the information.* **POTENTIAL ASSESSMENT METHODS AND OBJECTS:** **Examine:** [*SELECT FROM:* Information system media protection policy; procedures addressing media sanitization and disposal; media sanitization records; audit records; other relevant documents or records]. **Interview:** [*SELECT FROM:* Organizational personnel with information system media sanitization responsibilities].

MP-6(1) — **MEDIA SANITIZATION**
MP-6(1).1 — **ASSESSMENT OBJECTIVE:** *Determine if the organization tracks, documents, and verifies media sanitization and disposal actions.* **POTENTIAL ASSESSMENT METHODS AND OBJECTS:** **Examine:** [*SELECT FROM:* Information system media protection policy and procedures; media sanitization records; audit records; other relevant documents or records]. **Interview:** [*SELECT FROM:* Organizational personnel with information system media sanitization responsibilities].

MP-6(2) — **MEDIA SANITIZATION**
MP-6(2).1 — **ASSESSMENT OBJECTIVE:** *Determine if:* (i)   *the organization defines the frequency for testing sanitization equipment and procedures to verify correct performance; and* (ii) *the organization tests sanitization equipment and procedures to verify correct performance in accordance with organization-defined frequency.* **POTENTIAL ASSESSMENT METHODS AND OBJECTS:** **Examine:** [*SELECT FROM:* Information system media protection policy; procedures addressing media sanitization and disposal; media sanitization equipment test records; information system audit records; other relevant documents or records]. **Interview:** [*SELECT FROM:* Organizational personnel with information system media sanitization responsibilities].

MP-6(3)	MEDIA SANITIZATION
MP-6(3).1	**ASSESSMENT OBJECTIVE:** *Determine if:* (i) *the organization defines circumstances requiring sanitization of portable, removable storage devices prior to connecting such devices to the information system; and* (ii) *the organization sanitizes portable, removable storage devices prior to connecting such devices to the information system under organization-defined circumstances.* **POTENTIAL ASSESSMENT METHODS AND OBJECTS:** **Examine**: [*SELECT FROM:* Information system media protection policy and procedures; media sanitization records; audit records; other relevant documents or records]. **Interview**: [*SELECT FROM:* Organizational personnel with information system media sanitization responsibilities].

MP-6(4)	MEDIA SANITIZATION
MP-6(4).1	**ASSESSMENT OBJECTIVE:** *Determine if the organization sanitizes information system media containing CUI or other sensitive information in accordance with applicable organizational and/or federal standards and policies.* **POTENTIAL ASSESSMENT METHODS AND OBJECTS:** **Examine**: [*SELECT FROM:* Information system media protection policy; procedures addressing media sanitization and disposal; media sanitization equipment test records; information system audit records; other relevant documents or records]. **Interview**: [*SELECT FROM:* Organizational personnel with information system media sanitization responsibilities].

MP-6(5)	MEDIA SANITIZATION
MP-6(5).1	**ASSESSMENT OBJECTIVE:** *Determine if the organization sanitizes information system media containing classified information in accordance with NSA standards and policies.* **POTENTIAL ASSESSMENT METHODS AND OBJECTS:** **Examine**: [*SELECT FROM:* Information system media protection policy and procedures; media sanitization records; audit records; other relevant documents or records]. **Interview**: [*SELECT FROM:* Organizational personnel with information system media sanitization responsibilities].

MP-6(6)	MEDIA SANITIZATION
MP-6(6).1	**ASSESSMENT OBJECTIVE:** *Determine if the organization implements the media destruction process for information system media that cannot be sanitized.* **POTENTIAL ASSESSMENT METHODS AND OBJECTS:** **Examine**: [*SELECT FROM:* Information system media protection policy; procedures addressing media sanitization and disposal; media sanitization equipment test records; information system audit records; other relevant documents or records]. **Interview**: [*SELECT FROM:* Organizational personnel with information system media sanitization responsibilities].

FAMILY: PHYSICAL AND ENVIRONMENTAL PROTECTION   **CLASS:** OPERATIONAL

ASSESSMENT PROCEDURE	
PE-1	**PHYSICAL AND ENVIRONMENTAL PROTECTION POLICY AND PROCEDURES**

PE-1.1	**ASSESSMENT OBJECTIVE:**
	Determine if:
	(i) *the organization develops and formally documents physical and environmental protection policy;*
	(ii) *the organization physical and environmental protection policy addresses:*
	    - *purpose;*
	    - *scope;*
	    - *roles and responsibilities;*
	    - *management commitment;*
	    - *coordination among organizational entities; and*
	    - *compliance;*
	(iii) *the organization disseminates formal documented physical and environmental protection policy to elements within the organization having associated physical and environmental protection roles and responsibilities;*
	(iv) *the organization develops and formally documents physical and environmental protection procedures;*
	(v) *the organization physical and environmental protection procedures facilitate implementation of the physical and environmental protection policy and associated physical and environmental protection controls; and*
	(vi) *the organization disseminates formal documented physical and environmental protection procedures to elements within the organization having associated physical and environmental protection roles and responsibilities.*
	POTENTIAL ASSESSMENT METHODS AND OBJECTS:
	Examine: [*SELECT FROM:* Physical and environmental protection policy and procedures; other relevant documents or records].
	Interview: [*SELECT FROM:* Organizational personnel with physical and environmental protection responsibilities].

PE-1.2	**ASSESSMENT OBJECTIVE:** *Determine if:* *(i)* *the organization defines the frequency of physical and environmental protection policy reviews/updates;* *(ii)* *the organization reviews/updates physical and environmental protection policy in accordance with organization-defined frequency; and* *(iii)* *the organization defines the frequency of physical and environmental protection procedure reviews/updates;* *(iv)* *the organization reviews/updates physical and environmental protection procedures in accordance with organization-defined frequency.* **POTENTIAL ASSESSMENT METHODS AND OBJECTS:** **Examine:** [*SELECT FROM:* Physical and environmental protection policy and procedures; other relevant documents or records]. **Interview:** [*SELECT FROM:* Organizational personnel with physical and environmental protection responsibilities].

FAMILY: PHYSICAL AND ENVIRONMENTAL PROTECTION   **CLASS:** OPERATIONAL

ASSESSMENT PROCEDURE	
PE-2	**PHYSICAL ACCESS AUTHORIZATIONS**
PE-2.1	**ASSESSMENT OBJECTIVE:** *Determine if:* (i) *the organization identifies areas within the facility that are publicly accessible;* (ii) *the organization develops and keeps current lists of personnel with authorized access to the facility where the information system resides (except for those areas within the facility officially designated as publicly accessible); and* (iii) *the organization issues authorization credentials (e.g., badges, identification cards, smart cards).* **POTENTIAL ASSESSMENT METHODS AND OBJECTS:** **Examine:** [*SELECT FROM:* Physical and environmental protection policy; procedures addressing physical access authorizations; authorized personnel access list; authorization credentials; list of areas that are publicly accessible; other relevant documents or records].
PE-2.2	**ASSESSMENT OBJECTIVE:** *Determine if:* (i) *the organization defines the frequency for review and approval of the physical access list and authorization credentials for the facility;* (ii) *organization reviews and approves the access list and authorization credentials in accordance with the organization-defined frequency; and* (iii) *the organization removes from the access list personnel no longer requiring access.* **POTENTIAL ASSESSMENT METHODS AND OBJECTS:** **Examine:** [*SELECT FROM:* Physical and environmental protection policy; procedures addressing physical access authorizations; security plan; authorized personnel access list; authorization credentials; other relevant documents or records].

PE-2(1)	**PHYSICAL ACCESS AUTHORIZATIONS**
PE-2(1).1	**ASSESSMENT OBJECTIVE:** *Determine if:* (i) *the organization identifies personnel positions or roles authorized for physical access to the facility where the information system resides; and* (ii) *the organization authorizes physical access to the facility where the information system resides based on position or role.* **POTENTIAL ASSESSMENT METHODS AND OBJECTS:** **Examine:** [*SELECT FROM:* Physical and environmental protection policy; procedures addressing physical access authorizations; physical access control logs or records; information system entry and exit points; other relevant documents or records].

PE-2(2)	PHYSICAL ACCESS AUTHORIZATIONS
PE-2(2).1	**ASSESSMENT OBJECTIVE:** *Determine if the organization requires two forms of identification to gain access to the facility where the information system resides.* **POTENTIAL ASSESSMENT METHODS AND OBJECTS:** **Examine:** [*SELECT FROM:* Physical and environmental protection policy; procedures addressing physical access authorizations; physical access control logs or records; information system entry and exit points; other relevant documents or records]. **Interview:** [*SELECT FROM:* Organizational personnel with physical access authorization responsibilities; organizational personnel with physical access to information system facility].

PE-2(3)	PHYSICAL ACCESS AUTHORIZATIONS
PE-2(3).1	**ASSESSMENT OBJECTIVE:** *Determine if:* *(i) the organization identifies authorized personnel with appropriate clearances and access authorizations for gaining physical access to the facility containing an information system that processes classified information; and* *(ii) the organization restricts physical access to the facility containing an information system that processes classified information to authorized personnel with appropriate clearances and access authorizations.* **POTENTIAL ASSESSMENT METHODS AND OBJECTS:** **Examine:** [*SELECT FROM:* Physical and environmental protection policy; procedures addressing physical access authorizations; authorized personnel access list; physical access control logs or records; information system entry and exit points; other relevant documents or records].

FAMILY: PHYSICAL AND ENVIRONMENTAL PROTECTION   **CLASS:** OPERATIONAL

ASSESSMENT PROCEDURE	
PE-3	**PHYSICAL ACCESS CONTROL**
PE-3.1	**ASSESSMENT OBJECTIVE:** *Determine if:* (i) *the organization enforces physical access authorizations for all physical access points (including designated entry/exit points) to the facility where the information system resides (excluding those areas within the facility officially designated as publicly accessible);* (ii) *the organization verifies individual access authorizations before granting access to the facility;* (iii) *the organization controls entry to the facility containing the information system using physical access devices (e.g., keys, locks, combinations, card readers) and/or guards;* (iv) *the organization controls access to areas officially designated as publicly accessible in accordance with the organization's assessment of risk; and* (v) *the organization secures keys, combinations, and other physical access devices.* **POTENTIAL ASSESSMENT METHODS AND OBJECTS:** **Examine:** [*SELECT FROM:* Physical and environmental protection policy; procedures addressing physical access control; physical access control logs or records; information system entry and exit points; storage locations for physical access devices; other relevant documents or records]. **Interview:** [*SELECT FROM:* Organizational personnel with physical access control responsibilities]. **Test:** [*SELECT FROM:* Physical access control capability; physical access control devices].
PE-3.2	**ASSESSMENT OBJECTIVE:** *Determine if:* (i) *the organization defines the frequency for conducting inventories of physical access devices;* (ii) *the organization inventories physical access devices in accordance with the organization-defined frequency;* (iii) *the organization defines the frequency of changes to combinations and keys; and* (iv) *the organization changes combinations and keys in accordance with the organization-defined frequency, and when keys are lost, combinations are compromised, or individuals are transferred or terminated.* **POTENTIAL ASSESSMENT METHODS AND OBJECTS:** **Examine:** [*SELECT FROM:* Physical and environmental protection policy; procedures addressing physical access control; security plan; physical access control logs or records; inventory records of physical access devices; records of key and lock combination changes; storage locations for physical access devices; other relevant documents or records]. **Test:** [*SELECT FROM:* Physical access control devices].

PE-3(1)	PHYSICAL ACCESS CONTROL

PE-3(1).1	**ASSESSMENT OBJECTIVE:** *Determine if the organization enforces physical access authorizations to the information system independent of the physical access controls for the facility.* **POTENTIAL ASSESSMENT METHODS AND OBJECTS:** **Examine:** [*SELECT FROM:* Physical and environmental protection policy; procedures addressing physical access control; physical access control logs or records; information system entry and exit points; list of areas within the facility containing high concentrations of information system components or information system components requiring additional physical protection; other relevant documents or records].

PE-3(2)	PHYSICAL ACCESS CONTROL

PE-3(2).1	**ASSESSMENT OBJECTIVE:** *Determine if the organization performs security checks at the physical boundary of the facility or information system for unauthorized exfiltration of information or information system components.* **POTENTIAL ASSESSMENT METHODS AND OBJECTS:** **Examine:** [*SELECT FROM:* Physical and environmental protection policy; procedures addressing physical access control; physical access control logs or records; records of security checks; facility layout documentation; information system entry and exit points; other relevant documents or records]. **Interview:** [*SELECT FROM:* Organizational personnel with physical access control responsibilities].

PE-3(3)	PHYSICAL ACCESS CONTROL

PE-3(3).1	**ASSESSMENT OBJECTIVE:** *Determine if the organization guards, alarms, and monitors every physical access point to the facility where the information system resides 24 hours per day, 7 days per week.* **POTENTIAL ASSESSMENT METHODS AND OBJECTS:** **Examine:** [*SELECT FROM:* Physical and environmental protection policy; procedures addressing physical access control; physical access control logs or records; facility surveillance records; facility layout documentation; information system entry and exit points; other relevant documents or records]. **Interview:** [*SELECT FROM:* Organizational personnel with physical access control responsibilities].

PE-3(4)	PHYSICAL ACCESS CONTROL
PE-3(4).1	**ASSESSMENT OBJECTIVE:** *Determine if:* (i) the organization defines information system components to be protected from unauthorized physical access using lockable physical casings; and (ii) the organization uses lockable physical casings to protect organization-defined information system components from unauthorized physical access. **POTENTIAL ASSESSMENT METHODS AND OBJECTS:** **Examine**: [*SELECT FROM:* Physical and environmental protection policy; procedures addressing physical access control; security plan; list of information system components requiring protection through lockable physical casings; lockable physical casings; other relevant documents or records].

PE-3(5)	PHYSICAL ACCESS CONTROL
PE-3(5).1	**ASSESSMENT OBJECTIVE:** *Determine if the information system detects/prevents physical tampering or alteration of hardware components within the system.* **POTENTIAL ASSESSMENT METHODS AND OBJECTS:** **Examine**: [*SELECT FROM:* Physical and environmental protection policy; procedures addressing physical access control; physical access control logs or records; information system design documentation; other relevant documents or records]. **Test**: [*SELECT FROM:* Physical access control capability].

PE-3(6)	PHYSICAL ACCESS CONTROL
PE-3(6).1	**ASSESSMENT OBJECTIVE:** *Determine if:* (i) the organization defines the frequency of unannounced attempts to be included in a penetration testing process to bypass or circumvent security controls associated with physical access points to the facility; and (ii) the organization employs a penetration testing process that includes unannounced attempts, in accordance with the organization-defined frequency, to bypass or circumvent security controls associated with physical access points to the facility. **POTENTIAL ASSESSMENT METHODS AND OBJECTS:** **Examine**: [*SELECT FROM:* Physical and environmental protection policy; procedures addressing physical access control; procedures addressing penetration testing; rules of engagement and associated documentation; penetration test results; security plan; other relevant documents or records].

FAMILY: PHYSICAL AND ENVIRONMENTAL PROTECTION   **CLASS:** OPERATIONAL

ASSESSMENT PROCEDURE	
PE-4	ACCESS CONTROL FOR TRANSMISSION MEDIUM
PE-4.1	**ASSESSMENT OBJECTIVE:** *Determine if the organization controls physical access to information system distribution and transmission lines within organizational facilities.* **POTENTIAL ASSESSMENT METHODS AND OBJECTS:** **Examine:** [*SELECT FROM:* Physical and environmental protection policy; procedures addressing access control for transmission medium; information system design documentation; facility communications and wiring diagrams; other relevant documents or records].

FAMILY: PHYSICAL AND ENVIRONMENTAL PROTECTION   **CLASS:** OPERATIONAL

ASSESSMENT PROCEDURE	
PE-5	**ACCESS CONTROL FOR OUTPUT DEVICES**
PE-5.1	**ASSESSMENT OBJECTIVE:** *Determine if the organization controls physical access to information system output devices to prevent unauthorized individuals from obtaining the output.* **POTENTIAL ASSESSMENT METHODS AND OBJECTS:** **Examine:** [*SELECT FROM:* Physical and environmental protection policy; procedures addressing access control for display medium; facility layout of information system components; actual displays from information system components; other relevant documents or records].

FAMILY: PHYSICAL AND ENVIRONMENTAL PROTECTION   **CLASS:** OPERATIONAL

ASSESSMENT PROCEDURE

PE-6	MONITORING PHYSICAL ACCESS
PE-6.1	**ASSESSMENT OBJECTIVE:** *Determine if:* (i) the organization monitors physical access to the information system to detect and respond to physical security incidents; (ii) the organization defines the frequency to review physical access logs; (iii) the organization reviews physical access logs in accordance with the organization-defined frequency; and (iv) the organization coordinates results of reviews and investigations with the organization's incident response capability. **POTENTIAL ASSESSMENT METHODS AND OBJECTS:** **Examine:** [*SELECT FROM:* Physical and environmental protection policy; procedures addressing physical access monitoring; security plan; physical access logs or records; other relevant documents or records]. **Interview:** [*SELECT FROM:* Organizational personnel with physical access monitoring responsibilities]. **Test:** [*SELECT FROM:* Physical access monitoring capability].

PE-6(1)	MONITORING PHYSICAL ACCESS
PE-6(1).1	**ASSESSMENT OBJECTIVE:** *Determine if the organization monitors real-time physical intrusion alarms and surveillance equipment.* **POTENTIAL ASSESSMENT METHODS AND OBJECTS:** **Examine:** [*SELECT FROM:* Physical and environmental protection policy; procedures addressing physical access monitoring; physical intrusion alarm/surveillance equipment logs or records; other relevant documents or records]. **Interview:** [*SELECT FROM:* Organizational personnel with physical access monitoring responsibilities]. **Test:** [*SELECT FROM:* Physical access monitoring capability].

PE-6(2)	MONITORING PHYSICAL ACCESS
PE-6(2).1	**ASSESSMENT OBJECTIVE:** *Determine if the organization employs automated mechanisms to recognize potential intrusions and initiate designated response actions.* **POTENTIAL ASSESSMENT METHODS AND OBJECTS:** **Examine:** [*SELECT FROM:* Physical and environmental protection policy; procedures addressing physical access monitoring; information system design documentation; other relevant documents or records]. **Test:** [*SELECT FROM:* Automated mechanisms implementing physical access monitoring capability].

FAMILY: PHYSICAL AND ENVIRONMENTAL PROTECTION   **CLASS:** OPERATIONAL

ASSESSMENT PROCEDURE	
PE-7	**VISITOR CONTROL**
PE-7.1	**ASSESSMENT OBJECTIVE:** *Determine if the organization controls physical access to the information system by authenticating visitors before authorizing access to the facility where the information system resides other than areas designated as publicly accessible.* **POTENTIAL ASSESSMENT METHODS AND OBJECTS:** **Examine:** [*SELECT FROM:* Physical and environmental protection policy; procedures addressing visitor access control; visitor access control logs or records; other relevant documents or records]. **Interview:** [*SELECT FROM:* Organizational personnel with visitor access control responsibilities]. **Test:** [*SELECT FROM:* Visitor access control capability].

PE-7(1)	**VISITOR CONTROL**
PE-7(1).1	**ASSESSMENT OBJECTIVE:** *Determine if the organization escorts visitors and monitors visitor activity, when required.* **POTENTIAL ASSESSMENT METHODS AND OBJECTS:** **Examine:** [*SELECT FROM:* Physical and environmental protection policy; procedures addressing visitor access control; visitor access control logs or records; other relevant documents or records]. **Interview:** [*SELECT FROM:* Organizational personnel with visitor access control responsibilities].

PE-7(2)	**VISITOR CONTROL**
PE-7(2).1	**ASSESSMENT OBJECTIVE:** *Determine if the organization requires two forms of identification for visitor access to the facility.* **POTENTIAL ASSESSMENT METHODS AND OBJECTS:** **Examine:** [*SELECT FROM:* Physical and environmental protection policy; procedures addressing visitor access control; visitor access control logs or records; other relevant documents or records]. **Interview:** [*SELECT FROM:* Organizational personnel with visitor access control responsibilities].

FAMILY: PHYSICAL AND ENVIRONMENTAL PROTECTION   **CLASS:** OPERATIONAL

ASSESSMENT PROCEDURE	
PE-8	**ACCESS RECORDS**
PE-8.1	**ASSESSMENT OBJECTIVE:** *Determine if:* *(i) the organization maintains visitor access records to the facility where the information system resides (except for those areas within the facility officially designated as publicly accessible);* *(ii) the organization defines the frequency to review visitor access records;* *(iii) the organization reviews the visitor access records in accordance with the organization-defined frequency.* **POTENTIAL ASSESSMENT METHODS AND OBJECTS:** **Examine:** [*SELECT FROM:* Physical and environmental protection policy; procedures addressing facility access records; security plan; facility access control records; other relevant documents or records]. **Interview:** [*SELECT FROM:* Organizational personnel with responsibilities for reviewing physical access records].

PE-8(1)	**ACCESS RECORDS**
PE-8(1).1	**ASSESSMENT OBJECTIVE:** *Determine if the organization employs automated mechanisms to facilitate the maintenance and review of access records.* **POTENTIAL ASSESSMENT METHODS AND OBJECTS:** **Examine:** [*SELECT FROM:* Physical and environmental protection policy; procedures addressing facility access records; automated mechanisms supporting management of access records; facility access control logs or records; other relevant documents or records]. **Interview:** [*SELECT FROM:* Organizational personnel with responsibilities for reviewing physical access records].

PE-8(2)	**ACCESS RECORDS**
PE-8(2).1	**ASSESSMENT OBJECTIVE:** *Determine if the organization maintains a record of all physical access, both visitor and authorized individuals.* **POTENTIAL ASSESSMENT METHODS AND OBJECTS:** **Examine:** [*SELECT FROM:* Physical and environmental protection policy; procedures addressing facility access records; facility access control logs or records; other relevant documents or records].

FAMILY: PHYSICAL AND ENVIRONMENTAL PROTECTION   **CLASS:** OPERATIONAL

ASSESSMENT PROCEDURE

PE-9	POWER EQUIPMENT AND POWER CABLING
PE-9.1	**ASSESSMENT OBJECTIVE:** *Determine if the organization protects power equipment and power cabling for the information system from damage and destruction.* **POTENTIAL ASSESSMENT METHODS AND OBJECTS:** **Examine:** [*SELECT FROM:* Physical and environmental protection policy; procedures addressing power equipment and cabling protection; facility housing power equipment and cabling; other relevant documents or records].

PE-9(1)	POWER EQUIPMENT AND POWER CABLING
PE-9(1).1	**ASSESSMENT OBJECTIVE:** *Determine if the organization employs redundant and parallel power cabling paths.* **POTENTIAL ASSESSMENT METHODS AND OBJECTS:** **Examine:** [*SELECT FROM:* Physical and environmental protection policy; procedures addressing power equipment and cabling protection; facility housing power equipment and cabling; other relevant documents or records].

PE-9(2)	POWER EQUIPMENT AND POWER CABLING
PE-9(2).1	**ASSESSMENT OBJECTIVE:** *Determine if:* (i) *the organization defines the critical information system components that require automatic voltage controls; and* (ii) *the organization employs automatic voltage controls for organization-defined critical information system components* **POTENTIAL ASSESSMENT METHODS AND OBJECTS:** **Examine:** [*SELECT FROM:* Physical and environmental protection policy; procedures addressing voltage control; security plan; list of critical information system components requiring automatic voltage controls; other relevant documents or records].

FAMILY: PHYSICAL AND ENVIRONMENTAL PROTECTION   **CLASS:** OPERATIONAL

ASSESSMENT PROCEDURE

PE-10	EMERGENCY SHUTOFF

PE-10.1	**ASSESSMENT OBJECTIVE:** *Determine if:* *(i) the organization provides the capability of shutting off power to the information system or individual system components in emergency situations;* *(ii) the organization defines the location of emergency shutoff switches or devices by information system or system component;* *(iii) the organization places emergency shutoff switches or devices in an organization-defined location by information system or system component to facilitate safe and easy access for personnel; and* *(iv) the organization protects the emergency power shutoff capability from unauthorized activation.* **POTENTIAL ASSESSMENT METHODS AND OBJECTS:** **Examine**: [*SELECT FROM:* Physical and environmental protection policy; procedures addressing power source emergency shutoff; security plan; emergency shutoff controls or switches; other relevant documents or records].

PE-10(1)	EMERGENCY SHUTOFF [Withdrawn: Incorporated into PE-10].
PE-10(1).1	**ASSESSMENT OBJECTIVE:** [Withdrawn: Incorporated into PE-10]. **POTENTIAL ASSESSMENT METHODS AND OBJECTS:** [Withdrawn: Incorporated into PE-10].

FAMILY: PHYSICAL AND ENVIRONMENTAL PROTECTION   **CLASS:** OPERATIONAL

ASSESSMENT PROCEDURE

PE-11	EMERGENCY POWER
PE-11.1	**ASSESSMENT OBJECTIVE:** *Determine if the organization provides a short-term uninterruptible power supply to facilitate an orderly shutdown of the information system in the event of a primary power source loss.* **POTENTIAL ASSESSMENT METHODS AND OBJECTS:** **Examine**: [*SELECT FROM:* Physical and environmental protection policy; procedures addressing emergency power; uninterruptible power supply documentation; uninterruptible power supply test records; other relevant documents or records]. **Test**: [*SELECT FROM:* Uninterruptible power supply].

PE-11(1)	EMERGENCY POWER
PE-11(1).1	**ASSESSMENT OBJECTIVE:** *Determine if the organization provides a long-term alternate power supply for the information system that is capable of maintaining minimally required operational capability in the event of an extended loss of the primary power source.* **POTENTIAL ASSESSMENT METHODS AND OBJECTS:** **Examine**: [*SELECT FROM:* Physical and environmental protection policy; procedures addressing emergency power; alternate power supply documentation; alternate power test records; other relevant documents or records]. **Test**: [*SELECT FROM:* Alternate power supply].

PE-11(2)	EMERGENCY POWER
PE-11(2).1	**ASSESSMENT OBJECTIVE:** *Determine if the organization provides a long-term alternate power supply for the information system that is self-contained and not reliant on external power generation.* **POTENTIAL ASSESSMENT METHODS AND OBJECTS:** **Examine**: [*SELECT FROM:* Physical and environmental protection policy; procedures addressing emergency power; alternate power supply documentation; alternate power test records; other relevant documents or records]. **Test**: [*SELECT FROM:* Alternate power supply].

FAMILY: PHYSICAL AND ENVIRONMENTAL PROTECTION   **CLASS:** OPERATIONAL

ASSESSMENT PROCEDURE

PE-12	EMERGENCY LIGHTING
PE-12.1	**ASSESSMENT OBJECTIVE:** *Determine if:* (i) *the organization employs automatic emergency lighting for the information system that activates in the event of a power outage or disruption;* (ii) *the organization employs automatic emergency lighting for the information system that covers emergency exits and evacuation routes within the facility; and* (iii) *the organization maintains the automatic emergency lighting for the information system.* **POTENTIAL ASSESSMENT METHODS AND OBJECTS:** **Examine**: [*SELECT FROM:* Physical and environmental protection policy; procedures addressing emergency lighting; emergency lighting documentation; emergency lighting test records; emergency exits and evacuation routes; other relevant documents or records]. **Interview**: [*SELECT FROM:* Organizational personnel with emergency planning responsibilities]. **Test**: [*SELECT FROM:* Emergency lighting capability].

PE-12(1)	EMERGENCY LIGHTING
PE-12(1).1	**ASSESSMENT OBJECTIVE:** *Determine if the organization provides emergency lighting for all areas within the facility supporting essential missions and business functions.* **POTENTIAL ASSESSMENT METHODS AND OBJECTS:** **Examine**: [*SELECT FROM:* Physical and environmental protection policy; procedures addressing emergency lighting; emergency lighting documentation; emergency lighting test records; emergency exits and evacuation routes; other relevant documents or records]. **Interview**: [*SELECT FROM:* Organizational personnel with emergency planning responsibilities]. **Test**: [*SELECT FROM:* Emergency lighting capability].

FAMILY: PHYSICAL AND ENVIRONMENTAL PROTECTION   **CLASS:** OPERATIONAL

ASSESSMENT PROCEDURE

PE-13	FIRE PROTECTION

PE-13.1	**ASSESSMENT OBJECTIVE:** *Determine if:* (i) *the organization employs fire suppression and detection devices/systems for the information system that are supported by an independent energy source; and* (ii) *the organization maintains fire suppression and detection devices/systems for the information system that are supported by an independent energy source.* **POTENTIAL ASSESSMENT METHODS AND OBJECTS:** **Examine:** [*SELECT FROM:* Physical and environmental protection policy; procedures addressing fire protection; fire suppression and detection devices/systems; fire suppression and detection devices/systems documentation; test records of fire suppression and detection devices/systems; other relevant documents or records]. **Interview:** [*SELECT FROM:* Organizational personnel with responsibilities for fire detection and suppression devices/systems].

PE-13(1)	FIRE PROTECTION

PE-13(1).1	**ASSESSMENT OBJECTIVE:** *Determine if the organization employs fire detection devices/systems for the information system that, without manual intervention, activate automatically and notify the organization and emergency responders in the event of a fire.* **POTENTIAL ASSESSMENT METHODS AND OBJECTS:** **Examine:** [*SELECT FROM:* Physical and environmental protection policy; procedures addressing fire protection; facility housing the information system; alarm service level agreements; test records of fire suppression and detection devices/systems; fire suppression and detection devices/systems documentation; other relevant documents or records]. **Interview:** [*SELECT FROM:* Organizational personnel with responsibilities for fire detection and suppression devices/systems]. **Test:** [*SELECT FROM:* Simulated activation of fire detection devices/systems and automated notifications].

PE-13(2)	FIRE PROTECTION

PE-13(2).1	**ASSESSMENT OBJECTIVE:** *Determine if the organization employs fire suppression devices/systems for the information system that provide automatic notification of any activation to the organization and emergency responders.* **POTENTIAL ASSESSMENT METHODS AND OBJECTS:** **Examine:** [*SELECT FROM:* Physical and environmental protection policy; procedures addressing fire protection; fire suppression and detection devices/systems documentation; facility housing the information system; alarm service level agreements; test records of fire suppression and detection devices/systems; other relevant documents or records]. **Interview:** [*SELECT FROM:* Organizational personnel with responsibilities for fire detection and suppression devices/systems]. **Test:** [*SELECT FROM:* Simulated activation of fire suppression devices/systems and automated notifications].

PE-13(3)	FIRE PROTECTION
PE-13(3).1	**ASSESSMENT OBJECTIVE:** *Determine if the organization employs an automatic fire suppression capability for the information system when the facility is not staffed on a continuous basis.* **POTENTIAL ASSESSMENT METHODS AND OBJECTS:** **Examine**: [*SELECT FROM:* Physical and environmental protection policy; procedures addressing fire protection; facility housing the information system; alarm service level agreements; facility staffing plans; test records of fire suppression and detection devices/systems; other relevant documents or records]. **Interview**: [*SELECT FROM:* Organizational personnel with responsibilities for fire detection and suppression devices/systems]. **Test**: [*SELECT FROM:* Simulated activation of fire suppression devices/systems].

PE-13(4)	FIRE PROTECTION
PE-13(4).1	**ASSESSMENT OBJECTIVE:** *Determine if:* *(i) the organization defines the frequency of fire marshal inspections for the facility;* *(ii) the facility undergoes fire marshal inspections in accordance with the organization-defined frequency; and* *(iii) the organization promptly resolves deficiencies identified by fire marshal inspections.* **POTENTIAL ASSESSMENT METHODS AND OBJECTS:** **Examine**: [*SELECT FROM:* Physical and environmental protection policy; procedures addressing fire protection; security plan; facility housing the information system; fire marshal inspection results; test records of fire suppression and detection devices/systems; other relevant documents or records]. **Interview**: [*SELECT FROM:* Organizational personnel with responsibilities for fire detection and suppression devices/systems].

FAMILY: PHYSICAL AND ENVIRONMENTAL PROTECTION   **CLASS:** OPERATIONAL

ASSESSMENT PROCEDURE

PE-14	TEMPERATURE AND HUMIDITY CONTROLS
PE-14.1	**ASSESSMENT OBJECTIVE:** *Determine if:* (i) *the organization defines the acceptable temperature and humidity levels within the facility where the information system resides;* (ii) *the organization maintains temperature and humidity levels within the facility where the information system resides in accordance with organization-defined acceptable levels;* (iii) *the organization defines the frequency to monitor temperature and humidity levels; and* (iv) *the organization monitors the temperature and humidity levels within the facility where the information system resides in accordance with the organization-defined frequency.* **POTENTIAL ASSESSMENT METHODS AND OBJECTS:** **Examine:** [*SELECT FROM:* Physical and environmental protection policy; procedures addressing temperature and humidity control; security plan; temperature and humidity controls; facility housing the information system; temperature and humidity controls documentation; temperature and humidity records; other relevant documents or records].

PE-14(1)	TEMPERATURE AND HUMIDITY CONTROLS
PE-14(1).1	**ASSESSMENT OBJECTIVE:** *Determine if the organization employs automatic temperature and humidity controls in the facility to prevent fluctuations potentially harmful to the information system.* **POTENTIAL ASSESSMENT METHODS AND OBJECTS:** **Examine:** [*SELECT FROM:* Physical and environmental protection policy; procedures addressing temperature and humidity controls; facility housing the information system; automated mechanisms for temperature and humidity; other relevant documents or records]. **Test:** [*SELECT FROM:* Automated mechanisms implementing temperature and humidity controls].

PE-14(2)	TEMPERATURE AND HUMIDITY CONTROLS
PE-14(2).1	**ASSESSMENT OBJECTIVE:** *Determine if the organization employs temperature and humidity monitoring that provides an alarm or notification of changes potentially harmful to personnel or equipment.* **POTENTIAL ASSESSMENT METHODS AND OBJECTS:** **Examine:** [*SELECT FROM:* Physical and environmental protection policy; procedures addressing temperature and humidity monitoring; facility housing the information system; logs or records of temperature and humidity monitoring; records of changes to temperature and humidity levels that generate alarms or notifications; other relevant documents or records]. **Test:** [*SELECT FROM:* Temperature and humidity monitoring capability].

FAMILY: PHYSICAL AND ENVIRONMENTAL PROTECTION   **CLASS:** OPERATIONAL

ASSESSMENT PROCEDURE	
PE-15	**WATER DAMAGE PROTECTION**
PE-15.1	**ASSESSMENT OBJECTIVE:** *Determine if:* *(i) the organization protects the information system from damage resulting from water leakage by providing master shutoff valves that are accessible and working properly; and* *(ii) key personnel within the organization have knowledge of the master water shutoff valves.* **POTENTIAL ASSESSMENT METHODS AND OBJECTS:** **Examine:** [*SELECT FROM:* Physical and environmental protection policy; procedures addressing water damage protection; facility housing the information system; master shutoff valves; list of key personnel with knowledge of location and activation procedures for master shutoff valves for the plumbing system; master shutoff valve documentation; other relevant documents or records]. **Interview:** [*SELECT FROM:* Organization personnel with physical and environmental protection responsibilities]. **Test:** [*SELECT FROM:* Master water-shutoff valves; process for activating master water-shutoff].

PE-15(1)	**WATER DAMAGE PROTECTION**
PE-15(1).1	**ASSESSMENT OBJECTIVE:** *Determine if the organization employs mechanisms that, without the need for manual intervention, protect the information system from water damage in the event of a water leak.* **POTENTIAL ASSESSMENT METHODS AND OBJECTS:** **Examine:** [*SELECT FROM:* Physical and environmental protection policy; procedures addressing water damage protection; facility housing the information system; automated mechanisms for water shutoff valves; other relevant documents or records]. **Test:** [*SELECT FROM:* Automated mechanisms implementing master water shutoff valve activation].

FAMILY: PHYSICAL AND ENVIRONMENTAL PROTECTION   **CLASS:** OPERATIONAL

ASSESSMENT PROCEDURE	
PE-16	**DELIVERY AND REMOVAL**
PE-16.1	**ASSESSMENT OBJECTIVE:** *Determine if:* *(i) the organization defines the types of information system components to be authorized, monitored, and controlled as such components are entering or exiting the facility;* *(ii) the organization authorizes, monitors, and controls organization-defined information system components entering and exiting the facility; and* *(iii) the organization maintains records of information system components entering and exiting the facility.* **POTENTIAL ASSESSMENT METHODS AND OBJECTS:** **Examine:** [*SELECT FROM:* Physical and environmental protection policy; procedures addressing delivery and removal of information system components from the facility; security plan; facility housing the information system; records of items entering and exiting the facility; other relevant documents or records]. **Interview:** [*SELECT FROM:* Organization personnel with responsibilities for controlling information system components entering and exiting the facility]. **Test:** [*SELECT FROM:* Process for controlling information system-related items entering and exiting the facility].

FAMILY: PHYSICAL AND ENVIRONMENTAL PROTECTION   **CLASS:** OPERATIONAL

ASSESSMENT PROCEDURE	
PE-17	**ALTERNATE WORK SITE**
PE-17.1	**ASSESSMENT OBJECTIVE:** *Determine if:* *(i) the organization defines the management, operational, and technical information system security controls to be employed at alternate work sites;* *(ii) the organization employs organization-defined management, operational, and technical information system security controls at alternate work sites;* *(iii) the organization assesses, as feasible, the effectiveness of security controls at alternate work sites; and* *(iv) the organization provides a means for employees to communicate with information security personnel in case of security incidents or problems.* **POTENTIAL ASSESSMENT METHODS AND OBJECTS:** **Examine**: [*SELECT FROM:* Physical and environmental protection policy; procedures addressing alternate work sites for organizational personnel; security plan; list of management, operational, and technical security controls required for alternate work sites; assessments of security controls at alternate work sites; other relevant documents or records]. **Interview**: [*SELECT FROM:* Organization personnel using alternate work sites].

FAMILY: PHYSICAL AND ENVIRONMENTAL PROTECTION   **CLASS:** OPERATIONAL

ASSESSMENT PROCEDURE

PE-18	LOCATION OF INFORMATION SYSTEM COMPONENTS
PE-18.1	**ASSESSMENT OBJECTIVE:** *Determine if:* (i) *the organization positions information system components within the facility to minimize potential damage from physical and environmental hazards; and* (ii) *the organization positions information system components within the facility to minimize the opportunity for unauthorized access.* **POTENTIAL ASSESSMENT METHODS AND OBJECTS:** **Examine:** [*SELECT FROM:* Physical and environmental protection policy; procedures addressing positioning of information system components; documentation providing the location and position of information system components within the facility; other relevant documents or records].

PE-18(1)	LOCATION OF INFORMATION SYSTEM COMPONENTS
PE-18(1).1	**ASSESSMENT OBJECTIVE:** *Determine if:* (i) *the organization plans the location or site of the facility where the information system resides with regard to physical and environmental hazards; and* (ii) *the organization, for existing facilities, considers the physical and environmental hazards in its risk mitigation strategy.* **POTENTIAL ASSESSMENT METHODS AND OBJECTS:** **Examine:** [*SELECT FROM:* Physical and environmental protection policy; physical site planning documents; organizational assessment of risk, contingency plan; other relevant documents or records]. **Interview:** [*SELECT FROM:* Organization personnel with site selection responsibilities for the facility housing the information system].

FAMILY: PHYSICAL AND ENVIRONMENTAL PROTECTION   **CLASS:** OPERATIONAL

ASSESSMENT PROCEDURE	
PE-19	**INFORMATION LEAKAGE**
PE-19.1	**ASSESSMENT OBJECTIVE:** *Determine if the organization protects the information system from information leakage due to electromagnetic signals emanations.* **POTENTIAL ASSESSMENT METHODS AND OBJECTS:** **Examine**: [*SELECT FROM:* Physical and environmental protection policy; procedures addressing information leakage due to electromagnetic signals emanations; mechanisms protecting the information system against electronic signals emanation; facility housing the information system; records from electromagnetic signals emanation tests; other relevant documents or records]. **Test**: [*SELECT FROM:* Information system for information leakage due to electromagnetic signals emanations].

PE-19(1)	INFORMATION LEAKAGE	
PE-19(1).1	**ASSESSMENT OBJECTIVE:** *Determine if the information system components, associated data communications, and networks are protected in accordance with:* – *national emissions and TEMPEST policies and procedures; and* – *the sensitivity of the information being transmitted.* **POTENTIAL ASSESSMENT METHODS AND OBJECTS:** **Examine**: [*SELECT FROM:* Physical and environmental protection policy; procedures addressing information leakage that comply with national emissions and TEMPEST policies and procedures; information system component design documentation; information system configuration settings and associated documentation other relevant documents or records]. **Test**: [*SELECT FROM:* Information system components for compliance with national emissions and TEMPEST policies and procedures].	

FAMILY: PLANNING   **CLASS:** MANAGEMENT

ASSESSMENT PROCEDURE	
PL-1	**SECURITY PLANNING POLICY AND PROCEDURES**

PL-1.1	**ASSESSMENT OBJECTIVE:**
	Determine if:
	(i) the organization develops and formally documents security planning policy;
	(ii) the organization security planning policy addresses:
	    - *purpose;*
	    - *scope;*
	    - *roles and responsibilities;*
	    - *management commitment;*
	    - *coordination among organizational entities; and*
	    - *compliance;*
	(iii) the organization disseminates formal documented security planning policy to elements within the organization having associated security planning roles and responsibilities;
	(iv) the organization develops and formally documents security planning procedures;
	(v) the organization security planning procedures facilitate implementation of the security planning policy and associated security planning controls; and
	(vi) the organization disseminates formal documented security planning procedures to elements within the organization having associated security planning roles and responsibilities.
	
	POTENTIAL ASSESSMENT METHODS AND OBJECTS:
	Examine: [*SELECT FROM:* Security planning policy and procedures; other relevant documents or records].
	Interview: [*SELECT FROM:* Organizational personnel with security planning responsibilities].

PL-1.2	**ASSESSMENT OBJECTIVE:** *Determine if:* *(i) the organization defines the frequency of security planning policy reviews/updates;* *(ii) the organization reviews/updates security planning policy in accordance with organization-defined frequency; and* *(iii) the organization defines the frequency of security planning procedure reviews/updates;* *(iv) the organization reviews/updates security planning procedures in accordance with organization-defined frequency.* **POTENTIAL ASSESSMENT METHODS AND OBJECTS:** **Examine:** [*SELECT FROM:* Security planning policy and procedures; other relevant documents or records]. **Interview:** [*SELECT FROM:* Organizational personnel with security planning responsibilities].

FAMILY: PLANNING   **CLASS:** MANAGEMENT

ASSESSMENT PROCEDURE
PL-2   **SYSTEM SECURITY PLAN**

PL-2.1	**ASSESSMENT OBJECTIVE:**

Determine if:

(i)   the organization develops a security plan for the information system that:

- is consistent with the organization's enterprise architecture;

- explicitly defines the authorization boundary for the system;

- describes the operational context of the information system in terms of mission and business processes;

- provides the security categorization of the information system including supporting rationale;

- describes the operational environment for the information system;

- describes relationships with or connections to other information systems;

- provides an overview of the security requirements for the system;

- describes the security controls in place or planned for meeting those requirements including a rationale for the tailoring and supplemental decisions; and

- is reviewed and approved by the authorizing official or designated representative prior to plan implementation;

(ii)   the organization defines the frequency of security plan reviews;

(iii) the organization reviews the security plan in accordance with the organization-defined frequency; and

(iv) the organization updates the plan to address changes to the information system/environment of operation or problems identified during plan implementation or security control assessments.

POTENTIAL ASSESSMENT METHODS AND OBJECTS:

Examine: [*SELECT FROM:* Security planning policy; procedures addressing security plan development and implementation; procedures addressing security plan reviews and updates; enterprise architecture documentation; security plan for the information system; records of security plan reviews and updates; other relevant documents or records].

Interview: [*SELECT FROM:* Organization personnel with security planning and plan implementation responsibilities for the information system].

PL-2(1)	SYSTEM SECURITY PLAN
PL-2(1).1	**ASSESSMENT OBJECTIVE:** *Determine if:* (i) *the organization develops a security Concept of Operations (CONOPS) for the information system containing, at a minimum:* - *the purpose of the system;* - *a description of the system architecture;* - *the security authorization schedule; and* - *the security categorization and associated factors considered in determining the categorization;* (ii) *the organization defines the frequency of reviews and updates to the CONOPS; and* (iii) *the organization reviews and updates the CONOPS in accordance with the organization-defined frequency.* **POTENTIAL ASSESSMENT METHODS AND OBJECTS:** **Examine**: [*SELECT FROM*: Security planning policy; procedures addressing security CONOPS development; procedures addressing security CONOPS reviews and updates; security CONOPS for the information system; security plan for the information system; records of security CONOPS reviews and updates; other relevant documents or records]. **Interview**: [*SELECT FROM*: Organization personnel with security planning and plan implementation responsibilities for the information system].

PL-2(2)	SYSTEM SECURITY PLAN
PL-2(2).1	**ASSESSMENT OBJECTIVE:** *Determine if the organization develops a functional architecture for the information system that identifies and maintains:* – *external interfaces, the information being exchanged across the interfaces, and the protection mechanisms associated with each interface;* – *user roles and the access privileges assigned to each role;* – *unique security requirements;* – *types of information processed, stored, or transmitted by the information system and any specific protection needs in accordance with applicable federal laws, Executive Orders, directives, policies, regulations, standards, and guidance; and* – *restoration priority of information or information system services.* **POTENTIAL ASSESSMENT METHODS AND OBJECTS:** **Examine**: [*SELECT FROM*: Security planning policy; access control policy; contingency planning policy; security plan for the information system; contingency plan for the information system; information system design documentation; other relevant documents or records]. **Interview**: [*SELECT FROM*: Organization personnel with security planning and plan implementation responsibilities for the information system].

FAMILY: PLANNING

CLASS: MANAGEMENT

ASSESSMENT PROCEDURE	
PL-3	**SYSTEM SECURITY PLAN UPDATE** [Withdrawn: Incorporated into PL-2].
PL-3.1	**ASSESSMENT OBJECTIVE:** [Withdrawn: Incorporated into PL-2]. **POTENTIAL ASSESSMENT METHODS AND OBJECTS:** [Withdrawn: Incorporated into PL-2].

FAMILY: PLANNING

CLASS: MANAGEMENT

ASSESSMENT PROCEDURE

PL-4	RULES OF BEHAVIOR
PL-4.1	**ASSESSMENT OBJECTIVE:** *Determine if:* (i) *the organization establishes the rules that describe information system user responsibilities and expected behavior with regard to information and information system usage;* (ii) *the organization makes the rules available to all information system users; and* (iii) *the organization receives a signed acknowledgement from users indicating that they have read, understand, and agree to abide by the rules of behavior, before authorizing access to information and the information system.* **POTENTIAL ASSESSMENT METHODS AND OBJECTS:** **Examine:** [*SELECT FROM:* Security planning policy; procedures addressing rules of behavior for information system users; rules of behavior; other relevant documents or records]. **Interview:** [*SELECT FROM:* Organizational personnel who are authorized users of the information system and have signed rules of behavior].

PL-4(1)	RULES OF BEHAVIOR
PL-4(1).1	**ASSESSMENT OBJECTIVE:** *Determine if the organization includes in the rules of behavior:* − *explicit restrictions on the use of social networking sites;* − *posting information on commercial Web sites; and* − *sharing information system account information.* **POTENTIAL ASSESSMENT METHODS AND OBJECTS:** **Examine:** [*SELECT FROM:* Security planning policy; procedures addressing rules of behavior for information system users; rules of behavior; other relevant documents or records]. **Interview:** [*SELECT FROM:* Organizational personnel who are authorized users of the information system and have signed rules of behavior].

FAMILY: PLANNING   **CLASS:** MANAGEMENT

ASSESSMENT PROCEDURE	
PL-5	**PRIVACY IMPACT ASSESSMENT**
PL-5.1	**ASSESSMENT OBJECTIVE:** *Determine if:* *(i) the organization conducts a privacy impact assessment on the information system; and* *(ii) the privacy impact assessment is in accordance with OMB policy.* **POTENTIAL ASSESSMENT METHODS AND OBJECTS:** **Examine:** [*SELECT FROM:* Security planning policy; procedures addressing privacy impact assessments on the information system; privacy impact assessment; other relevant documents or records].

FAMILY: PLANNING

CLASS: MANAGEMENT

ASSESSMENT PROCEDURE	
PL-6	**SECURITY-RELATED ACTIVITY PLANNING**
PL-6.1	**ASSESSMENT OBJECTIVE:** *Determine if the organization plans and coordinates security-related activities affecting the information system before conducting such activities in order to reduce the impact on organizational operations (i.e., mission, functions, image, and reputation), organizational assets, and individuals.* **POTENTIAL ASSESSMENT METHODS AND OBJECTS:** **Examine:** [*SELECT FROM:* Security planning policy; procedures addressing security-related activity planning for the information system; other relevant documents or records]. **Interview:** [*SELECT FROM:* Organizational personnel with security planning and plan implementation responsibilities].

FAMILY: PROGRAM MANAGEMENT   **CLASS:** MANAGEMENT

ASSESSMENT PROCEDURE	
PM-1	**INFORMATION SECURITY PROGRAM PLAN**
PM-1.1	**ASSESSMENT OBJECTIVE:** *Determine if:* *(i) the organization develops an information security program plan for the organization that:* - *provides an overview of the requirements for the security program;* - *provides a description of the security program management controls and common controls in place or planned for meeting security program requirements;* - *provides sufficient information about the program management controls and common controls (including specification of parameters for any assignment and selection operations either explicitly or by reference) to enable an implementation that is unambiguously compliant with the intent of the plan and a determination of the risk to be incurred if the plan is implemented as intended;* - *includes roles, responsibilities, management commitment, coordination among organizational entities, and compliance;* - *is approved by a senior official with responsibility and accountability for the risk being incurred to organizational operations (including mission, functions, image, and reputation), organizational assets, individuals, other organizations and the Nation;* *(ii) the organization defines the frequency of information security program plan reviews;* *(iii) the organization reviews the organization-wide information security program plan in accordance with the organization-defined frequency;* *(iv) the organization revises the plan to address organizational changes and problems identified during plan implementation or security control assessments; and* *(v) the organization disseminates the most recent information security program plan to appropriate entities in the organization.* **POTENTIAL ASSESSMENT METHODS AND OBJECTS:** **Examine:** [*SELECT FROM:* Information security program policy; procedures addressing information security program plan development and implementation; procedures addressing information security program plan reviews and updates; information security program plan; program management controls documentation; common controls documentation; records of information security program plan reviews and updates; other relevant documents or records]. **Interview:** [*SELECT FROM:* Organizational personnel with security planning and plan implementation responsibilities for the information security program].

FAMILY: PROGRAM MANAGEMENT   **CLASS:** MANAGEMENT

ASSESSMENT PROCEDURE
PM-2	**SENIOR INFORMATION SECURITY OFFICER**

| PM-2.1 | **ASSESSMENT OBJECTIVE:**
Determine if:

(i)   *organization appoints a senior information security officer to coordinate, develop, implement, and maintain an organization-wide information security program; and*

(ii)   *the organization empowers the senior information security officer with the mission and resources required to coordinate, develop, implement, and maintain an organization-wide information security program.*

POTENTIAL ASSESSMENT METHODS AND OBJECTS:
Examine: [*SELECT FROM:* Information security program policy; information security program plan; documentation addressing roles and responsibilities of the senior information security officer position; information security program mission statement; other relevant documents or records].

Interview: [*SELECT FROM:* Organizational person appointed to the senior information security officer position]. |

FAMILY: PROGRAM MANAGEMENT   **CLASS:** MANAGEMENT

ASSESSMENT PROCEDURE	
PM-3	**INFORMATION SECURITY RESOURCES**
PM-3.1	**ASSESSMENT OBJECTIVE:** *Determine if:* *(i) the organization includes in its capital planning and investment requests the resources needed to implement the information security program;* *(ii) the organization documents all exceptions to the requirement that all capital planning and investment requests include the resources needed to implement the information security program;* *(iii) the organization employs a business case/Exhibit 300/Exhibit 53 to record the resources required; and* *(iv) the organization makes the required information security resources available for expenditure as planned.* **POTENTIAL ASSESSMENT METHODS AND OBJECTS:** **Examine**: [*SELECT FROM:* Information security program policy; capital planning and investment policy; procedures addressing management and oversight for information security-related aspects of the capital planning and investment control process; capital planning and investment documentation; documentation of exceptions supporting capital planning and investment requests; business cases; Exhibit 300; Exhibit 53; other relevant documents or records]. **Interview**: [*SELECT FROM:* Organizational personnel managing and overseeing the information security-related aspects of the capital planning and investment control process].

FAMILY: PROGRAM MANAGEMENT   **CLASS:** MANAGEMENT

ASSESSMENT PROCEDURE
PM-4	**PLAN OF ACTION AND MILESTONES PROCESS**

| PM-4.1 | **ASSESSMENT OBJECTIVE:**
Determine if:

(i) *the organization implements a process to maintain plans of action and milestones for the security program and the associated organizational information systems; and*

(ii) *the organization implements a process to document the remedial information security actions that mitigate risk to organizational operations and assets, individuals, other organizations, and the Nation.*

POTENTIAL ASSESSMENT METHODS AND OBJECTS:
Examine: [*SELECT FROM:* Information security program policy; plan of action and milestones policy; procedures addressing plan of action and milestones process; plan of action and milestones for the security program; plan of action and milestones for organizational information systems; other relevant documents or records].
Interview: [*SELECT FROM:* Organizational personnel with plan of action and milestones development and implementation responsibilities]. |

FAMILY: PROGRAM MANAGEMENT   **CLASS:** MANAGEMENT

ASSESSMENT PROCEDURE
PM-5   **INFORMATION SYSTEM INVENTORY**
PM-5.1   **ASSESSMENT OBJECTIVE:** *Determine if:* (i)   *the organization develops an inventory of its information systems; and* (ii)   *the organization maintains an inventory of its information systems.* **POTENTIAL ASSESSMENT METHODS AND OBJECTS:** **Examine**: [*SELECT FROM:* Information security program policy; procedures addressing information system inventory development and maintenance; information system inventory records, other relevant documents or records]. **Interview**: [*SELECT FROM:* Organizational personnel with information system inventory development and maintenance responsibilities].

FAMILY: PROGRAM MANAGEMENT   **CLASS:** MANAGEMENT

ASSESSMENT PROCEDURE	
PM-6	**INFORMATION SECURITY MEASURES OF PERFORMANCE**
PM-6.1	**ASSESSMENT OBJECTIVE:** *Determine if:* *(i) the organization develops information security measures of performance;* *(ii) the organization monitors information security measures of performance; and* *(iii) the organization reports on the results of information security measures of performance.* **POTENTIAL ASSESSMENT METHODS AND OBJECTS:** **Examine**: [*SELECT FROM:* Information security program policy; procedures addressing development, monitoring, and reporting of information security performance measures; information security performance metrics; information security performance measures; results of information security performance measures; other relevant documents or records].

FAMILY: PROGRAM MANAGEMENT   **CLASS:** MANAGEMENT

ASSESSMENT PROCEDURE	
PM-7	**ENTERPRISE ARCHITECTURE**
PM-7.1	**ASSESSMENT OBJECTIVE:** *Determine if the organization develops an enterprise architecture with consideration for information security and the resulting risk to organizational operations, organizational assets, individuals, other organizations, and the Nation.* **POTENTIAL ASSESSMENT METHODS AND OBJECTS:** **Examine**: [*SELECT FROM:* Information security program policy; enterprise architecture policy; procedures addressing information security-related aspects of enterprise architecture development; system development life cycle documentation; enterprise architecture documentation; enterprise security architecture documentation; other relevant documents or records].

FAMILY: PROGRAM MANAGEMENT   **CLASS:** MANAGEMENT

ASSESSMENT PROCEDURE	
PM-8	**CRITICAL INFRASTRUCTURE PLAN**
PM-8.1	**ASSESSMENT OBJECTIVE:** *Determine if:* (i) *the organization develops and documents a critical infrastructure and key resource protection plan;* (ii) *the organization updates the critical infrastructure and key resource protection plan; and* (iii) *the organization addresses information security issues in the critical infrastructure and key resource protection plan.* **POTENTIAL ASSESSMENT METHODS AND OBJECTS:** **Examine:** [*SELECT FROM:* Information security program policy; critical infrastructure protection policy; procedures addressing critical infrastructure plan development and implementation; procedures addressing critical infrastructure plan reviews and updates; records of critical infrastructure plan reviews and updates; other relevant documents or records]. **Interview:** [*SELECT FROM:* Organizational personnel with critical infrastructure plan development and implementation responsibilities].

FAMILY: PROGRAM MANAGEMENT   **CLASS:** MANAGEMENT

ASSESSMENT PROCEDURE
PM-9	**RISK MANAGEMENT STRATEGY**

| PM-9.1 | **ASSESSMENT OBJECTIVE:**
Determine if:

(i)   *the organization develops a comprehensive strategy to manage risk to organizational operations and assets, individuals, other organizations, and the Nation associated with the operation and use of information systems; and*

(ii) *the organization implements that strategy consistently across the organization.*

POTENTIAL ASSESSMENT METHODS AND OBJECTS:
Examine: [*SELECT FROM:* Information security program policy; risk management policy; procedures addressing risk management strategy development and implementation; risk management strategy (including risk identification, assessment, mitigation, acceptance, and monitoring methodologies); other relevant documents or records].

Interview: [*SELECT FROM:* Organizational personnel with risk management strategy development and implementation responsibilities]. |

FAMILY: PROGRAM MANAGEMENT   **CLASS:** MANAGEMENT

ASSESSMENT PROCEDURE	
PM-10	**SECURITY AUTHORIZATION PROCESS**
PM-10.1	**ASSESSMENT OBJECTIVE:** *Determine if:* (i) *the organization manages (i.e., documents, tracks, and reports) the security state of organizational information systems through security authorization processes;* (ii) *the organization designates individuals to fulfill specific roles and responsibilities within the organizational risk management process; and* (iii) *the organization fully integrates the security authorization processes into an organization-wide risk management program.* **POTENTIAL ASSESSMENT METHODS AND OBJECTS:** **Examine:** [*SELECT FROM:* Information security program policy; security assessment and authorization policy; risk management policy; procedures addressing security authorization processes; security authorization package (including security plan, security assessment report, plan of action and milestones, authorization statement); other relevant documents or records]. **Interview:** [*SELECT FROM:* Organizational personnel with security authorization responsibilities for information systems; organizational personnel with risk management responsibilities].

FAMILY: PROGRAM MANAGEMENT   **CLASS:** MANAGEMENT

ASSESSMENT PROCEDURE	
PM-11	**MISSION / BUSINESS PROCESS DEFINITION**
PM-11.1	**ASSESSMENT OBJECTIVE:** *Determine if:* *(i) the organization defines mission/business processes with consideration for information security and the resulting risk to organizational operations, organizational assets, individuals, other organizations, and the Nation; and* *(ii) the organization determines information protection needs arising from the defined mission/business processes and revises the processes as necessary, until an achievable set of protection needs is obtained.* **POTENTIAL ASSESSMENT METHODS AND OBJECTS:** **Examine**: [*SELECT FROM:* Information security program policy; risk management policy; procedures addressing security categorization of organizational information and information systems; organizational mission/business processes; risk management strategy (including risk identification, assessment, mitigation, acceptance, and monitoring methodologies); other relevant documents or records]. **Interview**: [*SELECT FROM:* Organizational personnel with mission/business process definition responsibilities; organizational personnel with security categorization and risk management responsibilities for the information security program].

FAMILY: PERSONNEL SECURITY   **CLASS:** OPERATIONAL

ASSESSMENT PROCEDURE	
PS-1	**PERSONNEL SECURITY POLICY AND PROCEDURES**

PS-1.1	**ASSESSMENT OBJECTIVE:**
	Determine if:
	(i) the organization develops and formally documents personnel security policy;
	(ii) the organization personnel security policy addresses:
	  - *purpose;*
	  - *scope;*
	  - *roles and responsibilities;*
	  - *management commitment;*
	  - *coordination among organizational entities; and*
	  - *compliance;*
	(iii) the organization disseminates formal documented personnel security policy to elements within the organization having associated personnel security roles and responsibilities;
	(iv) the organization develops and formally documents personnel security procedures;
	(v) the organization personnel security procedures facilitate implementation of the personnel security policy and associated personnel security controls; and
	(vi) the organization disseminates formal documented personnel security procedures to elements within the organization having associated personnel security roles and responsibilities.
	
	POTENTIAL ASSESSMENT METHODS AND OBJECTS:
	Examine: [*SELECT FROM*: Personnel security policy and procedures, other relevant documents or records].
	Interview: [*SELECT FROM*: Organizational personnel with personnel security responsibilities].

PS-1.2	**ASSESSMENT OBJECTIVE:** *Determine if:* *(i) the organization defines the frequency of personnel security policy reviews/updates;* *(ii) the organization reviews/updates personnel security policy in accordance with organization-defined frequency; and* *(iii) the organization defines the frequency of personnel security procedure reviews/updates;* *(iv) the organization reviews/updates personnel security procedures in accordance with organization-defined frequency.* **POTENTIAL ASSESSMENT METHODS AND OBJECTS:** **Examine**: [*SELECT FROM*: Personnel security policy and procedures; other relevant documents or records]. **Interview**: [*SELECT FROM*: Organizational personnel with personnel security responsibilities].

FAMILY: PERSONNEL SECURITY   **CLASS:** OPERATIONAL

ASSESSMENT PROCEDURE	
PS-2	**POSITION CATEGORIZATION**
PS-2.1	**ASSESSMENT OBJECTIVE:** *Determine if:* (i) *the organization assigns a risk designation to all positions within the organization;* (ii) *the organization establishes a screening criteria for individuals filling organizational positions;* (iii) *the organization defines the frequency of risk designation reviews and updates for organizational positions; and* (iv) *the organization reviews and revises position risk designations in accordance with the organization-defined frequency.* **POTENTIAL ASSESSMENT METHODS AND OBJECTS:** **Examine**: [*SELECT FROM:* Personnel security policy; procedures addressing position categorization; appropriate codes of federal regulations; list of risk designations for organizational positions; security plan; records of risk designation reviews and updates; other relevant documents or records]. **Interview**: [*SELECT FROM:* Organizational personnel with personnel security responsibilities].

FAMILY: PERSONNEL SECURITY   **CLASS:** OPERATIONAL

ASSESSMENT PROCEDURE	
PS-3	**PERSONNEL SCREENING**
PS-3.1	**ASSESSMENT OBJECTIVE:** *Determine if:* (i) *the organization screens individuals prior to authorizing access to the information system;* (ii) *the organization defines conditions requiring re-screening and, where re-screening is so indicated, the frequency of such re-screening; and* (iii) *the organization re-screens individuals according to organization-defined conditions requiring re-screening and, where re-screening is so indicated, the organization-defined frequency of such re-screening.* **POTENTIAL ASSESSMENT METHODS AND OBJECTS:** **Examine**: [*SELECT FROM:* Personnel security policy; procedures addressing personnel screening; records of screened personnel; security plan; other relevant documents or records]. **Interview**: [*SELECT FROM:* Organizational personnel with personnel security responsibilities].

PS-3(1)	**PERSONNEL SCREENING**
PS-3(1).1	**ASSESSMENT OBJECTIVE:** *Determine if:* (i) *the organization ensures that every user accessing an information system processing, storing, or transmitting classified information is cleared to the highest classification level of the information on the system; and* (ii) *the organization ensures that every user accessing an information system processing, storing, or transmitting classified information is indoctrinated to the highest classification level of the information on the system.* **POTENTIAL ASSESSMENT METHODS AND OBJECTS:** **Examine**: [*SELECT FROM:* Personnel security policy; procedures addressing personnel screening; records of screened personnel; other relevant documents or records]. **Interview**: [*SELECT FROM:* Organizational personnel with personnel security responsibilities].

PS-3(2)	**PERSONNEL SCREENING**
PS-3(2).1	**ASSESSMENT OBJECTIVE:** *Determine if the organization formally indoctrinates every user accessing an information system that processes, stores, or transmits types of classified information requiring formal indoctrination for all of the relevant types of information on the system.* **POTENTIAL ASSESSMENT METHODS AND OBJECTS:** **Examine**: [*SELECT FROM:* Personnel security policy; procedures addressing personnel screening; records of screened personnel; other relevant documents or records]. **Interview**: [*SELECT FROM:* Organizational personnel with personnel security responsibilities].

FAMILY: PERSONNEL SECURITY   **CLASS:** OPERATIONAL

ASSESSMENT PROCEDURE	
PS-4	**PERSONNEL TERMINATION**
PS-4.1	**ASSESSMENT OBJECTIVE:**

	Determine if:
	(i) *the organization terminates information system access upon termination of individual employment;*
	(ii) *the organization conducts exit interviews of terminated personnel;*
	(iii) *the organization retrieves all security-related organizational information system-related property from terminated personnel; and*
	(iv) *the organization retains access to organizational information and information systems formerly controlled by terminated personnel.*
	POTENTIAL ASSESSMENT METHODS AND OBJECTS:
	Examine: [*SELECT FROM:* Personnel security policy; procedures addressing personnel termination; records of personnel termination actions; list of information system accounts; other relevant documents or records].
	Interview: [*SELECT FROM:* Organizational personnel with personnel security responsibilities].

FAMILY: PERSONNEL SECURITY

CLASS: OPERATIONAL

ASSESSMENT PROCEDURE	
PS-5	**PERSONNEL TRANSFER**
PS-5.1	**ASSESSMENT OBJECTIVE:** *Determine if:* (i) *the organization reviews logical and physical access authorizations to information systems/facilities when personnel are reassigned or transferred to other positions within the organization;* (ii) *the organization defines the transfer or reassignment actions and the time period within which the actions must occur following formal transfer or reassignment; and* (iii) *the organization initiates the organization-defined transfer or reassignment actions within an organization-defined time period following formal transfer or reassignment.* **POTENTIAL ASSESSMENT METHODS AND OBJECTS:** **Examine**: [*SELECT FROM:* Personnel security policy; procedures addressing personnel transfer; security plan; records of personnel transfer actions; list of information system and facility access authorizations; other relevant documents or records]. **Interview**: [*SELECT FROM:* Organizational personnel with personnel security responsibilities].

FAMILY: PERSONNEL SECURITY   **CLASS:** OPERATIONAL

ASSESSMENT PROCEDURE	
PS-6	**ACCESS AGREEMENTS**
PS-6.1	**ASSESSMENT OBJECTIVE:** *Determine if:* *(i) the organization identifies appropriate access agreements for individuals requiring access to organizational information and information systems;* *(ii) individuals requiring access to organizational information and information systems sign appropriate access agreements prior to being granted access;* *(iii) the organization defines the frequency of reviews/updates for access agreements; and* *(iv) the organization reviews/updates the access agreements in accordance with the organization-defined frequency.* **POTENTIAL ASSESSMENT METHODS AND OBJECTS:** **Examine:** [*SELECT FROM:* Personnel security policy; procedures addressing access agreements for organizational information and information systems; security plan; access agreements; records of access agreement reviews and updates; other relevant documents or records]. **Interview:** [*SELECT FROM:* Organizational personnel with personnel security responsibilities].

PS-6(1)	**ACCESS AGREEMENTS**
PS-6(1).1	**ASSESSMENT OBJECTIVE:** *Determine if the organization grants access to information with special protection measures only to individuals who:* – *have a valid access authorization that is demonstrated by assigned official government duties; and* – *satisfy associated personnel security criteria.* **POTENTIAL ASSESSMENT METHODS AND OBJECTS:** **Examine:** [*SELECT FROM:* Personnel security policy; procedures addressing access agreements for organizational information and information systems; access agreements; access authorizations; personnel security criteria; other relevant documents or records]. **Interview:** [*SELECT FROM:* Organizational personnel with personnel security responsibilities].

PS-6(2)	ACCESS AGREEMENTS
PS-6(2).1	**ASSESSMENT OBJECTIVE:** *Determine if the organization grants access to classified information with special protection measures only to individuals who:* – *have a valid access authorization that is demonstrated by assigned official government duties;* – *satisfy associated personnel security criteria; and* – *have read, understood, and signed a nondisclosure agreement.* **POTENTIAL ASSESSMENT METHODS AND OBJECTS:** **Examine**: [*SELECT FROM:* Personnel security policy; procedures addressing access agreements for organizational information and information systems; access agreements; access authorizations; personnel security criteria; signed nondisclosure agreements; other relevant documents or records]. **Interview**: [*SELECT FROM:* Organizational personnel with personnel security responsibilities].

FAMILY: PERSONNEL SECURITY   **CLASS:** OPERATIONAL

ASSESSMENT PROCEDURE	
PS-7	**THIRD-PARTY PERSONNEL SECURITY**
PS-7.1	**ASSESSMENT OBJECTIVE:** *Determine if:* *(i) the organization establishes personnel security requirements, including security roles and responsibilities, for third-party providers* *(ii) the organization documents personnel security requirements for third-party providers; and* *(iii) the organization monitors third-party provider compliance with personnel security requirements.* **POTENTIAL ASSESSMENT METHODS AND OBJECTS:** **Examine:** [*SELECT FROM:* Personnel security policy; procedures addressing third-party personnel security; list of personnel security requirements; acquisition documents; compliance monitoring process; other relevant documents or records]. **Interview:** [*SELECT FROM:* Organizational personnel with personnel security responsibilities; third-party providers].

FAMILY: PERSONNEL SECURITY

CLASS: OPERATIONAL

ASSESSMENT PROCEDURE	
PS-8	**PERSONNEL SANCTIONS**
PS-8.1	**ASSESSMENT OBJECTIVE:** *Determine if the organization employs a formal sanctions process for personnel failing to comply with established information security policies and procedures.* **POTENTIAL ASSESSMENT METHODS AND OBJECTS:** **Examine**: [*SELECT FROM:* Personnel security policy; procedures addressing personnel sanctions; rules of behavior; records of formal sanctions; other relevant documents or records]. **Interview**: [*SELECT FROM:* Organizational personnel with personnel security responsibilities].

FAMILY: RISK ASSESSMENT   **CLASS:** MANAGEMENT

ASSESSMENT PROCEDURE	
RA-1	**RISK ASSESSMENT POLICY AND PROCEDURES**

RA-1.1	**ASSESSMENT OBJECTIVE:**
	Determine if:
	
	(i) *the organization develops and formally documents risk assessment policy;*
	
	(ii) *the organization risk assessment policy addresses:*
	
	  - *purpose;*
	  - *scope;*
	  - *roles and responsibilities;*
	  - *management commitment;*
	  - *coordination among organizational entities; and*
	  - *compliance;*
	
	(iii) *the organization disseminates formal documented risk assessment policy to elements within the organization having associated risk assessment roles and responsibilities;*
	
	(iv) *the organization develops and formally documents risk assessment procedures;*
	
	(v) *the organization risk assessment procedures facilitate implementation of the risk assessment policy and associated risk assessment controls; and*
	
	(vi) *the organization disseminates formal documented risk assessment procedures to elements within the organization having associated risk assessment roles and responsibilities.*
	
	POTENTIAL ASSESSMENT METHODS AND OBJECTS:
	Examine: [*SELECT FROM*: Risk assessment policy and procedures; other relevant documents or records].
	Interview: [*SELECT FROM*: Organizational personnel with risk assessment responsibilities].

RA-1.2	**ASSESSMENT OBJECTIVE:** *Determine if:* (i) *the organization defines the frequency of risk assessment policy reviews/updates;* (ii) *the organization reviews/updates risk assessment policy in accordance with organization-defined frequency; and* (iii) *the organization defines the frequency of risk assessment procedure reviews/updates;* (iv) *the organization reviews/updates risk assessment procedures in accordance with organization-defined frequency.* **POTENTIAL ASSESSMENT METHODS AND OBJECTS:** **Examine**: [*SELECT FROM*: Risk assessment policy and procedures; other relevant documents or records]. **Interview**: [*SELECT FROM*: Organizational personnel with risk assessment responsibilities].

FAMILY: RISK ASSESSMENT   **CLASS:** MANAGEMENT

ASSESSMENT PROCEDURE	
RA-2	**SECURITY CATEGORIZATION**
RA-2.1	**ASSESSMENT OBJECTIVE:** *Determine if:* *(i) the organization categorizes information and the information system in accordance with applicable federal laws, Executive Orders, directives, policies, regulations, standards, and guidance;* *(ii) the organization documents the security categorization results (including supporting rationale) in the security plan for the information system; and* *(iii) the authorizing official or authorizing official designated representative reviews and approves the security categorization decision.* **POTENTIAL ASSESSMENT METHODS AND OBJECTS:** **Examine**: [*SELECT FROM:* Risk assessment policy; procedures addressing security categorization of organizational information and information systems; security planning policy and procedures; security plan; security categorization documentation; other relevant documents or records]. **Interview**: [*SELECT FROM:* Organizational personnel with security categorization and risk assessment responsibilities].

FAMILY: RISK ASSESSMENT   **CLASS:** MANAGEMENT

ASSESSMENT PROCEDURE	
RA-3	**RISK ASSESSMENT**

RA-3.1	**ASSESSMENT OBJECTIVE:**
	Determine if:
	
	(i) the organization conducts an assessment of risk of the information system and the information it processes, stores, or transmits that includes the likelihood and magnitude of harm, from the unauthorized:
	
	   - *access;*
	   - *use;*
	   - *disclosure;*
	   - *disruption;*
	   - *modification; or*
	   - *destruction;*
	
	(ii) the organization defines the document in which risk assessment results are documented, selecting from the security plan, risk assessment report, or other organization-defined document;
	
	(iii) the organization documents risk assessment results in the organization-defined document;
	
	(iv) the organization defines the frequency for review of the risk assessment results;
	
	(v) the organization reviews risk assessment results in accordance with the organization-defined frequency;
	
	(vi) the organization defines the frequency that risk assessments are updated; and
	
	(vii) the organization updates the risk assessment in accordance with the organization-defined frequency or whenever there are significant changes to the information system or environment of operation, or other conditions that may impact the security state of the system.
	
	POTENTIAL ASSESSMENT METHODS AND OBJECTS:
	Examine: [*SELECT FROM:* Risk assessment policy; security planning policy and procedures; procedures addressing organizational assessments of risk; security plan; risk assessment; other relevant documents or records].
	Interview: [*SELECT FROM:* Organizational personnel with risk assessment responsibilities].

FAMILY: RISK ASSESSMENT   **CLASS:** MANAGEMENT

ASSESSMENT PROCEDURE	
RA-4	**RISK ASSESSMENT UPDATE** [Withdrawn: Incorporated into RA-3].
RA-4.1	**ASSESSMENT OBJECTIVE:** [Withdrawn: Incorporated into RA-3]. **POTENTIAL ASSESSMENT METHODS AND OBJECTS:** [Withdrawn: Incorporated into RA-3].

FAMILY: RISK ASSESSMENT   **CLASS:** MANAGEMENT

ASSESSMENT PROCEDURE	
RA-5	**VULNERABILITY SCANNING**

RA-5.1	**ASSESSMENT OBJECTIVE:**
	Determine if:
	
	(i) *the organization defines:*
	   - *the frequency for conducting vulnerability scans on the information system and hosted applications and/or;*
	   - *the organization-defined process for conducting random vulnerability scans on the information system and hosted applications;*
	
	(ii) *the organization scans for vulnerabilities in the information system and hosted applications in accordance with the organization-defined frequency and/or the organization-defined process for random scans;*
	
	(iii) *the organization scans for vulnerabilities in the information system and hosted applications when new vulnerabilities potentially affecting the system/applications are identified and reported;*
	
	(iv) *the organization employs vulnerability scanning tools and techniques that use standards to promote interoperability among tools and automate parts of the vulnerability management process that focus on:*
	   - *enumerating platforms, software flaws, and improper configurations;*
	   - *formatting/and making transparent checklists and test procedures; and*
	   - *measuring vulnerability impact, and*
	
	(v) *the organization analyzes vulnerability scan reports and results from security control assessments.*
	
	POTENTIAL ASSESSMENT METHODS AND OBJECTS:
	Examine: [*SELECT FROM:* Risk assessment policy; procedures addressing vulnerability scanning; risk assessment; security plan; vulnerability scanning results; patch and vulnerability management records; other relevant documents or records].
	Interview: [*SELECT FROM:* Organizational personnel with risk assessment and vulnerability scanning responsibilities].

RA-5.2	**ASSESSMENT OBJECTIVE:** *Determine if:* (i) *the organization defines the response times for remediating legitimate vulnerabilities in accordance with an organizational assessment of risk;* (ii) *the organization remediates legitimate vulnerabilities in accordance with organization-defined response times; and* (iii) *the organization shares information obtained from the vulnerability scanning process and security control assessments with designated personnel throughout the organization to help eliminate similar vulnerabilities in other information systems (i.e., systemic weaknesses or deficiencies).* **POTENTIAL ASSESSMENT METHODS AND OBJECTS:** **Examine:** [*SELECT FROM:* Risk assessment policy; procedures addressing vulnerability scanning; risk assessment; security plan; vulnerability scanning results; patch and vulnerability management records; other relevant documents or records]. **Interview:** [*SELECT FROM:* Organizational personnel with risk assessment and vulnerability scanning responsibilities].

RA-5(1)	VULNERABILITY SCANNING
RA-5(1).1	**ASSESSMENT OBJECTIVE:** *Determine if the organization uses vulnerability scanning tools that have the capability to readily update the list of information system vulnerabilities scanned.* **POTENTIAL ASSESSMENT METHODS AND OBJECTS:** **Examine**: [*SELECT FROM:* Risk assessment policy; procedures addressing vulnerability scanning; vulnerability scanning tools and techniques documentation; records of updates to vulnerabilities scanned; other relevant documents or records]. **Test**: [*SELECT FROM:* Vulnerability scanning capability and associated scanning tools].

RA-5(2)	VULNERABILITY SCANNING
RA-5(2).1	**ASSESSMENT OBJECTIVE:** *Determine if:* *(i) the organization defines the frequency of updates for information system vulnerabilities scanned; and* *(ii) the organization updates the list of information system vulnerabilities scanned in accordance with the organization-defined frequency or when new vulnerabilities are identified and reported.* **POTENTIAL ASSESSMENT METHODS AND OBJECTS:** **Examine**: [*SELECT FROM:* Risk assessment policy; procedures addressing vulnerability scanning; risk assessment; security plan; list of vulnerabilities scanned; records of updates to vulnerabilities scanned; other relevant documents or records].

RA-5(3)	VULNERABILITY SCANNING
RA-5(3).1	**ASSESSMENT OBJECTIVE:** *Determine if:* *(i) the organization employs vulnerability scanning procedures that can demonstrate the breadth of coverage (i.e., information system components scanned); and* *(ii) the organization employs vulnerability scanning procedures that can demonstrate the depth of coverage (i.e., vulnerabilities checked).* **POTENTIAL ASSESSMENT METHODS AND OBJECTS:** **Examine**: [*SELECT FROM:* Risk assessment policy; procedures addressing vulnerability scanning; risk assessment; list of vulnerabilities scanned and information system components checked; other relevant documents or records].

RA-5(4)	VULNERABILITY SCANNING
RA-5(4).1	**ASSESSMENT OBJECTIVE:** *Determine if the organization attempts to discern what information about the information system is discoverable by adversaries.* **POTENTIAL ASSESSMENT METHODS AND OBJECTS:** **Examine**: [*SELECT FROM:* Risk assessment policy; procedures addressing vulnerability scanning; penetration test results; vulnerability scanning results; other relevant documents or records].

RA-5(5)	VULNERABILITY SCANNING
RA-5(5).1	**ASSESSMENT OBJECTIVE:** *Determine if:* *(i) the organization defines the list of information system components to which privileged access is authorized for selected vulnerability scanning activities; and* *(ii) the organization includes privileged access authorization to organization-defined information system components identified for selected vulnerability scanning activities to facilitate more thorough scanning.* **POTENTIAL ASSESSMENT METHODS AND OBJECTS:** **Examine**: [*SELECT FROM:* Risk assessment policy; procedures addressing vulnerability scanning; security plan; list of information system components for vulnerability scanning; personnel access authorization list; authorization credentials; access authorization records; other relevant documents or records].

RA-5(6)	VULNERABILITY SCANNING
RA-5(6).1	**ASSESSMENT OBJECTIVE:** *Determine if the organization employs automated mechanisms to compare the results of vulnerability scans over time to determine trends in information system vulnerabilities.* **POTENTIAL ASSESSMENT METHODS AND OBJECTS:** **Examine**: [*SELECT FROM:* Risk assessment policy; procedures addressing vulnerability scanning; vulnerability scanning tools and techniques documentation; vulnerability scanning results; other relevant documents or records]. **Test**: [*SELECT FROM:* Vulnerability scanning capability and associated scanning tools].

RA-5(7)	VULNERABILITY SCANNING
RA-5(7).1	**ASSESSMENT OBJECTIVE:** *Determine if:* *(i) the organization defines the frequency for employing automated mechanisms to detect the presence of unauthorized software on organizational information systems and notify designated organizational officials; and* *(ii) the organization employs automated mechanisms to detect the presence of unauthorized software on organizational information systems and notify designated officials in accordance with the organization-defined frequency.* **POTENTIAL ASSESSMENT METHODS AND OBJECTS:** **Examine**: [*SELECT FROM:* Risk assessment policy; procedures addressing vulnerability scanning; security plan; information system design documentation; list of unauthorized software; notifications or alerts of unauthorized software on organizational information systems; other relevant documents or records]. **Test**: [*SELECT FROM:* Vulnerability scanning capability and associated scanning tools].

RA-5(8)	VULNERABILITY SCANNING
RA-5(8).1	**ASSESSMENT OBJECTIVE:** *Determine if the organization reviews historic audit logs to determine if a vulnerability identified in the information system has been previously exploited.* **POTENTIAL ASSESSMENT METHODS AND OBJECTS:** **Examine**: [*SELECT FROM:* Risk assessment policy; procedures addressing vulnerability scanning; audit logs; vulnerability scanning results; patch and vulnerability management records; other relevant documents or records]. **Interview**: [*SELECT FROM:* Organizational personnel with vulnerability scanning responsibilities].

RA-5(9)	VULNERABILITY SCANNING
RA-5(9).1	**ASSESSMENT OBJECTIVE:** *Determine if the organization employs an independent penetration agent or penetration team to:* – *conduct a vulnerability analysis on the information system; and* – *perform penetration testing on the information system based on the vulnerability analysis to determine the exploitability of identified vulnerabilities.* **POTENTIAL ASSESSMENT METHODS AND OBJECTS:** **Examine**: [*SELECT FROM:* Risk assessment policy; security assessment policy; procedures addressing vulnerability analysis; risk assessment; security plan; other relevant documents or records]. **Interview:** [*SELECT FROM:* Organizational personnel with vulnerability scanning and analysis responsibilities].

FAMILY: SYSTEM AND SERVICES ACQUISITION   **CLASS:** MANAGEMENT

ASSESSMENT PROCEDURE	
SA-1	**SYSTEM AND SERVICES ACQUISITION POLICY AND PROCEDURES**

SA-1.1	**ASSESSMENT OBJECTIVE:**
	Determine if:
	(i) *the organization develops and formally documents system services and acquisition policy;*
	(ii) *the organization system services and acquisition policy addresses:*
	    - *purpose;*
	    - *scope;*
	    - *roles and responsibilities;*
	    - *management commitment;*
	    - *coordination among organizational entities; and*
	    - *compliance;*
	(iii) *the organization disseminates formal documented system services and acquisition policy to elements within the organization having associated system services and acquisition roles and responsibilities;*
	(iv) *the organization develops and formally documents system services and acquisition procedures;*
	(v) *the organization system services and acquisition procedures facilitate implementation of the system and services acquisition policy and associated system services and acquisition controls; and*
	(vi) *the organization disseminates formal documented system services and acquisition procedures to elements within the organization having associated system services and acquisition roles and responsibilities.*
	
	POTENTIAL ASSESSMENT METHODS AND OBJECTS:
	Examine: [*SELECT FROM:* System and services acquisition policy and procedures; other relevant documents or records].
	Interview: [*SELECT FROM:* Organizational personnel with system and services acquisition responsibilities].

SA-1.2	**ASSESSMENT OBJECTIVE:** *Determine if:* *(i)* *the organization defines the frequency of system services and acquisition policy reviews/updates;* *(ii)* *the organization reviews/updates system services and acquisition policy in accordance with organization-defined frequency; and* *(iii)* *the organization defines the frequency of system services and acquisition procedure reviews/updates;* *(iv)* *the organization reviews/updates system services and acquisition procedures in accordance with organization-defined frequency.* **POTENTIAL ASSESSMENT METHODS AND OBJECTS:** **Examine**: [*SELECT FROM:* System and services acquisition policy and procedures; other relevant documents or records]. **Interview**: [*SELECT FROM:* Organizational personnel with system and services acquisition responsibilities].

FAMILY: SYSTEM AND SERVICES ACQUISITION   **CLASS:** MANAGEMENT

ASSESSMENT PROCEDURE	
SA-2	**ALLOCATION OF RESOURCES**
SA-2.1	**ASSESSMENT OBJECTIVE:** *Determine if:* (i) *the organization includes a determination of the information security requirements for the information system in mission/business process planning;* (ii) *the organization determines, documents, and allocates the resources required to protect the information system as part of its capital planning and investment control process; and* (iii) *the organization establishes a discrete line item for information security in organizational programming and budgeting documentation.* **ASSESSMENT METHODS AND OBJECTS:** **Examine**: [*SELECT FROM:* System and services acquisition policy; procedures addressing the allocation of resources to information security requirements; organizational programming and budgeting documentation; other relevant documents or records]. **Interview**: [*SELECT FROM:* Organizational personnel with capital planning and investment responsibilities].

FAMILY: SYSTEM AND SERVICES ACQUISITION   **CLASS:** MANAGEMENT

ASSESSMENT PROCEDURE	
SA-3	**LIFE CYCLE SUPPORT**
SA-3.1	**ASSESSMENT OBJECTIVE:** *Determine if:* (i) the organization manages the information system using a system development life cycle methodology that includes information security considerations; (ii) the organization defines and documents information system security roles and responsibilities throughout the system development life cycle; and (iii) the organization identifies individuals having information system security roles and responsibilities. **POTENTIAL ASSESSMENT METHODS AND OBJECTS:** **Examine**: [*SELECT FROM:* System and services acquisition policy; procedures addressing the integration of information security into the system development life cycle process; information system development life cycle documentation; other relevant documents or records]. **Interview**: [*SELECT FROM:* Organizational personnel with information security and system life cycle development responsibilities].

FAMILY: SYSTEM AND SERVICES ACQUISITION   **CLASS:** MANAGEMENT

ASSESSMENT PROCEDURE	
SA-4	**ACQUISITIONS**
SA-4.1	**ASSESSMENT OBJECTIVE:** *Determine if the organization includes the following requirements and/or specifications, explicitly or by reference, in information system acquisition contracts based on an assessment of risk and in accordance with applicable federal laws, Executive Orders, directives, policies, regulations, and standards:* – *security functional requirements/specifications;* – *security-related documentation requirements; and* – *developmental and evaluation-related assurance requirements.* **POTENTIAL ASSESSMENT METHODS AND OBJECTS:** **Examine:** [*SELECT FROM:* System and services acquisition policy; procedures addressing the integration of information security requirements and/or security specifications into the acquisition process; acquisition contracts for information systems or services; other relevant documents or records]. **Interview:** [*SELECT FROM:* Organizational personnel with information system security, acquisition, and contracting responsibilities].

SA-4(1)	**ACQUISITIONS**
SA-4(1).1	**ASSESSMENT OBJECTIVE:** *Determine if the organization requires in acquisition documents that vendors/contractors provide information describing in the functional properties of the security controls to be employed within the information system, information system components, or information system services in sufficient detail to permit analysis and testing of the controls.* **POTENTIAL ASSESSMENT METHODS AND OBJECTS:** **Examine:** [*SELECT FROM:* System and services acquisition policy; procedures addressing the integration of information security requirements and/or security specifications into the acquisition process; solicitation documents; acquisition documentation; acquisition contracts for information systems or services; other relevant documents or records].

SA-4(2)	**ACQUISITIONS**
SA-4(2).1	**ASSESSMENT OBJECTIVE:** *Determine if the organization requires in acquisition documents that vendors/contractors provide information describing the design and implementation details of the security controls to be employed within the information system, information system components, or information system services (including functional interfaces among control components) in sufficient detail to permit analysis and testing of the controls.* **POTENTIAL ASSESSMENT METHODS AND OBJECTS:** **Examine:** [*SELECT FROM:* System and services acquisition policy; procedures addressing the integration of information security requirements and/or security specifications into the acquisition process; solicitation documents; acquisition documentation; acquisition contracts for information systems or services; other relevant documents or records].

SA-4(3)	ACQUISITIONS
SA-4(3).1	**ASSESSMENT OBJECTIVE:** *Determine if the organization requires software vendors/manufacturers to minimize flawed or malformed software by demonstrating that their software development processes employ:* - *state-of-the-practice software and security engineering methods;* - *quality control processes; and* - *validation techniques.* **POTENTIAL ASSESSMENT METHODS AND OBJECTS:** **Examine:** [*SELECT FROM:* System and services acquisition policy; procedures addressing the integration of information security requirements and/or security specifications into the acquisition process; solicitation documents; acquisition documentation; acquisition contracts for information systems or services; other relevant documents or records].

SA-4(4)	ACQUISITIONS
SA-4(4).1	**ASSESSMENT OBJECTIVE:** *Determine if:* (i) *the organization explicitly assigns each acquired information system component to an information system; and* (ii) *the owner of the system acknowledges each assignment of information system components to the information system.* **POTENTIAL ASSESSMENT METHODS AND OBJECTS:** **Examine:** [*SELECT FROM:* System and services acquisition policy; procedures addressing the integration of information security requirements and/or security specifications into the acquisition process; solicitation documents; acquisition documentation; acquisition contracts for information systems or services; other relevant documents or records]. **Interview:** [*SELECT FROM:* Organizational personnel with information system security, acquisition, and contracting responsibilities; information system owner].

SA-4(5)	ACQUISITIONS
SA-4(5).1	**ASSESSMENT OBJECTIVE:** *Determine if:* (i) *the organization requires in acquisition documents that information system components are delivered in a secure, documented configuration; and* (ii) *the organization requires in acquisition documents that the secure configuration is the default configuration for any software reinstalls or upgrades.* **POTENTIAL ASSESSMENT METHODS AND OBJECTS:** **Examine:** [*SELECT FROM:* System and services acquisition policy; procedures addressing the integration of information security requirements and/or security specifications into the acquisition process; solicitation documents; acquisition documentation; acquisition contracts for information systems or services; other relevant documents or records].

SA-4(6)	ACQUISITIONS

SA-4(6).1	**ASSESSMENT OBJECTIVE:** *Determine if:* (i) *the organization employs only government off-the-shelf (GOTS) or commercial off-the-shelf (COTS) information assurance (IA) and IA-enabled information technology products that compose an NSA-approved solution to protect classified information when the networks used to transmit the information are at a lower classification level than the information being transmitted; and* (ii) *the organization ensures that these products have been evaluated and/or validated by the NSA or in accordance with NSA-approved procedures.* **POTENTIAL ASSESSMENT METHODS AND OBJECTS:** **Examine:** [*SELECT FROM:* System and services acquisition policy; procedures addressing the integration of information security requirements and/or security specifications into the acquisition process; solicitation documents; acquisition documentation; acquisition contracts for information systems or services; other relevant documents or records]. **Interview:** [*SELECT FROM:* Organizational personnel with information system security, acquisition, and contracting responsibilities].

SA-4(7)	ACQUISITIONS

SA-4(7).1	**ASSESSMENT OBJECTIVE:** *Determine if:* (i) *the organization limits the use of commercially-provided information technology products to those products that have been successfully evaluated against a validated U.S. Government Protection Profile for a specific technology type, if such a profile exists;* (ii) *the organization requires a commercially-provided information technology product to rely on cryptographic functionality to enforce its security policy when no U.S. Government Protection Profile exists for such a specific technology type; and* (iii) *the organization requires the use of a FIPS-validated, cryptographic module for a technology product that relies on cryptographic functionality to enforce its security policy when no U.S. Government Protection Profile exists for such a specific technology type.* **POTENTIAL ASSESSMENT METHODS AND OBJECTS:** **Examine:** [*SELECT FROM:* System and services acquisition policy; procedures addressing the integration of information security requirements and/or security specifications into the acquisition process; solicitation documents; acquisition documentation; acquisition contracts for information systems or services; other relevant documents or records]. **Interview:** [*SELECT FROM:* Organizational personnel with information system security, acquisition, and contracting responsibilities].

FAMILY: SYSTEM AND SERVICES ACQUISITION   **CLASS:** MANAGEMENT

ASSESSMENT PROCEDURE

SA-5	INFORMATION SYSTEM DOCUMENTATION

SA-5.1	**ASSESSMENT OBJECTIVE:**
	Determine if:
	
	(i) *the organization obtains, protects as required, and makes available to authorized personnel, administrator documentation for the information system that describes:*
	   - *secure configuration, installation, and operation of the information system;*
	   - *effective use and maintenance of the security features/functions; and*
	   - *known vulnerabilities regarding configuration and use of administrative (i.e., privileged) functions;*
	
	(ii) *the organization obtains, protects as required, and makes available to authorized personnel, user documentation for the information system that describes:*
	   - *user-accessible security features/functions and how to effectively use those security features/functions;*
	   - *methods for user interaction with the information system, which enables individuals to use the system in a more secure manner; and*
	   - *user responsibilities in maintaining the security of the information and information system; and*
	
	(iii) *the organization documents attempts to obtain information system documentation when such documentation is either unavailable or nonexistent.*
	
	POTENTIAL ASSESSMENT METHODS AND OBJECTS:
	Examine: [*SELECT FROM:* System and services acquisition policy; procedures addressing information system documentation; information system documentation including administrator and user guides; records documenting attempts to obtain unavailable or nonexistent information system documentation; other relevant documents or records].
	Interview: [*SELECT FROM:* Organizational personnel with information system documentation responsibilities; organizational personnel operating, using, and/or maintaining the information system].

SA-5(1)	INFORMATION SYSTEM DOCUMENTATION
SA-5(1).1	**ASSESSMENT OBJECTIVE:** *Determine if the organization obtains, protects as required, and makes available to authorized personnel, vendor/manufacturer documentation that describes the functional properties of the security controls employed within the information system with sufficient detail to permit analysis and testing.* **POTENTIAL ASSESSMENT METHODS AND OBJECTS:** **Examine:** [*SELECT FROM:* System and services acquisition policy; procedures addressing information system documentation; information system design documentation; other relevant documents or records]. **Interview:** [*SELECT FROM:* Organizational personnel with information system security, acquisition, and contracting responsibilities; organizational personnel operating, using, and/or maintaining the information system].

SA-5(2)	INFORMATION SYSTEM DOCUMENTATION
SA-5(2).1	**ASSESSMENT OBJECTIVE:** *Determine if the organization obtains, protects as required, and makes available to authorized personnel, vendor/manufacturer documentation that describes the security-relevant external interfaces to the information system with sufficient detail to permit analysis and testing.* **POTENTIAL ASSESSMENT METHODS AND OBJECTS:** **Examine**: [*SELECT FROM:* System and services acquisition policy; procedures addressing information system documentation; information system design documentation; other relevant documents or records]. **Interview**: [*SELECT FROM:* Organizational personnel with information system security documentation responsibilities; organizational personnel operating, using, and/or maintaining the information system].

SA-5(3)	INFORMATION SYSTEM DOCUMENTATION
SA-5(3).1	**ASSESSMENT OBJECTIVE:** *Determine if the organization obtains, protects as required, and makes available to authorized personnel, vendor/manufacturer documentation that describes the high-level design of the information system in terms of subsystems and implementation details of the security controls employed within the system with sufficient detail to permit analysis and testing.* **POTENTIAL ASSESSMENT METHODS AND OBJECTS:** **Examine**: [*SELECT FROM:* System and services acquisition policy; procedures addressing information system documentation; information system design documentation; other relevant documents or records]. **Interview**: [*SELECT FROM:* Organizational personnel with information system security, acquisition, and contracting responsibilities; organizational personnel operating, using, and/or maintaining the information system].

SA-5(4)	INFORMATION SYSTEM DOCUMENTATION
SA-5(4).1	**ASSESSMENT OBJECTIVE:** *Determine if the organization obtains, protects as required, and makes available to authorized personnel, vendor/manufacturer documentation that describes the low-level design of the information system in terms of modules and implementation details of the security controls employed within the system with sufficient detail to permit analysis and testing.* **POTENTIAL ASSESSMENT METHODS AND OBJECTS:** **Examine**: [*SELECT FROM:* System and services acquisition policy; procedures addressing information system documentation; information system design documentation; other relevant documents or records]. **Interview**: [*SELECT FROM:* Organizational personnel with information system security documentation responsibilities; organizational personnel operating, using, and/or maintaining the information system].

SA-5(5)	INFORMATION SYSTEM DOCUMENTATION
SA-5(5).1	**ASSESSMENT OBJECTIVE:** *Determine if the organization obtains, protects as required, and makes available to authorized personnel, the source code for the information system to permit analysis and testing.* **POTENTIAL ASSESSMENT METHODS AND OBJECTS:** **Examine:** [*SELECT FROM:* System and services acquisition policy; procedures addressing information system documentation; information system design documentation; information system source code documentation; other relevant documents or records]. **Interview:** [*SELECT FROM:* Organizational personnel with information system security, acquisition, and contracting responsibilities; organizational personnel operating, using, and/or maintaining the information system].

FAMILY: SYSTEM AND SERVICES ACQUISITION   **CLASS:** MANAGEMENT

ASSESSMENT PROCEDURE

SA-6	SOFTWARE USAGE RESTRICTIONS
SA-6.1	**ASSESSMENT OBJECTIVE:** *Determine if:* (i) *the organization uses software and associated documentation in accordance with contract agreements and copyright laws;* (ii) *the organization employs tracking systems for software and associated documentation protected by quantity licenses to control copying and distribution; and* (iii) *the organization controls and documents the use of peer-to-peer file sharing technology to ensure that this capability is not used for the unauthorized distribution, display, performance, or reproduction of copyrighted work.* **POTENTIAL ASSESSMENT METHODS AND OBJECTS:** **Examine:** [*SELECT FROM:* System and services acquisition policy; procedures addressing software usage restrictions; site license documentation; list of software usage restrictions; other relevant documents or records]. **Interview:** [*SELECT FROM:* Organizational personnel with information system administration responsibilities; organizational personnel operating, using, and/or maintaining the information system].

SA-6(1)	SOFTWARE USAGE RESTRICTIONS
SA-6(1).1	**ASSESSMENT OBJECTIVE:** *Determine if:* (i) *the organization prohibits the use of binary or machine executable code from sources with limited or no warranty without accompanying source code;* (ii) *the organization provides exceptions to the source code requirement only when no alternative solutions are available to support compelling mission/operational requirements; and* (iii) *the organization obtains express written consent of the authorizing official for exceptions to the source code requirement.* **POTENTIAL ASSESSMENT METHODS AND OBJECTS:** **Examine:** [*SELECT FROM:* System and services acquisition policy; procedures addressing the integration of information security requirements and/or security specifications into the acquisition process; solicitation documents; acquisition documentation; acquisition contracts for information systems or services; other relevant documents or records]. **Interview:** [*SELECT FROM:* Organizational personnel with information system administration responsibilities; organizational personnel operating, using, and/or maintaining the information system].

FAMILY: SYSTEM AND SERVICES ACQUISITION   **CLASS:** MANAGEMENT

ASSESSMENT PROCEDURE	
SA-7	**USER-INSTALLED SOFTWARE**
SA-7.1	**ASSESSMENT OBJECTIVE:** *Determine if:* *(i) the organization identifies and documents (as appropriate) explicit rules to be enforced when governing the installation of software by users; and* *(ii) the organization (or information system) enforces explicit rules governing the installation of software by users.* **POTENTIAL ASSESSMENT METHODS AND OBJECTS:** **Examine**: [*SELECT FROM:* System and services acquisition policy; procedures addressing user installed software; list of rules governing user installed software; network traffic on the information system; other relevant documents or records]. **Interview**: [*SELECT FROM:* Organizational personnel with information system administration responsibilities; organizational personnel operating, using, and/or maintaining the information system]. **Test**: [*SELECT FROM:* Enforcement of rules for user installed software on the information system; information system for prohibited software].

FAMILY: SYSTEM AND SERVICES ACQUISITION   **CLASS:** MANAGEMENT

ASSESSMENT PROCEDURE	
SA-8	**SECURITY ENGINEERING PRINCIPLES**
SA-8.1	**ASSESSMENT OBJECTIVE:** *Determine if:* *(i)* *The organization applies information system security engineering principles in the specification of the information system;* *(ii)* *the organization applies information system security engineering principles in the design of the information system;* *(iii)* *the organization applies information system security engineering principles in the development of the information system;* *(iv)* *the organization applies information system security engineering principles in the implementation of the information system; and* *(v)* *the organization applies information system security engineering principles in the modification of the information system.* **POTENTIAL ASSESSMENT METHODS AND OBJECTS:** **Examine:** [*SELECT FROM:* System and services acquisition policy; procedures addressing security engineering principles used in the development and implementation of the information system; information system design documentation; security requirements and security specifications for the information system; other relevant documents or records]. **Interview:** [*SELECT FROM:* Organizational personnel with information system design, development, implementation, and modification responsibilities].

FAMILY: SYSTEM AND SERVICES ACQUISITION   **CLASS:** MANAGEMENT

ASSESSMENT PROCEDURE

SA-9	EXTERNAL INFORMATION SYSTEM SERVICES
SA-9.1	**ASSESSMENT OBJECTIVE:** *Determine if:* (i) the organization requires that providers of external information system services comply with organizational information security requirements and employ appropriate security controls in accordance with applicable federal laws, Executive Orders, directives, policies, regulations, standards, and guidance; (ii) the organization defines and documents government oversight, and user roles and responsibilities with regard to external information system services; and (iii) the organization monitors security control compliance by external service providers. **POTENTIAL ASSESSMENT METHODS AND OBJECTS:** **Examine:** [*SELECT FROM:* System and services acquisition policy; procedures addressing external information system services; acquisition contracts and service level agreements; organizational security requirements and security specifications for external provider services; security control assessment evidence from external providers of information system services; other relevant documents or records]. **Interview:** [*SELECT FROM:* Organizational personnel with system and services acquisition responsibilities; external providers of information system services].

SA-9(1)	SOFTWARE USAGE RESTRICTIONS
SA-9(1).1	**ASSESSMENT OBJECTIVE:** *Determine if:* (i) the organization conducts an organizational assessment of risk prior to the acquisition or outsourcing of dedicated information security services; (ii) the organization defines the senior organizational official designated to approve the acquisition or outsourcing of dedicated information security services; and (iii) the designated senior organizational official approves the acquisition or outsourcing of dedicated information security services. **POTENTIAL ASSESSMENT METHODS AND OBJECTS:** **Examine:** [*SELECT FROM:* System and services acquisition policy; procedures addressing the integration of information security requirements and/or security specifications into the acquisition process; solicitation documents; acquisition documentation; acquisition contracts for information systems or services; risk assessment reports; other relevant documents or records]. **Interview:** [*SELECT FROM:* Organizational personnel with information system security, acquisition, and contracting responsibilities].

FAMILY: SYSTEM AND SERVICES ACQUISITION   **CLASS:** MANAGEMENT

ASSESSMENT PROCEDURE	
SA-10	**DEVELOPER CONFIGURATION MANAGEMENT**
SA-10.1	**ASSESSMENT OBJECTIVE:** *Determine if the organization requires that information system developers/integrators:* *(i) perform configuration management during information system:* - *design;* - *development;* - *implementation; and* - *operation;* *(ii) manage and control changes to the information system during:* - *design;* - *development;* - *implementation; and* - *modification;* *(iii) implement only organization-approved changes;* *(iv) document approved changes to the information system; and* *(v) track security flaws and flaw resolution.* **POTENTIAL ASSESSMENT METHODS AND OBJECTS:** **Examine:** [*SELECT FROM:* System and services acquisition policy; procedures addressing information system developer/integrator configuration management; acquisition contracts and service level agreements; information system developer/integrator configuration management plan; security flaw tracking records; system change authorization records; other relevant documents or records]. **Interview:** [*SELECT FROM:* Organization personnel with information system security, acquisition, and contracting responsibilities; organization personnel with configuration management responsibilities].

SA-10(1)	**DEVELOPER CONFIGURATION MANAGEMENT**
SA-10(1).1	**ASSESSMENT OBJECTIVE:** *Determine if the organization requires that information system developers/integrators provide an integrity check of software to facilitate organizational verification of software integrity after delivery.* **POTENTIAL ASSESSMENT METHODS AND OBJECTS:** **Examine:** [*SELECT FROM:* System and services acquisition policy; procedures addressing information system developer/integrator configuration management; acquisition contracts and service level agreements; information system developer/integrator configuration management plan; security flaw tracking records; system change authorization records; other relevant documents or records].

SA-10(2)	DEVELOPER CONFIGURATION MANAGEMENT
SA-10(2).1	**ASSESSMENT OBJECTIVE:** *Determine if the organization provides an alternative configuration management process with organizational personnel in the absence of a dedicated developer/integrator configuration management team.* **POTENTIAL ASSESSMENT METHODS AND OBJECTS:** **Examine:** [*SELECT FROM:* System and services acquisition policy; procedures addressing information system developer/integrator configuration management; acquisition contracts and service level agreements; information system configuration management plan; security flaw tracking records; system change authorization records; other relevant documents or records].

FAMILY: SYSTEM AND SERVICES ACQUISITION   **CLASS:** MANAGEMENT

	ASSESSMENT PROCEDURE
SA-11	**DEVELOPER SECURITY TESTING**
SA-11.1	**ASSESSMENT OBJECTIVE:** *Determine if the organization requires that information system developers/integrators, in consultation with associated security personnel (including security engineers):* – *create and implement a security test and evaluation plan;* – *implement a verifiable flaw remediation process to correct weaknesses and deficiencies identified during the security testing and evaluation process; and* – *document the results of the security testing/evaluation and flaw remediation processes.* **POTENTIAL ASSESSMENT METHODS AND OBJECTS:** **Examine:** [*SELECT FROM:* System and services acquisition policy; procedures addressing information system developer/integrator security testing; acquisition contracts and service level agreements; information system developer/integrator security test plans; records of developer/integrator security testing results for the information system; security flaw tracking records; other relevant documents or records]. **Interview:** [*SELECT FROM:* Organizational personnel with developer security testing responsibilities].

SA-11(1)	**DEVELOPER SECURITY TESTING**
SA-11(1).1	**ASSESSMENT OBJECTIVE:** *Determine if:* (i) *the organization requires that information system developers/integrators employ code analysis tools to examine software for common flaws; and* (ii) *the organization requires that information system developers/integrators document the results of the analysis.* **POTENTIAL ASSESSMENT METHODS AND OBJECTS:** **Examine:** [*SELECT FROM:* System and services acquisition policy; procedures addressing information system developer/integrator security testing; acquisition contracts and service level agreements; information system developer/integrator security test plans; records of developer/integrator security testing results for the information system; security flaw tracking records; other relevant documents or records]. **Interview:** [*SELECT FROM:* Organizational personnel with developer security testing responsibilities].

SA-11(2)	DEVELOPER SECURITY TESTING
SA-11(2).1	**ASSESSMENT OBJECTIVE:** *Determine if the organization requires that information system developers/integrators perform a vulnerability analysis to document vulnerabilities, exploitation potential, and risk mitigations.* **POTENTIAL ASSESSMENT METHODS AND OBJECTS:** **Examine**: [*SELECT FROM:* System and services acquisition policy; procedures addressing information system developer/integrator security testing; acquisition contracts and service level agreements; information system developer/integrator security test plans; records of developer/integrator security testing results for the information system; vulnerability scanning results; information system risk assessment report; other relevant documents or records]. **Interview**: [*SELECT FROM:* Organizational personnel with developer security testing responsibilities].

SA-11(3)	DEVELOPER SECURITY TESTING
SA-11(3).1	**ASSESSMENT OBJECTIVE:** *Determine if:* (i) *the organization requires that information system developers/integrators create a security test and evaluation plan; and* (ii) *the organization requires that information system developers/integrators implement the plan under the witness of an independent verification and validation agent.* **POTENTIAL ASSESSMENT METHODS AND OBJECTS:** **Examine**: [*SELECT FROM:* System and services acquisition policy; procedures addressing information system developer/integrator security testing; solicitation documents; acquisition documentation; acquisition contracts for information systems or services; security test and evaluation plan; security test and evaluation results report; other relevant documents or records]. **Interview**: [*SELECT FROM:* Organizational personnel with information system security, acquisition, and contracting responsibilities; organizational personnel with developer security testing responsibilities; independent verification and validation agent].

FAMILY: SYSTEM AND SERVICES ACQUISITION   **CLASS:** MANAGEMENT

	ASSESSMENT PROCEDURE
SA-12	**SUPPLY CHAIN PROTECTION**
SA-12.1	**ASSESSMENT OBJECTIVE:** *Determine if:* *(i) the organization defines the measures to be employed to protect against supply chain threats; and* *(ii) the organization protects against supply chain threats by employing organization-defined measures as part of a comprehensive, defense-in-breadth information security strategy.* **POTENTIAL ASSESSMENT METHODS AND OBJECTS:** **Examine:** [*SELECT FROM:* System and services acquisition policy; procedures addressing supply chain protection; procedures addressing the integration of information security requirements and/or security specifications into the acquisition process; acquisition contracts and service level agreements; list of supply chain threats; list of measures to be taken against supply chain threats; information system development life cycle documentation; other relevant documents or records].

SA-12(1)	**SUPPLY CHAIN PROTECTION**
SA-12(1).1	**ASSESSMENT OBJECTIVE:** *Determine if the organization purchases all anticipated information system components and spares in the initial acquisition.* **POTENTIAL ASSESSMENT METHODS AND OBJECTS:** **Examine:** [*SELECT FROM:* System and services acquisition policy; procedures addressing supply chain protection; procedures addressing the integration of information security requirements and/or security specifications into the acquisition process; solicitation documents; acquisition documentation; acquisition contracts for information systems or services; other relevant documents or records].

SA-12(2)	**SUPPLY CHAIN PROTECTION**
SA-12(2).1	**ASSESSMENT OBJECTIVE:** *Determine if the organization conducts a due diligence review of suppliers prior to entering into contractual agreements to acquire information system hardware, software, firmware, or services.* **POTENTIAL ASSESSMENT METHODS AND OBJECTS:** **Examine:** [*SELECT FROM:* System and services acquisition policy; procedures addressing supply chain protection; procedures addressing the integration of information security requirements and/or security specifications into the acquisition process; due diligence reviews documentation; acquisition documentation; acquisition contracts for information systems or services; other relevant documents or records]. **Interview:** [*SELECT FROM:* Organizational personnel with supply chain protection responsibilities; organizational personnel with information system security, acquisition, and contracting responsibilities].

SA-12(3)	SUPPLY CHAIN PROTECTION

SA-12(3).1	**ASSESSMENT OBJECTIVE:**
	Determine if the organization uses trusted shipping and warehousing for:
	   – *information systems;*
	   – *information system components; and*
	   – *information technology products.*
	
	POTENTIAL ASSESSMENT METHODS AND OBJECTS:
	Examine: [*SELECT FROM:* System and services acquisition policy; procedures addressing supply chain protection; procedures addressing the integration of information security requirements and/or security specifications into the acquisition process; solicitation documents; acquisition documentation; acquisition contracts for information systems or services; other relevant documents or records].
	Interview: [*SELECT FROM:* Organizational personnel with supply chain protection responsibilities; organizational personnel with information system security, acquisition, and contracting responsibilities].

SA-12(4)	SUPPLY CHAIN PROTECTION

SA-12(4).1	**ASSESSMENT OBJECTIVE:**
	Determine if the organization employs a diverse set of suppliers for:
	   – *information systems;*
	   – *information system components;*
	   – *information technology products; and*
	   – *information system services.*
	
	POTENTIAL ASSESSMENT METHODS AND OBJECTS:
	Examine: [*SELECT FROM:* System and services acquisition policy; procedures addressing supply chain protection; procedures addressing the integration of information security requirements and/or security specifications into the acquisition process; solicitation documents; acquisition documentation; acquisition contracts for information systems or services; other relevant documents or records].

SA-12(5)	SUPPLY CHAIN PROTECTION

SA-12(5).1	**ASSESSMENT OBJECTIVE:**
	Determine if the organization employs standard configurations for:
	   – *information systems;*
	   – *information system components; and*
	   – *information technology products.*
	
	POTENTIAL ASSESSMENT METHODS AND OBJECTS:
	Examine: [*SELECT FROM:* System and services acquisition policy; procedures addressing supply chain protection; procedures addressing the integration of information security requirements and/or security specifications into the acquisition process; configuration management policy; procedures addressing the baseline configuration of the information system; configuration management plan; information system design documentation; information system architecture and configuration documentation; acquisition documentation; acquisition contracts for information systems or services; other relevant documents or records].

SA-12(6)	SUPPLY CHAIN PROTECTION
SA-12(6).1	**ASSESSMENT OBJECTIVE:** *Determine if the organization minimizes the time between purchase decisions and delivery of:* – *information systems;* – *information system components; and* – *information technology products.* **POTENTIAL ASSESSMENT METHODS AND OBJECTS:** **Examine**: [*SELECT FROM:* System and services acquisition policy; procedures addressing supply chain protection; procedures addressing the integration of information security requirements and/or security specifications into the acquisition process; solicitation documents; acquisition documentation; acquisition contracts for information systems or services; shipment records; other relevant documents or records].

SA-12(7)	SUPPLY CHAIN PROTECTION
SA-12(7).1	**ASSESSMENT OBJECTIVE:** *Determine if the organization employs independent analysis and penetration testing against delivered:* – *information systems;* – *information system components; and* – *information technology products.* **POTENTIAL ASSESSMENT METHODS AND OBJECTS:** **Examine**: [*SELECT FROM:* System and services acquisition policy; procedures addressing supply chain protection; procedures addressing the integration of information security requirements and/or security specifications into the acquisition process; penetration testing records; security test and evaluation results reports; other relevant documents or records].

FAMILY: SYSTEM AND SERVICES ACQUISITION   **CLASS:** MANAGEMENT

ASSESSMENT PROCEDURE	
SA-13	**TRUSTWORTHINESS**
SA-13.1	**ASSESSMENT OBJECTIVE:** *Determine if:* *(i) the organization defines the organization's level of trustworthiness; and* *(ii) the organization requires that the information system meet the organization-defined level of trustworthiness.* **POTENTIAL ASSESSMENT METHODS AND OBJECTS:** **Examine**: [*SELECT FROM:* System and services acquisition policy; procedures addressing security engineering principles used in the development and implementation of the information system; information system design documentation; security requirements and security specifications for the information system; penetration test and vulnerability scan reports; security test and evaluation results; authority to operate documentation; other relevant documents or records]. **Interview**: [*SELECT FROM:* Organizational personnel with system and services acquisition responsibilities; information system authorizing official].

FAMILY: SYSTEM AND SERVICES ACQUISITION

CLASS: MANAGEMENT

ASSESSMENT PROCEDURE	
SA-14	**CRITICAL INFORMATION SYSTEM COMPONENTS**
SA-14.1	**ASSESSMENT OBJECTIVE:** *Determine if:* *(i) the organization defines the critical information system components that require re-implementation; and* *(ii) the organization re-implements organization-defined critical information system components.* **POTENTIAL ASSESSMENT METHODS AND OBJECTS:** **Examine:** [*SELECT FROM:* System and services acquisition policy; configuration management plan; list of critical information system components requiring re-implementation; configuration baseline for critical information system components; configuration management records; other relevant documents or records]. **Interview:** [*SELECT FROM:* Organizational personnel implementing, operating, and/or maintaining the information system].

SA-14(1)	**CRITICAL INFORMATION SYSTEM COMPONENTS**
SA-14(1).1	**ASSESSMENT OBJECTIVE:** *Determine if:* *(i) the organization identifies information system components for which alternative sourcing is not viable;* *(ii) the organization defines the measures to be employed to prevent critical security controls for information system components from being compromised; and* *(iii) the organization employs organization-defined measures to ensure that critical security controls for information system components are not compromised.* **POTENTIAL ASSESSMENT METHODS AND OBJECTS:** **Examine:** [*SELECT FROM:* System and services acquisition policy; information system design documentation; information system configuration settings and associated documentation; list of information system components; security requirements and security specifications for the information system; penetration test and vulnerability scan reports; security test and evaluation results; other relevant documents or records].

FAMILY: SYSTEM AND COMMUNICATIONS PROTECTION   **CLASS:** TECHNICAL

ASSESSMENT PROCEDURE	
SC-1	**SYSTEM AND COMMUNICATIONS PROTECTION POLICY AND PROCEDURES**

SC-1.1	**ASSESSMENT OBJECTIVE:**
	Determine if:
	
	(i) *the organization develops and formally documents system and communications protection policy;*
	
	(ii) *the organization system and communications protection policy addresses:*
	
	    - *purpose;*
	    - *scope;*
	    - *roles and responsibilities;*
	    - *management commitment;*
	    - *coordination among organizational entities; and*
	    - *compliance;*
	
	(iii) *the organization disseminates formal documented system and communications protection policy to elements within the organization having associated system and communications protection roles and responsibilities;*
	
	(iv) *the organization develops and formally documents system and communications protection procedures;*
	
	(v) *the organization system and communications protection procedures facilitate implementation of the system and communications protection policy and associated system and communications protection controls; and*
	
	(vi) *the organization disseminates formal documented system and communications protection procedures to elements within the organization having associated system and communications protection roles and responsibilities.*
	
	POTENTIAL ASSESSMENT METHODS AND OBJECTS:
	Examine: [*SELECT FROM:* System and communications protection policy and procedures; other relevant documents or records].
	Interview: [*SELECT FROM:* Organizational personnel with system and communications protection responsibilities].

SC-1.2	**ASSESSMENT OBJECTIVE:** *Determine if:* (i) *the organization defines the frequency of system and communications protection policy reviews/updates;* (ii) *the organization reviews/updates system and communications protection policy in accordance with organization-defined frequency; and* (iii) *the organization defines the frequency of system and communications protection procedure reviews/updates;* (iv) *the organization reviews/updates system and communications protection procedures in accordance with organization-defined frequency.* **POTENTIAL ASSESSMENT METHODS AND OBJECTS:** **Examine**: [*SELECT FROM:* System and communications protection policy and procedures; other relevant documents or records]. **Interview**: [*SELECT FROM:* Organizational personnel with system and communications protection responsibilities].

FAMILY: SYSTEM AND COMMUNICATIONS PROTECTION   **CLASS:** TECHNICAL

ASSESSMENT PROCEDURE

SC-2	APPLICATION PARTITIONING
SC-2.1	**ASSESSMENT OBJECTIVE:** *Determine if the information system separates user functionality (including user interface services) from information system management functionality.* **POTENTIAL ASSESSMENT METHODS AND OBJECTS:** **Examine:** [*SELECT FROM:* System and communications protection policy; procedures addressing application partitioning; information system design documentation; information system configuration settings and associated documentation; other relevant documents or records]. **Test:** [*SELECT FROM:* Separation of user functionality from information system management functionality].

SC-2(1)	APPLICATION PARTITIONING
SC-2(1).1	**ASSESSMENT OBJECTIVE:** *Determine if the information system prevents the presentation of information system management-related functionality at an interface for general (i.e., non-privileged) users.* **POTENTIAL ASSESSMENT METHODS AND OBJECTS:** **Examine:** [*SELECT FROM:* System and communications protection policy; procedures addressing application partitioning; information system design documentation; information system configuration settings and associated documentation; other relevant documents or records]. **Test:** [*SELECT FROM:* Separation of user functionality from information system management functionality].

FAMILY: SYSTEM AND COMMUNICATIONS PROTECTION   **CLASS:** TECHNICAL

ASSESSMENT PROCEDURE	
SC-3	**SECURITY FUNCTION ISOLATION**
SC-3.1	**ASSESSMENT OBJECTIVE:** *Determine if:* *(i) the organization defines the security functions of the information system to be isolated from nonsecurity functions; and* *(ii) the information system isolates security functions from nonsecurity functions.* **POTENTIAL ASSESSMENT METHODS AND OBJECTS:** **Examine**: [*SELECT FROM:* System and communications protection policy; procedures addressing security function isolation; list of security functions to be isolated from nonsecurity functions; information system design documentation; information system configuration settings and associated documentation; other relevant documents or records]. **Test**: [*SELECT FROM:* Separation of security functions from nonsecurity functions within the information system].

SC-3(1)	**SECURITY FUNCTION ISOLATION**
SC-3(1).1	**ASSESSMENT OBJECTIVE:** *Determine if the information system implements underlying hardware separation mechanisms to facilitate security function isolation.* **POTENTIAL ASSESSMENT METHODS AND OBJECTS:** **Examine**: [*SELECT FROM:* System and communications protection policy; procedures addressing security function isolation; information system design documentation; hardware separation mechanisms; information system configuration settings and associated documentation; other relevant documents or records]. **Test**: [*SELECT FROM:* Hardware separation mechanisms facilitating security function isolation].

SC-3(2)	**SECURITY FUNCTION ISOLATION**
SC-3(2).1	**ASSESSMENT OBJECTIVE:** *Determine if the information system isolates security functions enforcing access and information flow control from both nonsecurity functions and other security functions.* **POTENTIAL ASSESSMENT METHODS AND OBJECTS:** **Examine**: [*SELECT FROM:* System and communications protection policy; procedures addressing security function isolation; list of critical security functions; information system design documentation; information system configuration settings and associated documentation; other relevant documents or records]. **Test**: [*SELECT FROM:* Isolation of security functions enforcing access and information flow control].

SC-3(3)	SECURITY FUNCTION ISOLATION
SC-3(3).1	**ASSESSMENT OBJECTIVE:** *Determine if the organization implements an information system isolation boundary to minimize the number of nonsecurity functions included within the boundary containing security functions.* **POTENTIAL ASSESSMENT METHODS AND OBJECTS:** **Examine**: [*SELECT FROM:* System and communications protection policy; procedures addressing security function isolation; information system design documentation; information system configuration settings and associated documentation; other relevant documents or records].

SC-3(4)	SECURITY FUNCTION ISOLATION
SC-3(4).1	**ASSESSMENT OBJECTIVE:** *Determine if the organization implements security functions as largely independent modules that avoid unnecessary interactions between modules.* **POTENTIAL ASSESSMENT METHODS AND OBJECTS:** **Examine**: [*SELECT FROM:* System and communications protection policy; procedures addressing security function isolation; information system design documentation; information system configuration settings and associated documentation; other relevant documents or records].

SC-3(5)	SECURITY FUNCTION ISOLATION
SC-3(5).1	**ASSESSMENT OBJECTIVE:** *Determine if the organization implements security functions as a layered structure minimizing interactions between layers of the design and avoiding any dependence by lower layers on the functionality or correctness of higher layers.* **POTENTIAL ASSESSMENT METHODS AND OBJECTS:** **Examine**: [*SELECT FROM:* System and communications protection policy; procedures addressing security function isolation; information system design documentation; information system configuration settings and associated documentation; other relevant documents or records].

FAMILY: SYSTEM AND COMMUNICATIONS PROTECTION　　　　**CLASS:** TECHNICAL

ASSESSMENT PROCEDURE	
SC-4	**INFORMATION IN SHARED RESOURCES**
SC-4.1	**ASSESSMENT OBJECTIVE:** *Determine if the information system prevents unauthorized and unintended information transfer via shared system resources.* **POTENTIAL ASSESSMENT METHODS AND OBJECTS:** **Examine:** [*SELECT FROM:* System and communications protection policy; procedures addressing information remnance; information system design documentation; information system configuration settings and associated documentation; other relevant documents or records]. **Test:** [*SELECT FROM:* Information system for unauthorized and unintended transfer of information via shared system resources].

SC-4(1)	**INFORMATION IN SHARED RESOURCES**
SC-4(1).1	**ASSESSMENT OBJECTIVE:** *Determine if the information system does not share resources that are used to interface with systems operating at different security levels.* **POTENTIAL ASSESSMENT METHODS AND OBJECTS:** **Examine:** [*SELECT FROM:* System and communications protection policy; procedures addressing information remnance; information system design documentation; information system configuration settings and associated documentation; other relevant documents or records].

FAMILY: SYSTEM AND COMMUNICATIONS PROTECTION   **CLASS:** TECHNICAL

ASSESSMENT PROCEDURE

SC-5	DENIAL OF SERVICE PROTECTION
SC-5.1	**ASSESSMENT OBJECTIVE:** *Determine if:* *(i) the organization defines the types of denial of service attacks (or provides references to sources of current denial of service attacks) that can be addressed by the information system; and* *(ii) the information system protects against or limits the effects of the organization-defined or referenced types of denial of service attacks.* **POTENTIAL ASSESSMENT METHODS AND OBJECTS:** **Examine**: [*SELECT FROM:* System and communications protection policy; procedures addressing denial of service protection; information system design documentation; security plan; information system configuration settings and associated documentation; other relevant documents or records]. **Test**: [*SELECT FROM:* Information system for protection against or limitation of the effects of denial of service attacks].

SC-5(1)	DENIAL OF SERVICE PROTECTION
SC-5(1).1	**ASSESSMENT OBJECTIVE:** *Determine if the information system restricts the ability of users to launch denial of service attacks against other information systems or networks.* **POTENTIAL ASSESSMENT METHODS AND OBJECTS:** **Examine**: [*SELECT FROM:* System and communications protection policy; procedures addressing denial of service protection; information system design documentation; information system configuration settings and associated documentation; other relevant documents or records]. **Test**: [*SELECT FROM:* Information system for protection against or limitation of the effects of denial of service attacks].

SC-5(2)	DENIAL OF SERVICE PROTECTION
SC-5(2).1	**ASSESSMENT OBJECTIVE:** *Determine if the information system manages excess capacity, bandwidth, or other redundancy to limit the effects of information flooding types of denial of service attacks.* **POTENTIAL ASSESSMENT METHODS AND OBJECTS:** **Examine**: [*SELECT FROM:* System and communications protection policy; procedures addressing denial of service protection; information system design documentation; information system configuration settings and associated documentation; other relevant documents or records]. **Test**: [*SELECT FROM:* Automated mechanisms implementing information system bandwidth, capacity, and redundancy management].

FAMILY: SYSTEM AND COMMUNICATIONS PROTECTION   **CLASS:** TECHNICAL

ASSESSMENT PROCEDURE	
SC-6	**RESOURCE PRIORITY**
SC-6.1	**ASSESSMENT OBJECTIVE:** *Determine if the information system limits the use of resources by priority.* **POTENTIAL ASSESSMENT METHODS AND OBJECTS:** **Examine**: [*SELECT FROM:* System and communications protection policy; procedures addressing prioritization of information system resources; information system design documentation; information system configuration settings and associated documentation; other relevant documents or records]. **Test**: [*SELECT FROM:* Automated mechanisms implementing resource allocation capability].

FAMILY: SYSTEM AND COMMUNICATIONS PROTECTION   **CLASS:** TECHNICAL

ASSESSMENT PROCEDURE	
SC-7	**BOUNDARY PROTECTION**
SC-7.1	**ASSESSMENT OBJECTIVE:** *Determine if:* *(i) the organization defines the external boundary of the information system;* *(ii) the organization defines key internal boundaries of the information system;* *(iii) the information system monitors and controls communications at the external boundary of the information system and at key internal boundaries within the system; and* *(iv) the information system connects to external networks or information systems only through managed interfaces consisting of boundary protection devices arranged in accordance with an organizational security architecture.* **POTENTIAL ASSESSMENT METHODS AND OBJECTS:** **Examine:** [*SELECT FROM:* System and communications protection policy; procedures addressing boundary protection; list of key internal boundaries of the information system; information system design documentation; boundary protection hardware and software; information system configuration settings and associated documentation; enterprise security architecture documentation; other relevant documents or records]. **Interview:** [*SELECT FROM:* Selected organizational personnel with boundary protection responsibilities]. **Test:** [*SELECT FROM:* Automated mechanisms implementing boundary protection capability within the information system].

SC-7(1)	**BOUNDARY PROTECTION**
SC-7(1).1	**ASSESSMENT OBJECTIVE:** *Determine if the organization physically allocates publicly accessible information system components to separate subnetworks with separate, physical network interfaces.* **POTENTIAL ASSESSMENT METHODS AND OBJECTS:** **Examine:** [*SELECT FROM:* System and communications protection policy; procedures addressing boundary protection; information system design documentation; information system hardware and software; information system architecture; information system configuration settings and associated documentation; other relevant documents or records].

SC-7(2)	BOUNDARY PROTECTION
SC-7(2).1	**ASSESSMENT OBJECTIVE:** *Determine if:* *(i) the organization defines the mediation necessary for public access to the organization's internal networks; and* *(ii) the information system prevents public access into the organization's internal networks except as appropriately mediated by managed interfaces employing boundary protection devices.* **POTENTIAL ASSESSMENT METHODS AND OBJECTS:** **Examine**: [*SELECT FROM:* System and communications protection policy; procedures addressing boundary protection; list of mediation vehicles for allowing public access to the organization's internal networks; information system design documentation; boundary protection hardware and software; information system configuration settings and associated documentation; other relevant documents or records]. **Test**: [*SELECT FROM:* Automated mechanisms implementing access controls for public access to the organization's internal networks].

SC-7(3)	BOUNDARY PROTECTION
SC-7(3).1	**ASSESSMENT OBJECTIVE:** *Determine if the organization limits the number of access points to the information system to allow for more comprehensive monitoring of inbound and outbound communications and network traffic.* **POTENTIAL ASSESSMENT METHODS AND OBJECTS:** **Examine**: [*SELECT FROM:* System and communications protection policy; procedures addressing boundary protection; information system design documentation; boundary protection hardware and software; information system architecture and configuration documentation; information system configuration settings and associated documentation; communications and network traffic monitoring logs; other relevant documents or records].

SC-7(4)	BOUNDARY PROTECTION
SC-7(4).1	**ASSESSMENT OBJECTIVE:** *Determine if:* *(i) the organization defines the frequency for reviewing exceptions to traffic flow policy;* *(ii) the organization implements a managed interface for each external telecommunication service;* *(iii) the organization establishes a traffic flow policy for each managed interface;* *(iv) the organization employs security controls as needed to protect the confidentiality and integrity of the information being transmitted;* *(v) the organization documents each exception to the traffic flow policy with a supporting mission/business need and duration of that need;* *(vi) the organization reviews exceptions to the traffic flow policy in accordance with the organization-defined frequency; and* *(vii) the organization removes traffic flow policy exceptions that are no longer supported by an explicit mission/business need.* **POTENTIAL ASSESSMENT METHODS AND OBJECTS:** **Examine**: [*SELECT FROM:* System and communications protection policy; procedures addressing boundary protection; traffic flow policy; information system security architecture; information system design documentation; boundary protection hardware and software; information system architecture and configuration documentation; information system configuration settings and associated documentation; records of traffic flow policy exceptions; other relevant documents or records]. **Interview**: [*SELECT FROM:* Selected organizational personnel with boundary protection responsibilities]. **Test**: [*SELECT FROM:* Managed interfaces implementing organizational traffic flow policy].

SC-7(5)	BOUNDARY PROTECTION
SC-7(5).1	**ASSESSMENT OBJECTIVE:** *Determine if:* *(i) the information system, at managed interfaces, denies network traffic by default; and* *(ii) the information system, at managed interfaces, allows network traffic by exception.* **POTENTIAL ASSESSMENT METHODS AND OBJECTS:** **Examine**: [*SELECT FROM:* System and communications protection policy; procedures addressing boundary protection; information system design documentation; information system configuration settings and associated documentation; other relevant documents or records]. **Interview**: [*SELECT FROM:* Selected organizational personnel with boundary protection responsibilities].

SC-7(6)	BOUNDARY PROTECTION

SC-7(6).1	**ASSESSMENT OBJECTIVE:** *Determine if:* (i) *the organization prevents the unauthorized release of information outside of the information system boundary; or* (ii) *the organization prevents any unauthorized communication through the information system boundary when there is an operational failure of the boundary protection mechanisms.* **POTENTIAL ASSESSMENT METHODS AND OBJECTS:** **Examine**: [*SELECT FROM:* System and communications protection policy; procedures addressing boundary protection; information system design documentation; information system configuration settings and associated documentation; information system audit records; other relevant documents or records]. **Test**: [*SELECT FROM:* Automated mechanisms supporting the fail-safe boundary protection capability within the information system].

SC-7(7)	BOUNDARY PROTECTION

SC-7(7).1	**ASSESSMENT OBJECTIVE:** *Determine if the information system prevents remote devices that have established a non-remote connection with the system from communicating outside of that communications path with resources in external networks.* **POTENTIAL ASSESSMENT METHODS AND OBJECTS:** **Examine**: [*SELECT FROM:* System and communications protection policy; procedures addressing boundary protection; information system design documentation; information system hardware and software; information system architecture; information system configuration settings and associated documentation; other relevant documents or records]. **Test**: [*SELECT FROM:* Automated mechanisms supporting non-remote connections with the information system].

SC-7(8)	BOUNDARY PROTECTION

SC-7(8).1	**ASSESSMENT OBJECTIVE:** *Determine if:* (i) *the organization defines the internal communications traffic to be routed to external networks;* (ii) *the organization defines the external networks to which the organization-defined internal communications traffic should be routed; and* (iii) *the information system routes organization-defined internal communications traffic to organization-defined external networks through authenticated proxy servers within the managed interfaces of boundary protection devices.* **POTENTIAL ASSESSMENT METHODS AND OBJECTS:** **Examine**: [*SELECT FROM:* System and communications protection policy; procedures addressing boundary protection; information system design documentation; information system hardware and software; information system architecture; information system configuration settings and associated documentation; other relevant documents or records]. **Test**: [*SELECT FROM:* Mechanisms implementing managed interfaces within information system boundary protection devices].

SC-7(9)	BOUNDARY PROTECTION
SC-7(9).1	**ASSESSMENT OBJECTIVE:** *Determine if:* *(i) the information system, at managed interfaces, denies network traffic; and* *(ii) the information system audits internal users (or malicious code) posing a threat to external information systems.* **POTENTIAL ASSESSMENT METHODS AND OBJECTS:** **Examine**: [*SELECT FROM:* System and communications protection policy; procedures addressing boundary protection; information system design documentation; information system hardware and software; information system architecture; information system configuration settings and associated documentation; information system audit records; other relevant documents or records]. **Test**: [*SELECT FROM:* Mechanisms implementing managed interfaces within information system boundary protection devices].

SC-7(10)	BOUNDARY PROTECTION
SC-7(10).1	**ASSESSMENT OBJECTIVE:** *Determine if the organization prevents the unauthorized exfiltration of information across managed interfaces.* **POTENTIAL ASSESSMENT METHODS AND OBJECTS:** **Examine**: [*SELECT FROM:* System and communications protection policy; procedures addressing boundary protection; information system design documentation; information system configuration settings and associated documentation; information system audit records; other relevant documents or records]. **Test**: [*SELECT FROM:* Automated mechanisms preventing unauthorized exfiltration of information across managed interfaces].

SC-7(11)	BOUNDARY PROTECTION
SC-7(11).1	**ASSESSMENT OBJECTIVE:** *Determine if the information system checks incoming communications to ensure:* – *the communications are coming from an authorized source; and* – *the communications are routed to an authorized destination.* **POTENTIAL ASSESSMENT METHODS AND OBJECTS:** **Examine**: [*SELECT FROM:* System and communications protection policy; procedures addressing boundary protection; information system design documentation; information system configuration settings and associated documentation; information system audit records; other relevant documents or records].

SC-7(12)	BOUNDARY PROTECTION
SC-7(12).1	**ASSESSMENT OBJECTIVE:** *Determine if the information system implements host-based boundary protection mechanisms for:* – *servers;* – *workstations; and* – *mobile devices.* **POTENTIAL ASSESSMENT METHODS AND OBJECTS:** **Examine**: [*SELECT FROM:* System and communications protection policy; procedures addressing boundary protection; information system design documentation; boundary protection hardware and software; information system configuration settings and associated documentation; other relevant documents or records]. **Test**: [*SELECT FROM:* Automated mechanisms implementing host-based boundary protection capability].

SC-7(13)	BOUNDARY PROTECTION
SC-7(13).1	**ASSESSMENT OBJECTIVE:** *Determine if:* (i) *the organization defines the key information security tools, mechanisms, and support components to be isolated from other internal information system components; and* (ii) *the organization isolates organization-defined key information security tools, mechanisms, and support components from other internal information system components via physically separate subnets with managed interfaces to other portions of the system.* **POTENTIAL ASSESSMENT METHODS AND OBJECTS:** **Examine**: [*SELECT FROM:* System and communications protection policy; procedures addressing boundary protection; information system design documentation; information system hardware and software; information system architecture; information system configuration settings and associated documentation; list of security tools and support components to be isolated from other internal information system components; other relevant documents or records].

SC-7(14)	BOUNDARY PROTECTION
SC-7(14).1	**ASSESSMENT OBJECTIVE:** *Determine if:* (i) *the organization defines the managed interfaces where boundary protections are to be implemented;* (ii) *the organization defines the measures to protect against unauthorized physical connections across boundary protections implemented at organization-defined managed interfaces; and* (iii) *the organization protects against unauthorized physical connections across the boundary protections implemented at organization-defined managed interfaces.* **POTENTIAL ASSESSMENT METHODS AND OBJECTS:** **Examine**: [*SELECT FROM:* System and communications protection policy; procedures addressing boundary protection; information system design documentation; information system hardware and software; information system architecture; information system configuration settings and associated documentation; facility communications and wiring diagram; other relevant documents or records]. **Test**: [*SELECT FROM:* Physical access capability implementing protections against unauthorized physical connections to the information system].

SC-7(15)	BOUNDARY PROTECTION
SC-7(15).1	**ASSESSMENT OBJECTIVE:** *Determine if:* (i) *the information system routes all networked, privileged accesses through a dedicated, managed interface for purpose of access control; and* (ii) *the information system routes all networked, privileged accesses through a dedicated, managed interface for purpose of auditing.* **POTENTIAL ASSESSMENT METHODS AND OBJECTS:** **Examine**: [*SELECT FROM:* System and communications protection policy; procedures addressing boundary protection; information system design documentation; information system hardware and software; information system architecture; information system configuration settings and associated documentation; audit logs; other relevant documents or records]. **Test**: [*SELECT FROM:* Mechanisms routing networked, privileged access through dedicated managed interfaces].

SC-7(16)	BOUNDARY PROTECTION
SC-7(16).1	**ASSESSMENT OBJECTIVE:** *Determine if the information system prevents discovery of specific system components (or devices) composing a managed interface.* **POTENTIAL ASSESSMENT METHODS AND OBJECTS:** **Examine**: [*SELECT FROM:* System and communications protection policy; procedures addressing boundary protection; information system design documentation; information system hardware and software; information system architecture; information system configuration settings and associated documentation; other relevant documents or records]. **Test**: [*SELECT FROM:* Mechanisms preventing discovery of system components at a managed interface].

SC-7(17)	BOUNDARY PROTECTION
SC-7(17).1	**ASSESSMENT OBJECTIVE:** *Determine if the organization employs automated mechanisms to enforce strict adherence to protocol format.* **POTENTIAL ASSESSMENT METHODS AND OBJECTS:** **Examine:** [*SELECT FROM:* System and communications protection policy; procedures addressing boundary protection; information system design documentation; information system architecture; information system configuration settings and associated documentation; other relevant documents or records].

SC-7(18)	BOUNDARY PROTECTION
SC-7(18).1	**ASSESSMENT OBJECTIVE:** *Determine if the information system fails securely in the event of an operational failure of a boundary protection device.* **POTENTIAL ASSESSMENT METHODS AND OBJECTS:** **Examine:** [*SELECT FROM:* System and communications protection policy; procedures addressing boundary protection; information system design documentation; information system architecture; information system configuration settings and associated documentation; other relevant documents or records].

FAMILY: SYSTEM AND COMMUNICATIONS PROTECTION   **CLASS:** TECHNICAL

ASSESSMENT PROCEDURE	
SC-8	**TRANSMISSION INTEGRITY**
SC-8.1	**ASSESSMENT OBJECTIVE:** *Determine if the information system protects the integrity of transmitted information.* **POTENTIAL ASSESSMENT METHODS AND OBJECTS:** **Examine:** [*SELECT FROM:* System and communications protection policy; procedures addressing transmission integrity; information system design documentation; information system configuration settings and associated documentation; other relevant documents or records]. **Test:** [*SELECT FROM:* Transmission integrity capability within the information system].

SC-8(1)	**TRANSMISSION INTEGRITY**
SC-8(1).1	**ASSESSMENT OBJECTIVE:** *Determine if the organization employs cryptographic mechanisms to recognize changes to information during transmission unless otherwise protected by alternative physical measures.* **POTENTIAL ASSESSMENT METHODS AND OBJECTS:** **Examine:** [*SELECT FROM:* System and communications protection policy; procedures addressing transmission integrity; information system design documentation; information system configuration settings and associated documentation; other relevant documents or records]. **Test:** [*SELECT FROM:* Cryptographic mechanisms implementing transmission integrity capability within the information system].

SC-8(2)	**TRANSMISSION INTEGRITY**
SC-8(2).1	**ASSESSMENT OBJECTIVE:** *Determine if the information system in preparation for transmission maintains the integrity of information during:* – *aggregation;* – *packaging; and* – *transformation.* **POTENTIAL ASSESSMENT METHODS AND OBJECTS:** **Examine:** [*SELECT FROM:* System and communications protection policy; procedures addressing transmission integrity; information system design documentation; information system configuration settings and associated documentation; other relevant documents or records]. **Test:** [*SELECT FROM:* Transmission integrity capability within the information system].

FAMILY: SYSTEM AND COMMUNICATIONS PROTECTION   **CLASS:** TECHNICAL

ASSESSMENT PROCEDURE

SC-9	TRANSMISSION CONFIDENTIALITY
SC-9.1	**ASSESSMENT OBJECTIVE:** *Determine if the information system protects the confidentiality of transmitted information.* **POTENTIAL ASSESSMENT METHODS AND OBJECTS:** **Examine:** [*SELECT FROM:* System and communications protection policy; procedures addressing transmission confidentiality; information system design documentation; contracts for telecommunications services; information system configuration settings and associated documentation; other relevant documents or records]. **Test:** [*SELECT FROM:* Transmission confidentiality capability within the information system].

SC-9(1)	TRANSMISSION CONFIDENTIALITY
SC-9(1).1	**ASSESSMENT OBJECTIVE:** *Determine if:* (i) *the organization optionally defines alternative physical measures to prevent unauthorized disclosure of information during transmission ; and* (ii) *the organization employs cryptographic mechanisms to prevent unauthorized disclosure of information during transmission unless otherwise protected by organization-defined alternative physical measures.* **POTENTIAL ASSESSMENT METHODS AND OBJECTS:** **Examine:** [*SELECT FROM:* System and communications protection policy; procedures addressing transmission confidentiality; information system design documentation; information system communications hardware and software or Protected Distribution System protection mechanisms; information system configuration settings and associated documentation; other relevant documents or records]. **Test:** [*SELECT FROM:* Cryptographic mechanisms implementing transmission confidentiality capability within the information system].

SC-9(2)	TRANSMISSION CONFIDENTIALITY
SC-9(2).1	**ASSESSMENT OBJECTIVE:** *Determine if the information system in preparation for transmission maintains the confidentiality of information during:* – *aggregation;* – *packaging; and* – *transformation.* **POTENTIAL ASSESSMENT METHODS AND OBJECTS:** **Examine:** [*SELECT FROM:* System and communications protection policy; procedures addressing transmission confidentiality; information system design documentation; information system communications hardware and software or Protected Distribution System protection mechanisms; information system configuration settings and associated documentation; other relevant documents or records]. **Test:** [*SELECT FROM:* Transmission confidentiality capability within the information system].

FAMILY: SYSTEM AND COMMUNICATIONS PROTECTION **CLASS:** TECHNICAL

ASSESSMENT PROCEDURE	
SC-10	**NETWORK DISCONNECT**
SC-10.1	**ASSESSMENT OBJECTIVE:** *Determine if:* (i) *the organization defines the time period of inactivity before the information system terminates a network connection associated with a communications session; and* (ii) *the information system terminates a network connection associated with a communication session at the end of the session or after the organization-defined time period of inactivity.* **POTENTIAL ASSESSMENT METHODS AND OBJECTS:** **Examine:** [*SELECT FROM:* System and communications protection policy; procedures addressing network disconnect; information system design documentation; organization-defined time period of inactivity before network disconnect; information system configuration settings and associated documentation; other relevant documents or records]. **Test:** [*SELECT FROM:* Network disconnect capability within the information system].

FAMILY: SYSTEM AND COMMUNICATIONS PROTECTION   **CLASS:** TECHNICAL

ASSESSMENT PROCEDURE	
SC-11	**TRUSTED PATH**
SC-11.1	**ASSESSMENT OBJECTIVE:** *Determine if:* *(i) the organization defines the security functions within the information system to be included in a trusted communications path;* *(ii) the organization-defined security functions include information system authentication and reauthentication; and* *(iii) the information system establishes a trusted communications path between the user and the organization-defined security functions within the information system.* **POTENTIAL ASSESSMENT METHODS AND OBJECTS:** **Examine:** [*SELECT FROM:* System and communications protection policy; procedures addressing trusted communications paths; security plan; information system design documentation; information system configuration settings and associated documentation; assessment results from independent, testing organizations; other relevant documents or records]. **Test:** [*SELECT FROM:* Automated mechanisms implementing trusted communications paths within the information system].

FAMILY: SYSTEM AND COMMUNICATIONS PROTECTION   **CLASS:** TECHNICAL

ASSESSMENT PROCEDURE

SC-12	CRYPTOGRAPHIC KEY ESTABLISHMENT AND MANAGEMENT
SC-12.1	**ASSESSMENT OBJECTIVE:** *Determine if the organization establishes and manages cryptographic keys for required cryptography employed within the information system.* **POTENTIAL ASSESSMENT METHODS AND OBJECTS:** **Examine:** [*SELECT FROM:* System and communications protection policy; procedures addressing cryptographic key management and establishment; information system design documentation; information system configuration settings and associated documentation; other relevant documents or records]. **Interview:** [*SELECT FROM:* Organizational personnel with responsibilities for cryptographic key establishment or management]. **Test:** [*SELECT FROM:* Automated mechanisms implementing cryptographic key management and establishment within the information system].

SC-12(1)	CRYPTOGRAPHIC KEY ESTABLISHMENT AND MANAGEMENT
SC-12(1).1	**ASSESSMENT OBJECTIVE:** *Determine if the organization maintains availability of information in the event of the loss of cryptographic keys by users.* **POTENTIAL ASSESSMENT METHODS AND OBJECTS:** **Examine:** [*SELECT FROM:* System and communications protection policy; procedures addressing cryptographic key management, establishment, and recovery; information system design documentation; information system configuration settings and associated documentation; other relevant documents or records].

SC-12(2)	CRYPTOGRAPHIC KEY ESTABLISHMENT AND MANAGEMENT
SC-12(2).1	**ASSESSMENT OBJECTIVE:** *Determine if:* (i) *the organization defines whether it will use NIST-approved or NSA-approved key management technology and processes; and* (ii) *the organization produces, controls, and distributes symmetric cryptographic keys using the organization-defined key management technology and processes.* **POTENTIAL ASSESSMENT METHODS AND OBJECTS:** **Examine:** [*SELECT FROM:* System and communications protection policy; procedures addressing cryptographic key management, establishment, and recovery; information system design documentation; information system configuration settings and associated documentation; other relevant documents or records]. **Interview:** [*SELECT FROM:* Organizational personnel with responsibilities for cryptographic key establishment or management].

SC-12(3)	CRYPTOGRAPHIC KEY ESTABLISHMENT AND MANAGEMENT
SC-12(3).1	**ASSESSMENT OBJECTIVE:** *Determine if the organization produces, controls, and distributes symmetric and asymmetric cryptographic keys using NSA-approved key management technology and processes.* **POTENTIAL ASSESSMENT METHODS AND OBJECTS:** **Examine:** [*SELECT FROM:* System and communications protection policy; procedures addressing cryptographic key management, establishment, and recovery; information system design documentation; information system configuration settings and associated documentation; other relevant documents or records]. **Interview:** [*SELECT FROM:* Organizational personnel with responsibilities for cryptographic key establishment or management].

SC-12(4)	CRYPTOGRAPHIC KEY ESTABLISHMENT AND MANAGEMENT
SC-12(4).1	**ASSESSMENT OBJECTIVE:** *Determine if the organization produces, controls, and distributes asymmetric cryptographic keys using approved PKI Class 3 certificates or prepositioned keying material.* **POTENTIAL ASSESSMENT METHODS AND OBJECTS:** **Examine:** [*SELECT FROM:* System and communications protection policy; procedures addressing cryptographic key management, establishment, and recovery; information system design documentation; information system configuration settings and associated documentation; information system cryptographic keys; other relevant documents or records].

SC-12(5)	CRYPTOGRAPHIC KEY ESTABLISHMENT AND MANAGEMENT
SC-12(5).1	**ASSESSMENT OBJECTIVE:** *Determine if the organization produces, controls, and distributes asymmetric cryptographic keys using approved PKI Class 3 or Class 4 certificates and hardware security tokens that protect the user's private key.* **POTENTIAL ASSESSMENT METHODS AND OBJECTS:** **Examine:** [*SELECT FROM:* System and communications protection policy; procedures addressing cryptographic key management, establishment, and recovery; information system design documentation; information system configuration settings and associated documentation; information system cryptographic keys; other relevant documents or records].

FAMILY: SYSTEM AND COMMUNICATIONS PROTECTION   **CLASS:** TECHNICAL

ASSESSMENT PROCEDURE

SC-13	USE OF CRYPTOGRAPHY
SC-13.1	**ASSESSMENT OBJECTIVE:** *Determine if the information system implements cryptographic protections using cryptographic modules that comply with applicable laws, Executive Orders, directives, policies, regulations, standards, and guidance.* **POTENTIAL ASSESSMENT METHODS AND OBJECTS:** **Examine**: [*SELECT FROM:* System and communications protection policy; procedures addressing use of cryptography; information system design documentation; information system configuration settings and associated documentation; cryptographic module validation certificates; other relevant documents or records].

SC-13(1)	USE OF CRYPTOGRAPHY
SC-13(1).1	**ASSESSMENT OBJECTIVE:** *Determine if the organization employs, at a minimum, FIPS-validated cryptography to protect unclassified information.* **POTENTIAL ASSESSMENT METHODS AND OBJECTS:** **Examine**: [*SELECT FROM:* System and communications protection policy; procedures addressing use of cryptography; FIPS cryptography standards; information system design documentation; information system configuration settings and associated documentation; cryptographic module validation certificates; other relevant documents or records].

SC-13(2)	USE OF CRYPTOGRAPHY
SC-13(2).1	**ASSESSMENT OBJECTIVE:** *Determine if the organization employs NSA-approved cryptography to protect classified information.* **POTENTIAL ASSESSMENT METHODS AND OBJECTS:** **Examine**: [*SELECT FROM:* System and communications protection policy; procedures addressing use of cryptography; NSA cryptography standards; information system design documentation; information system configuration settings and associated documentation; cryptographic module validation certificates; other relevant documents or records].

SC-13(3)	USE OF CRYPTOGRAPHY
SC-13(3).1	**ASSESSMENT OBJECTIVE:** *Determine if the organization employs, at a minimum, FIPS-validated cryptography to protect information when such information must be separated from individuals who have the necessary clearances yet lack the necessary access approvals.* **POTENTIAL ASSESSMENT METHODS AND OBJECTS:** **Examine**: [*SELECT FROM:* System and communications protection policy; procedures addressing use of cryptography; FIPS cryptography standards; information system design documentation; information system configuration settings and associated documentation; FIPS cryptographic module validation certificates; other relevant documents or records]. **Interview**: [*SELECT FROM:* Organizational personnel with responsibilities for implementing cryptography within the information system].

SC-13(4)	USE OF CRYPTOGRAPHY
SC-13(4).1	**ASSESSMENT OBJECTIVE:** *Determine if:* *(i) the organization defines whether it will use NIST-approved or NSA-approved cryptography to implement digital signatures; and* *(ii) the organization employs the organization-defined cryptography to implement digital signatures* **POTENTIAL ASSESSMENT METHODS AND OBJECTS:** **Examine**: [*SELECT FROM:* System and communications protection policy; procedures addressing use of cryptography; information system design documentation; information system configuration settings and associated documentation; cryptographic module validation certificates; other relevant documents or records].

FAMILY: SYSTEM AND COMMUNICATIONS PROTECTION   **CLASS:** TECHNICAL

ASSESSMENT PROCEDURE	
SC-14	**PUBLIC ACCESS PROTECTIONS**
SC-14.1	**ASSESSMENT OBJECTIVE:** *Determine if the information system protects the integrity and availability of publicly available information and applications.* **POTENTIAL ASSESSMENT METHODS AND OBJECTS:** **Examine**: [*SELECT FROM:* System and communications protection policy; procedures addressing public access protections; access control policy and procedures; boundary protection procedures; information system design documentation; information system configuration settings and associated documentation; other relevant documents or records]. **Test**: [*SELECT FROM:* Automated mechanisms protecting the integrity and availability of publicly available information and applications within the information system].

FAMILY: SYSTEM AND COMMUNICATIONS PROTECTION   **CLASS:** TECHNICAL

ASSESSMENT PROCEDURE	
SC-15	**COLLABORATIVE COMPUTING DEVICES**
SC-15.1	**ASSESSMENT OBJECTIVE:** *Determine if:* (i) the organization defines exceptions to the prohibiting of collaborative computing devices where remote activation is to be allowed; (ii) the organization prohibits remote activation of collaborative computing devices, excluding the organization-defined exceptions where remote activation is to be allowed; and (iii) the organization provides an explicit indication of use to users physically present at the devices. **POTENTIAL ASSESSMENT METHODS AND OBJECTS:** **Examine**: [*SELECT FROM:* System and communications protection policy; procedures addressing collaborative computing; access control policy and procedures; information system design documentation; information system configuration settings and associated documentation; other relevant documents or records]. **Test**: [*SELECT FROM:* Automated mechanisms implementing access controls for collaborative computing environments; alert notification for local users].

SC-15(1)	**COLLABORATIVE COMPUTING DEVICES**
SC-15(1).1	**ASSESSMENT OBJECTIVE:** *Determine if the information system provides physical disconnect of collaborative computing devices in a manner that supports ease of use.* **POTENTIAL ASSESSMENT METHODS AND OBJECTS:** **Examine**: [*SELECT FROM:* System and communications protection policy; procedures addressing collaborative computing; access control policy and procedures; information system design documentation; information system configuration settings and associated documentation; other relevant documents or records]. **Test**: [*SELECT FROM:* Physical disconnect of collaborative computing devices].

SC-15(2)	**COLLABORATIVE COMPUTING DEVICES**
SC-15(2).1	**ASSESSMENT OBJECTIVE:** *Determine if the information system or supporting environment blocks both inbound and outbound traffic between instant messaging clients that are independently configured by end users and external service providers.* **POTENTIAL ASSESSMENT METHODS AND OBJECTS:** **Examine**: [*SELECT FROM:* System and communications protection policy; procedures addressing collaborative computing; access control policy and procedures; information system design documentation; information system configuration settings and associated documentation; other relevant documents or records]. **Test**: [*SELECT FROM:* Mechanisms blocking inbound and outbound traffic between instant message clients that are independently configured].

SC-15(3)	COLLABORATIVE COMPUTING DEVICES
SC-15(3).1	**ASSESSMENT OBJECTIVE:** *Determine if:* (i) *the organization defines the secure work areas where collaborative computing devices are prohibited; and* (ii) *the organization disables or removes collaborative computing devices from information systems in organization-defined secure work areas.* **POTENTIAL ASSESSMENT METHODS AND OBJECTS:** **Examine:** [*SELECT FROM:* System and communications protection policy; procedures addressing collaborative computing; access control policy and procedures; information system design documentation; information system configuration settings and associated documentation; other relevant documents or records]. **Interview:** [*SELECT FROM:* Organizational personnel with device management responsibilities for collaborative computing].

FAMILY: SYSTEM AND COMMUNICATIONS PROTECTION   **CLASS:** TECHNICAL

ASSESSMENT PROCEDURE

SC-16	TRANSMISSION OF SECURITY ATTRIBUTES
SC-16.1	**ASSESSMENT OBJECTIVE:** *Determine if the information system associates security attributes with information exchanged between information systems.* **POTENTIAL ASSESSMENT METHODS AND OBJECTS:** **Examine:** [*SELECT FROM:* System and communications protection policy; procedures addressing transmission of security parameters; access control policy and procedures; boundary protection procedures; information system design documentation; information system configuration settings and associated documentation; other relevant documents or records]. **Test:** [*SELECT FROM:* Automated mechanisms supporting reliable transmission of security parameters between information systems].

SC-16(1)	TRANSMISSION OF SECURITY ATTRIBUTES
SC-16(1).1	**ASSESSMENT OBJECTIVE:** *Determine if the information system validates the integrity of security attributes exchanged between systems.* **POTENTIAL ASSESSMENT METHODS AND OBJECTS:** **Examine:** [*SELECT FROM:* System and communications protection policy; procedures addressing transmission of security parameters; access control policy and procedures; boundary protection procedures; information system design documentation; information system configuration settings and associated documentation; other relevant documents or records]. **Test:** [*SELECT FROM:* Automated mechanisms supporting reliable transmission of security parameters between information systems].

FAMILY: SYSTEM AND COMMUNICATIONS PROTECTION   **CLASS:** TECHNICAL

ASSESSMENT PROCEDURE	
SC-17	**PUBLIC KEY INFRASTRUCTURE CERTIFICATES**
SC-17.1	**ASSESSMENT OBJECTIVE:** *Determine if:* (i) *the organization defines a certificate policy for issuing public key certificates; and* (ii) *the organization issues public key certificates under the organization-defined certificate policy or obtains public key certificates under a certificate policy from an approved service provider.* **POTENTIAL ASSESSMENT METHODS AND OBJECTS:** **Examine:** [*SELECT FROM:* System and communications protection policy; procedures addressing public key infrastructure certificates; public key certificate policy or policies; public key issuing process; other relevant documents or records]. **Interview:** [*SELECT FROM:* Organizational personnel with public key infrastructure certificate issuing responsibilities].

FAMILY: SYSTEM AND COMMUNICATIONS PROTECTION   **CLASS:** TECHNICAL

ASSESSMENT PROCEDURE	
SC-18	**MOBILE CODE**
SC-18.1	**ASSESSMENT OBJECTIVE:** *Determine if:* (i) *the organization defines acceptable and unacceptable mobile code and mobile code technologies;* (ii) *the organization establishes usage restrictions and implementation guidance for acceptable mobile code and mobile code technologies; and* (iii) *the organization authorizes, monitors, and controls the use of mobile code within the information system.* **POTENTIAL ASSESSMENT METHODS AND OBJECTS:** **Examine**: [*SELECT FROM:* System and communications protection policy; procedures addressing mobile code; mobile code usage restrictions, mobile code implementation policy and procedures; list of acceptable mobile code and mobile code technologies; other relevant documents or records]. **Interview**: [*SELECT FROM:* Organizational personnel with mobile code authorization, monitoring, and control responsibilities]. **Test**: [*SELECT FROM:* Mobile code authorization and monitoring capability for the organization].

SC-18(1)	MOBILE CODE	
SC-18(1)	**MOBILE CODE**	
SC-18(1).1	**ASSESSMENT OBJECTIVE:** *Determine if:* (i) *the information system implements detection and inspection mechanisms to identify unauthorized mobile code; and* (ii) *the information system takes corrective action when unauthorized mobile code is identified.* **POTENTIAL ASSESSMENT METHODS AND OBJECTS:** **Examine**: [*SELECT FROM:* System and communications protection policy; procedures addressing mobile code; mobile code usage restrictions, mobile code implementation policy and procedures; information system design documentation; information system configuration settings and associated documentation; information system audit records; other relevant documents or records]. **Test**: [*SELECT FROM:* Automated mechanisms implementing mobile code detection and inspection capability].	

SC-18(2)	MOBILE CODE

SC-18(2).1	**ASSESSMENT OBJECTIVE:** *Determine if:* (i) *the organization defines requirements for the acquisition, development and/or use of mobile code; and* (ii) *the organization ensures the acquisition, development, and/or use of mobile code to be deployed in information systems meets the organization-defined mobile code requirements.* **POTENTIAL ASSESSMENT METHODS AND OBJECTS:** **Examine**: [*SELECT FROM:* System and communications protection policy; procedures addressing mobile code; mobile code usage restrictions, mobile code implementation policy and procedures; acquisition documentation; acquisition contracts for information systems or services; other relevant documents or records]. **Interview**: [*SELECT FROM:* Organizational personnel with mobile code management responsibilities; organizational personnel with information system security, acquisition, and contracting responsibilities].

SC-18(3)	MOBILE CODE

SC-18(3).1	**ASSESSMENT OBJECTIVE:** *Determine if the information system prevents the download and execution of prohibited mobile code.* **POTENTIAL ASSESSMENT METHODS AND OBJECTS:** **Examine**: [*SELECT FROM:* System and communications protection policy; procedures addressing mobile code; mobile code usage restrictions, mobile code implementation policy and procedures; information system design documentation; information system configuration settings and associated documentation; information system audit records; other relevant documents or records]. **Test**: [*SELECT FROM:* Automated mechanisms preventing download and execution of prohibited mobile code].

SC-18(4)	MOBILE CODE

SC-18(4).1	**ASSESSMENT OBJECTIVE:** *Determine if:* (i) *the organization defines software applications for which automatic mobile code execution is to be prohibited;* (ii) *the organization defines actions required by the information system before executing mobile code;* (iii) *the information system prevents the automatic execution of mobile code in the organization-defined software applications; and* (iv) *the information system requires organization-defined actions before executing mobile code.* **POTENTIAL ASSESSMENT METHODS AND OBJECTS:** **Examine**: [*SELECT FROM:* System and communications protection policy; procedures addressing mobile code; mobile code usage restrictions; information system design documentation; information system configuration settings and associated documentation; list of applications for which automatic execution of mobile code must be prohibited; list of actions required before execution of mobile code; other relevant documents or records]. **Test**: [*SELECT FROM:* Automated mechanisms preventing mobile code execution within the information system].

FAMILY: SYSTEM AND COMMUNICATIONS PROTECTION   **CLASS:** TECHNICAL

ASSESSMENT PROCEDURE	
SC-19	**VOICE OVER INTERNET PROTOCOL**
SC-19.1	**ASSESSMENT OBJECTIVE:** *Determine if:* (i) *the organization establishes usage restrictions and implementation guidance for Voice over Internet Protocol (VoIP) technologies based on the potential to cause damage to the information system if used maliciously; and* (ii) *the organization authorizes, monitors, and controls the use of VoIP within the information system.* **POTENTIAL ASSESSMENT METHODS AND OBJECTS:** **Examine**: [*SELECT FROM:* System and communications protection policy; procedures addressing VoIP; VoIP usage restrictions; other relevant documents or records]. **Interview**: [*SELECT FROM:* Organizational personnel with VoIP authorization and monitoring responsibilities]. **Test**: [*SELECT FROM:* VoIP authorization and monitoring capability for the organization].

FAMILY: SYSTEM AND COMMUNICATIONS PROTECTION   **CLASS:** TECHNICAL

ASSESSMENT PROCEDURE	
SC-20	**SECURE NAME / ADDRESS RESOLUTION SERVICE (AUTHORITATIVE SOURCE)**
SC-20.1	**ASSESSMENT OBJECTIVE:** *Determine if the information system provides additional data origin and integrity artifacts along with the authoritative data the system returns in response to name/address resolution queries.* **POTENTIAL ASSESSMENT METHODS AND OBJECTS:** **Examine**: [*SELECT FROM:* System and communications protection policy; procedures addressing secure name/address resolution service (authoritative source); information system design documentation; information system configuration settings and associated documentation; other relevant documents or records]. **Test**: [*SELECT FROM:* Automated mechanisms implementing secure name/address resolution service (authoritative source)].

SC-20(1)	**SECURE NAME / ADDRESS RESOLUTION SERVICE (AUTHORITATIVE SOURCE)**
SC-20(1).1	**ASSESSMENT OBJECTIVE:** *Determine if* *(i) the information system, when operating as part of a distributed, hierarchical namespace, provides the means to indicate the security status of child subspaces; and* *(ii) the information system, when operating as part of a distributed, hierarchical namespace, enable verification of a chain of trust among parent and child domains (if the child supports secure resolution services).* **POTENTIAL ASSESSMENT METHODS AND OBJECTS:** **Examine**: [*SELECT FROM:* System and communications protection policy; procedures addressing secure name/address resolution service (authoritative source); information system design documentation; information system configuration settings and associated documentation; other relevant documents or records]. **Test**: [*SELECT FROM:* Automated mechanisms implementing child subspace security status indicators and chain of trust verification for resolution services].

FAMILY: SYSTEM AND COMMUNICATIONS PROTECTION   **CLASS:** TECHNICAL

ASSESSMENT PROCEDURE

SC-21	SECURE NAME / ADDRESS RESOLUTION SERVICE (RECURSIVE OR CACHING RESOLVER)
SC-21.1	**ASSESSMENT OBJECTIVE:** *Determine if the information system performs data origin authentication and data integrity verification on the name/address resolution responses the system receives from authoritative sources when requested by client systems.* **POTENTIAL ASSESSMENT METHODS AND OBJECTS:** **Examine:** [*SELECT FROM:* System and communications protection policy; procedures addressing secure name/address resolution service (recursive or caching resolver); information system design documentation; information system configuration settings and associated documentation; other relevant documents or records]. **Test:** [*SELECT FROM:* Automated mechanisms implementing data origin authentication and integrity verification for resolution services].

SC-21(1)	SECURE NAME / ADDRESS RESOLUTION SERVICE (RECURSIVE OR CACHING RESOLVER)
SC-21(1).1	**ASSESSMENT OBJECTIVE:** *Determine if the information system performs data origin authentication and data integrity verification on all resolution responses received whether or not client systems explicitly request this service.* **POTENTIAL ASSESSMENT METHODS AND OBJECTS:** **Examine:** [*SELECT FROM:* System and communications protection policy; procedures addressing secure name/address resolution service (recursive or caching resolver); information system design documentation; information system configuration settings and associated documentation; other relevant documents or records]. **Test:** [*SELECT FROM:* Automated mechanisms implementing data origin authentication and integrity verification for resolution services].

FAMILY: SYSTEM AND COMMUNICATIONS PROTECTION   **CLASS:** TECHNICAL

ASSESSMENT PROCEDURE	
SC-22	**ARCHITECTURE AND PROVISIONING FOR NAME / ADDRESS RESOLUTION SERVICE**
SC-22.1	**ASSESSMENT OBJECTIVE:** *Determine if:* (i) the information systems that collectively provide name/address resolution service for an organization are fault tolerant; and (ii) the information systems that collectively provide name/address resolution service for an organization implement internal/external role separation. **POTENTIAL ASSESSMENT METHODS AND OBJECTS:** **Examine**: [*SELECT FROM:* System and communications protection policy; procedures addressing architecture and provisioning for name/address resolution service; access control policy and procedures; information system design documentation; assessment results from independent, testing organizations; information system configuration settings and associated documentation; other relevant documents or records]. **Test**: [*SELECT FROM:* Automated mechanisms supporting name/address resolution service for fault tolerance and role separation].

FAMILY: SYSTEM AND COMMUNICATIONS PROTECTION   **CLASS:** TECHNICAL

ASSESSMENT PROCEDURE	
SC-23	**SESSION AUTHENTICITY**
SC-23.1	**ASSESSMENT OBJECTIVE:** *Determine if the information system provides mechanisms to protect the authenticity of communications sessions.* **POTENTIAL ASSESSMENT METHODS AND OBJECTS:** **Examine:** [*SELECT FROM:* System and communications protection policy; procedures addressing session authenticity; information system design documentation; information system configuration settings and associated documentation; other relevant documents or records]. **Test:** [*SELECT FROM:* Automated mechanisms implementing session authenticity].

SC-23(1)	**SESSION AUTHENTICITY**
SC-23(1).1	**ASSESSMENT OBJECTIVE:** *Determine if the information system invalidates session identifiers upon user logout or other session termination.* **POTENTIAL ASSESSMENT METHODS AND OBJECTS:** **Examine:** [*SELECT FROM:* System and communications protection policy; procedures addressing session authenticity; information system design documentation; information system configuration settings and associated documentation; other relevant documents or records]. **Test:** [*SELECT FROM:* Automated mechanisms implementing session identifier invalidation upon session termination].

SC-23(2)	**SESSION AUTHENTICITY**
SC-23(2).1	**ASSESSMENT OBJECTIVE:** *Determine if the information system provides a readily observable logout capability whenever authentication is used to gain access to Web pages.* **POTENTIAL ASSESSMENT METHODS AND OBJECTS:** **Examine:** [*SELECT FROM:* System and communications protection policy; procedures addressing session authenticity; information system design documentation; information system configuration settings and associated documentation; information system site designs; other relevant documents or records]. **Test:** [*SELECT FROM:* Automated mechanisms implementing logout capability for Web pages requiring user authentication].

SC-23(3)	SESSION AUTHENTICITY
SC-23(3).1	**ASSESSMENT OBJECTIVE:** *Determine if:* (i) *the information system generates a unique session identifier for each session; and* (ii) *the information system recognizes only session identifiers that are system-generated.* **POTENTIAL ASSESSMENT METHODS AND OBJECTS:** **Examine**: [*SELECT FROM:* System and communications protection policy; procedures addressing session authenticity; information system design documentation; information system configuration settings and associated documentation; other relevant documents or records]. **Test**: [*SELECT FROM:* Automated mechanisms generating and monitoring unique session identifiers].

SC-23(4)	SESSION AUTHENTICITY
SC-23(4).1	**ASSESSMENT OBJECTIVE:** *Determine if:* (i) *the organization defines requirements for randomly generating unique session identifiers; and* (ii) *the information system generates unique session identifiers in accordance with organization-defined randomness requirements.* **POTENTIAL ASSESSMENT METHODS AND OBJECTS:** **Examine**: [*SELECT FROM:* System and communications protection policy; procedures addressing session authenticity; information system design documentation; information system configuration settings and associated documentation; other relevant documents or records]. **Test**: [*SELECT FROM:* Automated mechanisms generating unique session identifiers].

FAMILY: SYSTEM AND COMMUNICATIONS PROTECTION   **CLASS:** TECHNICAL

ASSESSMENT PROCEDURE	
SC-24	**FAIL IN KNOWN STATE**
SC-24.1	**ASSESSMENT OBJECTIVE:** *Determine if:* *(i) the organization defines the known-states the information system should fail to in the event of a system failure;* *(ii) the organization defines types of failures for which the information system should fail to an organization-defined known-state;* *(iii) the organization defines the system state information that should be preserved in the event of a system failure;* *(iv) the information system fails to an organization-defined known-state for an organization-defined type of failure; and* *(v) the information system preserves organization-defined system state information in the event of a system failure.* **POTENTIAL ASSESSMENT METHODS AND OBJECTS:** **Examine**: [*SELECT FROM:* System and communications protection policy; procedures addressing information system failure; information system design documentation; information system configuration settings and associated documentation; list of failures requiring information system to fail in a known state; state information to be preserved in system failure; other relevant documents or records]. **Test**: [*SELECT FROM:* Automated mechanisms implementing fail-in-known-state capability].

FAMILY: SYSTEM AND COMMUNICATIONS PROTECTION   **CLASS:** TECHNICAL

ASSESSMENT PROCEDURE	
SC-25	**THIN NODES**
SC-25.1	**ASSESSMENT OBJECTIVE:** *Determine if the information system employs processing components that have minimal functionality and information storage.* **POTENTIAL ASSESSMENT METHODS AND OBJECTS:** **Examine**: [*SELECT FROM:* System and communications protection policy; procedures addressing use of thin nodes; information system design documentation; information system configuration settings and associated documentation; other relevant documents or records].

FAMILY: SYSTEM AND COMMUNICATIONS PROTECTION   **CLASS:** TECHNICAL

ASSESSMENT PROCEDURE	
SC-26	**HONEYPOTS**
SC-26.1	**ASSESSMENT OBJECTIVE:** *Determine if the information system includes components specifically designed to be the target of malicious attacks for the purpose of detecting, deflecting, and analyzing such attacks.* **POTENTIAL ASSESSMENT METHODS AND OBJECTS:** **Examine**: [*SELECT FROM:* System and communications protection policy; procedures addressing use of honeypots; information system design documentation; information system configuration settings and associated documentation; other relevant documents or records].

SC-26(1)	**HONEYPOTS**
SC-26(1).1	**ASSESSMENT OBJECTIVE:** *Determine if the information system includes components that proactively seek to identify Web-based malicious code.* **POTENTIAL ASSESSMENT METHODS AND OBJECTS:** **Examine**: [*SELECT FROM:* System and communications protection policy; procedures addressing use of honeypots; access control policy and procedures; boundary protection procedures; information system design documentation; information system configuration settings and associated documentation; other relevant documents or records]. **Test**: [*SELECT FROM:* Automated mechanisms proactively seeking Web-based malicious code].

FAMILY: SYSTEM AND COMMUNICATIONS PROTECTION   **CLASS:** TECHNICAL

ASSESSMENT PROCEDURE	
SC-27	**OPERATING SYSTEM-INDEPENDENT APPLICATIONS**
SC-27.1	**ASSESSMENT OBJECTIVE:** *Determine if:* *(i) the organization defines applications that are operating system-independent; and* *(ii) the information system includes organization-defined operating system-independent applications.* **POTENTIAL ASSESSMENT METHODS AND OBJECTS:** **Examine**: [*SELECT FROM:* System and communications protection policy; procedures addressing operating system-independent applications; information system design documentation; information system configuration settings and associated documentation; list of operating system-independent applications; other relevant documents or records].

FAMILY: SYSTEM AND COMMUNICATIONS PROTECTION   **CLASS:** TECHNICAL

ASSESSMENT PROCEDURE

SC-28	PROTECTION OF INFORMATION AT REST
SC-28.1	**ASSESSMENT OBJECTIVE:** *Determine if the information system protects the confidentiality and integrity of information at rest.* **POTENTIAL ASSESSMENT METHODS AND OBJECTS:** **Examine**: [*SELECT FROM:* System and communications protection policy; procedures addressing protection of information at rest; information system design documentation; information system configuration settings and associated documentation; cryptographic mechanisms and associated configuration documentation; list of information at rest requiring confidentiality and integrity protections; other relevant documents or records]. **Test**: [*SELECT FROM:* Automated mechanisms implementing confidentiality and integrity protections for information at-rest].

SC-28(1)	PROTECTION OF INFORMATION AT REST
SC-28(1).1	**ASSESSMENT OBJECTIVE:** *Determine if:* (i) *the organization employs cryptographic mechanisms to prevent unauthorized disclosure of information at rest unless otherwise protected by alternative physical measures; and* (ii) *the organization employs cryptographic mechanisms to prevent unauthorized modification of information at rest unless otherwise protected by alternative physical measures.* **POTENTIAL ASSESSMENT METHODS AND OBJECTS:** **Examine**: [*SELECT FROM:* System and communications protection policy; procedures addressing protection of information at rest; information system design documentation; information system configuration settings and associated documentation; cryptographic mechanisms and associated configuration documentation; other relevant documents or records]. **Test**: [*SELECT FROM:* Cryptographic mechanisms implementing confidentiality and integrity protections for information at-rest].

FAMILY: SYSTEM AND COMMUNICATIONS PROTECTION   **CLASS:** TECHNICAL

ASSESSMENT PROCEDURE	
SC-29	**HETEROGENEITY**
SC-29.1	**ASSESSMENT OBJECTIVE:** *Determine if the organization employs diverse information technologies in the implementation of the information system.* **POTENTIAL ASSESSMENT METHODS AND OBJECTS:** **Examine:** [*SELECT FROM:* System and communications protection policy; information system design documentation; information system configuration settings and associated documentation; list of technologies deployed in the information system; acquisition documentation; acquisition contracts for information system components or services; other relevant documents or records]. **Interview:** [*SELECT FROM:* Organizational personnel with information system acquisition, development, and implementation responsibilities].

FAMILY: SYSTEM AND COMMUNICATIONS PROTECTION   **CLASS:** TECHNICAL

ASSESSMENT PROCEDURE	
SC-30	**VIRTUALIZATION TECHNIQUES**
SC-30.1	**ASSESSMENT OBJECTIVE:** *Determine if the organization employs virtualization techniques to present information system components as other types of components, or components with differing configurations.* **POTENTIAL ASSESSMENT METHODS AND OBJECTS:** **Examine:** [*SELECT FROM:* System and communications protection policy; information system design documentation; information system configuration settings and associated documentation; information system architecture; list of virtualization techniques to be employed for organizational information systems; other relevant documents or records]. **Interview:** [*SELECT FROM:* Organizational personnel with responsibilities for implementing approved virtualization techniques for information systems].

SC-30(1)	VIRTUALIZATION TECHNIQUES	
SC-30(1).1	**ASSESSMENT OBJECTIVE:** *Determine if:* (i) *the organization defines the frequency of changes to operating systems and applications through the use of virtualization techniques; and* (ii) *the organization employs virtualization techniques to support the deployment of a diversity of operating systems and applications that are changed in accordance with organization-defined frequency.* **POTENTIAL ASSESSMENT METHODS AND OBJECTS:** **Examine:** [*SELECT FROM:* System and communications protection policy; configuration management policy and procedures; information system design documentation; information system configuration settings and associated documentation; information system architecture; other relevant documents or records]. **Interview:** [*SELECT FROM:* Organizational personnel with responsibilities for implementing approved virtualization techniques for information systems].	

SC-30(2)	VIRTUALIZATION TECHNIQUES	
SC-30(2).1	**ASSESSMENT OBJECTIVE:** *Determine if the organization employs randomness in the implementation of the virtualization techniques.* **POTENTIAL ASSESSMENT METHODS AND OBJECTS:** **Examine:** [*SELECT FROM:* System and communications protection policy; information system design documentation; information system configuration settings and associated documentation; information system architecture; other relevant documents or records]. **Interview:** [*SELECT FROM:* Organizational personnel with responsibilities for implementing approved virtualization techniques for information systems].	

FAMILY: SYSTEM AND COMMUNICATIONS PROTECTION   **CLASS:** TECHNICAL

ASSESSMENT PROCEDURE

SC-31	COVERT CHANNEL ANALYSIS
SC-31.1	**ASSESSMENT OBJECTIVE:** *Determine if the organization requires that information system developers/integrators perform a covert channel analysis to identify those aspects of system communication that are potential avenues for covert storage and timing channels.* **POTENTIAL ASSESSMENT METHODS AND OBJECTS:** **Examine:** [*SELECT FROM:* System and communications protection policy; procedures addressing covert channel analysis; information system design documentation; information system configuration settings and associated documentation; covert channel analysis documentation; other relevant documents or records]. **Interview:** [*SELECT FROM:* Organizational personnel with covert channel analysis responsibilities; information system developers/integrators].

SC-31(1)	COVERT CHANNEL ANALYSIS
SC-31(1).1	**ASSESSMENT OBJECTIVE:** *Determine if the organization tests a subset of the vendor-identified covert channel avenues to determine if such channels are exploitable.* **POTENTIAL ASSESSMENT METHODS AND OBJECTS:** **Examine:** [*SELECT FROM:* System and communications protection policy; procedures addressing covert channel analysis; information system design documentation; information system configuration settings and associated documentation; list of vendor-identified covert channel avenues or exploits; covert channel analysis documentation; other relevant documents or records]. **Interview:** [*SELECT FROM:* Organizational personnel with covert channel analysis responsibilities; information system developers/integrators]. **Test:** [*SELECT FROM:* Covert channel avenues to determine if such channels are exploitable].

FAMILY: SYSTEM AND COMMUNICATIONS PROTECTION   **CLASS:** TECHNICAL

ASSESSMENT PROCEDURE	
SC-32	**INFORMATION SYSTEM PARTITIONING**
SC-32.1	**ASSESSMENT OBJECTIVE:** *Determine if the organization partitions the information system into components residing in separate physical domains (or environments) as deemed necessary.* **POTENTIAL ASSESSMENT METHODS AND OBJECTS:** **Examine**: [*SELECT FROM:* System and communications protection policy; information system design documentation; information system configuration settings and associated documentation; information system architecture; list of information system physical domains (or environments); information system facility diagrams; other relevant documents or records]. **Interview**: [*SELECT FROM:* Organizational personnel installing, configuring, and/or maintaining the information system].

FAMILY: SYSTEM AND COMMUNICATIONS PROTECTION   **CLASS:** TECHNICAL

ASSESSMENT PROCEDURE	
SC-33	**TRANSMISSION PREPARATION INTEGRITY**
SC-33.1	**ASSESSMENT OBJECTIVE:** *Determine if the information system in preparation for transmission protects the integrity of information during the processes of:* – *data aggregation;* – *packaging; and* – *transformation.* **POTENTIAL ASSESSMENT METHODS AND OBJECTS:** **Examine**: [*SELECT FROM:* System and communications protection policy; procedures addressing transmission integrity; information system design documentation; information system configuration settings and associated documentation; other relevant documents or records]. **Test**: [*SELECT FROM:* Transmission integrity capability within the information system].

FAMILY: SYSTEM AND COMMUNICATIONS PROTECTION   **CLASS:** TECHNICAL

ASSESSMENT PROCEDURE

SC-34	NON-MODIFIABLE EXECUTABLE PROGRAMS
SC-34.1	**ASSESSMENT OBJECTIVE:** *Determine if:* (i) the organization defines the applications that are to be loaded and executed from hardware-enforced, read-only media; (ii) the organization defines the information system components for which the operating environment and organization-defined applications are loaded and executed from hardware-enforced, read-only media; and (iii) the information system, at organization-defined information system components, loads and executes: - the operating environment from hardware-enforced, read-only media; and - organization-defined applications from hardware-enforced, read-only media. **POTENTIAL ASSESSMENT METHODS AND OBJECTS:** **Examine**: [*SELECT FROM:* System and communications protection policy; information system design documentation; information system configuration settings and associated documentation; information system architecture; list of operating system components to be loaded from hardware-enforced, read-only media; list of applications to be loaded from hardware-enforced, read-only media; media used to load and execute information system operating environment; media used to load and execute information system applications; other relevant documents or records]. **Interview**: [*SELECT FROM:* Organizational personnel installing, configuring, and/or maintaining the information system].

SC-34(1)	NON-MODIFIABLE EXECUTABLE PROGRAMS
SC-34(1).1	**ASSESSMENT OBJECTIVE:** *Determine if:* (i) the organization defines the information system components to be employed with no writeable storage; and (ii) the organization employs organization-defined information system components with no writeable storage that are persistent across component restart or power on/off. **POTENTIAL ASSESSMENT METHODS AND OBJECTS:** **Examine**: [*SELECT FROM:* System and communications protection policy; information system design documentation; information system configuration settings and associated documentation; information system architecture; list of information system components to be employed without writeable storage capability; other relevant documents or records].

SC-34(2)	NON-MODIFIABLE EXECUTABLE PROGRAMS
SC-34(2).1	**ASSESSMENT OBJECTIVE:** *Determine if the organization protects the integrity of the information on read-only media.* **POTENTIAL ASSESSMENT METHODS AND OBJECTS:** **Examine**: [*SELECT FROM:* System and communications protection policy; procedures addressing protection of information on read-only media; information system design documentation; information system configuration settings and associated documentation; information system architecture; other relevant documents or records]. **Test**: [*SELECT FROM:* Organizational capability for protecting information integrity on read-only media].

FAMILY: SYSTEM AND INFORMATION INTEGRITY   **CLASS:** OPERATIONAL

ASSESSMENT PROCEDURE	
SI-1	**SYSTEM AND INFORMATION INTEGRITY POLICY AND PROCEDURES**

SI-1.1	**ASSESSMENT OBJECTIVE:**
	Determine if:
	(i) the organization develops and formally documents system and information integrity policy;
	(ii) the organization system and information integrity policy addresses:
	    - *purpose;*
	    - *scope;*
	    - *roles and responsibilities;*
	    - *management commitment;*
	    - *coordination among organizational entities; and*
	    - *compliance;*
	(iii) the organization disseminates formal documented system and information integrity policy to elements within the organization having associated system and information integrity roles and responsibilities;
	(iv) the organization develops and formally documents system and information integrity procedures;
	(v) the organization system and information integrity procedures facilitate implementation of the system and information integrity policy and associated system and information integrity controls; and
	(vi) the organization disseminates formal documented system and information integrity procedures to elements within the organization having associated system and information integrity roles and responsibilities.
	
	POTENTIAL ASSESSMENT METHODS AND OBJECTS:
	Examine: [*SELECT FROM:* System and information integrity policy and procedures; other relevant documents or records].
	Interview: [*SELECT FROM:* Organizational personnel with system and information integrity responsibilities].

SI-1.2	**ASSESSMENT OBJECTIVE:** *Determine if:* *(i) the organization defines the frequency of system and information integrity policy reviews/updates;* *(ii) the organization reviews/updates system and information integrity policy in accordance with organization-defined frequency;* *(iii) the organization defines the frequency of system and information integrity procedure reviews/updates; and* *(iv) the organization reviews/updates system and information integrity procedures in accordance with organization-defined frequency.* **POTENTIAL ASSESSMENT METHODS AND OBJECTS:** **Examine**: [*SELECT FROM:* System and information integrity policy and procedures; other relevant documents or records]. **Interview**: [*SELECT FROM:* Organizational personnel with system and information integrity responsibilities].

FAMILY: SYSTEM AND INFORMATION INTEGRITY   **CLASS:** OPERATIONAL

ASSESSMENT PROCEDURE
SI-2 **FLAW REMEDIATION**
SI-2.1 **ASSESSMENT OBJECTIVE:** *Determine if:*   (i) the organization identifies, reports, and corrects information system flaws;   (ii) the organization tests software updates related to flaw remediation for effectiveness before installation;   (iii) the organization tests software updates related to flaw remediation for potential side effects on organizational information systems before installation; and   (iv) the organization incorporates flaw remediation into the organizational configuration management process.   **POTENTIAL ASSESSMENT METHODS AND OBJECTS:**   **Examine**: [*SELECT FROM:* System and information integrity policy; procedures addressing flaw remediation; list of flaws and vulnerabilities potentially affecting the information system; list of recent security flaw remediation actions performed on the information system (e.g., list of installed patches, service packs, hot fixes, and other software updates to correct information system flaws); test results from the installation of software to correct information system flaws; other relevant documents or records].   **Interview**: [*SELECT FROM:* Organizational personnel with flaw remediation responsibilities].

SI-2(1)	FLAW REMEDIATION
SI-2(1).1	**ASSESSMENT OBJECTIVE:** *Determine if:* (i) the organization centrally manages the flaw remediation process; and (ii) the organization installs software updates automatically. **POTENTIAL ASSESSMENT METHODS AND OBJECTS:** **Examine**: [*SELECT FROM:* System and information integrity policy; procedures addressing flaw remediation; automated mechanisms supporting centralized management of flaw remediation and automatic software updates; information system design documentation; information system configuration settings and associated documentation; list of information system flaws; list of recent security flaw remediation actions performed on the information system; other relevant documents or records]. **Test**: [*SELECT FROM:* Automated mechanisms supporting centralized management of flaw remediation and automatic software updates].

SI-2(2)	FLAW REMEDIATION
SI-2(2).1	**ASSESSMENT OBJECTIVE:** *Determine if:* (i) *the organization defines the frequency of employing automated mechanisms to determine the state of information system components with regard to flaw remediation; and* (ii) *the organization employs automated mechanisms in accordance with the organization-defined frequency to determine the state of information system components with regard to flaw remediation.* **POTENTIAL ASSESSMENT METHODS AND OBJECTS:** **Examine**: [*SELECT FROM:* System and information integrity policy; procedures addressing flaw remediation; automated mechanisms supporting flaw remediation; information system design documentation; information system configuration settings and associated documentation; list of information system flaws; list of recent security flaw remediation actions performed on the information system; information system audit records; other relevant documents or records]. **Test**: [*SELECT FROM:* Automated mechanisms implementing information system flaw remediation update status].

SI-2(3)	FLAW REMEDIATION
SI-2(3).1	**ASSESSMENT OBJECTIVE:** *Determine if:* (i) *the organization defines the benchmarks to which the organization's measurement of time elapsed between flaw identification and flaw remediation should be compared;* (ii) *the organization measures the time between flaw identification and flaw remediation; and* (iii) *the organization compares the time measured between flaw identification and flaw remediation with organization-defined benchmarks.* **POTENTIAL ASSESSMENT METHODS AND OBJECTS:** **Examine**: [*SELECT FROM:* System and information integrity policy; procedures addressing flaw remediation; automated mechanisms supporting centralized management of flaw remediation and automatic software updates; information system design documentation; information system configuration settings and associated documentation; list of information system flaws; list of recent security flaw remediation actions performed on the information system; other relevant documents or records].

SI-2(4)	FLAW REMEDIATION
SI-2(4).1	**ASSESSMENT OBJECTIVE:** *Determine if:* *(i) the organization defines information system components for which automated patch management tools are to be employed to facilitate flaw remediation; and* *(ii) the organization employs automated patch management tools to facilitate flaw remediation to organization-defined information system components.* **POTENTIAL ASSESSMENT METHODS AND OBJECTS:** **Examine**: [*SELECT FROM:* System and information integrity policy; procedures addressing flaw remediation; automated mechanisms supporting flaw remediation; information system design documentation; information system configuration settings and associated documentation; list of information system flaws; list of recent security flaw remediation actions performed on the information system; information system audit records; other relevant documents or records]. **Test**: [*SELECT FROM:* Automated mechanisms facilitating flaw remediation to information system components].

FAMILY: SYSTEM AND INFORMATION INTEGRITY   **CLASS:** OPERATIONAL

ASSESSMENT PROCEDURE
SI-3   **MALICIOUS CODE PROTECTION**

| SI-3.1 | **ASSESSMENT OBJECTIVE:**
Determine if:

(i)   *the organization employs malicious code protection mechanisms at information system entry and exit points to detect and eradicate malicious code:*
   - *transported by electronic mail, electronic mail attachments, Web accesses, removable media, or other common means; or*
   - *inserted through the exploitation of information system vulnerabilities;*

(ii)   *the organization employs malicious code protection mechanisms at workstations, servers, or mobile computing devices on the network to detect and eradicate malicious code:*
   - *transported by electronic mail, electronic mail attachments, Web accesses, removable media, or other common means; or*
   - *inserted through the exploitation of information system vulnerabilities;*

(iii)   *the organization updates malicious code protection mechanisms (including signature definitions) whenever new releases are available in accordance with configuration management policy and procedures defined in CM-1;*

(iv)   *the organization defines the frequency of periodic scans of the information system by malicious code protection mechanisms;*

(v)   *the organization defines one or more of the following actions to be taken in response to malicious code detection:*
   - *block malicious code;*
   - *quarantine malicious code; and/or*
   - *send alert to administrator;*

(vi)   *the organization configures malicious code protection mechanisms to:*
   - *perform periodic scans of the information system in accordance with organization-defined frequency;*
   - *perform real-time scans of files from external sources as the files are downloaded, opened, or executed in accordance with organizational security policy; and*
   - *take organization-defined action(s) in response to malicious code detection; and*

(vii)   *the organization addresses the receipt of false positives during malicious code detection and eradication and the resulting potential impact on the availability of the information system.*

POTENTIAL ASSESSMENT METHODS AND OBJECTS:
Examine: [*SELECT FROM:* System and information integrity policy; procedures addressing malicious code protection; malicious code protection mechanisms; records of malicious code protection updates; information system configuration settings and associated documentation; other relevant documents or records].
Interview: [*SELECT FROM:* Organizational personnel with malicious code protection responsibilities].
Test: [*SELECT FROM:* Automated mechanisms implementing malicious code protection capability]. |

SI-3(1)	MALICIOUS CODE PROTECTION
SI-3(1).1	**ASSESSMENT OBJECTIVE:** *Determine if the organization centrally manages malicious code protection mechanisms.* **POTENTIAL ASSESSMENT METHODS AND OBJECTS:** **Examine**: [*SELECT FROM:* System and information integrity policy; procedures addressing malicious code protection; information system design documentation; malicious code protection mechanisms; records of malicious code protection updates; information system configuration settings and associated documentation; other relevant documents or records].

SI-3(2)	MALICIOUS CODE PROTECTION
SI-3(2).1	**ASSESSMENT OBJECTIVE:** *Determine if the information system automatically updates malicious code protection mechanisms, including signature definitions.* **POTENTIAL ASSESSMENT METHODS AND OBJECTS:** **Examine**: [*SELECT FROM:* System and information integrity policy; procedures addressing malicious code protection; information system design documentation; malicious code protection mechanisms; records of malicious code protection updates; information system configuration settings and associated documentation; other relevant documents or records].

SI-3(3)	MALICIOUS CODE PROTECTION
SI-3(3).1	**ASSESSMENT OBJECTIVE:** *Determine if the information system prevents non-privileged users from circumventing malicious code protection capabilities.* **POTENTIAL ASSESSMENT METHODS AND OBJECTS:** **Examine**: [*SELECT FROM:* System and information integrity policy; procedures addressing malicious code protection; information system design documentation; malicious code protection mechanisms; records of malicious code protection updates; information system configuration settings and associated documentation; other relevant documents or records]. **Test**: [*SELECT FROM:* Automated mechanisms implementing malicious code protection capability].

SI-3(4)	MALICIOUS CODE PROTECTION
SI-3(4).1	**ASSESSMENT OBJECTIVE:** *Determine if the information system updates malicious code protection mechanisms only when directed by a privileged user.* **POTENTIAL ASSESSMENT METHODS AND OBJECTS:** **Examine**: [*SELECT FROM:* System and information integrity policy; procedures addressing malicious code protection; information system design documentation; malicious code protection mechanisms; records of malicious code protection updates; information system configuration settings and associated documentation; other relevant documents or records]. **Test**: [*SELECT FROM:* Automated mechanisms implementing malicious code protection capability].

SI-3(5)	MALICIOUS CODE PROTECTION
SI-3(5).1	**ASSESSMENT OBJECTIVE:** *Determine if the organization does not allow users to introduce removable media into the information system.* **POTENTIAL ASSESSMENT METHODS AND OBJECTS:** **Examine**: [*SELECT FROM:* System and information integrity policy; procedures addressing malicious code protection; information system design documentation; malicious code protection mechanisms; records of malicious code protection updates; information system configuration settings and associated documentation; other relevant documents or records]. **Interview**: [*SELECT FROM:* Organizational personnel with malicious code protection responsibilities].

SI-3(6)	MALICIOUS CODE PROTECTION
SI-3(6).1	**ASSESSMENT OBJECTIVE:** *Determine if:* *(i) the organization defines the frequency of testing malicious code protection mechanisms; and* *(ii) the organization tests malicious code protection mechanisms, in accordance with organization-defined frequency, by introducing a known benign, non-spreading test case into the information system and subsequently verifying that both detection of the test case and associated incident reporting occur, as required.* **POTENTIAL ASSESSMENT METHODS AND OBJECTS:** **Examine**: [*SELECT FROM:* System and information integrity policy; procedures addressing malicious code protection; information system design documentation; malicious code protection mechanisms; records of malicious code protection updates; information system configuration settings and associated documentation; other relevant documents or records]. **Test**: [*SELECT FROM:* Automated mechanisms implementing malicious code protection capability].

FAMILY: SYSTEM AND INFORMATION INTEGRITY   **CLASS:** OPERATIONAL

ASSESSMENT PROCEDURE	
SI-4	**INFORMATION SYSTEM MONITORING**

SI-4.1	**ASSESSMENT OBJECTIVE:**
	Determine if:
	(i) the organization defines objectives for monitoring events on the information system;
	(ii) the organization monitors events on the information system in accordance with organization-defined objectives and detects information system attacks;
	(iii) the organization identifies unauthorized use of the information system;
	(iv) the organization deploys monitoring devices:
	    - *strategically within the information system to collect organization-determined essential information; and*
	    - *at ad hoc locations within the system to track specific types of transactions of interest to the organization;*
	(v) the organization heightens the level of information system monitoring activity whenever there is an indication of increased risk to organizational operations and assets, individuals, other organizations, or the Nation based on law enforcement information, intelligence information, or other credible sources of information; and
	(vi) the organization obtains legal opinion with regard to information system monitoring activities in accordance with applicable federal laws, Executive Orders, directives, policies, or regulations.
	
	POTENTIAL ASSESSMENT METHODS AND OBJECTS:
	Examine: [*SELECT FROM:* System and information integrity policy; procedures addressing information system monitoring tools and techniques; information system design documentation; information system monitoring tools and techniques documentation; information system configuration settings and associated documentation; other relevant documents or records].
	
	Interview: [*SELECT FROM:* Organizational personnel with information system monitoring responsibilities].

SI-4(1)	**INFORMATION SYSTEM MONITORING**
SI-4(1).1	**ASSESSMENT OBJECTIVE:** *Determine if the organization interconnects and configures individual intrusion detection tools into a system-wide intrusion detection system using common protocols.* **POTENTIAL ASSESSMENT METHODS AND OBJECTS:** **Examine:** [*SELECT FROM:* System and information integrity policy; procedures addressing information system monitoring tools and techniques; information system design documentation; information system monitoring tools and techniques documentation; information system configuration settings and associated documentation; information system protocols; other relevant documents or records]. **Test:** [*SELECT FROM:* Information system-wide intrusion detection capability].

SI-4(2)	INFORMATION SYSTEM MONITORING
SI-4(2).1	**ASSESSMENT OBJECTIVE:** *Determine if the organization employs automated tools to support near real-time analysis of events.* **POTENTIAL ASSESSMENT METHODS AND OBJECTS:** **Examine:** [*SELECT FROM:* System and information integrity policy; procedures addressing information system monitoring tools and techniques; information system design documentation; information system monitoring tools and techniques documentation; information system configuration settings and associated documentation; information system protocols documentation; other relevant documents or records]. **Test:** [*SELECT FROM:* Automated tools supporting near real-time event analysis].

SI-4(3)	INFORMATION SYSTEM MONITORING
SI-4(3).1	**ASSESSMENT OBJECTIVE:** *Determine if the organization employs automated tools to integrate intrusion detection tools into access control and flow control mechanisms for rapid response to attacks by enabling reconfiguration of these mechanisms in support of attack isolation and elimination.* **POTENTIAL ASSESSMENT METHODS AND OBJECTS:** **Examine:** [*SELECT FROM:* System and information integrity policy; procedures addressing information system monitoring tools and techniques; information system design documentation; information system monitoring tools and techniques documentation; information system configuration settings and associated documentation; information system protocols; other relevant documents or records]. **Test:** [*SELECT FROM:* Automated tools supporting the integration of intrusion detection tools and access/flow control mechanisms].

SI-4(4)	INFORMATION SYSTEM MONITORING
SI-4(4).1	**ASSESSMENT OBJECTIVE:** *Determine if the information system monitors inbound and outbound communications for unusual or unauthorized activities or conditions.* **POTENTIAL ASSESSMENT METHODS AND OBJECTS:** **Examine:** [*SELECT FROM:* System and information integrity policy; procedures addressing information system monitoring tools and techniques; information system design documentation; information system monitoring tools and techniques documentation; information system configuration settings and associated documentation; information system protocols; other relevant documents or records]. **Test:** [*SELECT FROM:* Automated tools supporting the integration of intrusion detection tools and access/flow control mechanisms].

SI-4(5)	INFORMATION SYSTEM MONITORING
SI-4(5).1	**ASSESSMENT OBJECTIVE:** *Determine if:* *(i) the organization defines indicators of compromise or potential compromise to the security of the information system; and* *(ii) the information system provides near real-time alerts when any of the organization-defined list of compromise or potential compromise indicators occurs.* **POTENTIAL ASSESSMENT METHODS AND OBJECTS:** **Examine**: [*SELECT FROM:* System and information integrity policy; procedures addressing information system monitoring tools and techniques; security plan; information system monitoring tools and techniques documentation; information system configuration settings and associated documentation; other relevant documents or records]. **Test**: [*SELECT FROM:* Information system monitoring real-time alert capability].

SI-4(6)	INFORMATION SYSTEM MONITORING
SI-4(6).1	**ASSESSMENT OBJECTIVE:** *Determine if the information system prevents non-privileged users from circumventing intrusion detection and prevention capabilities.* **POTENTIAL ASSESSMENT METHODS AND OBJECTS:** **Examine**: [*SELECT FROM:* System and information integrity policy; procedures addressing information system monitoring tools and techniques; information system design documentation; information system monitoring tools and techniques documentation; information system configuration settings and associated documentation; information system protocols; other relevant documents or records]. **Test**: [*SELECT FROM:* Information system-wide intrusion detection and prevention capability].

SI-4(7)	INFORMATION SYSTEM MONITORING
SI-4(7).1	**ASSESSMENT OBJECTIVE:** *Determine if:* *(i) the organization defines incident response personnel (identified by name and/or by role) to be notified of suspicious events;* *(ii) the organization defines least-disruptive actions to be taken by the information system to terminate suspicious events;* *(iii) the information system notifies organization-defined incident response personnel of suspicious events; and* *(iv) the information system takes organization-defined least-disruptive actions to terminate suspicious events.* **POTENTIAL ASSESSMENT METHODS AND OBJECTS:** **Examine**: [*SELECT FROM:* System and information integrity policy; procedures addressing information system monitoring tools and techniques; information system design documentation; information system monitoring tools and techniques documentation; information system configuration settings and associated documentation; information system protocols documentation; other relevant documents or records]. **Test**: [*SELECT FROM:* Information system notification capability].

SI-4(8)	INFORMATION SYSTEM MONITORING
SI-4(8).1	**ASSESSMENT OBJECTIVE:** *Determine if the organization protects information obtained from intrusion-monitoring tools from:* – *unauthorized access;* – *modification; and* – *deletion.* **POTENTIAL ASSESSMENT METHODS AND OBJECTS:** **Examine:** [*SELECT FROM:* System and information integrity policy; procedures addressing information system monitoring tools and techniques; information system design documentation; information system monitoring tools and techniques documentation; information system configuration settings and associated documentation; information system protocols; other relevant documents or records]. **Interview:** [*SELECT FROM:* Organizational personnel with information system monitoring responsibilities].

SI-4(9)	INFORMATION SYSTEM MONITORING
SI-4(9).1	**ASSESSMENT OBJECTIVE:** *Determine if:* (i) *the organization defines the time period for testing/exercising intrusion-monitoring tools; and* (ii) *the organization tests/exercises intrusion-monitoring tools in accordance with organization-defined time period.* **POTENTIAL ASSESSMENT METHODS AND OBJECTS:** **Examine:** [*SELECT FROM:* System and information integrity policy; procedures addressing information system monitoring tools and techniques; documentation providing evidence of testing intrusion monitoring tools; other relevant documents or records].

SI-4(10)	INFORMATION SYSTEM MONITORING
SI-4(10).1	**ASSESSMENT OBJECTIVE:** *Determine if the organization makes provisions so that encrypted traffic is visible to information system monitoring tools.* **POTENTIAL ASSESSMENT METHODS AND OBJECTS:** **Examine:** [*SELECT FROM:* System and information integrity policy; procedures addressing information system monitoring tools and techniques; information system design documentation; information system monitoring tools and techniques documentation; information system configuration settings and associated documentation; information system protocols; other relevant documents or records].

SI-4(11)	INFORMATION SYSTEM MONITORING
SI-4(11).1	**ASSESSMENT OBJECTIVE:** *Determine if the organization to discover anomalies analyzes outbound communications traffic at:* – *the external boundary of the system (i.e., system perimeter); and* – *as deemed necessary, at selected interior points within the system (e.g., subnets, subsystems).* **POTENTIAL ASSESSMENT METHODS AND OBJECTS:** **Examine**: [*SELECT FROM:* System and information integrity policy; procedures addressing information system monitoring tools and techniques; information system design documentation; information system monitoring tools and techniques documentation; information system configuration settings and associated documentation; information system monitoring logs or records; other relevant documents or records].

SI-4(12)	INFORMATION SYSTEM MONITORING
SI-4(12).1	**ASSESSMENT OBJECTIVE:** *Determine if:* (i) *the organization defines inappropriate or unusual activities with security implications that should trigger alerts to security personnel; and* (ii) *the organization employs automated mechanisms to alert security personnel of the organization-defined inappropriate or unusual activities with security implications.* **POTENTIAL ASSESSMENT METHODS AND OBJECTS:** **Examine**: [*SELECT FROM:* System and information integrity policy; procedures addressing information system monitoring tools and techniques; information system design documentation; information system monitoring tools and techniques documentation; information system configuration settings and associated documentation; list of inappropriate or unusual activities that trigger alerts; other relevant documents or records]. **Test**: [*SELECT FROM:* Automated mechanisms implementing alerts to security personnel for inappropriate or unusual activities].

SI-4(13)	INFORMATION SYSTEM MONITORING
SI-4(13).1	**ASSESSMENT OBJECTIVE:** *Determine if:* (i) *the organization analyzes communications traffic/event patterns for the information system;* (ii) *the organization develops profiles representing common traffic patterns and/or events;* (iii) *the organization defines the respective measurements to which the organization must tune system monitoring devices to reduce the number of false positives and false negatives; and* (iv) *the organization uses the traffic/event profiles in tuning system-monitoring devices to reduce the number of false positives and false negatives to their respective organization-defined measures.* **POTENTIAL ASSESSMENT METHODS AND OBJECTS:** **Examine:** [*SELECT FROM:* System and information integrity policy; procedures addressing information system monitoring tools and techniques; information system design documentation; information system monitoring tools and techniques documentation; information system configuration settings and associated documentation; list of common traffic patterns and/or events; information system protocols documentation; list of acceptable thresholds for false positives and false negatives; other relevant documents or records]. **Interview:** [*SELECT FROM:* Organizational personnel with information system monitoring responsibilities].

SI-4(14)	INFORMATION SYSTEM MONITORING
SI-4(14).1	**ASSESSMENT OBJECTIVE:** *Determine if the organization employs a wireless intrusion detection system to:* – *identify rogue wireless devices to the information system;* – *detect attack attempts to the information system; and* – *detect potential compromises/breaches to the information system.* **POTENTIAL ASSESSMENT METHODS AND OBJECTS:** **Examine:** [*SELECT FROM:* System and information integrity policy; procedures addressing information system monitoring tools and techniques; information system design documentation; information system monitoring tools and techniques documentation; information system configuration settings and associated documentation; information system protocols; other relevant documents or records]. **Test:** [*SELECT FROM:* Automated mechanisms implementing wireless communications intrusion detection capability].

SI-4(15)	INFORMATION SYSTEM MONITORING
SI-4(15).1	**ASSESSMENT OBJECTIVE:** *Determine if the organization employs an intrusion detection system to monitor wireless communications traffic as the traffic passes from wireless to wireline networks.* **POTENTIAL ASSESSMENT METHODS AND OBJECTS:** **Examine**: [*SELECT FROM:* System and information integrity policy; procedures addressing information system monitoring tools and techniques; information system design documentation; information system monitoring tools and techniques documentation; information system configuration settings and associated documentation; information system protocols documentation; other relevant documents or records]. **Test**: [*SELECT FROM:* Automated mechanisms implementing wireless communications intrusion detection capability].

SI-4(16)	INFORMATION SYSTEM MONITORING
SI-4(16).1	**ASSESSMENT OBJECTIVE:** *Determine if the organization correlates information from monitoring tools employed throughout the information system to achieve organization-wide situational awareness.* **POTENTIAL ASSESSMENT METHODS AND OBJECTS:** **Examine**: [*SELECT FROM:* System and information integrity policy; procedures addressing information system monitoring tools and techniques; information system design documentation; information system monitoring tools and techniques documentation; information system configuration settings and associated documentation; event correlation logs or records; other relevant documents or records]. **Interview**: [*SELECT FROM:* Organizational personnel with information system monitoring responsibilities].

SI-4(17)	INFORMATION SYSTEM MONITORING
SI-4(17).1	**ASSESSMENT OBJECTIVE:** *Determine if the organization correlates results from monitoring physical, cyber, and supply chain activities to achieve integrated situational awareness.* **POTENTIAL ASSESSMENT METHODS AND OBJECTS:** **Examine**: [*SELECT FROM:* System and information integrity policy; procedures addressing information system monitoring tools and techniques; information system design documentation; information system monitoring tools and techniques documentation; information system configuration settings and associated documentation; event correlation logs or records; other relevant documents or records]. **Interview**: [*SELECT FROM:* Organizational personnel with information system monitoring responsibilities].

FAMILY: SYSTEM AND INFORMATION INTEGRITY   **CLASS:** OPERATIONAL

ASSESSMENT PROCEDURE	
SI-5	**SECURITY ALERTS, ADVISORIES, AND DIRECTIVES**
SI-5.1	**ASSESSMENT OBJECTIVE:** *Determine if:* (i) *the organization receives information system security alerts, advisories, and directives from designated external organizations on an ongoing basis;* (ii) *the organization generates internal security alerts, advisories, and directives;* (iii) *the organization defines personnel (identified by name and/or by role) who should receive security alerts, advisories, and directives;* (iv) *the organization disseminates security alerts, advisories, and directives to organization-identified personnel; and* (v) *the organization implements security directives in accordance with established time frames, or notifies the issuing organization of the degree of noncompliance.* **POTENTIAL ASSESSMENT METHODS AND OBJECTS:** **Examine**: [*SELECT FROM:* System and information integrity policy; procedures addressing security alerts and advisories; records of security alerts and advisories; other relevant documents or records]. **Interview**: [*SELECT FROM:* Organizational personnel with security alert and advisory responsibilities; organizational personnel implementing, operating, maintaining, administering, and using the information system].

SI-5(1)	**SECURITY ALERTS, ADVISORIES, AND DIRECTIVES**
SI-5(1).1	**ASSESSMENT OBJECTIVE:** *Determine if the organization employs automated mechanisms to make security alert and advisory information available throughout the organization.* **POTENTIAL ASSESSMENT METHODS AND OBJECTS:** **Examine**: [*SELECT FROM:* System and information integrity policy; procedures addressing security alerts and advisories; information system design documentation; information system configuration settings and associated documentation; automated mechanisms supporting the distribution of security alert and advisory information; records of security alerts and advisories; other relevant documents or records]. **Test**: [*SELECT FROM:* Automated mechanisms implementing the distribution of security alert and advisory information].

FAMILY: SYSTEM AND INFORMATION INTEGRITY   **CLASS:** OPERATIONAL

ASSESSMENT PROCEDURE	
SI-6	**SECURITY FUNCTIONALITY VERIFICATION**
SI-6.1	**ASSESSMENT OBJECTIVE:** *Determine if:* (i) *the organization defines the appropriate conditions, including the system transitional states if applicable, for verifying the correct operation of security functions;* (ii) *the organization defines for periodic security function verification, the frequency of the verifications;* (iii) *the organization defines information system responses and alternative action(s) to anomalies discovered during security function verification;* (iv) *the information system verifies the correct operation of security functions in accordance with organization-defined conditions and in accordance with organization-defined frequency (if periodic verification); and* (v) *the information system responds to security function anomalies in accordance with organization-defined responses and alternative action(s).* **POTENTIAL ASSESSMENT METHODS AND OBJECTS:** **Examine**: [*SELECT FROM:* System and information integrity policy; procedures addressing security function verification; information system design documentation; security plan; information system configuration settings and associated documentation; other relevant documents or records]. **Test**: [*SELECT FROM:* Security function verification capability].

SI-6(1)	SECURITY FUNCTIONALITY VERIFICATION
SI-6(1).1	**ASSESSMENT OBJECTIVE:** *Determine if the information system provides notification of failed automated security tests.* **POTENTIAL ASSESSMENT METHODS AND OBJECTS:** **Examine**: [*SELECT FROM:* System and information integrity policy; procedures addressing security function verification; information system design documentation; security plan; information system configuration settings and associated documentation; automated security test results; other relevant documents or records]. **Test**: [*SELECT FROM:* Automated mechanisms implementing alerts and/or notifications for failed automated security tests].

SI-6(2)	SECURITY FUNCTIONALITY VERIFICATION
SI-6(2).1	**ASSESSMENT OBJECTIVE:** *Determine if the information system provides automated support for the management of distributed security testing.* **POTENTIAL ASSESSMENT METHODS AND OBJECTS:** **Examine:** [*SELECT FROM:* System and information integrity policy; procedures addressing security function verification; information system design documentation; security plan; information system configuration settings and associated documentation; other relevant documents or records]. **Test:** [*SELECT FROM:* Automated mechanisms supporting the management of distributed security function testing].

SI-6(3)	SECURITY FUNCTIONALITY VERIFICATION
SI-6(3).1	**ASSESSMENT OBJECTIVE:** *Determine if:* *(i) the organization identifies organizational officials with information security responsibilities designated to receive the results of security function verification; and* *(ii) the organization reports the results of security function verification to designated organizational officials with information security responsibilities.* **POTENTIAL ASSESSMENT METHODS AND OBJECTS:** **Examine:** [*SELECT FROM:* System and information integrity policy; procedures addressing security function verification; information system design documentation; security plan; information system configuration settings and associated documentation; other relevant documents or records]. **Interview:** [*SELECT FROM:* Organizational personnel with security functionality verification responsibilities; organizational personnel with information security responsibilities].

FAMILY: SYSTEM AND INFORMATION INTEGRITY   **CLASS:** OPERATIONAL

ASSESSMENT PROCEDURE	
SI-7	**SOFTWARE AND INFORMATION INTEGRITY**
SI-7.1	**ASSESSMENT OBJECTIVE:** *Determine if the information system detects unauthorized changes to software and information.* **POTENTIAL ASSESSMENT METHODS AND OBJECTS:** **Examine**: [*SELECT FROM:* System and information integrity policy; procedures addressing software and information integrity; information system design documentation; information system configuration settings and associated documentation; integrity verification tools and applications documentation; other relevant documents or records]. **Test**: [*SELECT FROM:* Software integrity protection and verification capability].

SI-7(1)	**SOFTWARE AND INFORMATION INTEGRITY**
SI-7(1).1	**ASSESSMENT OBJECTIVE:** *Determine if:* *(i) the organization defines the frequency of integrity scans to be performed on the information system; and* *(ii) the organization reassesses the integrity of software and information by performing integrity scans of the information system in accordance with the organization-defined frequency.* **POTENTIAL ASSESSMENT METHODS AND OBJECTS:** **Examine**: [*SELECT FROM:* System and information integrity policy; procedures addressing software and information integrity; security plan; information system configuration settings and associated documentation; integrity verification tools and applications documentation; records of integrity scans; other relevant documents or records].

SI-7(2)	**SOFTWARE AND INFORMATION INTEGRITY**
SI-7(2).1	**ASSESSMENT OBJECTIVE:** *Determine if the organization employs automated tools that provide notification to designated individuals upon discovering discrepancies during integrity verification.* **POTENTIAL ASSESSMENT METHODS AND OBJECTS:** **Examine**: [*SELECT FROM:* System and information integrity policy; procedures addressing software and information integrity; information system configuration settings and associated documentation; integrity verification tools and applications documentation; records of integrity scans; automated tools supporting alerts and notifications for integrity discrepancies; other relevant documents or records].

SI-7(3)	SOFTWARE AND INFORMATION INTEGRITY
SI-7(3).1	**ASSESSMENT OBJECTIVE:** *Determine if the organization employs centrally managed integrity verification tools.* **POTENTIAL ASSESSMENT METHODS AND OBJECTS:** **Examine**: [*SELECT FROM:* System and information integrity policy; procedures addressing software and information integrity; information system configuration settings and associated documentation; integrity verification tools and applications documentation; records of integrity scans; other relevant documents or records].

SI-7(4)	SOFTWARE AND INFORMATION INTEGRITY
SI-7(4).1	**ASSESSMENT OBJECTIVE:** *Determine if:* (i) *the organization defines information system components that require use of tamper-evident packaging;* (ii) *the organization defines the conditions (i.e., transportation from vendor to operational site, during operation, both) under which tamper-evident packaging must be used for organization-defined information system components; and* (iii) *the organization requires use of tamper-evident packaging for organization-defined information system components during organization-defined conditions.* **POTENTIAL ASSESSMENT METHODS AND OBJECTS:** **Examine**: [*SELECT FROM:* System and information integrity policy; procedures addressing software and information integrity; information system component packaging; other relevant documents or records].

FAMILY: SYSTEM AND INFORMATION INTEGRITY   **CLASS:** OPERATIONAL

ASSESSMENT PROCEDURE	
SI-8	**SPAM PROTECTION**

SI-8.1	**ASSESSMENT OBJECTIVE:** *Determine if:* (i) *the organization employs spam protection mechanisms at information system entry and exit points to detect and take action on unsolicited messages transported by electronic mail, electronic mail attachments, Web accesses, removable media, or other common means;* (ii) *the organization employs spam protection mechanisms at workstations, servers, or mobile computing devices on the network to detect and take action on unsolicited messages transported by electronic mail, electronic mail attachments, Web accesses, removable media, or other common means; and* (iii) *the organization updates spam protection mechanisms (including signature definitions) when new releases are available in accordance with organizational configuration management policy and procedures defined in CM-1.* **POTENTIAL ASSESSMENT METHODS AND OBJECTS:** **Examine:** [*SELECT FROM:* System and information integrity policy; procedures addressing spam protection; information system design documentation; spam protection mechanisms; information system configuration settings and associated documentation; other relevant documents or records]. **Interview:** [*SELECT FROM:* Organizational personnel with spam protection responsibilities]. **Test:** [*SELECT FROM:* Automated mechanisms implementing spam detection and handling capability].

SI-8(1)	**SPAM PROTECTION**
SI-8(1).1	**ASSESSMENT OBJECTIVE:** *Determine if the organization centrally manages spam protection mechanisms.* **POTENTIAL ASSESSMENT METHODS AND OBJECTS:** **Examine:** [*SELECT FROM:* System and information integrity policy; procedures addressing spam protection; information system design documentation; spam protection mechanisms; information system configuration settings and associated documentation; other relevant documents or records].

SI-8(2)	**SPAM PROTECTION**
SI-8(2).1	**ASSESSMENT OBJECTIVE:** *Determine if the information system automatically updates spam protection mechanisms (including signature definitions).* **POTENTIAL ASSESSMENT METHODS AND OBJECTS:** **Examine:** [*SELECT FROM:* System and information integrity policy; procedures addressing spam protection; information system design documentation; spam protection mechanisms; information system configuration settings and associated documentation; other relevant documents or records].

FAMILY: SYSTEM AND INFORMATION INTEGRITY   **CLASS:** OPERATIONAL

ASSESSMENT PROCEDURE	
SI-9	**INFORMATION INPUT RESTRICTIONS**
SI-9.1	**ASSESSMENT OBJECTIVE:** *Determine if the organization restricts the capability to input information to the information system to authorized personnel.* **POTENTIAL ASSESSMENT METHODS AND OBJECTS:** **Examine:** [*SELECT FROM:* System and information integrity policy; procedures addressing information input restrictions; access control policy and procedures; separation of duties policy and procedures; information system design documentation; information system configuration settings and associated documentation; other relevant documents or records]. **Interview:** [*SELECT FROM:* Organizational personnel with responsibilities for implementing restrictions on individual authorizations to input information into the information system].

FAMILY: SYSTEM AND INFORMATION INTEGRITY   **CLASS:** OPERATIONAL

ASSESSMENT PROCEDURE	
SI-10	**INFORMATION INPUT VALIDATION**
SI-10.1	**ASSESSMENT OBJECTIVE:** *Determine if the information system checks the validity of information inputs.* **POTENTIAL ASSESSMENT METHODS AND OBJECTS:** **Examine**: [*SELECT FROM:* System and information integrity policy; procedures addressing information validity; access control policy and procedures; separation of duties policy and procedures; documentation for automated tools and applications to verify validity of information; information system design documentation; information system configuration settings and associated documentation; other relevant documents or records]. **Test**: [*SELECT FROM:* Information system capability for checking validity of information inputs].

FAMILY: SYSTEM AND INFORMATION INTEGRITY   **CLASS:** OPERATIONAL

ASSESSMENT PROCEDURE	
SI-11	**ERROR HANDLING**
SI-11.1	**ASSESSMENT OBJECTIVE:** *Determine if:* *(i) the information system identifies potentially security-relevant error conditions;* *(ii) the organization defines sensitive or potentially harmful information that should not be contained in error logs and administrative messages;* *(iii) the information system generates error messages that provide information necessary for corrective actions without revealing organization-defined sensitive or potentially harmful information in error logs and administrative messages that could be exploited by adversaries; and* *(iv) the information system reveals error messages only to authorized personnel.* **POTENTIAL ASSESSMENT METHODS AND OBJECTS:** **Examine**: [*SELECT FROM:* System and information integrity policy; procedures addressing information system error handling; information system design documentation; information system configuration settings and associated documentation; other relevant documents or records]. **Test**: [*SELECT FROM:* Information system error handling capability].

FAMILY: SYSTEM AND INFORMATION INTEGRITY   **CLASS:** OPERATIONAL

ASSESSMENT PROCEDURE	
SI-12	**INFORMATION OUTPUT HANDLING AND RETENTION**
SI-12.1	**ASSESSMENT OBJECTIVE:** *Determine if:* *(i) the organization handles both information within and output from the information system in accordance with applicable federal laws, Executive Orders, directives, policies, regulations, standards, and operational requirements; and* *(ii) the organization retains both information within and output from the information system in accordance with applicable federal laws, Executive Orders, directives, policies, regulations, standards, and operational requirements.* **POTENTIAL ASSESSMENT METHODS AND OBJECTS:** **Examine**: [*SELECT FROM:* System and information integrity policy; procedures addressing information system output handling and retention; media protection policy and procedures; information retention records, other relevant documents or records]. **Interview**: [*SELECT FROM:* Organizational personnel with information output handling and retention responsibilities].

FAMILY: SYSTEM AND INFORMATION INTEGRITY   **CLASS:** OPERATIONAL

ASSESSMENT PROCEDURE

SI-13	PREDICTABLE FAILURE PREVENTION
SI-13.1	**ASSESSMENT OBJECTIVE:** *Determine if:* (i) *the organization defines information system components for which mean time to failure rates should be considered to protect the information system from harm;* (ii) *the organization protects the information system from harm by considering mean time to failure rates for organization-defined information system components in specific environments of operation;* (iii) *the organization provides substitute information system components, when needed; and* (iv) *the organization provides a mechanism to exchange active and standby roles of the components.* **POTENTIAL ASSESSMENT METHODS AND OBJECTS:** **Examine:** [*SELECT FROM:* System and information integrity policy; procedures addressing predictable failure prevention; information system design documentation; information system configuration settings and associated documentation; other relevant documents or records]. **Interview:** [*SELECT FROM:* Organizational personnel with predictable failure prevention responsibilities].

SI-13(1)	PREDICTABLE FAILURE PREVENTION
SI-13(1).1	**ASSESSMENT OBJECTIVE:** *Determine if:* (i) *the organization defines the maximum fraction or percentage of mean time to failure in order to transfer the responsibilities of an information system component that is out of service to a substitute component; and* (ii) *the organization takes the information system component out of service by transferring component responsibilities to a substitute component no later than the organization-defined fraction or percentage of mean time to failure.* **POTENTIAL ASSESSMENT METHODS AND OBJECTS:** **Examine:** [*SELECT FROM:* System and information integrity policy; procedures addressing predictable failure prevention; information system design documentation; information system configuration settings and associated documentation; other relevant documents or records]. **Interview:** [*SELECT FROM:* Organization personnel with predictable failure prevention responsibilities].

SI-13(2)	PREDICTABLE FAILURE PREVENTION
SI-13(2).1	**ASSESSMENT OBJECTIVE:** *Determine if:* *(i) the organization defines the time period that a process is allowed to execute without supervision; and* *(ii) the organization does not allow a process to execute without supervision for more than the organization-defined time period.* **POTENTIAL ASSESSMENT METHODS AND OBJECTS:** **Examine**: [*SELECT FROM:* System and information integrity policy; procedures addressing predictable failure prevention; information system design documentation; information system configuration settings and associated documentation; other relevant documents or records]. **Test**: [*SELECT FROM:* Information system predictable failure prevention capability].

SI-13(3)	PREDICTABLE FAILURE PREVENTION
SI-13(3).1	**ASSESSMENT OBJECTIVE:** *Determine if:* *(i) the organization defines the minimum frequency with which the organization manually initiates a transfer between active and standby information system components if the mean time to failure exceeds the organization-defined time period;* *(ii) the organization defines the time period that the mean time to failure must exceed before the organization manually initiates a transfer between active and standby information system components; and* *(iii) the organization manually initiates a transfer between active and standby information system components at least once per the organization-defined frequency if the mean time to failure exceeds the organization-defined time period.* **POTENTIAL ASSESSMENT METHODS AND OBJECTS:** **Examine**: [*SELECT FROM:* System and information integrity policy; procedures addressing predictable failure prevention; information system design documentation; information system configuration settings and associated documentation; other relevant documents or records]. **Interview**: [*SELECT FROM:* Organizational personnel with predictable failure prevention responsibilities]. **Test**: [*SELECT FROM:* Information system predictable failure prevention capability].

SI-13(4)	PREDICTABLE FAILURE PREVENTION

SI-13(4).1	**ASSESSMENT OBJECTIVE:**
	Determine if:
	
	(i) the organization defines the time period for a standby information system component to successfully and transparently assume the role of an information system component that has failed;
	
	(ii) the organization defines the organization-defined alarm when an information system component failure is detected; and
	
	(iii) the organization, if an information system component failure is detected:
	
	  - *ensures that the standby information system component successfully and transparently assumes its role within the organization-defined time period; and*
	
	  - *activates the organization-defined alarm and/or automatically shuts down the information system.*
	
	POTENTIAL ASSESSMENT METHODS AND OBJECTS:
	Examine: [*SELECT FROM:* System and information integrity policy; procedures addressing predictable failure prevention; information system design documentation; information system configuration settings and associated documentation; list of actions to be taken once information system component failure is detected; other relevant documents or records].
	
	Test: [*SELECT FROM:* Information system predictable failure prevention capability].

APPENDIX G

SECURITY ASSESSMENT REPORTS
DOCUMENTING THE FINDINGS FROM SECURITY CONTROL ASSESSMENTS

The primary purpose of the *security assessment report* is to convey the results of the security assessment to appropriate organizational officials. The security assessment report is included in the security authorization package along with the security plan (including an updated risk assessment), and the plan of action and milestones to provide authorizing officials with the information necessary to make credible, risk-based decisions on whether to place an information system into operation or continue its operation. As the security assessment and authorization process becomes more dynamic in nature, relying to a greater degree on the continuous monitoring aspects of the process as an integrated and tightly coupled part of the system development life cycle, the ability to update the security assessment report frequently becomes a critical aspect of an information security program.

It is important to emphasize the relationship, described in Special Publication 800-37, among the three key documents in the authorization package (i.e., the security plan, the security assessment report, and the plan of action and milestones). It is these documents that provide the most reliable indication of the overall security state of the information system and the ability of the system to protect to the degree necessary, the organization's operations and assets, individuals, other organizations, and the Nation. Updates to these key documents are provided on an ongoing basis in accordance with the continuous monitoring program established by the organization.

The security assessment report provides a disciplined and structured approach for documenting the findings of the assessor and the recommendations for correcting any weaknesses or deficiencies in the security controls.[51] This appendix provides a template for reporting the results from security control assessments. Organizations are not restricted to the specific template format; however, it is anticipated that the overall report of an assessment will include similar information to that detailed in the template for each security control assessed, preceded by a summary providing the list of all security controls assessed and the overall status of each control.

Key Elements for Assessment Reporting

The following elements are included in security assessment reports:[52]

- Information system name;

- Security categorization;

- Site(s) assessed and assessment date(s);

- Assessor's name/identification;

- Previous assessment results (if reused);

---

[51] While the rationale for each determination made is a part of the formal *Security Assessment Report*, the complete set of records produced as a part of the assessment is likely not included in the report. However, organizations retain the portion of these records necessary for maintaining an audit trail of assessment evidence, facilitating reuse of evidence as appropriate, and promoting repeatability of assessor actions.

[52] Information available in other key organizational documents (e.g., security plan, risk assessment, plan of action and milestones, or security assessment plan) need not be duplicated in the security assessment report.

- Security control or control enhancement designator;
- Selected assessment methods and objects;
- Depth and coverage attributes values;
- Assessment finding summary (indicating satisfied or other than satisfied);
- Assessor comments (weaknesses or deficiencies noted); and
- Assessor recommendations (priorities, remediation, corrective actions, or improvements).

The Assessment Findings

Each determination statement executed by an assessor results in one of the following findings: (i) satisfied (S); or (ii) other than satisfied (O). Consider the following example for security control CP-2. The assessment procedure for CP-2 consists of two assessment objectives denoted CP-2.1 and CP-2.2. The assessor initially executes CP-2.1 and produces the following findings:

CP-2.1	**ASSESSMENT OBJECTIVE:**
	Determine if:
	(i) *the organization develops a contingency plan for the information system that:*
	- *identifies essential missions and business functions and associated contingency requirements;* **(S)**
	- *provides recovery objectives, restoration priorities, and metrics;* **(S)**
	- *addresses contingency roles, responsibilities, assigned individuals with contact information;* **(O)**
	- *addresses maintaining essential missions and business functions despite an information system disruption, compromise, or failure;* **(S)**
	- *addresses eventual, full information system restoration without deterioration of the security measures originally planned and implemented;* **(S)** *and*
	- *is reviewed and approved by designated officials within the organization;* **(O)**
	(ii) *the organization defines key contingency personnel (identified by name and/or by role) and organizational elements designated to receive copies of the contingency plan;* **(O)** *and*
	(iii) *the organization distributes copies of the contingency plan to organization-defined key contingency personnel and organizational elements.* **(O)**
	Comments and Recommendations:
	CP-2.1 (i) is marked as *other than satisfied* because the contingency plan prepared by the organization did not assign individuals to contingency roles and provide contact information. There was also no evidence that the contingency plan had been reviewed and approved by designated organizational officials.
	CP-2.1 (iii) is marked as *other than satisfied* because the organization had not distributed copies of the contingency plan to key contingency personnel and organizational elements critical to executing the plan.

In a similar manner, the assessor executes CP-2.2 and produces appropriate findings. During an actual security control assessment, the assessment findings, comments, and recommendations are documented on a Security Assessment Reporting Form. Organizations are encouraged to develop standard templates for reporting that contain the key elements for assessment reporting described above. Whenever possible, automation is used to make assessment data collection and reporting cost-effective, timely, and efficient.

APPENDIX H

ASSESSMENT CASES

WORKED EXAMPLES OF ASSESSOR ACTIONS DERIVED FROM ASSESSMENT PROCEDURES

To provide assessors with additional tools and techniques for implementing the assessment procedures in Appendix F, NIST initiated the *Assessment Case Development Project.*[53] The purpose of the project is fourfold: (i) to actively engage experienced assessors from multiple organizations in recommending *assessment cases* that describe specific assessor actions to implement the assessment procedures in Appendix F; (ii) to provide organizations and the assessors supporting those organizations with an exemplary set of assessment cases for each assessment procedure in Appendix F; (iii) to provide a vehicle for ongoing community-wide review of the assessment cases to promote continuous improvement in the security control assessment process for more consistent, effective, and cost-effective security assessments of federal information systems; and (iv) to serve as a basis for reciprocity among various communities of interest. The assessment case development process is described in this appendix and several examples of assessment cases are provided.

Assessment Case Description and Template

The concept of assessment cases emerged during the development process of Special Publication 800-53A. Some organizations prefer the flexibility offered by the generalized assessment procedures in Appendix F, with the opportunity to tailor the procedures for specific organizational requirements and operational environments and to create specific assessor actions and activities for a particular security assessment. Other organizations prefer a more prescriptive approach and desire, to the greatest extent possible, a predefined set of specific assessor actions and activities needed to successfully carry out a security assessment. To facilitate the specificity of the latter approach while maintaining the flexibility of the former approach, assessment cases have been developed for all assessment procedures in Appendix F of this document.

An assessment case represents a worked example of an assessment procedure, identifying the specific actions that an assessor might carry out during the assessment of a security control or control enhancement in an information system. There is one assessment case per control, covering all assessment objectives from the assessment procedure in Appendix F for that control (both base control and all enhancements). The assessment case provides an example by experienced assessors of a potential set of specific assessor action steps to accomplish the assessment that were developed with consideration for the list of potential assessment methods and objects, and incorporating the level of coverage and depth to be applied and the specific purpose to be achieved by each assessor action. This additional level of detail in the assessment cases provides assessors with more prescriptive assessment information. Yet, while being more prescriptive, the assessment cases are not intended to restrict assessor flexibility provided as part of the design principles in Special Publication 800-53A. The assessor remains responsible for making the specified determinations and for providing adequate rationale for the determinations made.

---

[53] NIST initiated the *Assessment Case Development Project* in October 2007 in cooperation with the Departments of Justice, Energy, Transportation, and the Intelligence Community. The interagency task force developed a full suite of assessment cases based on the assessment procedures provided in Special Publication 800-53A. The assessment cases are available to all public and private sector organizations and can be downloaded from the NIST web site at http://csrc.nist.gov/sec-cert.

The following template is used to create the specific assessment cases for the assessment procedures in Appendix F.

ASSESSMENT CASE	
AA-N	**Security Control Name**
ASSESSMENT – Base Control, Part 1 of x (where x is the number of assessment objectives)	
Assessment Information from Special Publication 800-53A	
This section contains the *determinations* and *potential assessment methods and objects* from Special Publication 800-53A, with a separate row for each unique determination. The numbering in the column to the left associates a unique number with each specific determination. This numbering is used to link the assessor action steps below to the determinations.	
AA-N.1	*Determine if:*
AA-N.1.1	*(i) <determination statement 1>.*
⋮	⋮
AA-N.1.n	*(n) <determination statement n>.*

	POTENTIAL ASSESSMENT METHODS AND OBJECTS:
	Examine: [*ASSIGN ATTRIBUTE VALUES*: <depth>, <coverage>].
	  [*SELECT FROM*: <object-list>].
	Interview: [*ASSIGN ATTRIBUTE VALUES*: <depth>, <coverage>].
	  [*SELECT FROM*: <object-list>].
	Test: [*ASSIGN ATTRIBUTE VALUES*: <depth>, <coverage>].
	  [*SELECT FROM*: <object-list>].

Additional Assessment Case Information	
This section contains the additional information provided by the assessment case to help the assessor in planning and conducting the security control assessment.	
	POTENTIAL ASSESSMENT SEQUENCING: PRECURSOR CONTROLS: <security-control-list> CONCURRENT CONTROLS: <security-control-list> SUCCESSOR CONTROLS: <security-control-list>
	This section provides some initial suggestions with regard to sequencing of assessor actions for greater efficiency. *Precursor controls* are those controls whose assessment is likely to provide information either assisting in, or required for, the assessment of this control. *Concurrent controls* are those controls whose assessment is likely to require the assessor to assess similar objects and hence, the assessor may be able to obtain evidence for multiple control assessments at the same time. *Successor controls* are those controls whose assessment will likely need, or benefit from, information obtained from the assessment of this control.
Action Step	**Potential Assessor Evidence Gathering Actions**
Each step is numbered to align with a specific determination statement above.	Suggested assessor action (**Examine**, **Interview**, or **Test**) is identified, along with a likely set of objects to which that action would be applied. As the title of this column indicates, each action step does not necessarily result in a determination. Rather collectively, the set of assessor action steps aligned with a specific determination above provide the evidence necessary to make that determination.
AA-N.1.1.1	[<Assessment Method with assigned depth and coverage attribute values> <Assessment Object(s)>]
⋮	⋮
AA-N.1.1.m	[<Assessment Method with assigned depth and coverage attribute values> <Assessment Object(s)>]
Legend **AA:** Alphanumeric characters representing security control family in Special Publication 800-53. **N:** Numeric character representing the security control number within the family of controls. **n:** Number of determination statements in the assessment object. **m:** Number of action steps associated with a specific determination statement.	

Cautionary Note

The assessment cases developed for this project are not the *only* acceptable assessment cases; rather, the cases represent one possible set of assessor actions for organizations (and assessors supporting those organizations) to use in helping to determine the effectiveness of the security controls employed within the information systems undergoing assessments. The following assessment procedure for security control AC-3, illustrates how assessment cases are developed from the template on the preceding page. The assessment cases and any ongoing updates to the cases, will be published regularly on the FISMA Implementation Project Web site at http://csrc.nist.gov/sec-cert.

ASSESSMENT CASE EXAMPLE

ASSESSMENT CASE	
MP-2	**Media Access**

ASSESSMENT – Base Control	
Assessment Information from Special Publication 800-53A	
	ASSESSMENT OBJECTIVE:
MP-2.1	*Determine if:*

MP-2.1.1
MP-2.1.1a
MP-2.1.1b
MP-2.1.1c
	(i) the organization defines:
	  - *digital and non-digital media requiring restricted access;*
	  - *individuals authorized to access the media; and*
	  - *security measures taken to restrict access.*

MP-2.1.2	*(ii) the organization restricts access to organization-defined information system media to organization-defined authorized individuals using organization-defined security measures.*
	POTENTIAL ASSESSMENT METHODS AND OBJECTS: **Examine**: [*SELECT FROM:* Information system media protection policy; procedures addressing media access; access control policy and procedures; physical and environmental protection policy and procedures; media storage facilities; access control records; other relevant documents or records]. **Interview**: [*SELECT FROM:* Organizational personnel with information system media protection responsibilities].
Additional Assessment Case Information	
	POTENTIAL ASSESSMENT SEQUENCING: PRECURSOR CONTROLS: MP-3, MP-4, MP-5, MP-6. CONCURRENT CONTROLS: AC-2, AC-3, AC-19, AU-2, AU-3, CM-6, MP-6, PE-2, PE-3, PE-7, PE-8. SUCCESSOR CONTROLS: NONE.
	General notes to assessor for MP-2: The focus of this control is the organization restricting access to information system media, and not whether the media is allowed to be used (which is covered under AC-19). As indicated in the supplemental guidance for this control, this control addresses both digital and non-digital media.
Action Step	**Potential Assessor Evidence Gathering Actions**
MP-2.1.1a.1	**Examine** information system media protection policy and procedures, access control policy and procedures, physical and environmental protection policy and procedures, or other relevant documents (e.g., system security plan) reviewing for what the organization has defined as the digital and non-digital media requiring restricted access.
MP-2.1.1b.1	**Examine** information system media protection policy and procedures, access control policy and procedures, physical and environmental protection policy and procedures, or other relevant documents (e.g., system security plan) reviewing for what the organization has defined as individuals authorized to access the media identified in MP-2.1.1a.1.
MP-2.1.1c.1	**Examine** information system media protection policy and procedures, access control policy and procedures, physical and environmental protection policy and procedures, or other relevant documents (e.g., system security plan) reviewing for what the organization has defined as measures to be taken for the access of media identified in MP-2.1.1a.1.

ASSESSMENT CASE	
MP-2.1.2.1	**Examine** an agreed-upon representative sample of media access control records or other relevant records for an agreed-upon representative sample of information system media types identified in MP-2.1.1a.1; reviewing for evidence that the measures identified in MP-2.1.1c.1 are implemented as intended.
MP-2.1.2.2	**Examine** an agreed-upon representative sample of operations at media storage facilities and other relevant areas; observing for indication that the measures identified in MP-2.1.1c.1 are implemented as intended.
MP-2.1.2.3	**Examine** an agreed-upon representative sample of operations at media storage facilities and other relevant areas; inspecting for indication that the measures identified in MP-2.1.c.1 are implemented as intended.
MP-2.1.2.4	**Interview** an agreed-upon representative sample of organizational personnel identified in MP-2.1.1b.1 with information system media protection responsibilities; conducting focused discussions for further evidence that the measures identified in MP-2.1.1c.1 are implemented as intended. *Note to assessor:* To facilitate testing of this control, there should be an identified list of storage areas (e.g., identified in the security plan) where the system intends to apply the MP-2 control, and it is assumed that such designated storage areas that either house large concentrations of information system media (e.g., server rooms, communication centers) or house particularly important media with regard to potential impacts if not adequately protected.

ASSESSMENT – Control Enhancement 1	
Assessment Information from Special Publication 800-53A	
	ASSESSMENT OBJECTIVE:
MP-2(1).1	*Determine if:*
MP-2(1).1.1	(i) *the organization employs automated mechanisms to restrict access to media storage areas; and*
MP-2(1).1.2	(ii) *the organization employs automated mechanisms to audit access attempts and access granted to media storage areas.*
	POTENTIAL ASSESSMENT METHODS AND OBJECTS: **Examine**: [SELECT FROM: Information system media protection policy; procedures addressing media access; access control policy and procedures; physical and environmental protection policy and procedures; media storage facilities; access control devices; access control records; audit records; other relevant documents or records]. **Test**: [SELECT FROM: Automated mechanisms implementing access restrictions to media storage areas].
Additional Assessment Case Information	
	POTENTIAL ASSESSMENT SEQUENCING: PRECURSOR CONTROLS: MP-3, MP-4, MP-5, MP-6. CONCURRENT CONTROLS: AC-2, AC-3, AC-19, AU-2, AU-3, CM-6, MP-6, PE-2, PE-3, PE-7, PE-8. SUCCESSOR CONTROLS: NONE.
Action Step	**Potential Assessor Evidence Gathering Actions**
MP-2(1).1.1.1	**Examine** information system media protection policy and procedures, access control policy and procedures, physical and environmental protection policy and procedures, security plan, or other relevant documents; reviewing for the automated mechanisms and configuration settings to be employed to restrict access to designated media storage areas.

ASSESSMENT CASE	
MP-2(1).1.1.2	**Examine** documentation describing the current configuration settings for an agreed-upon specific sample of automated mechanisms identified in MP-2(1).1.1.1; reviewing for indication that the mechanisms are configured as identified in MP-2(1).1.1.1.
MP-2(1).1.1.3	**Examine** an agreed-upon specific sample of media storage facilities; observing for indication that the mechanisms identified in MP-2(1).1.1.1 are implemented as intended.
MP-2(1).1.1.4	**Examine** an agreed-upon specific sample of media storage facilities; inspecting for indication that the mechanisms identified in MP-2(1).1.1.1 are implemented as intended.
MP-2(1).1.1.5	**Test** an agreed-upon specific sample of automated mechanisms identified in MP-2(1).1.1.1; conducting focused testing for evidence that the mechanisms operate as intended.
MP-2(1).1.2.1	**Examine** information system media protection policy and procedures, audit and accountability policy and procedures, physical and environmental protection policy and procedures, security plan, or other relevant documents; reviewing for the automated mechanisms and configuration settings to be employed to audit access attempts and access granted to media access areas.
MP-2(1).1.2.2	**Examine** documentation describing the current configuration settings for an agreed-upon specific sample of automated mechanisms identified in MP-2(1)1.2.1; reviewing for indication that the mechanisms are configured as identified in MP-2(1).1.2.1. *Note to assessor:* Consideration for selecting the specific sample include: selected audit and accountability policies (access attempts/access granted), how many media storage areas should be included in the sample, and how many instances of access attempts are to be examined.
MP-2(1).1.2.3	**Test** an agreed-upon specific sample of automated mechanisms identified in MP-2(1).1.2.1; conducting focused testing for evidence that the mechanisms operate as intended. *Note to assessor:* See note for MP-2(1).1.2.2 above.

ASSESSMENT – Control Enhancement 2

Assessment Information from Special Publication 800-53A

	ASSESSMENT OBJECTIVE:
MP-2(2).1	*Determine if the information system uses cryptographic mechanisms to protect and restrict access to information on portable digital media.*
	POTENTIAL ASSESSMENT METHODS AND OBJECTS: **Examine**: [*SELECT FROM:* Information system media protection policy; procedures addressing media access; other relevant documents or records]. **Test**: [*SELECT FROM:* Cryptographic mechanisms protecting and restricting access to information system information on portable digital media].

Additional Assessment Case Information

	POTENTIAL ASSESSMENT SEQUENCING: PRECURSOR CONTROLS: NONE. CONCURRENT CONTROLS: NONE. SUCCESSOR CONTROLS: NONE.
Action Step	**Potential Assessor Evidence Gathering Actions**
MP-2(2).1.1.1	**Examine** information system media protection policy and procedures, audit and accountability policy and procedures, physical and environmental protection policy and procedures, security plan, or other relevant documents; reviewing for required use of the cryptographic mechanisms and the configuration settings to be employed to protect and restrict access to information on portable digital media.

ASSESSMENT CASE	
MP-2(2).1.1.2	**Examine** documentation describing the current configuration settings for an agreed-upon specific sample of automated mechanisms identified in MP-2(1)1.2.1; reviewing for indication that the mechanisms are configured as identified in MP-2(2).1.1.1. *Note to assessor:* Consideration for selecting the specific sample include: selected audit and accountability policies (access attempts/access granted), how many media storage areas should be included in the sample, and how many instances of access attempts are to be examined.
MP-2(2).1.1.3	**Test** an agreed-upon specific sample of automated mechanisms identified in MP-2(2).1.1.2; conducting focused testing for evidence that the mechanisms operate as intended. *Note to assessor:* See note for MP-2(2).1.1.2 above.

Made in the USA
Columbia, SC
21 April 2018